the

BIRTH DAY BOOK

the BIRTHDAY BOOK

what the day you were born says about you

SHELLEY VON STRUNCKEL

W
E
L
C
O
M
E

Aries

*MARCH 20 –
APRIL 18*

Taurus

*APRIL 19 –
MAY 19*

Leo

*JULY 22 –
AUGUST 21*

Virgo

*AUGUST 22 –
SEPTEMBER 21*

Sagittarius

*NOVEMBER 21 –
DECEMBER 20*

Capricorn

*DECEMBER 21 –
JANUARY 19*

Gemini

MAY 20 –
JUNE 19

Cancer

JUNE 20 –
JULY 21

Libra

SEPTEMBER 22 –
OCTOBER 21

Scorpio

OCTOBER 22 –
NOVEMBER 20

Aquarius

JANUARY 20 –
FEBRUARY 18

Pisces

FEBRUARY 19 –
MARCH 19

Introduction

Welcome to this tour of the astrological year. Everybody is intrigued by astrology – even those who don't "believe" in it. I know this because, having written columns that are published worldwide and in a number of languages, I've learnt that the fascination with the 12 signs of the zodiac, and the individual dates within each, is universal.

The columns I write for each star sign focus on the nature of each day for the 12 signs. However, there are shades of intensity and character that ebb and flow over the 30 or so days of each sign.

Many don't realise that the dates of the signs are linked to the seasons. For example, in the northern hemisphere, the first day of Aries is linked to the beginning of spring; Cancer to the first day of summer; Libra to autumn, and Capricorn to winter. While in the southern hemisphere the seasons are reversed, the dates are still linked to the start of each season.

And, as the day of each sign unfolds, elements of its character – its joys, charms

and challenges – arise in a unique form. So while the interpretation for your birthday will reveal insights, reading the interpretation for other days could prove fascinating, if not enlightening, as well.

Each day of the year has its own character but, as with a family, those of the same sign are bound to have similarities.

Knowing about the day's character is useful for everybody, whatever their sign, so at the bottom of each page, you'll find an entry called This Day for Everyone, which is exactly that – it's the nature of that day for those of any sign; astrological tips for your day, whatever your sign – check it out.

Questions about the dates of the signs? Find out more at shelleyvonstrunckel.com.

Enjoy your journey.

Aries

March 20 – April 18

Aries   Fiery Aries is the first sign of the zodiac. Being ruled by the warrior planet Mars, you are a forceful character who thrives on challenges in a range of forms. Each adds to your skills, wisdom and, ultimately, patience. Your plants and flowers reflect that sharpness, from thistles to gladioli, and your spice is, of course, red chilli. Your gemstones are red, too – ranging from ruby to coral.

A
R
I
E
S

GIFTS Forthright, Industrious, Athletic

CHALLENGES Impulsive, Demanding, Unbending

NUMBER 5

$(2+0) + (3) = 5$

Each day I'll surprise somebody – and in a wonderfully unexpected way

You

Not only are you an Aries, but you were born on the first day of Aries, which makes you about 150% Aries – the most Aries of all. And even if you're not into astrology, you're probably still proud of the energy and power that come with being an Aries and ruled by the dynamic planet Mars. In fact, you may even have a stubborn streak that comes as a result of this intense energy.

In your personal life and your personal style, you rarely compromise. However, that can lead to ups and downs, simply because you don't pause to consider whether what you're doing is worthwhile, or if it's time to make a change. Your enthusiasm, therefore, needs to be balanced with an awareness of what is actually in your best interests, which means pausing in a way that won't necessarily come naturally to you.

Yet when you begin to do this, not only will you enjoy life more, you'll also spot more subtle joys in your own day, in relationships with others and in what you do. You may even find yourself having fun doing things that you would once have dismissed as too dull. And this is your journey as an Aries. It's not just being true to yourself – it's discovering what life itself has to offer and enjoying every second of it. Master that and you'll have mastered life's biggest secret.

You and others

As an enthusiastic Aries, you've a knack for galvanising even those who are questioning whether certain ideas or, possibly, introductions are worth the bother. While, mostly, others profit from your encouragement, if they're seriously unwilling, then back off, at least for the moment.

Health and wellbeing

When you're in the mood to get moving, you're not just enthusiastic, you'll tire out others. The trick is keeping up the pace. Taking it more slowly may seem like a compromise, but it means you're more likely to continue in the future.

Goals and challenges

Admitting that your decisions were unwise may not be easy, but the sooner you do it, the more swiftly you'll be able to rethink the plans in question. Ask others for their guidance. They'll admire you for being so open about your problems.

THIS DAY FOR EVERYBODY

Obviously, it would be easier if you could deal with the range of changes currently reshaping various elements of your life all at once. But, not only are things moving too slowly for that, your own perspective is changing as well. The trick? It's to rethink plans but regard any decisions as tentative.

When things don't go according to plan, I'll figure out why, then learn from it

You

Your enthusiasm is a kind of magnetism that draws people to you. You don't understand why. In fact, because it's something you've had your whole life, you don't even think about it until others mention it. Yet that magnetism starts and stops. It seems to depend on your mood. And this is where your lesson lies, which is important for you, and that is to never compromise in what you're doing.

Don't act to please others, unless it's part of an arrangement at work or in a relationship where basically you have got to compromise in order to help each other. But, at the same time, be aware that there is very much the possibility of doing too much of a good thing. And when you sense that, you'll want to pause and consider whether what you're doing is actually in your best interests.

In fact, bizarrely, you can get so into the habit of dressing in a particular way, eating a particular food, or doing something else, that you don't even realise you could make a change. And that's one of your big lessons. When you become aware of that, you'll also begin to be a bit calmer and enjoy life itself and those around you all the more.

This is one of the greatest gifts for you. Your passion for life comes with who you are. The passion to enjoy the life around you and others is one of the skills you'll learn.

You and others

As someone who goes at full speed ahead, conducting a relationship, a friendship, a romantic liaison or even family relationships can be tricky. The secret? It's to ask others for their concerns and advice, then discuss their views frankly. Everybody will learn from the resulting exchanges.

Health and wellbeing

Being excited about an activity is great, but even when you're fully involved, you must remember to eat or even to rest. Once you've become so absorbed in an activity or regime that you were told was beneficial, you'll do nothing else. The fact is, there can be too much of a good thing, and this is it.

Goals and challenges

You're amazingly self-sufficient, and proud of it. Because of that, you could struggle to accept an offer as exciting as it is unexpected, simply because it is somebody else's idea. There are few greater gifts than being offered to be part of somebody else's project. Say a heart-warming and enthusiastic yes.

THIS DAY FOR EVERYBODY

Others are complaining about the time it's taking you to make simple decisions. They might be easy if circumstances stayed the same. But with changes – some minor and others major – demanding that you rethink even the simplest of ideas or arrangements, it's nearly impossible to make long-term plans.

A
\
R
/
I
\
E
/
S

GIFTS Dynamic, Enthusiastic, Passionate

CHALLENGES Rigid, Stubborn, Hasty

NUMBER 7

(2+2) + (3) = 7

When I'm feeling bored, I'll tackle dull tasks I've been ignoring for ages

You

Every Aries is ruled by the dynamic planet Mars, but in your case Mars can sometimes be too big a player in your life. Mars is the planet of energy, aggression, and sometimes war, which means that occasionally you can get involved in a plan, or become absorbed in learning something, but it's almost as if you intend to conquer it rather than enjoy it. Of course, what happens next is that you become exhausted and it all seems overwhelming. And then it loses its lustre.

So for you, the trick is to maintain the amazing enthusiasm that comes with your nature, but also to learn to spread it out over more than one thing, or to spend time with someone who helps you recognise when you're overdoing it. Not only is this important because it allows you to keep balance, it also means that you have time not only to enjoy achieving those goals, but for life itself.

As you're aware, there are times when you've completely ignored those who are closest to you, perhaps forgetting a birthday or an important date. Or maybe you've been madly in love with somebody, but haven't got in touch with them. Whatever the case, the lesson here too is to find balance. Do that and the feedback you get, the love you get and the joy you get, will not only make it worthwhile, it will remind you to do that all the more often.

You and others

With your passion for life, you attract everybody to you. But that doesn't mean you enjoy everybody's company or should make plans with them. If you do so unwisely, simply apologise and back out. This prevents you from making arrangements that are no fun. Better yet, it teaches you to carefully pick and choose those who you spend time with.

Health and wellbeing

You'll often become enthusiastic about eating something you were told was good for you, or doing an exercise or a sport because it's been recommended. However, these activities can become routine and soon achingly dull. The secret? Make changes, just for the fun of it.

Goals and challenges

Finding things that excite you is easy. But that excitement lasting is another matter. Usually, you're eager to move on to something new and equally exciting. The real challenge is finding the right balance for you, one that enables you to be true to yourself, which, as an Aries, is crucial.

THIS DAY FOR EVERYBODY

Understanding the need to be patient can be challenging, especially when others are in a hurry to make things happen. Yet at the moment, even you are struggling with the feeling things should be moving more swiftly. They will. But for now, you're better off taking it slowly.

Instead of doing a single good deed each day, I'll aim to do a dozen

You

As an Aries you've probably heard people say that they envy your enthusiasm. However, you may wonder why that is, because for you it comes so naturally that you don't even think about it. Yet, at the same time, the range of your feelings, from being on top of the world to exhausted, has to do with the need to find equilibrium between these two. It's something that doesn't come naturally to you, and is, in fact, one of your biggest lessons. This has to do with your energy levels and your enthusiasm, but also with the things you get involved in – your work, close relationships and romance. Also, how you live your daily life and how you organise your routine. Bizarrely, in your enthusiasm you can forget things you need to do, whether it's paying bills or even, occasionally, eating.

While, you can't always make notes about this kind of thing, what you can do is deal with one of the greatest challenges for you. That is to pause every once in a while, take a deep breath and realise how wonderful it is just to be you and to be alive. And if you're with somebody, have a brief chat about that. Once you begin, and as you do it more often, you'll not only enjoy the swings between the excitement and the stillness all the more, you'll also enjoy every single breath of life all the more as well.

You and others

The gift that you bring to relationships, whether with family, loved ones, or even a neighbour or colleague, is that you're entirely you. In fact, it puzzles you when others put up a fake front. Discuss this gently, because it probably means they're shy, nothing more.

Health and wellbeing

While sometimes you'll throw yourself into a way of eating or exercising that you've been told is good, or which you find particularly rewarding, at the same time you've a tendency to exclude other things. Then you'll tire of that regime, and move onto another. Moderation may not come naturally, but it's your best bet.

Goals and challenges

Being passionate by nature, you thrive on excess, overdoing things, then feeling exhausted. So not only is finding balance difficult, but you don't really enjoy it. What's more, inner stillness can be difficult to achieve. Still, at times it's not only wise – it also gives you space to recover from the past and to consider the future.

THIS DAY FOR EVERYBODY

Recent setbacks have freed you from a situation that, while seemingly worthwhile, was increasingly worrying. However, as that particular arrangement comes to an end, with each passing day, a far better one isn't just increasingly likely, it's showing amazing promise.

GIFTS Candid, Loving, Impulsive

CHALLENGES Self-involved, Unbending, Obsessive

NUMBER 9

(2+4) + (3) = 9

Is somebody dull? Chat with them, until you realise how amazing they are

You

Those around you will often remark on your enthusiasm, your zest for life and how involved you get in things. And, while it's true, sometimes that involvement can turn into an obsession, to the degree that you actually end up getting bored with your current passion. You'll note this when someone asks if you're still interested in something, whether it's a form of exercise, a particular eating regime or even a destination. And you'll almost have forgotten that it existed, because you got so tired of it, you moved on to something else.

One of your big lessons in life, therefore, is to find things that you can be passionate about, but without allowing that passion to overwhelm you. This has to do with activities but, even more, it has to do with how you work and your close relationships. It may well be that you've been so enthusiastic about a certain subject that you studied and earned a degree in it, and then found you didn't actually like. Or it could have been the same with a close alliance, a friendship or even a relationship. You overwhelmed yourself. For any Aries, finding balance is challenging, but it's especially important for you. Because once you acquire that skill, it will enable you to enjoy the subtleties in your own life, your close relationships and love in ways that you haven't been able to before.

You and others

One of your greatest gifts is the attention you pay to those you meet and get to know. However, one of your greatest obstacles is the degree to which that attention can become so intense that you forget there are other things around you. It may be a friend whose company you really enjoy. Or if you're in love, you will be madly in love. And the gift here is to learn, to take it easy, to take time with it. This won't come naturally, but it is one of the greatest challenges for you.

Health and wellbeing

In the same way, your health and wellbeing require balance – a thoughtful approach as to how you look after yourself, how you eat and possibly even moments of questioning or reflection. If you socialise constantly or are a movie addict, it might be time to cut back and, even more, consider what's next.

Goals and challenges

One of the greatest gifts for you is to have problems to solve and obstacles to overcome, each of which forces you to focus on elements of your life you often ignore. Initially, these won't seem exciting, yet while dealing with them you'll learn something very challenging for you, which is to live a balanced life.

THIS DAY FOR EVERYBODY

Listening with your heart as much as with your ears is always important, but even more so now. While certain individuals are eager to clear up persistent issues, their efforts to discuss these matters are only making things worse. Forget discussions. Instead, make it clear how much they mean to you.

Frustrated by the same tedious task?
Get others involved. Do it faster, better

You

One of your greatest characteristics is loyalty. When you believe in something or somebody, you'll stick with them through thick and thin. However, the difficulty is that you assume they feel the same. And if they don't behave the way you expect them to, you're not only disappointed, you can get angry – except, of course, the individual in question won't understand why.

This is also one of your most important journeys as an Aries, and one of your biggest lessons in life – to recognise that the intensity of the way you feel towards others, or an organisation, or perhaps a profession, can be overwhelming. It's also about how you negotiate. You can talk things over and, in doing so, you'll not only resolve those issues, you'll learn a lot about yourself too. It's said that life is a journey. And for you, that journey is not so much to do with finding that balance, because life is always changing, but with discovering the fact that, sometimes, you go so far that others can't understand where you're coming from.

Begin to talk that over with others, and you will have some of the most important discussions of your life. You'll find yourself coming closer enough to the centre and you'll be able to establish warm and stable relationships in your romantic life, your working life – and, most of all, with yourself.

You and others

Achieving a balance in close relationships is a challenge, yet it could become one of your greatest skills. You'll not only learn patience with those who are frustrating, but you'll also discover that, often, they are a mirror for many of your own characteristics. Recognise that, and even serious clashes with others will turn into incredibly useful lessons.

Health and wellbeing

You want to feel great, but are sometimes so overwhelmed that you can barely think, still less be enthusiastic. The trick? Make a few changes, health-wise. Find something fun yet physically challenging to take part in along with others. Then do it regularly. A few weeks of that regime, and you'll be a new person.

Goals and challenges

For you as an Aries, life is always full of challenges. That's the way you like it. If everything was easy or predictable, you'd soon get bored. Yet for you, choosing the right challenge, for the right time, is a complex skill – one you'll be learning to master every day of your life.

Few things upset you more than being forced to disappoint somebody. It's not only troubling, but you'll find it difficult to discuss the matter in question, so are tempted not to bring it up it at all. That's understandable. Still, you're urged to talk things over, in detail, and the sooner, the better.

A
\
R
/
I
\
E
/
S

GIFTS Passionate, Motivated, Warm

CHALLENGES Rash, Stubborn, Impatient

NUMBER 2

(2+6) + (3) = 11 = (1+1) = 2

If your goals seem distant, set new ones for now. Make them challenging, but possible

You

You sometimes wonder why other people aren't as enthusiastic as you are. Of course, it comes naturally to you, so there's a tendency to assume that everybody has this zest for life – and they don't. It's for this reason that you may feel frustrated when others don't respond in the way that you hope or expect when you're talking about what you're doing, or something you could do with them, or even just when you're asking what they're up to.

The important thing to remember is that it's not about being right or wrong, although there are certain people who will criticise you for your enthusiastic take on life. Rather, it's about being who you are and being true to yourself. And if someone isn't particularly enthusiastic about a certain activity, or even about spending time with you, it doesn't matter – you can move on.

That's the other skill that you'll develop during your life, to carefully pick and choose those you spend time with and the activities you pursue. Just because you're excited about something doesn't mean you need to commit to it for years, or even months. And it's the same with people. The skill of choosing what and who suits you is a skill that you'll be practising every day of your life. One at which you'll be getting better every day. And one that will allow you to enjoy life all the more.

You and others

Being a spontaneous fire sign, the idea of carefully selecting the people you hang out with seems strange. Yet you've learnt that while some people are fun and challenge you, others grow more boring by the minute. Selecting the right people to spend time with is as crucial how you eat and look after yourself.

Health and wellbeing

Long ago, it became obvious that you feel better when you eat wisely. Despite that, you occasionally rebel, only to discover that there's a price to pay for indulging yourself. The trick? It's to make a date with yourself to overdo it on some days, and make time to repair the damage, as well.

Goals and challenges

It may be that when you were very young, setting a single lifelong goal made sense. Since then, however, you've realised just how much there is to do and discover, and the more you fit into each day, the better it is is. As an Aries, the more passions you have, the better.

 THIS DAY FOR EVERYBODY

Somebody seems determined to corner you into doing something that will serve them well but not you. The real problem is that they haven't asked, thereby recognising this as a favour. They're manipulating you into offering. Don't. Instead, address this frankly. You won't regret it.

GIFTS Intense, Forthright, Athletic

CHALLENGES Reckless, Demanding, Rigid

NUMBER 3

(2+7) + (3) = 12 = (1+2) = 3

Restless? Ask somebody what they really enjoy doing. Then learn that skill from them

You

For you, life is full of challenges – not in a negative sense, it's just the way you learn things. Whereas others will often run from challenges, you may ask them to join you in trying something new. To your amazement, they'll say they actually aren't interested in altering certain elements of their lives. As an Aries, you were born to enjoy these challenges, to thrive on them. Sometimes they'll last for years, while at other times you'll learn what it is you need to know then move on.

Most of all, try to recognise that not everybody will want to share those challenges with you. It's the same with your own pursuits. It's important for you to find activities – personally, and at work – that allow you to do things in a new and different way. If not, you'll quickly grow tired of them. If your job is a bit predictable, perhaps it will be in your personal life that you'll discover those challenges. You may just decide to mix things up things from time to time, so you're always learning something.

Whatever the case – and it can be different at different times in your life – for you, those challenges, those lessons in doing things in a new way, are like taking a very special variety of Aries vitamins. Once you've learnt how to do that, you'll not only benefit from it, you'll want to do it for the rest of your life.

You and others

As an Aries, discovering that others think very differently from you can be a surprise, if not jarring. Tempting as it is to focus on those who are equally enthusiastic about life, often relationships thrive on contrast. In your case, learning to accept this, and enjoy others for what they are, is an art.

Health and wellbeing

While you can hurl yourself into certain activities, hoping they'll make you stronger and healthier, keeping at it is another matter. Ideally, you should aim to have a variety of activities and, equally, a varied and interesting diet. That way, you can have a blowout on some days, then be more moderate over the next few.

Goals and challenges

The secret isn't so much finding the single "right" goal or ambition as to have a whole series of them – some your current focus, others on the sidelines but by no means forgotten. Some involve other people; a few are yours alone. The thing they have in common is your passionate feeling for them all.

THIS DAY FOR EVERYBODY

What you're facing requires you to acknowledge the need to be patient, even while others are putting the pressure on to make things happen, and fast. Yet at the moment, you're questioning the idea that things should be moving more swiftly. They will. For now, you're better off taking it slowly.

A R I E S

GIFTS Strong, Enthusiastic, Loyal

CHALLENGES Impatient, Sullen, Single-minded

NUMBER 4

(2+8) + (3) = 13 = (1+3) = 4

Always being told what to do? Irritated? Ask for a list. That'll change everything

You

You don't usually think of this, but you tend to take on more than you can realistically manage. As a life enthusiast, anything new or challenging is appealing to you. You'll say yes immediately, assuming you can fit it into your schedule. While this means your life is rich, it can also be overwhelming, and either you don't have time to do things properly, or you're always catching up, so you're late for everything. What's more, the idea of cutting back is unappealing.

However, there is another approach. Pause every once in a while and do something out of character – ask for help. Find a friend, family member or even a professional who'll review your activities and diary and help you examine where your time and, possibly, money, are going. This isn't just about life's practicalities, but where you invest your deepest feelings, and whether that's wise and worthwhile.

This is because you're fiercely loyal and will sometimes stick with something just because you have made a commitment, when actually what you need is someone to suggest it's time to say farewell to that particular activity, ambition or, indeed, relationship. And that is one of your biggest lessons in this life. Not to pick and choose what you do, but to know when to say farewell to certain things so you can enjoy everything else all the more.

You and others

When you make a commitment to an activity, job, or individuals, whether it's family, loved ones or even colleagues, you feel that this connection is an important one and you do everything you can to honour it. But others must earn your loyalty. No excuses and no discussion.

Health and wellbeing

Being able to enjoy life and its pleasures, and enjoy feeling and eating well, is important. But, it's easy for you to overdo things, then adopt an extremely tough diet and fitness regime. While balance doesn't come naturally, it's the secret. The trick is to learn to say no, and at the right time.

Goals and challenges

If ever there was an individual who loves a challenge, it's you. And, what's more, you love achieving those goals. It's just that some of them don't mean as much to you as you once thought they would. It's okay to say no, to back out, and that's the big lesson for you, today and every day.

THIS DAY FOR EVERYBODY

What you're facing requires you to acknowledge the need to be patient, even while others are putting the pressure on to make things happen, and fast. Yet at the moment, you're questioning the idea things should be moving more swiftly. They will. But, for now, you're better off taking it slowly.

Stuck somewhere dull? Ask anybody, even a stranger, where you should go

You

One of your greatest characteristics is your zest for life. Of course, this comes with being an Aries and ruled by Mars. However, your particular nature is such that it needs new challenges – some small, others bigger – and in every case, it's exciting for you to learn how to do something, to achieve a skill, or even how to create the kind of relationship you want. The secret to all of this, however, is to recognise that some things are simply skills. They aren't challenges, and you don't need to put quite as much energy into them. You just need to figure out how to discern between the two. And this is where those closest – family, friends and even work colleagues – come in.

In the past, you wouldn't listen to their cautions that maybe you were doing too much, hurling yourself into one activity. Finally, you're learning to back off. This isn't just worthwhile. It means you'll gain time to explore other activities and, perhaps, even one or two challenges that will be rewarding. But most of all, it will give you time to be with those you care about most. To spend time with the number one person in your life – you – but, equally, to be with family, friends and colleagues who add to your life and whose company you enjoy. And, rather than worrying about having to get somewhere, you'll be able to truly relax with them.

You and others

It's rare that an Aries depends on another individual to fulfil their lives. Caring passionately about people and projects is normal. But putting yourself first is key. That's part of your lesson, and your journey. Do that, and work, live and love intensely, yet retain that all-important link with your deepest inner self.

Health and wellbeing

Knowing what's in your best interests seems simple. Yet you complicate it with complex fitness routines and demanding diets. Being good to yourself should be simple, and once you've linked up with your inner wisdom, you'll know exactly what to do. Until then, think carefully about whose ideas you embrace.

Goals and challenges

Some say that, ideally, you'll set challenges that are modest. However, not only is that completely out of character for you, but if you chat with friends, you'll find they're amazed and impressed by what you achieve on a daily basis. If you like the idea of a challenge, go for it, but knowing it won't prove anything to anybody.

THIS DAY FOR EVERYBODY

Few things are more rewarding than having struggled with difficult people and coming up with a plan that works for everybody. The good news is that's what you've done. The bad news is that these arrangements will change before you can regard anything as settled for good.

GIFTS Loving, Dynamic, Spontaneous

CHALLENGES Brash, Unbending, Impatient

NUMBER 6

(3+0) + (3) = 6

Unsure about your life goals? Maybe there's more than one on a path of self-discovery

You

It's always fascinated you when somebody has lived in the same home for their whole life, continued in the same job for years without considering changing it, or has stuck to a particular hobby – or a combination of all of three. As an Aries, you're passionate about life. Sometimes you will stick with a single, lifelong passion, but one side of your nature thrives on new discoveries and experiences that stretch you. This is important to you. While you enjoy meeting people and learning about them – and encountering new ideas – you can get lost in it. You then have to find your way back to yourself.

As an Aries and a fire sign, passion is in your nature. What's more, you're generous, and if someone's struggling or in need, you'll do whatever you can. However, in trying to help others, you sometimes neglect your own needs – home, family, loved ones or, quite possibly, your work – or you may be avoiding something that you don't enjoy doing.

Your challenge is to balance the two – maintaining your wonderful generous streak, but putting yourself and your commitments first instead of struggling to ensure that others are happy. Manage this, and you'll find you're able to enjoy life in a way you have never done before. It's an art and, most of all, it will be the greatest gift you could give to yourself.

You and others

Finding balance in close alliances, at home and out in the world, is important but can also be challenging. Often, the biggest lesson involves somebody who's your exact opposite. Where you're obsessive and impatient, they're easygoing. This can be at home with family or friends, or out in the world. Achieving this balance is one of life's greatest gifts.

Health and wellbeing

For many, but not all, Aries, looking after yourself – that is, your physical wellbeing and eating well – isn't of particular interest to you, which is itself an important challenge. The solution is to keep any regime simple, but make it exciting and, ideally, part of your life with others.

Goals and challenges

Goals are easy to define. However, overcoming obstacles is another matter. Instead of battling them, the trick is to define them very clearly, which, as an impatient Aries, annoys you. Tackle this now, and not only will you learn a lot, better yet, what you learn will be an asset for the rest of your life.

THIS DAY FOR EVERYBODY

Some problems can be defined and dealt within swiftly, then put behind you. However, those you're currently facing are more complex than they seem and so could take days to put to rest. Still, while this will require considerable patience, it will be justified by the results you achieve.

Are you often late, or forget something? Try showing up unexpectedly, but with gifts

You

There are two ways of viewing your nature. One is that you're flexible, and adapt swiftly to new and even very unexpected developments. While that means you're comfortable with the twists and turns of modern life, you're also easily bored. So when those around you – family, friends or even colleagues – settle into a routine, you're restlessly looking for something new. As a fire sign, this is natural.

Still, there's a secret to dealing with this. It's to allow yourself to be swept away by the moment you're in, whatever you're doing and whoever you're with. You'll either be thrilled by your enthusiasm, even with unfamiliar activities, or will recognise your deep, and touching, response to certain individuals. True, these experiences will be as unsettling as they are appealing, mostly because you've so valued your independence that, previously, you've brushed off any such feelings. This fresh perspective will shift your approach to the rest of life.

You may have been this passionately involved with your own pursuits, from your career to a challenging activity you enjoy, be that sports or a game of bridge. However, this will trigger a top-to-bottom review of your priorities. What's more, because this can't be done in a day, you'll find yourself asking questions about almost every area of your life.

You and others

As a fire sign, you have a well of passion waiting to be discovered. Certain situations or individuals will lead the way. And they'll take a special place, in your diary, your priorities and, possibly, your heart.

Health and wellbeing

Action makes you feel powerful. But learning from others touches your heart. If you slow your pace enough, soon you'll adore time spent in activities and with people who, previously, you barely noticed.

Goals and challenges

Your motto? Learn something new, and different, every year. You have a restless and inquisitive mind. It needs to be kept busy, ideally with suitable challenges. Physical fitness is fine but regular mental workouts will do the trick, exercising your mind as much as your body.

THIS DAY FOR EVERYBODY

You have been battling with certain individuals about important details. Now, looking back, you're beginning to realise that you were sidestepping the real issue. Deep down, you know what this is. The challenge is raising it. Once you do, everything else will be easy.

GIFTS Lively, Open-hearted, Frank

CHALLENGES Rash, Obsessive, Demanding

NUMBER 5

(0+1) + (4) = 5

Give yourself the challenge of surprising three people, in three wonderful ways, today

You

Being born on the first of the month brings a fresh energy to the world around you, into your life and, importantly, to your enthusiasm. You need to do things your way. That's typical, but, more so, this process of discovering your own approach to life isn't just exciting. It is almost as if you were Christopher Columbus on a ship sailing to the New World, unsure of what you were going to encounter. That sense of excitement and vitality fuels your life. Even if you're just going around the corner to do something ordinary, you never know who you'll run into or what you'll discover. And your enthusiasm rubs off on others, which means that they, in turn, want to spend time with you. This is a great gift.

However, your lesson is to ensure that you channel your lively energy into something that doesn't just benefit others, but also is of benefit to you personally – in your close relationships, out in the world, at work and in the activities you pursue. Even more think that these benefits need to feed your feelings, your mind, your heart and your soul. Because you're so busy thinking about things, you sometimes neglect to embrace those more subtle and more tender moments. The more that you learn to do that each day, the more you'll enjoy the day itself, and all the days to come as well.

You and others

Finding perfect friends, a perfect relationship with family and a perfect way of dealing with others is important to you, because you really believe that there's a kind of high that's possible. You've experienced it and you want to experience it again. It's just that this comes and goes. When it comes, it's a very special moment. And when it isn't there, it's important you realise it will come again.

Health and wellbeing

It's easy to say it's important to eat well. For you, it is simply because you're quite sensitive. And if you haven't had enough to eat, if your diet is out of balance, you can pay a price for it. If you eat too much sugar and then crash, you'll struggle. If you don't eat enough, you'll struggle, too. Finding a balance is important. And it's the same with movement. A brisk walk every day will make all the difference.

Goals and challenges

Life for you is nothing without at least three goals to pursue every day and one challenge to overcome. When you achieve that and find the perfect balance, you'll feel like you are taking the best vitamins in the world.

 THIS DAY FOR EVERYBODY

When you decided to sidestep certain potentially upsetting issues, they were minor, so of little concern anyway. However, now that these are out in the open, you must be frank about your concerns but, also, seek advice. Brainstorm solutions together. You'll be amazed how helpful others' ideas are.

Bored? Unsure what you enjoy? Ask what others do for fun, then explore together

You

For you, as an Aries, and somebody ruled by the passionate Mars, passion is itself a way of being. It's not something you simply experience from time to time.

However, you don't really think about this until you're around those who don't seem to be excited, much less passionate, about anything. Yet, at the same time, these individuals will be drawn to you because your warmth and your excitement and your enthusiasm are almost like taking a tonic for them. While, this is wonderful, it's also important that you provide your own passion in a way that satisfies you, not others. And finding that balance is important for you.

Also, much of life – close relationships, your job if you have one – varies from day to day. Routine tasks don't necessarily involve much passion, which means it's important that every day there's some component of it, whether that's in an activity you love, a variety of exercise that you enjoy or music you listen to. That means a lot. That balance can change from day to day, but for you in particular, as an Aries who thrives on this level of passion, finding ways to fit it into everyday life is like finding the right vitamins to take. And once you are sure you've included enough of that enthusiasm, passion and zest in some form every day, then each day will be a joy.

You and others

You realise that some individuals will never be excited about certain activities – they don't have that kind of nature. They're happier just to sit comfortably and quietly. Hopefully, this means you've given up trying to create excitement for them and discovered that despite this, often they're good company.

Health and wellbeing

Here too, passion is important, but in this particular case, it's your own passion for your wellbeing and for ensuring that over a period of time, you're eating well. Some people have an exact routine, but for most Aries, that's too dull. Besides, you need to change things around every once in a while. And it's the same with activities. Ensure that you've got plenty to keep you going.

Goals and challenges

For you, a challenge a day is essential to your zest for life It may be a small challenge or a big one, but the more you embrace these challenges, the better you'll feel about your day, your week, your month and your year.

THIS DAY FOR EVERYBODY (v)

Obviously, you're in no mood to confess that when you withdrew from one particular arrangement, you were dishonest about the reason why. Your objective was to avoid hurting anybody's feelings. Now that everything has come out, you have to be frank. Still, you can speak from the heart.

GIFTS Energetic, Frank, Affectionate

CHALLENGES Single-minded, Hasty, Excitable

NUMBER 7

(0+3) + (4) = 7

I'll play a game with myself. How many dull tasks can I do before getting bored?

You

If you're familiar with astrology, you'll know that you're ruled by the intense, passionate planet Mars, and you're a fire sign as well, both of which indicate that you have an incredible zest for life. Of course, you take this for granted most of the time, until you run into those individuals who don't share those qualities. You sometimes wonder what you can do to make life more exciting for them. And the answer is nothing. They are who they are.

Acknowledging this isn't easy, but it's like acknowledging that certain people are blonde while others have dark hair; some are tall, others short. The trick is recognising those differences, then learning to enjoy them. While your sheer enthusiasm for life is an amazing gift, it belongs to you. You can learn to enjoy those who are less easily excited, or who prefer to live life at a slower pace. It may be family, it may be colleagues or maybe it's someone you're close to.

Your romantic partner may be like that, yet, despite their slow pace, you still love them. In fact, it may well be that it is this slower pace and what it brings to your life that makes a relationship – whether it's personal, family, or even professional – so rewarding. Whatever its nature, know that this isn't about changing anybody, but about achieving balance.

You and others

Some relationships are about enjoying time with others. However, for you, often they're an invitation to broaden your horizons, in terms of the individuals in question. But, as much, you're discovering new ways of experiencing life, together and individually. It's a challenging, powerful and rewarding journey.

Health and wellbeing

Some say feeling your best is all about what you eat and how you exercise. For you, however, the emphasis is on communication, that is, understanding others. The more you discuss, the greater that understanding will be.

Goals and challenges

Nothing focuses your mind more than an exciting challenge. However, when you're short of facts or the circumstances are unclear, you can become so irritated that you find it impossible to be clear-minded. This is your greatest lesson – and challenge. Patience.

THIS DAY FOR EVERYBODY

Recently, you've struggled to keep certain long-standing arrangements going. And you've succeeded. Yet circumstances, and your own priorities, are shifting. While these changes are timely, they're also upsetting, because this means rethinking those arrangements you tried to keep afloat.

Are you always complaining? Ask others to rate your complaints. You'll end up laughing

You

Some say that you were born into a particular sign for a reason. If you're an Aries, you were born to discover the passion that comes with being a fire sign and to benefit from the energy associated with being ruled by the planet Mars. Yet, at the same time, there is a need for balance within every individual. And your particular chart shows that, while it's essential you use your Aries enthusiasm, to make the best of it, it's also important for you to discover that slower pace within you. This isn't just about living slowly. It's about being able to slow down so you can listen to and be with those you care about, whether that's family or loved ones, or even those out in the world – your friends or colleagues.

This discovery of this slower pace will also enable you to rethink certain elements of your life that have been a source of frustration. You may have kept trying to make things work when actually, they just aren't meant to be that exciting. Or you may have tried to force them into being worthwhile when, in reality, they aren't. And the greatest gift you could give to yourself is to let them go.

Whatever the case, and the situations will appear frequently from time to time, being able to say farewell to something that doesn't suit you isn't just wise – it may be the nicest thing you can do for yourself.

You and others

It's unusual for an Aries to compare themselves to others, because being born under the first sign of the zodiac, you're always thinking about what you've done in the past and your future goals. However, you care about those closest to you, and if they aren't happy, you worry. What means most to them is that you care. That alone is enough.

Health and wellbeing

Looking after yourself may seem selfish, yet in order to be at your best, it's an important variety of selfishness. Think of that each day and, when you can't be bothered to eat properly or do a little exercise or get enough rest, recognise that not only is self-care a gift to you, it's a gift to others as well.

Goals and challenges

Finding the balance between generosity to others and looking after yourself is one of your major challenges. However, because it's something you can control yourself, it's also something you can learn to resolve very quickly.

THIS DAY FOR EVERYBODY Ⓥ

Ages ago, your mind fastened on doing something, going somewhere or achieving a particular goal. But, despite your efforts, you've achieved nothing. Frustrating as this is, it isn't about what you can actually do, but having a challenge that stirs you up. It's about getting you doing, not getting it done.

GIFTS Robust, Strong, Honourable

CHALLENGES Unbending, Impatient, Thoughtless

NUMBER 9

(0+5) + (4) = 9

When I'm impatient, I'll make it a game. I'll guess how long things will take

You

The theme for your birthday is discovery. It's a wonderful theme to have, because it isn't about trying to keep things the same or even trying to make what you have better, it's about recognising that your life is going to be peppered with all kinds of exciting findings Some things you've been hoping for, others are unexpected.

If there's a challenge, it will be acknowledging those discoveries that you encounter as important, and something you should embrace. If you recognise them as something that will enhance your life, then, when they arise, you'll explore them. But in some cases, you're much more than this. They will add to your way of thinking, your way of living and possibly your way of working. And, in every case, you'll be discovering something new – and that is the key to it.

It's interesting, because as an Aries you're inquisitive, but you can also be a creature of habit and rather impatient about having to master new ways of doing things. Ironically, some of what you're learning may mean that you'll meet new people or have new experiences that will themselves be rewarding. That again brings us back to the theme of discovery. Think about it in the past, acknowledge and embrace it in the present and you will have a future full of delightful and rewarding discoveries.

You and others

You tend to want to share discoveries with others. Except each individual is here to learn their own lesson and to have their own experiences. And while there may be times when you're able to share them with those around you, just as often, it's important that you enjoy them yourself.

Health and wellbeing

You'll be surprised how unexpected events or encounters teach you new ways to look after yourself – activities that are worth your while, ways to eat that benefit you. More than that, recognise that this is an ongoing part of your life, so there will be further discoveries over the coming days, months, weeks and even years.

Goals and challenges

Making yourself number one is difficult for you, because you're generous by nature. But when you find the balance between looking after yourself first and foremost yet being generous with others, you'll also find that you experience great satisfaction.

THIS DAY FOR EVERYBODY

Unsettling as the revelations you're facing may be, deep down you've known something is amiss. The real shock is the extent of the issues and how secretive certain individuals were. From their perspective, this was wise. Yet the gulf between you is wide – so much so that it's unlikely you'll strike an accord.

Today, I'll lend my focus and enthusiasm to somebody who needs a boost

You

For you, as an Aries, the secret to making the best of your nature is to make a point of learning each day. That may sound strange, because you learn from all of life. Yet in this particular case, it's about being much closer to the day's events in a way that might be more usual if you were born in Taurus, an earth sign and the one next to yours, or in Virgo, another earth sign. Both these signs are very much into the details of the day as opposed to action, which is so much a part of your nature.

While by no means are you lacking the fiery nature of the Aries, you also need to pause – and pause regularly – to look at what you're doing each day. In doing so, think about whether it could be better, whether you need to take a new path. That's important. And this isn't just about achieving what you want. It's also about the time you spend with those around you, be they friends or family, and what you're doing for yourself. It might be termed checking in for yourself regularly.

Make a habit of this, and you'll find that not only will you achieve far more than you imagined you could in a day, but you'll also enjoy the day. You'll be far more aware of what you've achieved, what was a pleasure for you and the obstacles you've overcome. And each of those will put a smile on your face.

You and others

Often when dealing with others – family, colleagues, neighbours or friends – it's about keeping the peace and getting along with them. But in your case, you feel the responsibility to keep them happy. While this is wonderful, and shows your generous nature, it's also tricky because some individuals don't want to be happy. Acknowledging this will be difficult for you, but once you actually do, you'll find it a lot easier to deal with those around you.

Health and wellbeing

Tempting as it is to spoil others at the expense of your own pleasures, finding those little pleasures every day is important. They will add to your life in ways you can't imagine. And it's not just about pleasures in terms of what you eat. It's also the objects around you that add to your life, and even having things you enjoy doing, from exercises in a lovely setting to something else equally rewarding.

Goals and challenges

You have a strange challenge, and that's to learn to be a little more self-centred. This is unusual for an Aries, but as you'll be aware, it's an important one for you.

THIS DAY FOR EVERYBODY

Ordinarily, you're frank with others. Recently, however, a lack of communication about certain pivotal matters has been a problem. Overcoming your discomfort and raising this may be a challenge. Once you do, and are talking things through, the confusion behind those problems will vanish.

GIFTS Enthusiastic, Passionate, Spontaneous

CHALLENGES Driven, Relentless, Single-minded

NUMBER 2

(0+7) + (4) = 11 = (1+1) = 2

Are certain individuals bossy? Turn it around. Actually ask them to tell you what to do

You

Most Aries think and move swiftly. So swiftly, in fact, that often they won't catch the things that need to be reflected on, thought about or analysed. In your particular case, though, this variety of analysis is so rare in your sign that it doesn't come naturally. Sometimes you wonder and worry whether you might actually be missing something important.

However, this also allows you to enjoy what you're achieving in a way that isn't common for others who were also born under the sign of Aries. It allows you to slow down. And if there's any challenge, it's being able to pick up and move swiftly when you need to, and to back off from that process of analysis.

Of course, you are ruled by the dynamic and courageous Mars. If you let that side of you kick in at those times when you need to move quickly, to be dynamic or possibly even courageous, if you allow Mars to take the lead when you need to take a stand with somebody, you'll know exactly what to do.

But most of all, you might want to borrow an idea, a concept from the sign opposite yours, Libra, which is all about finding that balance of the analytical, helpful side, with the passion that is so central to you being an Aries.

You and others

Often when people ask how you are, they don't care. Of course, you do care, and it's one of your greatest gifts. And others need to care about you. It's not that you're secretive, but sometimes you need to let others know what's going on inside.

Health and wellbeing

Making the best of life has to do with its pleasures, but it also has to do with being in both a physical condition and state of mind that allow you to enjoy every day. Ironically, sometimes you can be a bit lazy about that, simply because your mind takes you elsewhere. One of the lessons for you is to turn looking after yourself into a joy.

Goals and challenges

The passion that you have for life and for everything good is admirable, but sometimes you can take such a long time organising things that you won't achieve what you want as swiftly as you might hope. However, if you bring a little Aries passion into that, things would happen more swiftly.

THIS DAY FOR EVERYBODY

The time has come to take a tough line with one particularly tricky individual. While you're usually able to sidestep their manoeuvres or stage a diplomatic confrontation, neither of those has worked. Bizarre as it seems, the fact is that they want to talk things through, but are too shy to ask.

If you find you don't care about your goals, start making ones you're passionate about

You

If there's anything irritating for you – in the world around you, in the lives of others and in your own life – it's that things start and stop so much. As an Aries, and somebody ruled by fiery Mars, the planet of focus and action, when you tackle something, it's natural for you to plunge in. And once you've plunged in, you expect to get things done fast. In fact, the most difficult thing in the world for you is to begin a task, whether it's something at home involving a friend or at work, and then be forced to stop. But every once in a while, you must. Being easy-going in this way is one of your biggest lessons in this life.

What's more, if you battle those situations, you'll either end up more frustrated or could actually make things more complicated. Instead, try going with the flow. Then you'll realise there's a lot of other things to pay attention to – to do and to enjoy. And that many of those things that you'd otherwise have missed out on will be great fun if not a real joy. This is the reason that achieving a balance in your life is so important.

While your drive to get things done and to turn your goals into reality is important, focusing on enjoying what the moment offers is a big lesson for you. And what you learn will become increasingly rewarding, so make the best of it.

You and others

Sometimes you feel so impatient with certain individuals that you want to explode. Once that mood passes, you're more relaxed and would do anything for them. Then, after you've had time to talk and realise what they're struggling with, instead of being annoyed, you understand them much better.

Health and wellbeing

Few things make you feel better than getting out in the fresh air and moving swiftly. But, frustratingly, that's not always possible. The secret is to find minor ways to achieve that same feeling wherever you are, and even when there's not much time. It's challenging, but feels terrific when you manage it.

Goals and challenges

When you know what you're going after, there's no stopping you. However, when your options – or, worse, your own priorities – are unclear, making decisions can be complicated. True, you could act on impulse. Take time to ensure your decisions are wise ones.

THIS DAY FOR EVERYBODY

For ages there's been talk of changes in the circumstances of somebody close to you, events that would be as disruptive as they might be exciting. While, thus far, nothing has happened, suddenly things are moving swiftly. However unsettling this is in the short term, it's in everyone's best interests.

APRIL

09

A R I E S

GIFTS Passionate, Forthright, Loving

CHALLENGES Fixed, Demanding, Self-involved

NUMBER 4

(0+9) + (4) = 13 = (1+3) = 4

Stuck with somebody boring? Ask what's magical in their life. Their answer will amaze you

You

If there's a single lesson for you, it's summed up in the phrase "less is more". It has long been said that living simply is both wise and a virtue. What's more, there is a growing passion for decluttering.

But this lesson is about more than that. It's actually about recognising that sometimes what you're already doing or what you have is plenty. Despite that, this can be challenging for you as an Aries, a fire sign, and somebody who thrives on a challenge, because you want something more to do, and often that will translate into creating or acquiring more of what you already have.

The lesson for you, though, is to pause and recognise what you have and to enjoy it, then to begin to explore. And this is where it can be tricky, because for you as an Aries, and someone who is both passionate by nature and impatient, you'll be eager to do, acquire or achieve what you have in mind right away.

However, the trick is to take it slowly. Ordinarily, this would be frustrating for you. The idea of allowing things to unfold at their own pace is seriously aggravating. The remedy? Finding a balance. Do that, and you'll benefit in ways you couldn't have imagined possible. And that is the path to joy for you in this particular life, as the very special kind of Aries that you are.

You and others

Often, you're the most enthusiastic person in a relationship, and consequently, whatever its nature, whether it's family, romance or career, you'll probably be taking the lead. Yet, it's important that you encourage others to express their views or take action, even if their pace is slower than yours.

Health and wellbeing

The tendency to want to do things with others is so strong in your birthday chart that you'll want to match up to the joys and desires of others. Whether it's the way they like to eat or exercise, it's about teamwork, except you are very much an individual which means learning to pursue that and share joys is a great art.

Goals and challenges

Sharing life is a gift, and this is a gift that you have. Being true to yourself while you're sharing that life is the challenge for you. Once you learn how to do it, not only will this challenge become a joy, you'll find that you're all the closer to others in your life as well.

THIS DAY FOR EVERYBODY

You've no problem airing your views. And, if challenged, you'll make an effort to ensure others understand what's behind those convictions. However, certain individuals are in a tricky mood. So be careful what you say, or minor differences could turn into a major, and completely unnecessary, blow-up.

Set yourself a challenge a week, and see how exciting life becomes

You

The 10th of any month, which is numerologically a "one" day, underlines the importance of doing things on your own. Not necessarily tackling them solo, but you must do what is of personal significance to you.

While that can't always be the case because of obligations to family, work, friends and to yourself, at the same time seek out activities that are rewarding or mean a great deal to you. These can have to do with your physical wellbeing and with developing new and rewarding challenges. It might be that you decide to become so skilled at a particular pursuit that you'll know you've achieved something. Or it could involve a range of activities; and, while it's your decision, it may be something that's visible to others or something you're doing quietly on your own.

This balance between taking action and getting others involved is always shifting, and those changes are of significance in your relationships. You may not actually discuss this with others. However, the fact you're doing something because it's important to you will substantially alter the way you deal with others and, interestingly, mean you're more easygoing with them and enjoy their company more. What's more, you'll feel less pressure to do things your way just to show you're in control, and that alone will bring you huge joy.

You and others

As a fire sign, you're okay with life's ups and downs, although living with constant tension with others isn't easy. Yet certain individuals like it that way. Acknowledging this seems like a defeat until you realise their problems aren't yours to solve. It's not about what others think or do, it's about what you do for yourself.

Health and wellbeing

You have a tendency to put off looking after yourself physically, your excuse being that it can wait until everything else has been dealt with, and everybody else is happy. That will be a long wait. The best approach? Make looking after yourself your priority now.

Goals and challenges

You realise that your biggest goal is to put yourself first. As an Aries, this is not unusual, because being born under the first sign of the zodiac, you know this kind of individuality comes naturally. But in your case, it is a skill you'll be developing for much of your life.

THIS DAY FOR EVERYBODY

Life would be a lot easier if you could make decisions about certain complex situations, then turn those into lasting plans. However, with the foundation on which these are based shifting so swiftly and dramatically, the more flexible your thinking and your long-term vision, the better.

GIFTS Frank, Unconventional, Sincere

CHALLENGES Single-minded, Stubborn, Abrupt

NUMBER 6

(1+1) + (4) = 6

Do you sometimes annoy others? Make it a game. Ask what you can change

You

As an Aries, you were born to face challenges. That may sound like you're in for a struggle, but it's the reverse. You're enthusiastic, if not obsessive, by nature about what you want to do. Having been born under this passionate fire sign, you've a gift for turning merely good ideas into something exciting and, equally, for overcoming obstacles. Your challenge? It's carefully selecting your obsessions.

Sometimes you can get so involved in something, or with somebody, that it becomes central to your life. Only later do you realise that either it's impossible or, if you had achieved your goal, it wouldn't be nearly as rewarding as you'd hoped. This may have to do with an activity, a relationship or even your physical wellbeing. But in every situation, it's vital that you pause and consider whether what seems so important to you now will mean as much next month or next year.

Once you're looking at life from a clearer perspective, you'll be able to view many other elements with new clarity. This will enable you to identify and also to consider ending the pursuit of aims or goals that are unrewarding. It will allow you to recognise how much you've already achieved, and that if you invest more time, energy, thought and, indeed, heart into those activities, life will be richer as the years unfold.

You and others

Finding a balance in relationships is difficult for anybody. But it's particularly the case for you, as an intense and passionate Aries. You'll often put others and their needs first, and in a way that's out of balance. While relationships are always in flux, one of your biggest lessons is focusing on that balance.

Health and wellbeing

Looking after your wellbeing is an important journey for you. However, unless you consciously decide it will be fun, it could seem seriously dull. Finding a way to make it exciting may take a while, but you will. And, what's more, the results will more than justify the effort you've made.

Goals and challenges

For you, life's dull without challenges, but it's important they aren't just challenging physically – they must lift your spirits, too. Simply defining that is itself a challenge. But that's the point. Each day and each step will add to your knowledge, and that increases your joy in what you're doing and achieving.

THIS DAY FOR EVERYBODY

Be watchful of conversations about certain tricky issues. One or two individuals are trying to measure, then compare, the sincerity of others. While this will never work, they need to discover it for themselves. Until then, back off and leave them to their debates, while you busy yourself elsewhere.

Learn to make tasks fun. Then you'll be able to enjoy anything and everything

A
\
R
/
I
\
E
/
S

You

For an April 12th Aries, facing challenges isn't so much what you want to do, but such experiences will strengthen both your identity and confidence. The trick? It's finding a balance between your capacity to face those challenges, in your life and the world you're living in, and being able to relax. It's about knowing when to pause. That may sound strange in situations where you felt frustrated. This isn't because of your success or failure, but because your expectations were very different from the actual circumstances.

Yet one of your greatest gifts is your ability to ignore restrictions. Many Aries achieve a great deal doing that, whether it's climbing peaks – both literal, such as mountains, or those in business – or creating a happy family under difficult circumstances.

But in your particular case, the journey is about situations where you'll need to be aware that making changes requires you to be persistent. This is also about personal goals, especially being close with others. Sometimes you're impatient, because certain individuals don't understand how much you care about your plans, or their ideas differ from yours.

However, the resulting discussions will not only be enormously rewarding, they will also deepen your connection with the individuals in question.

You and others

So often in life, you've wondered if you and those around you were speaking the same language. As an Aries, you're passionate about what you want to do, and about connecting with others, and you're sometimes impatient, because others act at their own, usually slower, pace. The challenge? It's about being patient.

Health and wellbeing

Waking up brimming with energy is fabulous. However, that can be complicated. There are all sorts of ways to make this happen, but you get distracted, Or bored. The trick? Do things that boost your energy, wellbeing and spirits, and change your routine frequently. This won't just make you feel better, you'll be creating a valuable lifelong habit.

Goals and challenges

Keeping life interesting is not an issue. There's always something or somebody to deal with. Your problem? Once you've dealt with a challenge, whether major or minor, you need to pause to enjoy your victory and congratulate yourself. This may seem pointless, but those good feelings are a variety of emotional vitamins, to be taken daily.

THIS DAY FOR EVERYBODY

In raising certain persistent issues, your intention is to speak from the heart. However, the resulting discussions could easily slip into the type of brutally frank exchanges you dread. Tempting as it is to avoid these, don't. Actually, they won't just be timely, they'll do wonders to clear the air.

A
\
R
/
I
\
E
/
S

GIFTS Candid, Vivid, Enthusiastic

CHALLENGES Edgy, Unrelenting, Brash

NUMBER 8

(1+3) + (4) = 8

Want to be the best at something but struggling? Tackle another challenge. Then try again

You

As you know, as an Aries, you can be impulsive. In fact, that's one of your greatest gifts – the ability to think and act swiftly and to be authentic and true to yourself, whatever the situation. Yet, at the same time, there's a tremendous emphasis on the practical side of life and on the doubts that acting with passion raises. This discussion and the resulting process of exploration – either to justify your decisions to yourself, or to explain your thoughts to others – may seem annoying, but, intriguingly, it will bring you closer to others.

The trick, therefore, is not to find the swiftest answer, but to delve deeply and then to talk with those closest, whether it's family, friends or in a work setting. It doesn't matter where. This process will go on in various ways, in various elements of your life. And, in each case, the things you learn while doing this will help you understand yourself better and understand your priorities better, and it will also deepen your relationships.

Even more than that, these discussions will bring a certain joy to exploring situations that you might once have regarded as explosive. While at one point you might be right, as you learn more about who you are, and about how to discuss even very sensitive matters, you'll not only enjoy those discussions, but you will deepen the resulting relationships too.

You and others

As an Aries, you're all or nothing. When you care, it's total – you're honest with others and will support them through thick and thin. But when there are differences, or you can't be there for them, you worry. Sometimes letting go and believing others will survive without you is the challenge. What's most important is how much you care.

Health and wellbeing

You'll sometimes hurl yourself into a diet or exercise routine with admirable enthusiasm. The problem? Often it won't last, because the programme in question didn't suit you personally and you got bored. While many activities are worth your while, make sure you search out the right one.

Goals and challenges

Being comfortable with yourself is essential for you, because it affects your confidence. This creates the foundation for your worldly success at work or with plans or projects. Each day will bring progress. Rejoice in this broader, more exciting world, and the powerful insights it brings about the future.

THIS DAY FOR EVERYBODY

Recently, you've not only discussed matters that, at one point, you'd never have dared even mention, you've learnt a great deal. Tempting as it is to withdraw and mull things over, you're far better off keeping the lines of communication open. Amazingly, you'll soon begin to enjoy those frank exchanges.

Turn boring commitments into a game. Figure out how to make them fun

You

By nature, you're self-sufficient. Your ruling planet is the powerful Mars, which means you tend to feel it's your duty to deal with everything that comes your way. You're actually really good at that. What's more, you enjoy overcoming challenges, because this process both broadens your horizons and teaches you about new people, situations and settings. Even more, it's a measure of your capacity to handle all such matters. Yet certain elements of your life are so important to you that if issues involve them, you'll worry. A lot. You'll be concerned about doing things right, about the impact of plans on circumstances or about upsetting others.

And this is the big lesson for you – to understand that the passion you bring to any situation is important, but if you make decisions based on the past, then you're only complicating your life. The trick? It's to shift your focus from managing the present, the here and now, to focusing on the future.

This is especially important for you as an Aries, because you feel it's so essential to act swiftly. But if you take a deep breath and reflect slowly on your options, extending your thinking into the future, your perspective will change. And, instead of acting swiftly – but, possibly, unwisely – you'll act slowly and with wisdom.

You and others

Sometimes those around you are seriously upset about your plans or ideas. Ordinarily, you'd say nothing but proceed, knowing that success will win them over faster than words. Still, at times, you've no choice but to listen to others' concerns. What they say is one thing, but a serious exchange of ideas matters even more. The secret? Truly listen to what others are thinking, You'll learn a lot.

Health and wellbeing

You're happily involved in what you're doing and enthusiastic about life. As a result, you're so busy you don't notice you're tired. Or, because you're living at a swift pace, you forget to eat. That results in a mood that's difficult for you and for others. It's easy to forget about these things. But remember, and the rewards are huge.

Goals and challenges

There are many varieties of success. Some are about achieving goals of your own, but others are to do with work or affect others. You can get so involved in these that you neglect to set your own targets, from each day being a joy to achieving your own personal successes. These goals matter most of all.

GIFTS Strong, Spontaneous, Dynamic

CHALLENGES Thoughtless, Rigid, Hasty

NUMBER 1

$(1+5) + (4) = 10 = (1+0) = 1$

Is somebody boring? Ask them questions until you discover amazing facts about them

You

For you, life's a constant juggling act, trying to balance everything that you've achieved and the resulting demands on your time versus the dream of getting rid of it all so you can pause and take a deep breath. These extremes are typically Aries. Juggling your time and having too much on your plate is typical. Yet there's a remedy other than making everything go away because you're feeling overwhelmed. It's how you deal with it.

As an Aries and a fire sign ruled by Mars, you are by nature dynamic. You were designed for ongoing excitement. The trick, however, is to know where and what form that excitement will take, how you'll employ that energy and how you can benefit from your actions. And, equally, you'll learn when you need to slow down and cut back on your commitments. This is the tricky part, because "doing less" doesn't come naturally to you.

This is one of your greatest lessons. Firstly, knowing when you need to slow down. Secondly, learning how to pause, to think about what's next and decide whether what you're doing is truly in your best interests. And it's also about cutting back, possibly even letting go of familiar plans or passions. Achieve this balance now, and you'll be able to live it out every day. And that is one of the greatest goals for you.

You and others

Your passion for life is natural. You're intense, sometimes overwhelmingly so. However, reducing that vibe isn't easy. And finding common ground between you and others can be challenging. But it's possible. And doing so will enable you to spend stress-free time with others –family, close friends and colleagues.

Health and wellbeing

You want projects to succeed instantly. That includes looking after yourself, from working out or watching what you eat. And if you aren't successful, you give up. Your challenge? Being patient. But, also, finding ways to look after yourself that excite you and that you enjoy.
Do that, and the rest will be much easier.

Goals and challenges

Some goals can be achieved swiftly. But, as you're well aware, others take much longer. The secret for you is to line up short-term objectives when you're facing something that requires patience, but which you really care about. That simple strategy is the difference between enjoyment and frustration.

THIS DAY FOR EVERYBODY

Certain individuals or, possibly, destiny itself, are trying to take over. Your plans have been disrupted, if not radically changed, and more than once. It may seem that you're alone in these struggles. But look around you and you'll soon realise this is not the case. Everybody is facing similar difficulties.

You can make joy your best friend. It's all about how you decide to live your day – and life

You

Making compromises is difficult for any Aries. It seems as if you're undermining your convictions as an individual. Yet, long ago, you learnt that in certain situations your refusal to compromise will only create complications in your plans and even your life. The challenge is finding a balance between the two. This has to do with how you live, how you think and even your personal style.

Yet, at the same time, you're generous by nature, and if what you do makes others unhappy, then you'll work hard to remedy the situation. The trick in all of this is to borrow a characteristic from the sign opposite yours, Libra, and find a balance between your passion for life and your impatience when it comes to allowing others to take the time they need. It's about each of you understanding the other better. While this is important in close relationships, it's also an amazing tool when it comes to life in general.

As a fire sign, you rarely struggle with the twists and turns and unexpected events that trouble others. You recognise them as an invitation to experience something new, even if that isn't always clear at the time. And that's the skill in learning to slow down and communicate with others at their pace. Make it your objective and not only will you learn a great deal, but also you'll enjoy the process.

You and others

One of your greatest challenges is also one of your greatest gifts. That is your ability to inspire others, yet also to stand up to them. The challenge is recognising the line between the two. The solution? When you discuss such matters, learn to listen more and talk less. It won't be easy, but will change everything.

Health and wellbeing

Sometimes your concerns about things not going as swiftly as they should emerges as being uptight, if not short-tempered, with others. This undermines your own wellbeing. The solution? Back off. Chill. It's the reverse of your instincts, but can improve your mood and lead to brilliant solutions as well.

Goals and challenges

Even when you're living life to the full and when you have what you need, you still have a tendency to want to reinvent things. And that process can steal the joy from the here and now. How to overcome it? Simply be in the moment and rejoice in those achievements.

You could easily misinterpret a change in attitude or plans, or even both, by one particular individual as no more than a bad mood, one from which they'll recover swiftly. Actually, they've misunderstood something that you said or did. This isn't serious but needs attention, and the sooner, the better.

A
\
R
/
I
\
E
/
S

Make bringing happiness to three other people your project. Then see what happens

You

As an April 17th Aries, energy and enthusiasm are your bywords. Although you thrive on it, life itself is a stop-and-go affair, and the resulting changes in pace are as sudden as they are unexpected. It's about observing these rhythms. Some are predictable – days and nights and, even more, the seasons of the year, in which nature reminds us about timing.

For you, it's about allowing certain plans, arrangements and passions to develop at their own pace. This doesn't come naturally to you. Being a fire sign and ruled by the dynamic Mars, your impatience is understandable. Yet one of your lessons is to accept nature's pace and, equally, that projects won't always move at the rate you're planning. The solution? Learn to allow things to grow at their own speed. This isn't just important, it's vital.

If you had a vegetable garden, you couldn't just pull up a carrot to check if it was growing. Instead, you'd simply have to learn how to observe its growth and to patiently wait. In the same way, in other areas of your life you're learning to allow things to grow. Once you understand the process, you'll not only enjoy it and the people involved as well, you'll want to do more of it. That understanding of allowing things to grow, in a garden and in life, is one of the greatest gifts anybody can be given.

You and others

Often when dealing with others, the question isn't what they're doing, but why they're avoiding certain situations – some that involve you but as many that do not. This question links to a frequent irritation with friends, family and, if you work, close colleagues. And that is, why they take so long discussing or dealing with things. There's a simple answer. They're not you. They're not an Aries. Simple.

Health and wellbeing

As a fire sign, you thrive on life lived in the fast lane. Thinking and moving swiftly are your strengths. The problem? Circumstances aren't always in a cooperative mood, and delays are inevitable. The solution? Don't push. Do something out of character and cool it. This may seem a compromise, until you realise options beyond anything you'd imagined possible have appeared from nowhere.

Goals and challenges

It's said that the greatest advice often given to anybody is also the simplest: Be. Here. Now. For you, as an Aries, that can be very difficult, because most of the time your mind is focused on where you're going, not on the present moment. That's your greatest challenge, and achieving it will be your greatest gift.

THIS DAY FOR EVERYBODY

For ages you've been nursing certain long-cherished plans, ideas or alliances that once held promise but are increasingly burdensome. Difficult as saying farewell to these would be, the moment you let go of them, you'll create space in your life for the thrilling events or ideas waiting in the wings.

Don't give up on tough tasks. It will be great remembering how you battled to do them

You

Balancing enthusiasm and optimism with concerns or even pessimism is tricky. Of course, you expect your efforts to do well. And because you're full of that marvellous Aries energy, often they do. Yet there are periods when bad timing, minor obstacles or serious challenges force you to rethink arrangements. However, instead of recognising that changes are necessary, you can get upset or even back off, as if you're almost demanding that nature finds a remedy.

The solution? It's to acknowledge that you're in a period that's forcing you to slow your pace and rethink things – not just your short-term plans but, possibly, life in general. You could battle those changes or, instead, recognise that something new and exciting, but as yet unknown to you, is developing behind the scenes. You need to recognise and embrace nature's pace.

Next, it's about freeing yourself from the past so you can welcome the changes as they take form. You could struggle or embrace this process. If it's the latter, you'll recognise this as the adventure it is. What's more, you'll be in the here and now, and enjoy what you have, without tinkering with things just to keep yourself busy. Take this approach and, without doing a thing, you'll discover a whole new world in the present.

You and others

There are times in life when you haven't just been over-enthusiastic, you've almost bullied others into feeling the way you do. Then you wondered why they were grumpy. This is a real Aries challenge: sometimes your enthusiasm overwhelms others. Still, that shows how much you care. And that's what's important.

Health and wellbeing

The trick to feeling wonderful is twofold. One is to look after your physical body, which you do with enthusiasm, but can also forget to do. However, being happy in your head is mostly the result of being contented with life as it is, even if things aren't going as swiftly as you want, or you have to rethink plans. Finding that balance is a challenge and a gift.

Goals and challenges

The most important thing for you as an Aries to discover is that life is full of exciting challenges, most of which are goals, but in disguise. Once you discover that, you'll think carefully about what the outcome will be. And if you're happy with it, you'll hurl yourself into dealing with those challenges – the sooner, the better.

A
\
R
/
I
\
E
/
S

THIS DAY FOR EVERYBODY ♈

You're eager to take a break from the rather intense discussions of the past few days. But you've learnt so much, and not only about where others stand on certain matters, that your own perspective has changed. Continue to talk things through. The results will amaze you.

Taurus

April 19 – May 19

Taurus   Sensuality and practicality are fundamental to you as a Taurus, the first of the earth signs. While your ruling planet, Venus, accents life's pleasures, it's also about assets, which means you are a gracious individual who lives both well and wisely. That's reflected in your flower, the orchid, and your aromatic spices – cloves and sorrel. Your tree is crabapple, while your stones reflect Venus's pastel shades in both jade and emerald.

T
A
U
R
U
S

GIFTS Persistent, Good taste, Stylish

CHALLENGES Headstrong, Contrary, Lazy

NUMBER 5

$(1+9) + (4) = 14 = (1+4) = 5$

Instead of questioning the unexpected, embrace it with enthusiasm

You

As somebody born under the first day of your sign, you could be termed pure Taurus. You benefit from all of the assets of your sign, but are occasionally bewildered by the rest of the world, especially those who don't see things the way you do. As an earth sign, you're practical and benefit from an ability to enjoy life. And, equally, you've a strong sense of beauty. You appreciate it in life, in food, even in the character of others. What's more, you've a gift for bringing joy to those around you.

This, in turn, benefits your relationships, from family to personal and even more worldly links. Your gift for enjoying the physical side of life extends from your own body to an appreciation of movement and music, possibly even dancing. And then there's food, and often amazing gardens. If there's any challenge, it is differences with others.

You're often puzzled that the values and interests of certain individuals are so at odds with yours. Once that's clear, even challenging relationships with others, and your own comfort with yourself, will grow enormously. We're all here to grow. And one of your most important journeys as someone born under the first day of Taurus is being able to truly savour the influence of your ruling planet, the harmonious Venus, and bring love, joy and pleasure into your life.

You and others

Venus, your ruling planet, accents harmony in all relations, from family and loved ones to friends and even colleagues. You're not casual about any of them. But it's confusing when others seem determined to do things that provoke clashes. Learning to understand each other is a valuable part of your journey.

Health and wellbeing

Because Venus accents beauty and abundance, you can sometimes overdo these. The trick? Look after yourself, but do it luxuriously, whether it's in a gym, on a walk or dancing. Balance the luscious food you enjoy with an activity you love, and you'll fit into the beautiful clothing you enjoy as well.

Goals and challenges

For you, once life is organised the way you want, you like to keep it that way. Consequently, sudden events that upset arrangements can be annoying. But not only are these changes vital, they encourage you to rethink what you enjoy and make improvements where they're needed.

 THIS DAY FOR EVERYONE

Mostly, you enjoy tackling issues as a team. Yet you're uneasy about trusting certain individuals. This is mostly because you're in unfamiliar territory, so feeling anxious in general. As with all feelings, however, these will pass. Knowing that, get involved, but adopt an uncharacteristically slow pace.

APRIL

Increasingly, I recognise the unexpected drawing me into rewarding experiences

20

T
/
A
\
U
/
R
\
U
/
S

You

All Taureans are ruled by the planet Venus, and, in fact, your birthday honours Venus, which is named after the beautiful goddess who signifies all of life's joys and pleasures – everything from scent to flowers to eating well. But it also accents what you own and earn; money and any assets.

What's more, the typical Taurus is interested in collecting, but not just anything. You enjoy acquiring knowledge that expands your appreciation and understanding of your treasures. These may not be objects, but could be a garden, or a skill. The most important thing is the pleasure they give you. It's the same with close alliances – with those you care about. It's not so much what you might call the quality of the character of the individual, but the place they hold in your life and what you give back to them.

And this is one of your greatest gifts and skills as a Taurus, and somebody ruled by charming Venus. It's not until you observe the behaviour of others that you recognise that, often, people simply don't know how to share the experience of being together. For you, it's not only your special gift, it's one that you generously share with others, that is, family, friends and your broader circle – something that improves your life, and theirs and, ultimately, in some ways, the world.

You and others

While spending time relaxing with family and friends is important, it's just as vital that special individuals bring something new into your life. Part of your nature thrives on discovery, on the magic of broadening your horizons. This is linked to your birthday, so it isn't just special – these experiences are like vitamins that will supercharge your life.

Health and wellbeing

You wouldn't necessarily think of health and wellbeing and sensuality in the same phrase. But for you especially, and your sensual Taurean nature, pleasure in the process is as important as the result. Once you discover how to turn achieving your objectives into a joyful endeavour, the rest is easy.

Goals and challenges

The trick to transforming challenges into a game involves exactly that – finding the fun in them. While, initially, this may not be easy for you, instead of dwelling on getting jobs done, try focusing on the joy of discovery. Do that, and each task will become exactly that – a joy.

APRIL

21

T
/
A
\
U
/
R
\
U
/
S

Each time I say no, I explore what a yes would bring my way

You

As an April 21st Taurus, there are big questions in your life. They are important for you, as an earth sign and somebody who appreciates what you have. These questions are, am I what I possess? Am I what I've created? While you should take pride in that, the question also is whether to go deeper in your thinking and to consider if other elements of your life that aren't involved with what you, as an individual, have created are as important.

We're in a world that places emphasis on material things, so it's easy to get lost in conversations about practical, financial or physical achievements. Yet being ruled by Venus, the planet of relationship and beauty, the less tangible, more intuitive side of life is equally important to you. That balance between assessing what you have and what you've achieved, and the nature of your relationships with others, and even with Mother Nature, is important.

In some ways, these relationships support you and feed you in ways that material possessions or achievements can't. This is an essential component – to examine what you're doing with your time and your priorities, and whether you're getting enough good feelings in the process. If these are lacking, it's not difficult to recognise them. It's simply a matter of spending time dwelling on them each day.

You and others

Family and old friends are important. As are those who remind you of the happiness that comes with life's simple pleasures, with nature, with small yet beautiful possessions – all add to your enjoyment of each day. One of the joys of this is that the balance changes, as each year moves on, and as you evolve as well.

Health and wellbeing

You can be a creature of habit. If you've found ways to look after yourself that work for you, that's great. You'll be eating, living and moving in ways you enjoy, but which also benefit your mind and body. However, from time to time, some of those habits may belong in the past, and need to be rethought, if not radically altered.

Goals and challenges

Few individuals are happier than a Taurus who appreciates what they have and has a few projects in mind or underway. Yet, as you know, it's easy to settle into a routine and to put off even exciting changes. That's your challenge and potentially a source of great excitement.

THIS DAY FOR EVERYONE

Although you may be short of facts about recent amazing developments, that shouldn't prevent you from taking action on what you do know. If others say you should organise plans beforehand, thank them politely but ignore them. With things moving swiftly, you'll need to think and act fast.

Just when life seems tough, I realise what an exciting adventure it is

You

You're often described as a sensual Taurus, but that suggests that you indulge yourself broadly. And while that's true – you enjoy your pleasures – another side of your nature, as an earth sign, prefers life to have a certain order, and you like making arrangements and setting goals. What's more, you'll ensure the process of achieving those goals will be fun. But you'll sometimes put off that gratification until you've achieved everything you have in mind, whether in regard to your personal life, your activities out in the world or a long-term goal, perhaps something at school or at work.

Similarly, this involves studying even when you're simply lounging around. You might set yourself the target of learning about art, or a particular sport. For you, this process of making plans and achieving goals is a kind of vitamin. However, finding harmony between this and two other parts of your life – building close alliances, and simply enjoying life for what it is – is one of your challenges.

Once you manage to achieve this – linking certain goals with the pleasure of others' company while learning something new, or simply allowing exciting developments to take over your life for a few days, weeks or even months – you'll find a balance that will turn a life of objectives into a life of joy as well.

You and others

With Venus ruling Taurus, you care deeply about the happiness and wellbeing of others. And if you're asked to do too much or someone else becomes overwhelmed, you'll try to achieve a balance. The trick? Recognise that there are cycles – times to give and times to receive. Find that balance, and you'll achieve peace where, previously, there's been tension.

Health and wellbeing

When it comes to looking after yourself, finding an equilibrium can be challenging. While a regime is tempting, being by nature sensual you must be able to enjoy it. Seek out and find a form of fitness or a way of eating that's a joy, and you'll achieve both health and happiness.

Goals and challenges

Sometimes you become so addicted to certain challenges and how to face them that you forget to stop and embrace partway goals, small achievements that become your priority each day. Equally, it's vital you congratulate yourself on what you've done each day. Do that, and your joys will blossom abundantly.

GIFTS Sensual, Appreciates value, Affectionate

CHALLENGES Unbending, Lazy, Self-indulgent

NUMBER 9

(2+3) + (4) = 9

Every day, love appears in many forms, some as unexpected as they are powerful

You

The theme of your Taurus birthday is the appreciation of beauty. It's likely that you are already well aware of the beauty of the world around you and have been since you were very young, recognising it in your own toys or the things you saw. It may be that something you viewed in your parents' home or were given so fascinated you that it has become a source of interest, if not study. Or, alternatively, it may have been the starting point for exploration of another variety.

Whatever the case – and there could be a range of situations as your life has unfolded – you'll have learnt a lot, not just about those objects, but about the value of time, of your own efforts and even about money itself. While this is important to you, especially as someone born under the sign that's said to rule money, it's also vital for you to spot and deal with habits that could limit your thinking, or your capacity to investigate or enjoy new activities.

This forms a link to the planet that rules your sign – Venus, also ruler of the sign of Libra, which is about balance. Make this your objective, your theme, for today and every day. Do this, and not only will you enjoy these discoveries, you'll also develop a growing awareness of what there is to enjoy in each day of your life.

You and others

You sometimes get short-tempered with family, friends or colleagues, wondering why they waste time on unimportant matters when other activities are more important. However, they aren't you, and probably aren't Taureans. Your challenge? Recognising that others live in their own world, and it's completely different from yours. That's the key to true harmony.

Health and wellbeing

When you're passionately involved in an activity or time with loved ones, the day will fly by and you won't even have taken a walk. You may grab a bite or, alternatively, share a delicious meal with others. Great. But then compensate with the gift of getting out, and getting your own energy going.

Goals and challenges

If there's a single word that could sum up your goals and challenges, it's balance. Too much never works, and struggling is no fun. Focus on balancing what you're always seeking and what you already have in the here and now. Achieve this, and life will become far more joyous day by day.

 THIS DAY FOR EVERYONE

Being told you're about to be disillusioned may not sound like good news. Yet when you think about it, you're trading in a fantasy, one that's likely to be disappointing, for the facts. If you're facing any challenge, it's narrowing down your range of options and deciding what you'll do next.

Beauty and kindness are easy to recognise but, often, generosity isn't as clear-cut

You

For you, Taurus, the twist and turns you face during your day, week or throughout your life can be puzzling, simply because you've worked so hard to organise things and to create the stability that enables you to enjoy life. But then something happens and a plan you've made, your vision, is thrown into disarray – or so it seems. But, actually, it's simply that life is about change. The weather changes, clouds pass in the sky and the plants around you grow.

And, indeed, your own life and relationships with others will also change and grow. Still, you'll often put off, if not battle, changes, because you fear the disarray they'll bring. It's true, the process of change and growth can be unsettling, if not untidy. Yet making plans is one thing, taking action on them is another. What's more, finding a balance between those plans and allowing space for growth is a crucial challenge – and a skill. Once you understand how it's done, you'll also develop the ability to turn the process of exploration into something you enjoy. As a Taurus, and a sensual earth sign, life isn't just about being practical. Deep down, you feel that living well is an art. Once you recognise it as such – an art you can enjoy in ways small and large, in every day of your life – everything else will be so much more exciting, and more worthwhile.

You and others

Sometimes you make plans with others, then they change them. You're irritated, and ask why. They'll detail sudden changes, which intrigue you. This balance in all close relationships shifts constantly and is always informative. The key? First, ask questions. Second, recognise twists and turns are normal. Support each other through those, and learn and share together.

Health and wellbeing

Here the key to finding pleasure in looking after yourself is so important. For you, going to a gym where everyone's sweaty may work, but won't necessarily be as rewarding as taking a walk in the countryside, or even being around those who are doing something that is as energising as it is worthwhile.

Goals and challenges

You can be a creature of habit. It's predictable, but also comfortable. And you then realise life's no longer exciting. For you the great skill is spotting that rut before you become so accustomed to it that any change seems impossible. Actually, you can make those changes right now.

GIFTS Tough, Generous, Music-lover

CHALLENGES Immoderate, Wilful, Insensitive

NUMBER 2

(2+5) + (4) = 11 = (1+1) = 2

Joy comes in new and unexpected ways, making each day an adventure

You

For you as an April 25th Taurus, life centres on balance, living well and love. It's about finding the capacity to be true to yourself, to enjoy what life has to offer, yet also to love those around you – your family, friends and romantic partners.

However, at the same time, you must face the fact that this requires you to love yourself first. This may sound like psychobabble, but as somebody ruled by Venus, the planet of love, it's essential. This requires a degree of analysis that may not come naturally to you as a Taurus and an earth sign. You are, of course, very logical. But the kind of detached analysis that's so important for any personal growth may take time. Deep down, you feel that you and those you're with simply understand each other. Often, getting to know others is like learning a foreign language, and while you can do it on your own, it's worth getting guidance.

Talking things over gives you a chance to look at what you're doing, and what your priorities are, from a fresh perspective. This also offers a glimpse of new ways of dealing with existing issues and possibilities for the future. Do this from time to time, and be reminded there's always yet more to discover and yet more joys to share with those around you, whether it's those closest, those you work with or those you're about to meet.

You and others

Close alliances are important. However, even these can settle into a routine that's reassuring and easy yet restrictive. It may even mean that you miss out on taking opportunities on your own, with others or to meet new people. Balancing stability with the unexpected is an important skill. Achieve it, and you'll soon be exploring exciting new activities.

Health and wellbeing

True, habits are important. Theoretically, you needn't change worthwhile habits. But, both in relationships and in looking after yourself, breaking habits can introduce new magic into your life. Tempting as it is to get into a routine, be bold. Make changes just to make them. You'll soon realise how exciting looking after yourself can be.

Goals and challenges

Discovery is the key here. When you begin to recognise how much there is out there for you to not only experience but also enjoy, rather than settling into a familiar routine, which, as a Taurus, you can do, you'll make a deal with yourself to discover something new and wonderful every single day of your life.

 THIS DAY FOR EVERYONE

Every once in a while, life is good, so much so that there's no need to query ideas or offers. All that's necessary is that you respond to events as they arise. Yet certain well-meaning individuals are warning you things are just too easy. At other times, that might be true. But not now.

The unexpected is, increasingly, the highlight of my day

You

From your point of view, you're a pretty straightforward person – someone who loves life and beauty and tries to use your time wisely. However, destiny seems determined to make this difficult for you. There's a secret to this. It's about achieving balance in several areas of your life. It's about what you intend to do, and those things that pop up that often distract or annoy you. Then, eventually, you realise that, actually, these unexpected events are an invitation that's leading you into new territory.

While this may involve your daily routine, it's also about your social life, from family and relationships to your job and pursuits you're passionate about. Unsettling as those twists and turns may seem, they're about breaking habits, which in turn lead to unexpected discoveries. While planning ahead is important, this is about organising your life so you can embrace the unexpected. Go with the flow, and you'll discover how much fun you can have venturing into the unknown.

Yes, this is out of character for you. However, those relationships and activities – and even certain once burdensome duties – will become more fun every day. In fact, you might even find yourself going off in new and rewarding directions and enjoying them before you even realise it.

You and others

Often, chatting with certain individuals is such hard work that you wonder why you bother. However, others don't think this. They have lower expectations. For you, finding those individuals with whom you have a special spark is vital, and enjoying others is an essential skill. Discover that and, bizarrely, you'll have the key to the joy you're seeking.

Health and wellbeing

Every Taurus has experienced the feeling that when they're doing one thing, they should be doing something else. While you might say it's because you have a rich imagination, it could also be because you're avoiding getting out and about when you're so comfortable. The secret? Take that imagination out for a brisk walk, and ask your body to come along too.

Goals and challenges

In general, it's your goals and challenges that we've been talking about here. Familiar habits are holding you back. Note those, and each day break a habit – a little one maybe, then a medium-sized one and, once a week, a big one. Not only will your life be a lot more fun, the results could be miraculous.

THIS DAY FOR EVERYONE

Sometimes even the simplest of plans take ages to organise. Yet now, and over the coming days, things will move with astonishing swiftness. This is wonderful. Bear in mind, however, that you'd best have all the details beforehand, because you'll have no opportunity afterwards.

GIFTS Luxury-loving, Persistent, Affectionate

CHALLENGES Single-minded, Insensitive, Headstrong

NUMBER 4

$(2+7) + (4) = 13 = (1+3) = 4$

Making plans boosts my sense of control, yet the unexpected brings magical moments

You

If there were a single motto for your life, it would be summed up in the hopeful phrase, "One day, everything will work out." As a Taurus ruled by Venus, the planet of beauty and order, it's understandable that this is your ideal. But the fact is that each day the sun rises and each evening it sets; the world changes and so do you. And while that idealistic order you're seeking may be achieved on one particular day, with the world itself changing, life itself must shift, change – and on occasion, reform itself – as well.

And that's the big lesson for you – in general, and very much as the future unfolds. Appealing as the thought of getting things organised perfectly may be, you'll be far better off simply accepting the disarray in which events unfold, and to find the beauty in that.

As someone ruled by Venus, once you can discover beauty in anything, including the way things unfold, you'll also have answered all the questions and dealt with all the obstacles that otherwise would seem to keep popping up. You'll see the beauty in growth. And that, as a Taurus, is essential for you. You'll be able to tackle even the tricky situations and difficult individuals with a delight that previously wouldn't have been possible. And you'll also have the key to planning the future as well.

You and others

As desirable as creating and maintaining harmony in relationships is, sometimes you learn most and gain a greater understanding of others when you're working out your differences. The trick? It's to pause, review what you've learnt and, if any apologies are due, to make them then.

Health and wellbeing

When you were very young, there was everyday life and everyday eating, and then there were treat times. These occurred during seasonal holidays, when away on a break or, of course, as part of a birthday or celebration. The secret is to include those mini-treats in everyday life, just often enough to lift your spirits and remind you how special life can be.

Goals and challenges

From your earliest days, you were probably asked what you wanted to be when you grew up. Since then, a lot has changed – for you, and also the world. However, there may still be a part of you that feels you really should be pursuing that childhood dream, however unappealing or inappropriate it is. If so, the best time to say farewell to it is now. It's time to embrace the future.

THIS DAY FOR EVERYONE

Most questions have relatively straightforward answers. However, several aren't just perplexing – you're under pressure from certain demanding individuals to come up with answers fast. They're being unrealistic. Explain diplomatically but firmly that there's no way you can fulfil their demands.

While changes can be puzzling, I welcome a thrilling surprise

You

For you, as an April 28th Taurus, living well and with joy is a priority. That may sound strange, because you'd imagine that everyone thinks that way. Yet they don't. This also means that if you intend to spend time with those around you, whether it's family, friends or colleagues, it's your responsibility to organise things. While that's sometimes annoying, it also means those arrangements will be far more interesting than if you left plans to others.

Yet, being a Taurus and ruled by Venus, which also rules Libra, the relationship sign, it's all about collaboration. Getting others involved in plans is an art. What's more, those around you may have very different views about what they'd enjoy. In fact, when they come up with something, you may wonder what on earth they're thinking. Actually, they're revealing their point of view to you.

Recognising this is part of your journey. The more you listen to, learn about and experience what others find joy in, the better you'll understand them, and you'll gain a better understanding of yourself as well. While you could sit back and try to figure things out, your birthday is linked to learning. The more you explore and the more you experiment, the more you'll discover and the more joy you'll have with every passing day.

You and others

As a Taurus and an earth sign, you're often the person who everybody expects to make decisions. However, sometimes you're too cautious. That's one of your biggest lessons. Make a deal with yourself to take a chance, on your own and with others. You'll not only learn a lot, but even seemingly challenging relationships will suddenly begin to be fun.

Health and wellbeing

Life's about breakthroughs. Once, you enjoyed doing certain things and eating foods that were good for you. But you've changed and times have changed so those habits need to change as well. It's all about experimentation. Take chances with eating, with what you do and with how you live. What you discover will be as unexpected as it is exciting.

Goals and challenges

The biggest challenge for you is to resist settling into a familiar activity. Instead do something new – if not every day, then at least once a week. Get yourself into this routine, and what you discover, who you meet and the delights you encounter will feed you in ways beyond anything you'd imagined possible.

THIS DAY FOR EVERYONE

Urgent as certain decisions seem, don't allow anyone to corner you into committing to something you're unsure about. The problem isn't a lack of options but too many. You need to explore and experiment. Let others know that's the approach you're taking and that you will finalise plans later.

GIFTS Stylish, Sensual, Appreciates quality

CHALLENGES Wilful, Excessive, Inflexible

NUMBER 6

(2+9) + (4) = 15 = (1+5) = 6

I recognise that disappointments are often thrilling surprises in disguise

You

As a Taurus, and an earth sign, you're a collector. You may collect objects, but you'll also collect experiences and, in the same way, friendships with people. And some of them – those objects, and those people – will stay in your life for a long time, and this familiarity gives you a kind of comfort.

Yet, at the same time, every once in a while, you need to allow changes to roll in your life. And it would appear that finding a balance between these two, between creating a collection of people and activities that are rewarding, and ensuring that changes take place, is a skill that it's important for you to develop as you live through the days and months and years of your life.

This is especially significant because otherwise you could easily settle into something that's appealing but which, when changes arise, as is inevitable in life, could lead to complications. You'll either worry that something's wrong and try to go back to the way things were, or instead you'll realise that, every once in a while, life is not about merely dealing with changes, but embracing them and, as a result, thinking and living in a new way. Once you've developed this skill, you'll be able to enjoy these changes, enjoy the changes in the lives of those around you and enjoy the changes in your world all the more.

You and others

Being close to others – from family and friends to certain special individuals – is important. So when they act unpredictably, you worry or become upset. The key? Discuss this, and everything else, often. They may question this. Fine. Slowly they, too, will realise how much they're benefitting from these changes. They might even begin to enjoy them.

Health and wellbeing

For you, habits are natural. And they're reassuring. Once something works for you, you'll stick with it. However, it may be that 20 years have passed, or your life's changed, yet you're still doing the same thing, the same way. Make a point of discovering things, and regularly. You'll be glad you did.

Goals and challenges

Sometimes a goal seems uncomplicated. Often it is. Learning a sport such as tennis, or appreciating jazz perhaps. But as important are shifting goals, some long-standing. Each day, say something new, try something new and agree to something unexpected. You'll soon realise how rewarding this is.

THIS DAY FOR EVERYONE

It doesn't matter whether the issues in question are personal or involve others. They're unsettling and therefore not easy to discuss. Despite that, the time has come to raise them. It won't be easy. Still, once you do, you'll notice how grateful others are that you had the courage to bring these up.

There's no wrong way to be thankful, yet it's a skill to receive gratitude

You

For you, the art of reviewing is an important one. This may seem strange, because most of the time, we focus on the present. However, this is actually about pausing to consider what you've done recently and, equally, to think about times in the past when it seemed as if things worked better, or life was easier. This may well have been true, but it could also be that in your imagination you remember things as being easier, simply because you've forgotten the parts that were difficult or challenging. This process of review isn't about idealising the past, but remembering challenges and what you learnt from them.

Every so often, life throws a twist or turn your way. And if you consider these to be a nuisance and do all you can to stop them, then life could turn into a battle. If, on the other hand, you remember times in the past when those twists and turns became joys, then you'll recognise that, even though what you're doing is unsettling, it, too, will become a joy.

It's the same with close alliances with others. Sometimes it may take a bit of imagination to picture where things are going, especially when you're having difficulty with family members or with somebody close. Yet, every once in a while, you've had to break through those difficult times and you always learn from them in amazing ways.

You and others

Your instincts say that relationships with close friends or partners are guided by destiny. Some go back ages and you've grown close slowly, while with others there was an instant connection. However, things move on. Understand that changes are like the seasons, and not only will you enjoy them, but you'll also discover how enriching they are.

Health and wellbeing

Yes, feeling well in life has lots to do with how you eat and the way you live. But, even more, it's about enjoying every minute. This may sound absurdly idealistic, but sometimes life seems an uphill climb. And the trick is to recognise that often these challenges are gifts in disguise.

Goals and challenges

Sometimes goals are clear-cut. However, often they come in the form of a challenge at the gym, sticking to a diet or undertaking studies. And those goals aren't always clear. So if you notice the challenge then you'll be aware at its conclusion that you've achieved far more than you ever conceived possible.

GIFTS Loving, Tough, Music-lover

CHALLENGES Lethargic, Headstrong, Unsympathetic

NUMBER 6

(0+1) + (5) = 6

Increasingly, I'm surprising myself at my joy when the unexpected shakes things up

You

Being a May 1st Taurus brings a complex range of options, opportunities and joys. May Day is one of the happiest days of the year – a celebration of spring, flowers, beauty and joy. It's a wonderful theme for your birthday. And it's also about the joys of family and friends and colleagues and loved ones; being able to truly enjoy time with them, and the pleasures that come with that.

However, there's a part of you that's very much about the first of the month, about action and getting things done. But some of those joys take time, just as being able to understand somebody doesn't happen overnight The flowers that are so much a part of the spring take a while to blossom. If you've planted a bulb, it may not yet be in flower.

The lesson for you is to recognise the passion you bring to the moment sometimes needs to be balanced with patience. And, occasionally, you need to remind others to do this as well. In fact, it may be that they're making demands on you to move more swiftly, or be more passionate, in ways that are unwise, if not impossible. They want you to care more about what they're doing in the ways they want. This is a valuable part of the journey, one that enables you to discuss differences and to learn from them, and in doing so, to deepen those relationships.

You and others

One of your greatest challenges is the conflict between your desire for harmony – and understanding of others – and certain issues that aren't easily resolved. Yet this is a rewarding lesson. It's the simple acknowledgement that those differences are a great gift. At last, you'll enjoy them for who they are, and they'll enjoy you as well.

Health and wellbeing

Often it's assumed that everybody's happy to pursue health and wellbeing by eating in one particular way and heading off to the gym. But, also, there's simply enjoying what each day brings and the company of others. When you find that single joy, the rest may or may not follow, but it won't matter nearly as much.

Goals and challenges

Some say that life's greatest joy is achieving your goals. But others say it's about savouring what the day brings. Certainly making that your priority will mean you will have a smile on your face when you wake up and when you go to bed at night.

THIS DAY FOR EVERYONE

The time has come to let go of familiar but restrictive arrangements. From time to time you've considered making changes but decided it would be too much bother. Now events are forcing your hand. Tempting as it is to do the bare minimum, you'd regret it. Muster your courage and plunge in.

Daily, I worry less, and my understanding of the power of kindness and generosity grows

You

True, you were born under the sensual and sensible earth sign of Taurus. However, to a certain degree, you share the sensibilities of Libra, the other sign associated with the planet Venus, which is always trying to balance things and make everybody happy. While you certainly want others to be happy, you'd never sacrifice your plans just for the sake of a good mood. As an earth sign, you have a strong instinct about what will work and what won't. You may have found that if you stick with those feelings and talk things through with others, you'll not only achieve an accord with them, but also figure out a way to do whatever needs to be done wisely and well. Better yet, in the process you'll deepen your relationship with those individuals.

You'll also enjoy the process of creating something, which is so central to being an earth sign and being a Taurus. This may be an object, a beautiful home or even a business. It could be something small or large. For you, the act of creating is an art. And there's also the art of sharing and exchanging ideas with others in a way that allows you to recognise that, often, they see things very differently from the way you do.

This recognition brings a certain peace to what may have been tricky relationships in the past and promises more in the future.

You and others

Being ruled by Venus means relationships are important to you. But finding harmony when it seems others are almost trying to create disarray isn't easy. However, their views about life and relationships may differ from yours. The secret? Get them to listen more. Then do the same. Instead of getting lost in those differences, you'll build a beautiful bridge between you.

Health and wellbeing

There are two perspectives on your health and wellbeing: one is purely about how you eat and look after yourself. But the other, inner point of view accents the joys in your life, those that bring a happiness that includes, but is beyond, the physical. The simple idea of inner wellbeing is key.

Goals and challenges

Setting goals is important, but turning them into challenges can make them difficult. Yet there is another way, and that is joy in exploring your goals. You will then focus on bringing your vision to reality. This is a variety of magic that you can use every day.

Inevitably, certain changes will mean leaving elements of the past behind. While in some situations this is a relief, others bring a pang of regret. If so, pause to reflect on what you've done, enjoyed or accomplished, then say farewell. At the moment, life's about discovery, not dwelling on the past.

GIFTS Good taste, Appreciates value, Realistic

CHALLENGES Immoderate, Selfish, Wilful

NUMBER 8

(0+3) + (5) = 8

What seems an insurmountable obstacle today will become tomorrow's joy

You

As a Taurus, you are often easy-going, and being ruled by Venus means you have a unique charm, one that's appealing to everyone. Yet, as a May 3rd Taurus, you can sometimes be on edge, if not impatient with yourself. You want things to work well, and you have goals – yet you can't quite figure out how to make these happen. The resulting impatience can lead to making plans that, because they're done in haste, are unpredictable and unreliable.

The trick to dealing with this is to spot that impatience and recognise that it won't make things happen any more swiftly. However, it does suggest that you could unintentionally do things that ultimately you'll regret. Firstly, you need to think about the past, and previous situations that turned out brilliantly, often because you gave them a certain special attention. It's the same now. And, in fact, this isn't about getting things done quickly, but about what you learn about yourself and this variety of patience.

These are some of your greatest challenges. However, not only will you overcome them, what you learn will turn into a skill. It's also about allowing your imagination to work, which means giving it time. This is all about trust, and when you eventually trust in this way, you'll find a new joy, not only in every day of your life, but in being you.

You and others

Every once in a while, you find yourself wondering why others behave as they do. It's puzzling why they argue about matters when it's clear what's right. However, their view of life differs from yours – it's as if you both see the same life but from a different angle. Realising that makes everything else much easier.

Health and wellbeing

Feeling positive isn't just about eating well and exercising. It's about being able to relax. Often you put so much pressure on yourself that you are on edge with others. Instead of analysing those problems, focus on something beautiful. Do it often. Gradually, you'll exchange those tensions for a smile.

Goals and challenges

Sometimes goals are very specific and challenges can be defined. But often you're impatient, and either obstacles are slowing your progress or there are problems with others. These happen, and sometimes you can't control them. But you can decide to relax and see what happens. There may well be progress without you doing a thing.

THIS DAY FOR EVERYONE

For weeks you've kept quiet about unsettling issues, thinking that others weren't ready to discuss them. While that's true, you were relieved to avoid them, too. Now that circumstances are forcing these out in the open, waste no time on analysis. The faster you begin discussing them openly, the better.

GIFTS Well-presented, Loving, Hospitable

CHALLENGES Stubborn, Excessive, Arrogant

NUMBER 9

$(0+4) + (5) = 9$

Wise ideas guide the way, but laughter makes persistence easy – and a joy

You

For you, Taurus, as an earth sign ruled by Venus, the planet that has to do with beauty and balance, figuring out a plan is essential. Once you know this, then you can think about each stage, what you'll do and also about others' responsibilities. Then you can relax. While this makes sense, it's likely minor events or unexpected developments could trigger doubts, or even undermine your plan. It's happened before, so you may wonder if there's a flaw in your thinking. Actually, you're approaching things perfectly. These doubts can overshadow the here and now if you let them. Tempting as it is to focus on past experiences, it often means you're stuck with the familiar when it's better to take chances – although not in a way that triggers those previously mentioned doubts.

Important as making plans may be, make sure they're flexible. They may have to do with your personal life, close alliances, your work or how you organise long-term plans. In every case, it's about knowing what you want and setting yourself goals, yet also including a kind of flexibility that you sometimes regard as being weak. Most of all, learn to view making plans and life itself as a great adventure. The more chances you take, the more fun you'll have – and the greater your rewards will be.

You and others

Being ruled by Venus means that for you relationships are precious. Whether it's family, friends or loved ones, you want others to know how important they are to you. Yet sometimes, their way of looking at things differs from yours so much, you've no idea what to say. The trick? Recognising how very differently each individual see things. Acknowledging that alone will change everything.

Health and wellbeing

Looking after your health is one thing, and if you do, that's great. However, stress can be unsettling and may even interfere with your sleep. But you aren't always sure what exactly is causing that stress. Amazingly, you don't need to know. Just employ a trick designed for Taureans – take a deep breath, and, as you do so, simply accept life as it is, even if just for that moment.

Goals and challenges

What's most important is living a happy life. You'd think as a Taurus, you'd be easy-going, but you put lots of pressure on yourself in terms of how you live, work or even your style. Actually, the highest achievement is simply living each day with joy.

THIS DAY FOR EVERYONE

There are few things as bitter as being disappointed by somebody you've trusted. Before you draw any conclusions, however, ask a few questions. And be forthright. The odds are good that they were dealing with issues of which you were unaware. Once you learn about these, all will be forgiven.

I'm learning to ask whether those who give advice are themselves happy

You

As a Taurus and an earth sign, you don't particularly think of life as being about cycles, but as a May 5th Taurus, life isn't just about cycles. It's about new discoveries, and the excitement that comes with them. This can be in terms of people or activities, then the process of learning about those – and the doubts and concerns that arise. Perhaps, in some cases, you're even feeling disillusioned, and then doing it all over again.

This journey is important to understand, because it's actually about life. In life itself, there are seasons. There's spring, when you were born and everything is bursting with bloom. There's summer's heat and there's autumn, when the blooms vanish and the leaves fall from the trees. Then there's the stillness of winter, leading to spring again. In your life too, it's about this cycle.

When you become comfortable with this, then you'll also understand that, important as certain relationships are, they'll have their ups and downs. As exciting as certain discoveries may be, whether they relate to personal goals or activities out in the world, each will be about a journey that may occasionally be easy, but will often have twists and turns. You'll also discover how exciting and rewarding these are. Once you do that, you'll have learnt one of life's most important lessons.

You and others

Few things upset you as much as when somebody you've trusted disappoints you. The big question is, have you learnt that the issue is not their actions, but your own expectations? There may have been a misunderstanding or an unexpected problem. It's happened to you before and will again. The secret is to realise mistakes are human and there's nothing to forgive.

Health and wellbeing

While it's good to eat healthily and move well, stress can be one of the most challenging elements of your life. Learning to undo that stress is one of the major themes for you as a May 5th Taurus. The trick is to disentangle yourself from situations that ordinarily you might get wound up about, and to learn to be relaxed.

Goals and challenges

Having goals is important, as is spotting challenges. Learning how to dance around those goals is the biggest trick of all. This is the lesson for you, to recognise that it isn't about getting things resolved on any particular day, but simply enjoying what each day brings.

THIS DAY FOR EVERYONE

Life is full of minor disagreements that often lead to valuable discussions and rewarding new ideas. Now, however, you're taking one particular issue too seriously, mostly because it involves a matter about which you have intense feelings. Admitting this won't be easy, but it is essential.

GIFTS Values Investments, Persistent, Tough

CHALLENGES Wilful, Uncooperative, Immoderate

NUMBER 2

$(0+6) + (5) = 11 = (1+1) = 2$

I'm drawn to elegance, yet am increasingly aware of the beauty of wisdom

You

As a May 6th Taurus, you'll find that every once in a while you face a puzzle – one that's more or less unique to you. It's not unusual because, as a practical earth sign – and also what is termed one of the fixed signs of the zodiac, that is, the signs born in the middle of each season – once you understand a situation or figure out a plan, you'll stick with it. Yet, you frequently seem to encounter individuals who have an entirely different approach to certain situations.

If you make suggestions but are ignored, this can be puzzling, if not a very real challenge. The trick is to realise that your understanding of how things work is yours and yours alone. The perspective of others about the same thing can be very different. Acknowledge that, and the resulting exchange of ideas can bring amazing insights.

This is actually about broadening your horizons. Why? Because another point that's key to your birth date is the importance of being flexible, rethinking plans and altering goals as you go along. While you may make arrangements based on the past – which makes sense because they've already worked – if you use that approach now, with things having changed, you could miss a whole new world of discovery, excitement and experiences just waiting for you to become part of it.

You and others

You've decided to embrace a new, flexible approach to life. Great. What about others? Forget about discussion and just live it, day by day, and see what happens. Your concerns may be about old habits that you're changing anyway. You may even welcome ideas you've dismissed as unrealistic or unwise. Better yet, you could create a new way of being together, one that's all about discovery.

Health and wellbeing

Tension can undermine your health. You may be doing what you need to do – eating right, getting out and about – but if you're uptight, this can overshadow the sense of health and wellbeing that you've created. Finding this balance and ensuring it includes joy is one of your biggest challenges.

Goals and challenges

While some challenges have to do with finding that joy, being able to roll with ups and downs is the most important component for you. In some cases, this means going along with what others think. Initially, you might question them, but soon you'll discover just how clever they were.

As much as you enjoy talking over intriguing ideas, ensure others understand you're doing no more than that – exploring possibilities. Certain individuals will mistake your enthusiasm for serious interest in getting involved. Explain that clearly and you'll avoid misunderstandings, if not hurt feelings, later.

GIFTS Luxury-loving, Insistent, Hospitable

CHALLENGES Self-indulgent, Immoderate, Unbending

NUMBER 3

(0+7) + (5) = 12 = (1+2) = 3

Seeking the perfect plan tempts fate, whereas a flexible vision welcomes it

You

The theme for you as a May 7th Taurus is building your best life. Of course, as a Taurus ruled by the elegant Venus, this isn't anything new. Except in your particular case it is, because your ideas about what's best are themselves shifting. There's a part of you that's impatient. Once you get things organised, if they aren't quite as good as you'd hoped, you'll need to change something – and then something else again.

It seems like one thing after the other changes, but you're never quite satisfied. Yet the joy actually comes from what's inside you. It's being able to savour the process of making those changes, whether it involves you on your own, whether it has to do with your relationship with Mother Nature, whether it has to do with family or friends or even a business. It may be all of these things. Whatever it is, the joy also stems from recognising the role you're taking on your own or with others in those changes, and that's the greatest discovery for you.

When you do that, you'll also get in touch with a creative side of your own nature, something it's easy to miss out on in a time that emphasises chatting about things and doing so much. Your love affair with Mother Nature is one of the most important aspects of your life. This encourages you to explore it.

You and others

Your theme is teamwork, but not as you've thought of it previously. It's spotting those who are struggling with an issue that's very different from what you're facing. The trick is not to focus on the goal, but to turn each day's challenges, however minor, into a lesson. Together, you'll learn to master them, then turn them to your advantage.

Health and wellbeing

There are all sorts of formulas for waking up with a spring in your step, including exercise, vitamins and the right diet. However useful these are, there's a secret rarely mentioned – and that is to expect the best, and in turn, ensure that's what you give to others. Simple. And it works miracles.

Goals and challenges

Some people are obsessive list-makers, but everybody makes a list at some point in their lives. Really, you only need one thing on your list. To choose the most exciting, promising approach to any task, then tackle it right away. That alone will ensure you get everything done, with a few adventures along the way.

THIS DAY FOR EVERYONE

After a fast-paced and exciting period, things are slowing down and you're able to focus on the practical side of things. You'll realise you're just in time. If you don't act swiftly, certain obligations or financial issues could become troublesome. The sooner you tackle these, the better.

Sometimes I seek others' advice when I could simply ask them for a hand

You

As a May 8th Taurus, the big question revolves around the pleasure you take in what you do or in what you acquire. True, you've no choice about many elements of your life. However, you've a range of options in terms of timing, the people involved and the extent of your commitment. This isn't about money, investment or status, it's about the quality of your experience, so even simple arrangements are appealing, if not just plain wonderful.

That different kind of satisfaction has less to do with settings, situations or objects and more to do with lifting your spirits, being quiet and feeling inner peace. Of course, even thinking this way is new for many, and organising your life so events include experiences like this may seem unlikely, if not impossible. Yet you're already recalling certain times this happened, so you know it's possible.

Knowing you can do this is one thing. Doing it is another. But when it comes to your everyday life, it may seem that bringing a similar joy would be asking too much, if not impossible. However, it's the feeling behind it all, the beauty in the mood and the spirit of those involved, even in nature around you, that add to the enchantment. Take that approach and you'll begin to relax and simply enjoy dealing with a bright day or a sunlit evening, or even with simply taking a breath.

You and others

You are all about quality of life. Explaining that to others isn't easy, mostly because their ideas will differ from yours. What's more, because you sometimes question your own priorities, discussions with others can be confusing. The solution? If their ideas are unlikely to enrich your thinking, change the subject. Save deep discussions for those who have something to offer.

Health and wellbeing

Health can be achieved by looking after yourself, by eating well and by exercising. However, wellbeing comes with inner peace, and that's about your own journey, as an individual, as a May 8th Taurus. It's also about the kind of discoveries that are so important. Recognise those and you'll also find joy.

Goals and challenges

Achieving a goal seems clear cut. It's about building something, acquiring a certain amount of money or arranging a successful event. However, enjoying the challenge is something else entirely. That involves balancing those goals with your own nature. Instead of tackling challenges because they're there, first ask yourself how much you care about them to begin with.

THIS DAY FOR EVERYONE

When it comes to certain rather tricky matters, timing is as crucial as your strategy. What appear to be setbacks are actually preventing you taking action now. Frustrating as this is at the moment, you'll be more than compensated by what comes your way very soon.

T
/
A
\
U
/
R
\
U
/
S

GIFTS Animal-lover, Generous, Realistic

CHALLENGES Unsympathetic, Uncompromising, Idle

NUMBER 5

(0+9) + (5) = 14 = (1+4) = 5

Love can be shown with affection or gifts, yet it can be felt from far away

You

For you, one particularly big question comes to mind again and again. It's actually the core of being ruled by the planet Venus. On the one hand Venus, the goddess of love, has to do with exactly that – loving those around you, your family, offspring and even close friends – and sometimes it's about loving what you do. Yet, equally, being a Taurus and therefore conscious of every element of your wellbeing, living well but wisely is important, too.

One of the questions that often arises is whether this stability is more important than those loving bonds with others. Which should you put first? The answer is neither. Instead, you must find yourself, and the centre of your being within. This will enable you to love life, whatever you're doing. And, while life inevitably has its ups and downs – and even the most careful, thorough and calculating Taurus will experience these – learning how to enjoy who you are and, at the same time, how to enjoy those around you is a vital skill.

Ironically, this isn't about passionate love as much as it's about the sheer joy of life itself, and being able to take pleasure in that is one of life's greatest gifts. The secret is learning to enjoy it, whatever the setting and whoever you're with. The more you develop this ability, the happier life will be.

You and others

Often our standards vary. We tolerate one thing from family and close friends, another from neighbours or colleagues and yet another from strangers. But, being ruled by Venus, which accents what you both value and love, the trick is to view all of these individuals as fellow human beings. It may seem strange, but it's easier and will make you happier.

Health and wellbeing

For you, health is one thing, but enjoying life is quite another. That means being so "together" that you don't allow even unsettling events to upset you. That may sound idealistic, because all sorts of things happen. But part of your journey is learning to recognise them as passing, which they will.

Goals and challenges

There is no simple way to overcome a challenge, but there's a very simple way to deal with it. That's to recognise that, instead of battling it, you can seek a new approach. When you spot it, you make it possible to exchange the concept of goals and challenges for a creative way of living life itself.

THIS DAY FOR EVERYONE

Having dealt with a series of unsettling situations, the last thing you want is yet more unexpected developments. However, disruptive as these may be, you'll soon realise how much you'll benefit from them, and exchange irritation for enthusiasm about changes that you recently dreaded.

Certain individuals bring out the worst in me, but what I learn is worthwhile

You

As a May 10th Taurus, you live life with an understated passion. Of course, as a Taurus, you're perfectly capable of free-flowing passion. But, normally, you try to avoid allowing this to dominate your life. You also give considerable thought to what's in your best interests and, equally, the price you'd pay if you allowed that passion to take over. While that's wise, every once in a while it's important that you let go. This is about the feelings of passion you experience when a plan or project comes together – it could involve anything from a garden to a business, or even a long conversation with another. Once you've experienced this, you'll know it's worth the risk.

Still, finding and maintaining the balance that's so important for you can be difficult, if not actually challenging. The trick is to realise how much you relish and, in fact, benefit from the action, and the heat of it all. But, also, you'll develop the stillness of finding your way back to your own centre.

That's the secret – to have that passion in some element of your life, yet to remain connected to your centre. Do this, and you'll have accomplished one of the greatest lessons of this life, one that's about being who you are – a passionate and intense individual, yet one who retains a powerful link to your fundamental nature as a grounded Taurus.

You and others

Obviously, relationships matter. While many are easy-going, those involving certain individuals take a very special role, and demand a particular kind of attention. In these, you try to figure them out, to anticipate if not control their behaviour. Yet it's actually about caring about them, and living in the moment, enjoying it for what it offers – even if it's not what you expected.

Health and wellbeing

Talking about life's tensions, you'll find that in achieving a balance in those stressful elements of your life, you need to work less at being comfortable and move on to being healthy. Those ups and downs can take a toll or provide an excuse for not looking after yourself.

Goals and challenges

You've set so many different goals, most of them focusing on achieving your objectives, and in the way you planned. However, your challenge is recognising that as the world changes, so must those goals. Letting old ones go clears the way for new and potentially more rewarding aims and objectives.

Certain individuals regard change as worrying, if not an enemy – something to analyse at length. You avoid such discussions. Now, however, you must keep these individuals updated on your plans. Explain your intentions concisely and in a manner that invites neither comment nor discussion.

GIFTS Practical, Flower-lover, Affectionate

CHALLENGES Excessive, Inflexible, Selfish

NUMBER 7

(1+1) + (5) = 7

Practical decisions bring pleasure, while helping others brings a more lasting joy

You

The theme for your birthday is the joy of order. As a Taurus and an earth sign, you appreciate the beauty of life in so many ways. You value the beauty of nature, but also the beauty of kind gestures, as well as beautiful objects. They don't necessarily need to be valuable, but simply something that brings joy to your heart. And, at the same time, you need your own life to be in order as well.

Obviously, it's nice if what's around you is in order, but the pace of events and the role those around you play is also important. Yet, things don't always work out as you expect. When you're so busy that it's impossible to be organised, you'll still try to be orderly. However, at times, that temporary chaos can become a permanent variety of disarray.

Bizarrely, often that disarray might lead to a fresh viewpoint on elements of your life that you hadn't realised need to change. Alternatively, it could introduce new activities or objectives that hadn't crossed your mind, possibly because you were so focused on what you were already doing. The key is to balance your pleasure in life's beauty and also to recognise that, occasionally, what seem to be unsettling changes are actually breakthroughs – changes that will add to your life in ways that you couldn't possibly have conceived of when those events first arose.

You and others

Hoping for relaxation, order and joy with others is wonderful. But this may mean something entirely different to them. Discuss it? Maybe, but that, too, can create confusion. The solution? Recognising that their views are, and always will be, different from yours. Find a middle ground – one that holds the promise of joyous times together.

Health and wellbeing

It's easy to blame stress, from others or from things that aren't working, for undermining your enthusiasm for life. It's true – challenges can be overwhelming. The remedy isn't battling them but simply stopping for a moment, taking a deep breath and being still. It's by far the best strategy.

Goals and challenges

Whatever your lifestyle – at home, at work or juggling lots of duties – everybody needs a goal. Challenges are important too, although undoubtedly there are times when you wish they'd disappear. Approach these as offering you the potential to celebrate achievements both major and minor, and you'll be amazed how much you learn from each one.

THIS DAY FOR EVERYONE

Tensions with loved ones or close friends isn't easy. They've been behaving oddly but made no explanation, so you assume they'd rather keep things to themselves. Perhaps. Yet it's just as likely they don't realise how much certain concerns have altered their behaviour. A frank discussion will do wonders.

Justifying your decisions to those who are critical achieves little

You

Many think of profit in financial terms. But often it's said you've profited from dealing with, and overcoming, a serious challenge – one you've dealt with by employing thought, analysis of others' perspectives and, most of all, patience. Profit doesn't always refer to finances – you'll also have learnt how time, effort and a willingness to wait, watch and learn from others can also be profitable. What's more, this reminds you that the time, effort, energy and heart you put into whatever you're doing creates the end result.

This, in turn, highlights the importance of the word "joy", which is often used in ceremonies such as weddings and the wonder of holidays. Here, it has to do with a leap in your heart, a real and personal joy that comes from having done something you know will benefit you, others and, possibly, even the world. With this as a theme for your birthday, it's important that you find a balance between doing what you need to do and being able to savour life's joys. True, often it's believed the world isn't designed in this way.

Dealing with finances involves dull duty and challenges. However, in your particular case, the capacity to get things going and to bring money and joy into your life – and at the same time – is both a skill and an art, and one that you're always learning about and refining.

You and others

Making the best of life is one thing, discussing it with others is quite another. When at your best, you've a talent for creating magic. It's important to share this gift with those who you were destined to be with – family, loved ones or friends. While there isn't a single right way to do it, every effort adds its own magic.

Health and wellbeing

We all have moments when things just don't feel right. That can mean you need to rest or have a touch of something. But, as often, it's because you're worrying and don't realise it. The key? Pausing long enough to find the joy in your life. That, in turn, will give you a clearer sense of what's needed to restore your health and wellbeing.

Goals and challenges

Often people are encouraged to set very specific goals then make a list so they can achieve them. While at times this is useful, it can also be restrictive. For you as an individual, not only is that restrictive, but it also interferes with using your intuition to achieve those goals and to celebrate them.

MAY

13

T
/
A
\
U
/
R
\
U
/
S

Some insist being kind is weak. Nevertheless, do it anyway

You

For Taurus, as an earth sign, imposing order on life is important. Even when there's disarray, you like to know where you're standing, what needs to be done to create calm, what comes first and, perhaps, what you can put off until next week or next month. Yet, at the same time, there are twists and turns that can upset your plans. The trick is to recognise how much you can achieve, or not, on any one day. And then take a deep breath, knowing the rest will simply have to wait.

Yet there's a part of you that truly enjoys this challenge. Without it, life can be dull, if not predictable. You may complain about such challenges, but the creativity they spark is important. What's more, they expose you to new ideas and new people, which brings very real rewards.

So the secret is learning to recognise how much you benefit from the resulting twists and turns and, in doing so, possibly complaining less, too. The problem with complaining? It prevents you from viewing difficulties as challenges that you can conquer and, in the process, learn from. Better yet, when you have conquered them, you can celebrate not only your conquest but also what you've learnt. Abandoning complaints may seem strange. Still, once you do, it will be like clouds vanishing, leaving you with sunny sky.

You and others

We all face practical challenges. But you may encounter somebody who enjoys creating obstacles – possibly a family member, friend or colleague. As a determined Taurus, your instinct is to stand up to them. Yet, this only complicates matters. Back off. Let them be who they are. This may seem weak, yet you'll soon discover the peace it brings to your life.

Health and wellbeing

While there are all sorts of diets and regimes to follow, true inner wellbeing is another matter. It's about allowing certain individuals, or even circumstances, to be the nuisance they're meant to be. You enjoy battling to make improvements, even if it means facing one battle after another. By simply letting them unfold, you'll give yourself peace.

Goals and challenges

You wouldn't think achieving goals begins with stillness. But this variety of reflection prepares you to fight for what you intend to achieve. True, this may not come naturally to you. But once you realise achieving that stillness is the challenge you're meeting, then you'll not only enjoy it – you'll be proud of yourself for doing it.

THIS DAY FOR EVERYONE

Usually, you'd check out the facts before getting involved in life-changing arrangements, whether personal or professional. Yet things are moving so swiftly that it's a matter of now or never. Waste no time debating the pros and cons. At moments like this, your instincts are far more reliable.

Ignore others' manoeuvres – and have a grand time regardless

You

For you, the process of planning – of imposing order on life, or turning ideas into reality – isn't just about getting things done. It's a pleasure and, even more, it's one of your real gifts as a Taurus. While you're a practical earth sign, born with the relationship planet Venus as your ruler, you've a talent for managing such matters naturally. Yet there's also a challenge. Once you've formed a plan and made things happen, it feels like a letdown, because you no longer have a project.

The question is, what will you do next? Will you make another plan, plant a garden? The fact is, you can do any of that. Your journey is about being able to exercise your creative muscles in every way and, even more, to experience the joy of that creativity every day in how you live, how you think and your plans and projects.

As an earth sign, you tend to focus on the physical world around you. One of your greatest challenges is to go within, while still enjoying what nature offers you. Find the balance between the two, and every day will be a joy. You'll enjoy the plants around you and the heavens in the sky. What's more, you'll enjoy the love of those you care about all the more. While you can't weigh or measure this, it's still deeply touching. Achieving that balance can be one of your greatest gifts.

You and others

You take pride in the fact that those around you – family, colleagues, even neighbours and friends – rely on you. They come to you for support, they ask questions, and, as a clever earth sign, you've got solutions. Yet, while you're delighted to lend them a hand, it doesn't boost your spirits. Learn to embrace others' joy and discover your own.

Health and wellbeing

There's all sorts of advice out there about looking after yourself. However, your starting point is whatever excites you and gives you a sense of promise. It may simply mean exercising in the way you want, by walking or going somewhere lovely, or it may be enjoying a beautiful meal or a massage. Whatever it is, it's something that's just for you.

Goals and challenges

Life, your background, school and, if you work, your job, will all have given you clear information on how to achieve. None of this is about enjoying yourself. But increasingly, it's time to both deal with life's practicalities and be excited by what each day brings. The starting point? Be generous with yourself.

THIS DAY FOR EVERYONE

Ordinarily you'd be uncomfortable handing a task that's your responsibility over to somebody else. However, at the moment, that individual is eager to deal with the matter in question and, perhaps, better equipped than you are. Knowing that, waste no time on debate. Simply leave it to them.

MAY

15

T
/
A
\
U
/
R
\
U
/
S

Those who insist you show your love in a certain way don't know how to receive it

You

For you, the path to joy can be a confusing one. That may seem a strange statement, because you have a talent for making life seem easy. Even when you're facing challenges on your own, somehow you manage to help others glide past obstacles they're facing. Often people tell you how much they envy you. It's true, you're accomplished at this.

Actually, it's not until you notice how much others struggle with certain practicalities that you realise what a knack you have for dealing with even very tricky situations. Of course, some would say that being charitable with others is important. However, you do so much. In this particular case, it's about you and you alone – and discovering what brings you joy. That may be the challenge, because you've focused so much on others that you're not really sure what you, personally, want to do or what will bring that special kind of joy.

The solution? Waste no time on discussion and experiment. Where to begin? Think small. Maybe it's about studying something that interests you. Maybe it's about taking a walk, thinking about how or what you eat, or even taking time alone or with a certain individual. Whatever the case, this part of your journey is one of discovery, and what you've learnt about yourself during the process will benefit you now and for the rest of your life.

You and others

Often, when you speak, it's about your hopes. You say, "If only I could...", followed by ideas about helping a particular person, or rethinking certain past arrangements. Some are possible, most are not. Your path has reached a fork. You can continue focusing on impossible situations, or forget them and employ your mind, energy and effort into the future, where you can make a difference.

Health and wellbeing

There's a tendency to feel that if you look after yourself adequately, then you should be fine and happy. But in your particular case, life's about discovering ways of thinking and activities that lift your spirits. Focus on these, and on making them a part of your life every day for a week or a month, and note how much things change.

Goals and challenges

It's easy to turn big challenges into big ongoing projects. But with these, a sense of achievement is in the distant future. Try adding everyday tasks, some easy, others challenging. They're like taking daily vitamins. They'll enrich your wellbeing, day by day. Do both. That's the skill – and the challenge.

THIS DAY FOR EVERYONE

Having struggled to get the attention of one particular individual about certain concerns and complaints, you're exasperated. You're both annoyed and concerned about the situation in question. Soon you'll have a chance to confront them. Be ready to act on it – and fast.

There is no greater gesture of love than that which is as sudden as it is unexpected

You

As a Taurus, and an earth sign, you have a knack for managing the physical world – from finances to acquiring beautiful and often valuable possessions. You also benefit from a powerful and analytical mind. Yet it's not only about what you think. The direction in which your mind takes you is also of considerable significance, because while you're clever, and good at thinking things through, you can sometimes get lost in those thoughts.

There's a fine line between being creative – that is, using your excellent mind to come up with ideas – and doing what might be called daydreaming, allowing your mind to wander off in all sorts of directions. And, on occasion, you come back 15 minutes or even an hour later, feeling relaxed but wondering exactly where you've been.

While this is OK, in your particular case, learning to master that capacity to create visions, not just to relax but for your benefit, is a powerful and important part of your journey. And one that, as your awareness of it grows, will become exciting. It will open the door to ideas that may have been on the edges of your thoughts, but will take centre stage. Next, you'll think about making them reality, and even part of your way of living, working or loving. Do that and you will discover joys that once seemed far beyond your reach.

You and others

You have an imaginative and rich side to your nature. Yet, it's difficult to describe, so you've shared it with few people. Mostly, with others, you focus on more "Taurus" topics – the world, what you enjoy, your achievements. However, certain individuals share that imaginative vision. Chat with them about it. Those discussions won't just be enriching – you could create some projects together.

Health and wellbeing

While often health and wellbeing is thought of as fitness, diet and exercise, sometimes it is more about your capacity to realise a vision. And that's very much the case for you. Ironically, sometimes if you get involved physically walking or while envisioning your desires, you'll be able to combine that vision with looking after yourself.

Goals and challenges

Figuring out what's next from a practical point of view is sometimes wise. But, as you're increasingly aware, often you need to allow your imagination to shape your thinking. Do that, and you'll be planning the direction you'll be taking over the coming days, weeks, months and possibly even years.

THIS DAY FOR EVERYONE

Usually, you stick with who or what you believe in through thick and thin. Yet even you could discover that you're unable to ride out the coming weeks' tricky events without making changes. No matter how much of a compromise this may seems at the time, those changes are in your best interests.

MAY

17

T
/
A
\
U
/
R
\
U
/
S

The love that comes from a flower or a newborn can help you express your feelings

You

As a Taurus, the idea of turning concepts into action may be an appealing one, but being a thorough Taurus, naturally, you'll check out the facts first. However, these days, with things moving so swiftly, or being so different from elements of the past, there really are no facts to check out. You can talk to other people about what they've done. But, mostly, you need to trust another element of your nature – your intuition. While you're well aware of it, you're sometimes reluctant to even mention it, just because you're unsure of the reaction you'll get. Yet, increasingly, you're learning to rely on it, even with practical matters. What's more, this is very much what your journey as an individual is about.

It's about combining your amazing ability to enjoy life's pleasures and to manage its demands. When necessary, you employ your intuition, which can often bring a fresh view to arrangements. Yet, at the same time, in certain situations, you to want to plan ahead. And this is where it gets tricky, because when you're using your intuition, often half of what you're envisioning is based on the past, while the rest has to do with a future that hasn't yet taken place. This is where the process of developing your trust and true vision comes in. As you master this, you'll embrace a rewarding skill and deepen your wisdom about life.

You and others

Your gift for understanding others is wonderful, although you don't always realise how much your knack for knowing what those around you are working on, dealing with or passionate about means to them. Better yet, you know what to say, and when. The irony is that your kindness or patience don't always extend to yourself. That's your next project.

Health and wellbeing

Sometimes the emphasis on health is on physical wellbeing alone. In your case, the emphasis is also on your mental and even emotional wellbeing. As much as you care about others, sometimes that concern becomes worry, which can undermine your mood. Learning to spot that and, where appropriate, shift your focus, is a vital skill.

Goals and challenges

Some would say putting life in order and outlining what needs to be done is vital. And often it is, but in your particular case, because you have such a strong practical streak, your instincts will tell you when to get in touch with somebody, when to rethink a plan or when to undertake something new. Trust those feelings, they're a powerful gift.

THIS DAY FOR EVERYONE

It seems you need only say yes, and a series of brilliant events will unfold. Yet, appealing as this is, it's sudden enough that you've no time to consider these. Judging by the pace of events, however, you won't have the luxury of such reflection. In fact, it's now or never.

GIFTS Affectionate, Generous, Well-presented

CHALLENGES Selfish, Lazy, Inflexible

NUMBER 5

(1+8) + (5) = 14 = (1+4) = 5

If you debate the rights and wrongs of joy, it becomes an impossibility

You

For you, as a Taurus and an earth sign – and somebody who likes to get things organised – life should be fairly straightforward, except that you have a tinge of the sign next to yours. It's Gemini, which has to do with a different kind of vision – with having a lively mind, with picking up what's happening in the world, with noting what's going on, what people are talking about and new ideas.

Sometimes you don't even realise you're doing that. Yet at the same time, it's all about a kind of discovery that is important, because occasionally those insights, completely unconsciously, add to your life and come up as ideas later – and you don't even know where they came from. Being able to take advantage of them is the important thing. And the trick is to refuse to get caught up having to explain or justify your ideas, or to come up with facts to support them. Simply dive in. That may seem unwise, but you've done it before.

And you'll do it again now that you're increasingly aware of this very special skill – swinging from being a solid Taurus to being inquisitive, a visionary, which is what you can be at times. And will be, the more you recognise it. This is an important part of your journey. The more you embrace this visionary part of you, the more you'll accomplish and the more you'll enjoy life itself.

You and others

There have been many times that you've been confronted by those who are so narrow-minded that there's no point in even discussing ideas different from theirs. Still, their persistence can undermine your confidence. The fact is, part of the challenge is to trust yourself and your feelings over those who seem determined to raise doubts.

Health and wellbeing

Your passion about certain ideas or activities can mean you forget obligations, including looking after yourself. While that's unusual for a Taurus, you're borrowing that from the sign next to yours, Gemini, which can get so absent-minded that they forget to eat or sleep. The solution? Return to your core nature, and look after yourself, like a good earth sign.

Goals and challenges

For you, life is about discovery. While one part of your nature is tempted to stick with the safe and familiar, you thrive on new ideas and even unfamiliar settings. The more you venture into that new territory in terms of ideas and activities, the more you will get out of life.

THIS DAY FOR EVERYONE

Don't be surprised if certain individuals aren't as enthusiastic about new ideas or potential changes as you are. While you've already explored these possibilities in depth, they're new to others. Knowing that, invest time in explaining exactly what is behind your feelings of enthusiasm. That should do the trick.

MAY

19

T
/
A
\
U
/
R
\
U
/
S

You move fewer muscles when you smile than when you frown, so it's more relaxing

You

The theme running through your life is rediscovering yourself. You were born sharing the influence of Taurus, one of the most down-to-earth signs, with the creative, restless, imaginative Gemini. And with the toughness of Gemini in your nature, you're always aware of future possibilities. This insight prevents you from getting overly stuck in Taurean activities alone, as important as they can be. However, it can also mean that you sometimes get caught off guard. It could be that you're thinking about a new idea or possibly swept away by something exciting. An encounter will have inspired you, or you have a vision of something you really must do.

The problem isn't yours. While those closest to you are aware of the two sides of your nature, if somebody knows only the down-to-earth Taurean side, the individual in question could misunderstand you. Using those Gemini vibes and chatting about new ideas with others who, like you, share these wonderful qualities of practicality and vision, will be huge fun. There are those who understand you. And as much as you enjoy the company of others, of family and friends, there will always be a few whose company not only inspires you, but gives you the kind of appreciation that is heart-warming. It's almost like a variety of vibrational vitamins.

You and others

Dealing with others is easy if you employ your Taurean side, which is as charming as it is practical. But, as you've learnt increasingly over the past years, you've a visionary side, too. And it's almost as if you're speaking two different languages. The trick? Learn to live with both sides of your nature, then share it with others. They'll benefit, and so will you.

Health and wellbeing

Contending with pressure from others is nothing new. Mostly, they need to be convinced that your plans or ideas have promise or will actually work. But, in every case, struggling achieves nothing. Instead, it's about relaxing and allowing things to come together in their own time. This may seem difficult, but once you take a deep breath, those ideas will begin to fit together like magic.

Goals and challenges

You have a tendency to get bored. The remedy? Explore. If ever there was a time to begin, it's now. Learn the art of exploration, and not only will you enjoy life and achieve a lot, you'll begin to live your own vision.

THIS DAY FOR EVERYONE

If ever there was a time to take certain ventures you're passionate about further, it's now. The planets' favour is likely to take the form of certain extremely helpful individuals. You've done all you can. So sit back and allow those who are both able and eager to give you a boost.

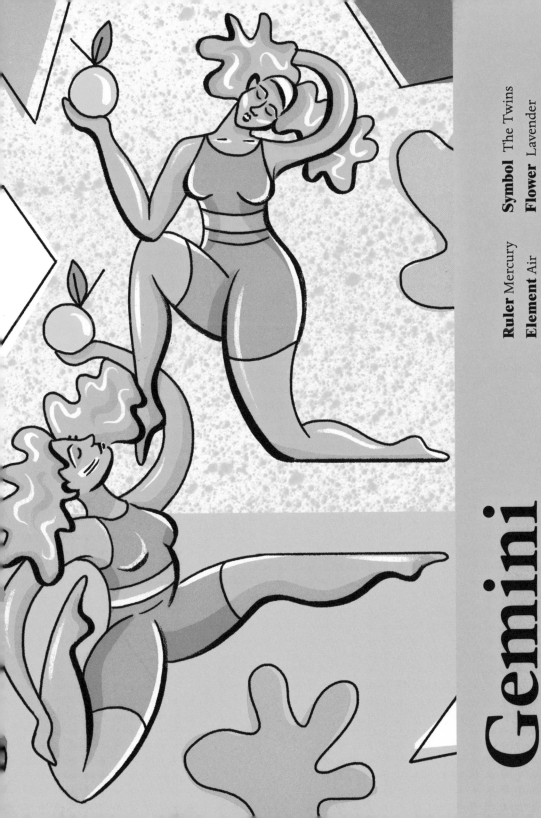

Gemini

Ruler Mercury
Element Air

Symbol The Twins
Flower Lavender

May 20 – June 19

Gemini The first of the three inquisitive air signs, Gemini – the twins – benefits from the rule of restless Mercury, the god of communication, charm and, especially, a lively mind. You are endlessly curious individuals, often with many sides to your lives, interests and tastes. Your flower is lavender, your herb is savoury marjoram and your tree is the hazel. Your stone is agate, with its endless range of colours.

G
\
 E
/
 M
\
 I
/
 N
\
 I

The power of a golden moment of insight changes your life forever

MAY

20

G
\
E
/
M
\
I
/
N
\
I

You

You are the very essence of Gemini, born on the day the sign starts. You carry the clever wit and enthusiasm of your ruling planet, Mercury, and of the theme for your sign, which is communication – it's about ideas, not only communicating with others, but paying attention to what's going on in the world around you and learning from that. Sometimes, however, your enthusiasm can turn into impatience, so you may take action or even commit before you know all the facts.

Of course, you don't think about this until later, when you find you must extract yourself from certain arrangements or commitments, personal or even of a business nature. That's part of your style as a Gemini. It's said that many of you born under this sign live several lives, with a range of activities, and in many different settings. Certainly your symbol – the twins – suggests that you may even live all of those lives at one time.

The trick to making the best of this is to enjoy the diversity, and to take advantage of it. There may be those around you who are jealous, but it's your life to live. And your own day isn't just about experiencing all those ideas, it's about making them a part of your life. Focus on these, and not only will you be spectacularly good at them, you'll enjoy what each and every day brings your way.

You and others

You don't just enjoy the company of others, often your life is built around those you're close to – family, friends, even neighbours and colleagues. However, this can mean that often you're the one who's creating all the excitement. The secret? It's encouraging others to learn how to add magic to their own lives. You'll be doing yourself, and them, a favour.

Health and wellbeing

As you're aware, sometimes you can be tired or hungry and not even realise it. That's because you get so involved in what you're doing, and in your enthusiasm for life itself, that you forget to eat. But, on the other hand, you also can eat so much that you feel exhausted. Finding a balance is a challenge, but once you do, you'll feel much better.

Goals and challenges

This has to do not so much with life out in the world as your inner life and the challenges you set for yourself. This isn't about a single day or challenge, or even a single year. It's about finding a way to live that allows you to use your active mind and your energy to set up challenges that aren't just worthwhile, but bring you personal satisfaction as well.

For every step you take forward, you're leaving something behind. That may seem obvious, yet you're battling that fact now in one situation you've strong feelings about. While letting go of both that emotional attachment and certain arrangements won't be easy, it's essential that you move on.

MAY

21

G
\
E
/
M
\
I
/
N
\
I

Discussing ideas can be informative –
Listening to others' words can be life-changing

You

Your birthday theme is inquisitiveness. You might think this comes naturally to every Gemini, but actually you benefit from a special, if not unique, level of interest in the world around you and the people in it. You enjoy each day for what you learn. You love collecting ideas and the experiences you have as a result of the circumstances you're in. And, even more than that, you love learning about what people are doing, not so much because you intend to become close friends or involved with them, but simply hearing about what they have in mind is enchanting.

At the same time, finding your own centre and finding people you can exchange ideas with, is as important. These discussions are a major part of what might be called your "personal vitamins". This has to do with you, as an individual, but also with your activities out in the world, your work, in your community or with your family. Here, too, while you'll listen to what others have to say, the exchange of ideas with them is what's most important to you.

As a result, your world becomes a broader and more exciting place. Not only do you pursue exciting goals, you could even take up something new. This isn't just important – this approach to life brings you a variety of joy in the present and promise for the future.

You and others

While relationships are important, when that word is used, it doesn't just apply to everyday relationships. Yes, it's about friendships, family and even neighbours. But it's just as much about those individuals you meet who add enormously to your life and, in fact, you add to theirs as well. Acknowledge that, and the richness of the links between you.

Health and wellbeing

On occasion, something hits you that doesn't just slow you down. It flattens you. It may seem you're ill, but actually it's fatigue. As a Gemini, you're both restless and endlessly inquisitive, so often you don't realise you've forgotten to eat or are exhausted. Recognising this involves simply noticing when you need to relax, then doing exactly that.

Goals and challenges

For you, as an inquisitive Gemini, a life without challenges would be very dull indeed. Yet you often get so involved in others' projects that you forget about your own. The remedy? Every once in a while, make a list. Then, from time to time, revisit it, and ensure that you're putting your own goals first.

THIS DAY FOR EVERYONE

It's worth considering the fact that while some decisions can be made once and will last forever, others really must be regarded as tentative. This means that, for now, things are settled, yet, at the same time, you'll have the freedom to explore the rather intriguing ideas or offers coming your way.

GIFTS Debater, Easy-going, Explorer

CHALLENGES Inquisitive, Changeable, Late

NUMBER 9

(2+2) + (5) = 9

Insights can appear in surprising settings. Often, what's least expected turns out best

MAY

22

You

There are vitamins you take, and there are vitamins in food. But for you, as an inquisitive Gemini, there are also what might be termed "vitamins" in ideas, and your active mind needs to be nourished with them. This isn't just about ideas, though – it also has to do with meeting people, getting out and about and finding yourself in situations where your restless need to know what's happening in the world is satisfied. Some get involved in a hobby. And while you might have one, observing others satisfies your desire to learn about what's happening around you, often by simply observing what people are doing. And being in unfamiliar situations always gives you an opportunity to broaden your horizons.

You're an inquisitive Gemini, but your character's a balance between simply learning what you can and taking action. While you might decide to turn some of what you discover into a part of your life, simply learning about what's going on around you, with others and in the wider world is vital, and rewarding. Whatever you're doing, explore. That simple process of exploring for the sake of what you experience can itself become a rewarding part of your life, something you do with friends, a vocation, a career or even a passion. The most important thing is to realise the joy in discovery that is core to your nature.

You and others

Often you're more aware of what's going on than those around you. Yet, at the same time, others' experiences and the places they'll take you will enhance your life. Once you recognise how vital this is, and how those experiences are truly meaningful, you'll ensure there are always one or two individuals who can add to your life in this unique way.

Health and wellbeing

As a Gemini and an air sign, you're easily distracted and can rapidly become impatient with dull routine when looking after your health or eating. As a result, you can overdo things until you're exhausted. The trick is to turn potentially beneficial activities into fun. Whatever it is, if you enjoy it, you'll do it.

Goals and challenges

Being curious by nature, you always need something new, and that could very well have to do with what's next in your life. Some people stumble over goals, but for you, the process of searching for them is as important as the discovery. What's more, being excited about what's next makes today's tasks more fun too.

G
\
E
/
M
\
I
/
N
\
I

Every day, exchange an old habit for a more upbeat one. Your life will take on a new glow

MAY

23

G
\
E
/
M
\
I
/
N
\
I

You

While you may not think about this, as a Gemini and somebody ruled by the planet Mercury, you have a sister sign, Virgo, which is also ruled by Mercury. It's an earth sign, and it's all about order. And your particular Gemini character has a touch of that Virgo need not only to create order, but also to organise your life in a way where you appreciate the beauty of what you're doing far more than the ordinary Gemini would. You appreciate the ideas and, once you've created a balance, you'll know how to create situations and a lifestyle that provide you with the activity and excitement you thrive on. But, again, this is about joy in terms of living well, which includes knowing interesting people and having an exciting life.

However, the earth sign aspect of your nature, linked to Virgo, is as important as the Gemini side. It's analytical. It considers what those who you spend time with bring into your life, from rewarding ideas and activities to sheer fun. It's not that you demand anything specific from them, but simply that because you offer so much as a friend or a colleague, you want others to bring something to the experience as well. The challenge? That tough analysis. Sometimes you're too generous. This isn't easy, yet it's one of your most important tasks as a Gemini – with a touch of Virgo.

You and others

Those around you, the individuals who you regularly spend time with, are important to you. This includes friends, family, colleagues or even just closer acquaintances. Each of them adds something, because each lives a life or has access to facts unfamiliar to you, so you find them fascinating. Not everyone understands this. Don't bother trying to explain. Just continue to enjoy people for what they are.

Health and wellbeing

As a Gemini who is influenced by Virgo, you'll analyse what's good for you, then worry about whether you're doing the right thing or not, and end up doing nothing. The trick? Try things out, from ways to eat and exercise to relaxation. See how they feel and, importantly, whether you want to stick with them. They'll stop you from getting bored.

Goals and challenges

While you'll often set far-reaching goals, minor goals for next week, next month or even tomorrow are just as important. They're a form of vitamins for you. As you begin your day, choose one goal, and by the day's close, you may have accomplished it – and other things too.

THIS DAY FOR EVERYONE

There's a difference between things going wonderfully and events being what you've planned or anticipated. Ironically, what's least expected could turn out to be best in the long run. Knowing that, explore absolutely every idea and offer that comes your way. You won't regret it.

A lively exchange of ideas is exciting. Learning what others feel touches your heart

MAY

24

G
\
E
/
M
\
I
/
N
\
I

You

The message for you as a May 24th Gemini is that every day is a new experience. This may seem obvious, but it's not the case for others. Many people set up their lives so that each day is basically the same, day after day. That would drive you crazy. As an inquisitive Gemini, especially one born on this day, you have a need to discover. While obviously there are certain things that are essential to your daily routine, if you set up things so that you have something new to do every day, then you'll gain a sense of accomplishment.

Whether it's taking a new route somewhere, trying a new food or chatting to somebody you've never met before, it doesn't really matter. In fact, it may happen spontaneously. But each will add to your life. Some may be memorable, others may be forgotten almost immediately. But each will increase your memory box of experiences.

Better yet, this will get you in the habit of searching for things that will be rewarding. And here again, rather than trying to figure out why something in the past wasn't that rewarding, instead of worrying, you'll forget about it and will, instead, derive great joy from the actual process of searching. And that's the key to being a Gemini born on this day – not just to search, but even more to enjoy the process of discovery.

You and others

Often when people meet, they'll exchange questions sometimes discreetly, sometimes forthright, about their lives or background. For you, that's natural. But it's important that you talk about yourself, too. And, sometimes, that exchange will grow, and become an essential and rewarding part of your life.

Health and wellbeing

For you, as a Gemini, serious workouts can be dull. But if you're able to find activities that lift your spirits, from eating well to fun exercise, you'll exchange boredom for enthusiasm and feel more energetic. Better yet, do it with someone whose company you enjoy. Then even jogging at home will bring you pleasure.

Goals and challenges

Many people love setting goals. But you'll think about such matters, then get distracted and end up doing a bit of this and a bit of that. One of your biggest challenges is remembering to set goals for yourself. Once it becomes a habit, you'll not only benefit from it, but you'll enjoy the process as well.

THIS DAY FOR EVERYONE

Some disappointments are a nuisance. However, one you're about to face could seem a disaster, at least initially. While, ordinarily, you'd respond swiftly to a situation of this nature, do some serious investigation first. Once you discover how timely those changes are, you'll exchange your panic for relief.

The more you try laughing, the more powerful you'll realise it is

MAY

25

G
\
E
/
M
\
I
/
N
\
I

You

If you're into astrology, you'll know Gemini is an air sign, which symbolises thought and ideas. And it's true. Most Geminis live in a world of concepts and possibilities – thinking about what they could be doing, what they've done in the past and the ideas they've exchanged with others. But you also focus on the tangible side of life, the world around you. That includes what you actually see, possibly the objects you own, the colours around you that create the texture of your life. And, equally, it's about the food you eat and the feelings you experience around others or when doing things. Each of these brings its own excitement to your day. The challenge? It's getting others to understand that, because, to your surprise, not everybody is as aware as you are of this special variety of joy.

However, gradually you'll connect with those who do appreciate that, and they'll become friends or, possibly, colleagues. The activity could become a hobby or even an element of your work. Your restless side needs a range of interests. Some will become a temporary obsession, while others will draw you in more. This could turn into a lasting hobby, from gardening to collecting something about which, gradually, you become an expert. And it could become a second career, one you don't just enjoy, you also share it with others.

You and others

One major focus is deepening your link with others. Some Geminis are happy just chatting with people, including those closest. However, it's important you find deeper links, those you can develop. This may be in terms of a personal relationship, but one that also extends out into the world. In every case, ensure you devote enough time to these enriching connections.

Health and wellbeing

The key here isn't what you do, it's how you approach it. Do something, say, work out at a gym, solely because it's good for you and soon you'll be unenthusiastic. If, instead, you're excited, whether it's salsa dancing or tennis, you'll actually do it. And, whatever it is, it will be helpful for you.

Goals and challenges

The real challenge for you is exactly what we've been discussing – making sure that you're able to appreciate that tangible side of your life and the way in which it excites and inspires you. These feelings may not come naturally, but the more you practise, the more you'll benefit from it, and the more you'll enjoy whatever it is you're doing.

THIS DAY FOR EVERYONE

It would seem that while problems cause dissent, everybody would agree that there are golden opportunities to be taken advantage of. Unfortunately, that's not the case. In fact, if you're to make the best of what comes your way, you may need to compromise – at least in the short term.

Be the student who discovers the perfect, yet unexpected, solution

MAY

26

G
\
E
/
M
\
I
/
N
\
I

You

While everybody sees the world around them in their own way, as an inquisitive Gemini you see a world that's wider than most. You're unusual in the sense that you don't just observe events, you also experience them in a very personal way. However, you may not be aware of that, unless you compare notes with others about what you see versus their experience.

Of course, this becomes an important part of your life at home and as you take a walk or look at a garden, you'll view the world around you with joy and pleasure. Yet, for many Geminis, this may actually be part of your work, something you do that allows you to analyse anything from fashion to architecture, perhaps even observing or being involved in something as mechanical as the way a car is built. Looking at and enjoying the world around you is one thing, but the process of discovery is also exciting. If you notice yourself feeling uncomfortable or critical about one particular matter, simply stop and back up to the point at which you began to think about, and appreciate the matter, idea or activity in question.

Do that, and you'll discover the joy that is very much a part of this side of your life. And even more, you'll discover the joy that comes with being able to spend time with and talk to others who also view life in this way.

You and others

For you, being able to hang out with others is so important. But, often, you find people overwhelming and enjoy being alone. The trick is achieving a balance. Ensure those around you add what might be called vitamins to your life – especially enthusiasm vitamins. That way, you don't just have a good time, your spirits get a very real boost.

Health and wellbeing

The funny thing about dealing with your own health and wellbeing is that it's influenced by the pleasure you take in looking after yourself. If what you're doing is no fun, you're unlikely to do much of it. Find a setting or an activity that satisfies your need for quality and beauty, and you actually take part, and will enjoy it.

Goals and challenges

Your challenge is living life a little bit better than others do. That may sound strange, but many people can't be bothered to make the effort you do to ensure that every day has its wonderful moments. As you do that, what you learn will add to your life and to your relationships and lead to achievements.

THIS DAY FOR EVERYONE

Sooner or later you'll need to disentangle yourself from an arrangement that once made sense but no longer does. The problem is that the actual process will involve facts, figures or the kind of formalities you loathe. Tempting as it is, putting it off achieves nothing. The sooner you tackle this, the better.

MAY

27

G
\
E
/
M
\
I
/
N
\
I

Your busy mind seeks ideas, unaware that the best ideas emerge from stillness

You

Your theme, as a May 27th Gemini, comes as the result of being ruled by the restless and inquisitive Mercury. It is "keep moving". Of course, there are lots of ways to do this. You can keep your body moving; take a walk or exercise. But as a Gemini, your constantly roaming mind is part of your nature. It's circulating around any room you're in. It's wandering, already thinking about what you'll be doing next. And sometimes it's moving around the world.

While many Geminis benefit from a restless mind, your vision and your mind's capacity to wander is both a joy and a skill. True, if you allow your mind to wander too far, or into thoughts that don't profit you, it can be exhausting. And this is very much the focus, because being aware of those mental journeys and of their impact on you is a challenge – and potentially a skill that will enable you to direct your mind along more rewarding paths. It allows you to think about what you need to organise and do, but also find those you enjoy.

Ironically, even when you're doing something you enjoy, your mind may wander and dwell on something less joyous. So for you, this process of learning to stick with the thoughts that elevate you isn't just useful, it's something that can actually reshape your life and bring true joy.

You and others

You may not think of it this way, but at times the negative attitude of others can be infectious, in the sense that after being around them a short while, you don't just feel lousy, but you are questioning why you're there – and with good reason. You can ensure the visit is brief. And also, you can learn how to actually improve on the vibes of the situation.

Health and wellbeing

Being in an upbeat mood is one thing; feeling well physically adds its own light to your life. Yet you sometimes get lost doing things you don't enjoy, even eating unwisely, and don't know why. Forget analysis. Simply change your habits. The payoff will come in how wonderful you feel.

Goals and challenges

The challenge for you is accepting the fact that you are an eternal explorer. You may stay in the same place, you may even remain in the same job, but that process of exploration is a wonderful part of your nature and one to be noted, discussed with others and savoured each and every day.

THIS DAY FOR EVERYONE

You've been concerned and upset by sudden developments. Since then, you've learnt a lot, which has both surprised and delighted you. Remember this when other, equally dramatic, developments arise over the coming weeks. Instead of battling them, focus on exploring what they offer.

GIFTS   Smart, Fluid, Communicator

CHALLENGES   Preoccupied, Undependable, Mercurial

NUMBER 6

$(2+8) + (5) = 15 = (1+5) = 6$

Helping others comes naturally to you. Accepting thanks doesn't

You

You don't think of yourself as being restless until you compare how you live and think to others, and then you realise that while those you're talking to have been doing the same things and living the same way as they were a month, a year, or possibly several years ago, you'll have explored all sorts of ideas. You'll have met people and gone places. This restless side of your nature comes naturally, but also there's a part that is seeking a single perfect moment in a day, a perfect link with others and possibly even the perfect activity.

This isn't simply about moving around or being restless, it's about a search. Yet the trouble is that life itself changes, which means that when you find a perfect activity or a link with somebody that brings a new glow to your life, you may well find that the next day it's not quite the same – which, of course, is natural.

And this is the lesson for you, to recognise that what seems like restlessness is a genuine, enthusiastic and what might be termed golden curiosity about life. Those perfect moments are wonderful, but they can't last, because life itself changes. Day comes, followed by night. Spring is replaced by summer, autumn and then winter. Each of these is about changes. So don't be surprised when those golden moments pass. They're simply clearing the way for the next ones.

You and others

Relationships, whether with family, friends or close emotional ties, can be confusing, simply because, for you, the need for variety is as natural as breathing. Yet certain individuals need to do things the same way, day in, day out. Obviously, this drives you crazy. The solution? It's not changing them. It's developing a sense of humour. That's the secret to many of life's crises, including this.

Health and wellbeing

That restless part of you, as you can imagine, needs a lot of different things to do with your mind, but also with your body. Your sense of wellbeing comes not only from physical movement and choosing wisely what you eat. Even more crucial is a positive mental attitude. This is about improvement. Once you find that centre, you're able to continue exploring.

Goals and challenges

One of your greatest challenges is not allowing other people's negativity to influence you. You wouldn't think it would actually have that much of an impact, but you'll find that if you can manage to avoid, if not shut off, discussions with individuals of that nature, not only does life seem a lot better, but you'll feel a lot better as well.

THIS DAY FOR EVERYONE

Life often brings surprises. Often those you remember best are those that were challenging. Yet the surprises that are coming your way now will be memorable for other reasons. While you may be short of reassuring facts to begin with, once you get involved, you'll recognise just how promising they are.

MAY

29

G
\
E
/
M
\
I
/
N
\
I

Turn setbacks into opportunities – it's easier than you imagine

You

Your birth date message is inspired not only by your ruling planet, Mercury, but also the Roman god Mercury himself. He's renowned for being swift of mind and fleet of foot. His influence accents these elements of your character, especially with your May 29th birthday, because you share those characteristics of being quick-thinking and fast-moving. If you've seen images of Mercury, you'll know he wore a winged helmet. And, just as is the case with him, you too have ideas that, when you release them, fly in so many directions, offering inspiration, insights and, on occasion, helping others resolve issues.

But Mercury's capacity to bring ideas is as important, and this is your gift as well. It comes so naturally that you don't even think about it. You're always trying something new, which for you is normal. However, certain individuals around you may complain about this, and that's simply because they don't have your inborn gift of curiosity.

Don't let complaints about your inquisitiveness bother you. This is your special gift and, in fact, many people appreciate being with you actually because of that enthusiasm. The more you appreciate yourself and the more you allow your characteristics to shape your life and your activities, the better.

You and others

Being an inquisitive Gemini, you're interested in a wide range of topics. For you, being fascinated by events is as natural as breathing, and the more you explore, the better. In some cases, you'll go one place, then another. But in others, you don't need to go any further, these will be a part of your life, forever.

Health and wellbeing.

As often as we're told it's good to get involved in a routine, the trick for you is to find a range of people to spend time with and, equally, activities. Similarly, you need variety in your way of eating. All of these are vital, and in fact, this variety comes naturally to you.

Goals and challenges

Setting a single goal seems crazy and, in fact, for you, it is. It's vital your life is organised around what might be termed mini-goals – that is, modest aims and challenges. But ensure you have one or two long-term, if not lifetime, goals. Combine those and not only will you enjoy every day of your life, you'll be amazed how swiftly you move towards achieving them.

THIS DAY FOR EVERYONE

The adage is "Never say never", and rarely was such advice more apt than now. In the past, you may have said there were certain things you'd wouldn't consider or even certain individuals you'd do anything to avoid. But that was then. Times have changed – and so have you.

GIFTS Flexible, Versatile, Listener

CHALLENGES Sporadic, Procrastinator, Changeable

Often, the most rewarding joys are entirely within your mind

You

As a May 30th Gemini, one of your greatest gifts is your broad interest in the world around you, in ideas and discussions and, especially, in people. However, you won't realise how wonderful and unique this is until you begin to chat with somebody and you realise that they don't ask questions of any variety.

For you, this process of exploring the world around you and what people do and the resulting discussions is like special vitamins that nourish you in the present.
And, even more, often those ideas you hear about will add to your awareness. While you may well collect things – anything from art to photographs and books – you're also collecting memories that will enrich your life, even when you aren't around the actual objects that you have in mind.

True, it's very easy for you to get so involved in the process that you get overwhelmed. This is partly because your inquisitive mind can expand. You may begin collection number one and then find you are also building collections two, three and four – and that's when it all starts to overwhelm your life.

This is where balance is important, because that process of discovery is wonderful and deepens your feelings so much, but even more important is recognising how much being with people alone benefits you.

You and others

Whether it's family, friends, colleagues or even neighbours, people add to your life. However, if you depend on them too much, you can forget about the pleasures of going solo. What's most important is to find that centre within yourself that, quite simply, enjoys life and being in the present. Your most important relationship? The one you have with yourself.

Health and wellbeing

Health is one thing, wellbeing another. They're separate, in the sense that you can feel terrific, even if you're tired or not eating well, simply because a sense of wellbeing comes from living an interesting and worthwhile life. However, it is vital that you balance the two, and manage to practise self-care. This brings a certain lightness to your day.

Goals and challenges

Often people are told to list their goals, but because you are by nature so inquisitive, things don't always work out that way. Rather, you discover one thing and then another, then another, and then you eliminate something. While that's one approach, it may not fit in with everyone else's idea of listing goals and challenges.

THIS DAY FOR EVERYONE

Being interested in others is one thing. But there are one or two individuals who seem to think you'll be there for them whatever your other commitments. Thus, saying a firm no can be very difficult indeed. That is, however, exactly what you'll have to do – or face yet more unrealistic demands.

True love? You'll be thrilled by what you discover because of it

You

The birthday theme for you – imagination – is something you rarely focus on, because it's so much a part of your way of thinking and living. You're imaginative – that is, rather than simply dealing with change swiftly, you benefit from new experiences and exposure to ideas that stimulate your thinking. Yet, at times, your mind can run away with you – you'll go from simply organising plans to imagining getting away from the everyday and taking off to somewhere far away. The trick here isn't what you imagine, but reining in your mind to focus on facts and potential solutions, and then on to exploring new possibilities.

It may well be that you're intrigued by certain new ideas but you didn't pursue them because you didn't know enough, there was no one to do it with or you were distracted. Yet, at the same time, for you, as an inquisitive Gemini, delving more deeply into these ideas and potential activities lifts your spirits. That, in turn, leads to meeting people with similar interests. True, this could mean rearranging your life. If so, it's worth beginning the process of broadening your horizons, which, accordingly, will boost your feelings and ultimately brighten your life.

Turn your imagination into an asset and, whatever else you're doing, your way of living, activities or work will benefit enormously.

You and others

Your links with others, from family to friends or colleagues, are a dance. Each has its own rhythm and style. Some are like a stately waltz, others rock'n'roll, possibly with frequent shake-ups. The resulting variety means you're never bored, and what's more, it encourages others to find, and live, according to their own rhythm. Nothing could be better than that.

Health and wellbeing

For you, as a restless Gemini, following others' rules for a healthy diet or routine is almost unbearable. Yet you need the energy that comes with eating well. There's a secret. Stock up on all sorts of nutritious food, so you've a choice, but having options will boost your spirits and your intake of vitamins.

Goals and challenges

Some people set goals for a year, even several years, ahead. You do, too, but because you're creative, you also need to be able to rethink your objectives, and often. Achieving a balance between planning and indulging the spontaneous side of your nature is itself a challenge, and one you'll actually enjoy wrestling with.

THIS DAY FOR EVERYONE

It may seem you're stuck in a rut. But actually you've been restricted by circumstances. Now, happily, those are about to change. So when sudden and unsettling events shake things up, welcome them – they're a first step to new and timely changes and, better yet, rewarding if unexpected adventures.

Discussing ideas wakes up your mind. Reflecting on life's joys delights your soul

JUNE

01

G
\
E
/
M
\
I
/
N
\
I

You

Your birthday theme is "fresh start". This is natural because, of course, it's the first of the month. But, also, being ruled by Mercury means you're inquisitive by nature, so every day is about discovery. In fact, you fear getting stuck in situations where you're prevented from exploring new ideas. For you, this is as natural as breathing. However, you can unintentionally catch yourself in restrictive habits. It's because they're so familiar that you don't realise their influence. The solution? Be aware of the moments when you feel you "must" do something. It's about balancing the discomfort of making frequent changes, doing things in a new way, yet being so organised that you can deal with events in your personal life, in your career, if you have one, and in close relationships. Ideally, this means you're not always doing things at the last minute.

While this may seem a lot to think about, once you've organised a routine, knowing what's next actually frees you. If that routine includes giving you the space to do things differently, then finding the balance in your thoughts and actions becomes a real joy. It may not be the way others want to live – and they may question this odd balance between freedom and your own version of a routine – but then, they don't have to live your life. You're doing a very good job of it.

You and others

You'd like to deepen links with others, but don't always do it. The reason? You're lively and inquisitive, and some criticise you for that. If it's family, simply agree to disagree. If it's friends, variety is crucial. They don't need to be like you. But it's vital they rejoice in who you are and enjoy being themselves with you.

Health and wellbeing

As you know, in the past you've sometimes been so uptight that even if you're eating well and exercising, you're still unsettled. Knowing this, aim to balance health and wellbeing with your way of thinking. Do that each day, and gradually you'll end up eating better and sleeping better without a strict routine, simply because you're more balanced.

Goals and challenges

As a Gemini, setting goals is one thing, but because of your changeable nature, those goals evolve as you do. They tend to do what might be described as morph into something else. As those goals change, you'll have the option to rethink your plans, in the unique way that's one of your greatest strengths.

THIS DAY FOR EVERYONE

Financial issues have been on your mind for weeks. While you've managed to resolve several, one or two others require the cooperation of a particular individual. Not only was it not forthcoming, but they wouldn't even discuss it. Try again. Recent events will force them to take such matters seriously.

Good ideas can bring relief, but laughter broadens your horizons

You

As a June 2nd Gemini, you tend to be a bit of a collector. You may collect objects, but what you really collect is ideas, that is memories of wonderful times, from places you've been and people you've been with. When you're reminiscing, you'll sometimes compare them to the here and now. That's risky. It's easy to focus on everyday struggles, then compare them with pleasant memories from the past.

However, you'll have forgotten about the problems you faced back then, such as difficult people or puzzling obstacles. This is the key to making the best of your life – to recognise that often you'll recall the past as far rosier than the present day. And, often, you'll anticipate great joys for the future, too. However, actually achieving joy in the here and now is another matter, and can be a real challenge for you.

You're not alone in this – there are plenty of others who'll join you in complaining. They'll merrily talk about how awful things are to the extent that, if you didn't begin the conversation in a bad mood, you'll be in one by the end. The lesson? It's to recognise that this is about where you allow your mind to go. Use the power of your unique Gemini vision as if you were directing a movie, and you'll create a happy and productive here and now and, ultimately, a happy future too.

You and others

As a Gemini, you're sometimes influenced by those you feel a link with. If so, you sometimes tend to agree, unthinkingly, with what they say. Do that, however, and you can be drawn into their world, one that may not suit you. Sometimes, you have to agree to disagree. Whatever the nature of the relationship, ensure you can be who you are.

Health and wellbeing

You've a knack for looking after yourself wisely. You get moving and, equally, you eat the right things. Yet, there are times when your joy vanishes, and a glum mood takes over, often influenced by others. Learning to acknowledge and deal with this, and create emotional links with others, especially if they're being moody, is a gift, and mastering it will bring you lifelong joy.

Goals and challenges

Sometimes goals can be listed, one by one. But in your particular case, your goal and your challenge is to learn to enjoy every moment for what it is. Worldly achievements are exciting. However, perhaps the greatest achievement for you is developing the ability to enjoy each and every moment of life, from its shadows to its sunniest moments.

THIS DAY FOR EVERYONE

Sometimes setbacks are exactly that. However, what seem to be problems are actually events prompting you to reconsider arrangements that have been a part of your life for such a long time that you wouldn't otherwise question them. But you must. Once you begin, you'll realise why changes are crucial.

Analyse what's wrong and needs fixing – or what you can learn from it

JUNE

03

G
\
E
/
M
\
I
/
N
\
I

You

The planet Mercury isn't just your ruler – it dominates your birthday reading. The ancient Roman god Mercury was a clever young man but also a trickster, with a reputation for surprising people with what he would or wouldn't do. For you, life can be like this. You'll commit to a situation, change your mind and then discover certain people are upset. Alternatively, it may be that those around you make the changes and you have to deal with the resulting fallout. In every case, however, it's about recognising that just as, inevitably, day follows night, long ago a part of you recognised that no matter how carefully you figure out details, things won't necessarily go according to plan. The irony is that in some cases, those changes are an improvement.

Ignore those who are upset by those unexpected developments. Instead, focus on figuring out a new way to work with what's happened versus what's necessary. Once you're doing that, you'll begin to use the creative side of your Gemini nature and, even better, the creative influence of Mercury.

You'll come up with plans far better than you'd have imagined possible. Live out your life, knowing that even unexpected twists will allow you to trigger this wonderfully creative side of your nature, and you'll not only make the best of it, you'll enjoy it as well.

You and others

Life is about change and evolution, especially in relationships, whether with friends, neighbours or colleagues. These changes are the result of decisions and, as often, shifts in circumstances or others' needs. Their complaints? Agree they're inconvenient, then say no more. Why? Because what seems most worrying in the short term may actually be a thrilling opportunity.

Health and wellbeing

Unsettling periods and sudden changes aren't just stressful – you'll sometimes forget about taking care of yourself. The trick is to recognise that, while life has twists and turns, you as an individual have a stable core that it's important to look after. That has to do with how you sleep, how you eat and finding the joy that's present in every moment.

Goals and challenges

Your greatest challenge is being able to recognise that when things aren't going as you expected you have an opportunity to create a breakthrough, a genuine golden moment. Focus on that, and not only will you become increasingly good at it, there'll be more and more of those shining moments in your life.

THIS DAY FOR EVERYONE

Obviously, you can't ignore the questions of certain individuals or the advice others insist on offering you. But you can explain you're busy and so would prefer to speak to them when things are a bit quieter. This allows you to make your own decisions, without justifying your plans to anybody.

Self-love can be confusing – savouring others' love is easier and more fun

You

You have a remarkable capacity for finding things to do, from exciting activities to interesting encounters. This a gift. But it's also a challenge, because when you're looking for that special something that will fulfil your objectives, it can mean you miss something that's closer to home, if not right in front of you. Something that might be even better.

The key is balancing the restlessness of your inquisitive Gemini side and the gift of being able to spot what works in the here and now. However, the things you're familiar with may not be as exciting as you'd hoped. What's more, there's always something thrilling about a new activity, something exotic about going to a new place. While that's true, the trick is reining in your inquisitive side, which wants to explore, so the part that actually needs to be in the here and now, can focus on practical matters as well.

That may not sound exciting but, ironically, what you learn and who you meet when dealing with those practicalities could be more rewarding than your gains from the activities or alliances you thought would add so much to your life. For you, change is like breathing. However, the only time you can actually take a deep breath is in the present, and that's the reason it's so important that you learn to enjoy what you have.

You and others

There's no doubting the excitement of meeting somebody new, and the joy of getting to know an individual who adds welcome inspiration to your life. Even more important, however, is enjoying your own company. You often assume others are more exciting. Achieve a balance between these, and you'll find amazing peace.

Health and wellbeing

In a way, dealing with health is easy. Eat well, live wisely and exercise in some way. However, if you're worrying about the future, or brooding about the past, you're gradually undermining your wellbeing. That's the big lesson for you. Yes, look after yourself physically but, even more, ensure that you feed your mind with nourishing thoughts.

Goals and challenges

Long ago, you realised that a good challenge gets you going. Yet, if things are predictable, you'll sometimes create a "do-it-yourself" challenge, deciding changes are urgent or that you must explore a new idea. While this brings welcome excitement, the trick is recognising you needn't explore, because what you're seeking is right there in front of you.

THIS DAY FOR EVERYONE

Timing is important in all of life. But in tricky situations involving those you're close to, personally or professionally, the moment you undertake certain discussions is crucial. Instead of focusing on analysis, trust your instincts. You'll find they prove far more reliable than you expect.

Can you plan for joy? No. But be ready for it, and embrace it when it arrives

JUNE

05

G
\
E
/
M
\
I
/
N
\
I

You

For you, as a June 5th Gemini, balance is the key to your life. You may already have sensed this because, at times, you've felt terrific, then something came along and your sense of wellbeing vanished. On the other hand, when you're worried or perhaps even feeling a bit grim, an event suddenly boosts your spirits. This is an element of your Gemini nature, the two aspects of your personality and mood.

While these sudden switches can be unsettling, you have a rich range of feelings, much broader than most. What's more, you can actually take advantage of these ups and downs in terms of your interests, activities and emotional life.

You understand the feelings of others better than most. In fact, you'll find certain individuals will join you in exploring these feelings. This process will enrich your life and deepen crucial relationships.

Whatever it is, rather than struggle to counter those "down" feelings, when you're ready, you'll simply give yourself a big dose of whatever shifts your focus.

It's not so much a case of things being better, more the way you're looking at them. Often, simply capturing that moment is what's important – and being able to do that is an essential skill.

You and others

Certain individuals lift your spirits, others don't. You know that. But you may not realise that there's a cost in spending time with those who bring you down. True, sometimes people like that can be puzzling. It's the same with what you eat. Balance indulgent food with fresh goodness– and take the same approach with those whose company you keep.

Health and wellbeing

There's a tendency for you to put off dealing with dull practicalities, but you must. Then, when you're feeling great, you'll revert. But, as a Gemini, you thrive on variety. The secret? Recognise that the simple act of eating a little better and doing something ordinary, such as taking a walk, will add enormously to your day, to your week and to your life.

Goals and challenges

As much as you enjoy achieving your goals, you have a short attention span. So you'll often redefine your objectives midway. While that keeps things more exciting, it's vital you let others know about changes. They may complain or, equally, be delighted. What's most important is keeping in touch.

THIS DAY FOR EVERYONE

Often, when making a decision, discussion isn't just wise, it's essential. While you may need to go to others for facts, one particular matter is complex. Practicalities alone aren't enough. And you'll soon realise why you must ignore those facts and rely entirely on your own views and feelings.

JUNE

06

G
\
E
/
M
\
I
/
N
\
I

Every sunrise is a special moment that lifts your vision in a new way for a new day

You

As a Gemini, you're one of three air signs. Along with Libra and Aquarius, you live in the realm of vision, thoughts and ideas, and all three are clever, quick thinkers. Plus, because your ruling planet is Mercury, which is about communication, you have a gift for learning about life and the world around you and discussing it with others.

Every sign accents a certain part of the body, and for Gemini it's the shoulders, arms and hands. Often Geminis will use these as a means of expression but also in sports. Equally, it's important that you focus on how you handle things, and whether you want people to be close to you or whether, in fact, you'd prefer to keep them at arm's length. This is the other element of your nature.

As an air sign, while you're very much about communication, you also like to keep certain ideas to yourself and discuss them only when you're ready to. What's more, if you spend time with those who ask too many questions, you may feel uncomfortable. Yet, at the same time, often these individuals will have good ideas, some that are worth listening to. An important part of your journey is to discover who is of benefit to you, and who isn't. And, equally, who you want to link your Gemini arms with, to play, to explore or to accompany you on a longer journey.

You and others

On rare occasions, you describe somebody as a true friend. However, there are questions about what friendship means. Is it something convenient for the moment, or lasting? What's more, it's worth considering whether in certain situations, you're doing more giving than receiving. What you learn could lead to timely discussions, if not changes.

Health and wellbeing

In order to feel well, you need to eat wisely, and will benefit from getting outside and moving. But the other question is whether your time with others is worthwhile. Do you benefit from the challenges? The trick, for you, as a Gemini, is your attitude towards all of this. Decide to be upbeat, and within a moment your mood will soar.

Goals and challenges

Everyone benefits from a challenge from time to time. But sometimes they can seem overwhelming. It's not necessarily what's happening, but that others have taken over, and their plans will benefit them, not you. Standing your ground won't be easy, at least not at first, but soon it will feel natural. You'll handle things wisely and, equally, will feel a tremendous sense of accomplishment.

THIS DAY FOR EVERYONE

Nobody minds sudden, and exciting, ideas or offers. Thrilling as what's happening may be, though, it could undermine arrangements you worked hard to organise. Seek some form of compromise, and you'll find that, with a combination of persistence and creativity, you're able to achieve great things.

Solving persistent dilemmas is easy. Finding the path to inner stillness isn't

JUNE

07

You

Your own ruling planet, Mercury, accents ideas and discussion. However, you sometimes get lost in those ideas. Equally, you can become so interested in discussing possibilities, you lose track of time. What's more, you enjoy gathering facts and analysing what you've learnt. Yet, fascinating as these may be, that's not all you need to know, because decisions involve feelings as much as facts.

Your usual approach to such matters is to get more information. That's often helpful, yet some matters require a different approach – shifting the focus to your own priorities. You may not be as clear about these as you imagined. Often there's no need to dwell on them until pivotal moments arise, as they sometimes do. These accent the importance of being aware of what, and who, you put first.

If you rely on others' views, those decisions are unlikely to last. So put your own priorities first, rather than going along with others. As a flexible Gemini, finding a balance can be challenging. Once your mind is clear, the resulting choices will be less complicated. From that point on, the trick is to avoid being distracted by intriguing but unreliable ideas and, equally, individuals, and stick with arrangements and people who bring stability and happiness to your life. Do that, and suddenly everything else will make sense.

You and others

The trick to dealing with situations involving you and others is to be alert to those where you're almost seduced into going along with them. You want their support or approval, or perhaps you're anxious about your own decisions. However, the only way you'll learn whether your ideas will work is by giving them a try. That's the message from the planets for you. Put yourself and your ideas first.

Health and wellbeing

For you, this should include the unsettling feelings you experience when struggling with indecision. It's also about learning to rein in your mind rather than allowing worry to take over. The solution? Take a walk, do yoga or some form of meditation. That leads to relaxation, unwinding and, ultimately, sleep.

Goals and challenges

Of course, life would be very dull without challenges to take on and goals to meet. You're more comfortable with those periods when there are twists and turns to deal with, too. Bear this in mind when those challenges arise, and recognise that they're giving you an opportunity to use an important muscle in your character. Not only will you use it well, you'll use it wisely.

G
\
E
/
M
\
I
/
N
\
I

The time has come to take a stand with somebody whose attitude or actions have been a constant source of irritation. You've mentioned this, but they've ignored you. Bring it up again, and be both frank and precise about what's bothering you. They've no idea what they're doing is so annoying.

JUNE

08

G
\
E
/
M
\
I
/
N
\
I

You debate ideas for fun – ensure others know what you stand for and believe

You

Your birthday theme is finding ways to use your energy wisely. That may seem strange, because as a Gemini and somebody ruled by the planet Mercury, your mind is more active than your body. In fact, directing your amazing mental energy can be a challenge. As a Gemini, you're an air sign, and live in the realm of thoughts and ideas. While that means you sometimes forget to eat, you occasionally struggle with mental exhaustion.

However, there's a solution that's about a union of the mind and body. Your challenge – and lesson – is balancing your physical and mental energy. While taking up certain sports, such as tennis or, say, fencing, will do the trick, walking is also great. Add a setting that requires concentrating on balance or agility, and do it with a friend. It could be a serious walk in the countryside, or hiking. The urban version is shopping– a variety of hiking, just from one store to another. What's more, if you're trying on lots of clothes in the process, that too requires agility.

The trick is to be in an appealing setting, and to keep moving. This can turn a walk around your neighbourhood into a joyous experience. Learn to employ your mind and body together in your day-to-day life, and in doing so, you'll begin to discover how the combination brings you joy and confidence.

You and others

Friends, colleagues and even family can be more of a distraction than a pleasure. You may enjoy family events. But relaxing can be quite another matter. It's a challenge – considering what you want to do, then selecting your companion accordingly. It's not obvious, but once you know what to do, it's easy.

Health and wellbeing

Focusing on how you eat is important, as is being attentive to your physical wellbeing. Yet you sometimes forget to eat altogether. It's the same with physical activities; if they're boring, you just want to escape. The trick? Discover something exciting that keeps your attention. Once you do this, the rest will come.

Goals and challenges

Setting goals is vital. However, with your roving mind, you're an expert at many areas, so many that you fear being trapped in one. While others have single goals, you have many, and they change. Actually, that's perfect. Don't let those whose minds and lives are narrow corner you into thinking or living like them. Commit to learning something today and tomorrow and the day after that. That's your ideal life plan.

THIS DAY FOR EVERYONE

Promising developments can be as exhausting as they are exciting, as you're currently discovering. One of the biggest challenges you're facing is the recognition that as you embrace the future, elements of the past must go. You could struggle to keep these afloat but, deep down, you know it's unwise.

Some difficulties can transform your vision of what's possible every day

You

For you, as a June 9th Gemini, the challenge is having too many options. That may not sound like anything to worry about, but there have been times in your life when there's been so much going on that you've felt overwhelmed. The issue may have been the people around you, things you were doing or even ideas that came your way. However, the confusion was a result of a single issue – having too much on your mind, combined with a sense of being unable to assess the situations in question or get a grip on the ideas involved.

And that's the secret for you. The key isn't figuring things out. It's learning to balance advice you're given and what you're told by others, including experts, with your own knowledge and experience. As a Gemini, you're inquisitive, and as an air sign you thrive on debate. What's more, you enjoy analysing what you hear about and observe. Then you weigh things up. You don't think in terms of things being interesting, but whether they're worth learning about – or not. And that's a skill you'll develop year by year.

It may have to do with your activities, the people you like to spend time with or even who or what you put first. In every case, achieving balance isn't about how interesting things are but, rather, how worthwhile they may prove to you, now and in the future.

You and others

While getting to know people is endlessly fascinating, it also drives you crazy. You'd rather create your circle, then get to know who's who. Yet because you're inquisitive, the list of people you'd like to get to know grows every day. The solution? Stick with long-term core friends. Ultimately, it's better than spending time with somebody new, only to discover how truly dull they are.

Health and wellbeing

You're one of those Geminis who has a natural kind of health and wellbeing, except when you get anxious about decisions. The trick is to take a break from decision-making and to learn from others. Do that, and you will start to thrive in the process.

Goals and challenges

One of the challenges in your life is that you're always working towards a goal, and because of that you are rarely happy with your current achievements. This is, in fact, your biggest lesson. That is, first, to enjoy what you have right now. And then, while you're doing that, you can begin to think about what might be your next project.

Ordinarily, it would be wise to analyse sudden changes before you get involved. However, with things moving so swiftly, there's no time. What you learn from even seemingly bizarre experiences will offer insights that will prove vital when the time comes to make lasting plans.

GIFTS Agile, Quick-thinking, Fair

NUMBER 7

CHALLENGES Inquisitive, Late, Undependable

(1+0) + (6) = 7

JUNE

10

G
\
E
/
M
\
I
/
N
\
I

Chatting with others is fun. Time spent with those you needn't talk to is a luxury

You

While every Gemini is ruled by Mercury, the planet associated with communication and a quick mind, its influence is especially strong for you. The benefits include your many interests and capacity to discuss new ideas and discover exciting people and places. Yet at the same time, your mind can run away with you.

Of course, as an air sign, this lively mind is one of your greatest gifts, and indicates your ability to come up with intriguing ideas. However, at times you also have a need for stillness – being free to concentrate on one thing, perhaps a plan or, in certain cases, a particular individual, The trick is being able to recognise that while your quick mind can be an asset, it can also break away, to the extent you need to rein it in. This is a lifetime skill, one you'll learn then, over the years, refine, until you're able to quieten your mind and access moments of inner calm.

And it's then that, often, you have your greatest discussions and most enjoy the here and now. The trick is to live with both sides of your nature, allowing each to emerge at the right moment. It's a skill, one you'll master gradually. You can undertake activities that keep you in the present. Ultimately, you'll enjoy both moments of liveliness and of peace, which is an achievement for anybody, especially a Gemini.

You and others

On one hand, you're the best company in the world. You're genuinely interested in others, and the questions you ask demonstrate that fascination. Yet you move swiftly from one topic to the next. For you, lasting connections with others demand that the individual in question is as passionate about life as you are. Your interests may differ, but your passion for them won't.

Health and wellbeing

Knowing who you are is an art, especially for a changeable Gemini. While you link up easily with others, if those connections dominate your way of living, working or thinking, you can lose track of your true self. This involves how you live, eat and look after yourself and your sense of wellbeing. Each is an essential part of your nature.

Goals and challenges

The irony is that you have an amazing knack for achieving goals others struggle with. Yet, at the same time, you have your own battles, some as frustrating as they are persistent. While they're annoying, seeking solutions for them broadens your circle, and you encounter fascinating people and exciting new ideas – so exciting they'll make up for those struggles.

THIS DAY FOR EVERYONE

You take great pride in standing up for what and who you believe in. You'll support those you care about and causes you regard as significant. However, there's one particular personal matter in which you're compromising. True, admitting this might be challenging. But once you do, the rest will be easy.

Your radar for those who are argumentative for the sake of it is good. Still, be wary

You

As a Gemini, you're an air sign, and because of that you are very good with ideas. You're inquisitive and you enjoy collecting things, not just possessing the actual object but, also because the story behind it interests you.

For you, the fun comes in learning about where something came from, what it's made of and how it's used. The item may be something small, like jewellery, or large, like a car; it could involve the outdoors, nature, from plants to crystals or even recipes. Whatever the case, you will revel in the sheer joy of learning about it. As an air sign, you'll find the real fun is not just owning an item – looking at it will bring back the story that came with it.

Rewarding as these interests or pursuits are, and however much they add to your own story, try mixing up your daily routine. You can become a creature of habit, doing the same things in the same way, day in, day out. While this streamlines your activities, try balancing that efficiency with changes that spice things up in daily life, This is vital. Yes, shaking things up is unsettling, but that's the point. Altering your routine can actually mean you will enjoy life more. Simply undertaking routine activities in a different order may make an amazing difference. Try it. Even minor shifts will add a new sparkle to your day and a new and welcome excitement to your life.

You and others

Many relationships are lasting – because of family links, or perhaps they go back years, possibly to school. However, as an inquisitive Gemini, when you meet somebody who shares your interests, you'll click, and those links will last as long as you're both involved. Yet, over time, you'll discover another, deeper link, and a special understanding that brings a joy which nothing and nobody can replace.

Health and wellbeing

There are two types of Gemini. If you're the type who lives in your head, you're interested in fitness because you want to look good and be energetic, but nothing more. Other Geminis, however, view sport as a mental exercise; some may even become professional. Whatever the case, this is an all-or-nothing relationship and, for a very few, it's a passion.

Goals and challenges

As much as you enjoy meeting new people and having new experiences, if you do too much you become overwhelmed. Finding a balance between routine and new pursuits is itself a challenge. However, once you do, not only is life more interesting, but those around you will profit from your inquisitiveness in many ways.

THIS DAY FOR EVERYONE

Sometimes plunging into something unfamiliar takes courage. At the moment, that's not the problem. It's letting go of the past that you're finding a challenge. You rarely encounter this sentimental side of your nature, so find it overwhelming. It's about saying goodbyes. Toast the past, then bid it farewell.

GIFTS Debater, Adaptable, Bright

CHALLENGES Changeable, Unreliable, Tardy

NUMBER 9

(1+2) + (6) = 9

JUNE

12

G
\
E
/
M
\
I
/
N
\
I

There's sense of warmth that's bringing wonderful changes into your life

You

For you, life's about discovery, a new relationship with change. Most Geminis have a fairly short attention span, so like to have lots to do and experience. However, you tend to settle into habits, so changes and challenges are needed to stimulate your mind and, even more, your imagination; it's like devising solutions for intriguing puzzles, and you enjoy tackling life's puzzles. These can be a part of your personal or working life. Ideally, however, you'll seek a range of different settings, as stimulating as they are diverse.

It's the same when it comes to taking breaks or holidays – as a Gemini, you thrive on variety. Even if you go to the same place, you'll vary the routine, checking out unfamiliar settings or new additions. The fun lies in discovering something new. Ideally, even relaxing won't just be fun, it will also challenge your mind, in ways you're unfamiliar with.

But whether you're away or living everyday life, you thrive on new ideas, experiences and interesting people. What's more, this links with another challenge. It's confronting the part of you that gets stuck with routine.

Here, too, the trick is the discovery that you could do things, live or love differently. The less restricted your thinking and the more you explore, the more magical your life will be.

You and others

Being understood by others is wonderful, yet it's something Geminis struggle with, mostly because family and colleagues view life from a different perspective. Despite your knowing this, every once in a while the realisation comes as a shock. When making plans, this demands careful discussion, and exploring with others why they enjoy or benefit from your ideas. It's not easy, but it is vital.

Health and wellbeing

Because you streamline your time, you're likely to devise a formula for health, too. Do that, however, and you could find yourself doing the same thing regularly but unenthusiastically. While you may feel better and fitter, you'll also be increasingly bored. The trick? Discovering new activities, from jumping rope to flamenco dancing, complete with castanets.

Goals and challenges

You've achieved goals that others only dream of. However, you're restless, and need new challenges, from personal objectives to more worldly pursuits. Your biggest challenge is actually enjoying what life brings you. That's very much about refusing to allow the routine that you've established to dominate life, making every day an adventure.

THIS DAY FOR EVERYONE

Rethinking plans is one thing. But revisiting the foundation on which certain arrangements are made may seem strange, if not impossible. Despite that, raise it with the individual in question and you'll find that you're not only able to clear up confusion easily, you'll discuss future plans with equal ease.

Strengthen your connection with your inner self, so you know what's best

JUNE

13

You

The theme for your birthday is finding balance between organising things in a way that makes life almost routine and having freedom. This is unusual for a Gemini, because normally you value freedom above all else.

However, because in the past you've found yourself in situations where you neglected one detail or another, you've developed a way of dealing with plans in a manner that leaves you little option to get creative or – and this is what's important to you – to make mistakes.

The trick is now to be less exact, and give yourself more space to deal with those tasks, and to enjoy life in a way that you probably haven't for a while. However, this is also about finding that balance between being organised, which is terrific, and being creative and allowing the moment to take over, especially when it's something that excites you – when you have encountered something new, or met someone who seems interesting to know.

If your plans are flexible enough to rethink things, initially for the time being, you'll be free to explore your options and, if necessary, consider making serious changes. So while achieving this balance takes effort, the reward is the freedom it gives you to explore. This isn't just about the here and now. It's also about what you'll be considering as the future unfolds as well.

You and others

When life's too predictable, you'll stir things up, reorganising existing arrangements or making changes. True, they'll be timely and beneficial, but others may complain. Explain, but briefly. Then, next time around, discuss your ideas as you proceed. This may seem a distraction, but in the long run it will save you time and stress.

Health and wellbeing

You could easily have a fixed relationship with your diet and activities, refusing to eat certain foods and always working out in a particular way at a particular hour. Except there's another kind of wellbeing, which involves self-awareness, the variety that's about truly feeling life's joys, and that can mean being more easy-going, whatever it is you're doing.

Goals and challenges

Because you're always thinking about what's next, you sometimes forget to look back and consider what you've done, the challenges you've met and the skills you've mastered. And, happily, there will be more challenges to keep you busy. But there's another, even more important challenge, which is being able to enjoy every minute of life itself, from its challenges to its joys.

G
\
E
/
M
\
I
/
N
\
I

THIS DAY FOR EVERYONE

Previously, you'd have made excuses for those whose actions and attitude have been disappointing. But now you realise that, in making those excuses, you were pretending you could trust them. Not only is that untrue, but the more you investigate, the more you'll discover about their deception.

JUNE

14

G
\
E
/
M
\
I
/
N
\
I

Those who give unsolicited advice are well-meaning but questionable advisors

You

Your quick mind is one of your greatest assets, but it can also be a liability – as you well know. True, you benefit from being ruled by the planet Mercury, whose legendary swiftness brings worldly skills that are employed in everything from politics to media and all forms of communication. However, if that active mind of yours isn't busy, it can overshadow life's joys. This can turn minor irritations into major concerns. Yet, when distracted by a new project or passion, those worries vanish.

Getting lost in doing things works for a while. But even a rewarding social life or a job you really enjoy won't calm your restless mind, which can be as much of an adversary as an ally. The secret is to find and maintain interests and alliances that don't just nurture you, but that are consistent, that you can rely on.

These can range from healthy habits, from eating well – many Geminis forget to eat – and doing some variety of exercise, to having people whose guidance you trust nearby. Once those stabilising habits are formed, you'll exchange the ups and downs that can become a way of life for a variety of balance that is rare these days, especially for Geminis. Once calm is yours, life becomes a very different, and more rewarding, adventure – less lived on the edge, and more centred in joy.

You and others

Finding friends and forging close emotional ties with people who are as inquisitive as you are isn't easy. But it's a skill you'll acquire, and you'll keep them close. Getting along with those whose company you can't choose, from family to colleagues, is an art – one that takes effort but is worth learning.

Health and wellbeing

Yes, you forget to eat. Some envy this, but it takes a toll on both your moods and energy levels. The irony is that while lots of Geminis are gourmets, unless you train yourself to enjoy it, eating and looking after your physical wellbeing can be more of a chore than a joy.

Goals and challenges

Your active mind is an asset – you're inquisitive. You notice more, and can enjoy all sorts of places and people, in your social life and work. Your challenge is ensuring there's variety, and that dull tasks are mixed with stimulating activities and fun companions.

THIS DAY FOR EVERYONE

Although you wouldn't describe yourself as being generous with others, it's true. This isn't about money as much as it involves thinking carefully about who and what matters to certain individuals – and doing what you can to enable them to connect. And, amazingly, often you'll do it in secret.

GIFTS Clever, Easy-going, Versatile

CHALLENGES Easily distracted, Forgetful, Scatty

NUMBER 3

(1+5) + (6) = 12 = (1+2) = 3

Celebrating before a victory indicates an excess of optimism and a lack of patience

JUNE

15

You

Others tell you how much they envy your easy charm and clever mind. While you enjoy being an object of admiration, this is strange, if not annoying. Why? Because these characteristics are as much of a nuisance as an asset. True, you've a knack for dealing swiftly and cleverly with a wide range of difficulties. But, ironically, it means there isn't much excitement in managing tricky situations or difficult people.

You've an amazing instinct for what to say or do to defuse even very complex problems. However, problems and practical matters are one thing. Those matters that involve close relationships, that call on your deeper feelings, your heart and intuition, are more complex.

However, what you're learning isn't just how to manage a tricky issue, it's about getting closer to those who matter most. Knowing you could distract everybody is a good idea, combined with your legendary Gemini charm. Or you could go deeper and talk things over. True, others may be uncomfortable and you could struggle. But what you learn about the situation in question – and the individuals involved – could allay these concerns. And it may create a new understanding and a new way of having relationships in general. You can make these changes at any time – don't wait for a drama. And the minute you begin, life will be a lot more fun.

You and others

Many Geminis are surprised by the number of people who regard them as best friends,or "one of the family". This is both heartwarming and puzzling, because you don't feel the same way. The confusion? Your interest in them. For you, these emotional links comes with time. Others are not nearly as skilled at it, so you being involved means all the more.

Health and wellbeing

Many Geminis benefit from the lanky body type that thrives on physical activity, from physically challenging activities or games. However, other Geminis tend to be round, Both find eating regularly and sensibly a challenge. The trick? Turn it into a hobby, one you can share and enjoying doing with everybody from family to friends.

Goals and challenges

You wouldn't think your quick mind is a problem. However, because you take on and overcome challenges easily, much of the time you are in what might be termed mental "top gear", which means that if there's no crisis to focus on, you'll feel the need to find one. On occasion, you may even become absorbed by others' dramas. Escaping this isn't easy. Once you do, you'll be relieved and grateful.

G
\
E
/
M
\
I
/
N
\
I

THIS DAY FOR EVERYONE

True, recently, you've achieved a great deal. But it's come at a cost to other plans and pursuits and caused a fair amount of aggravation with certain individuals. Now, finally, those matters are dealt with, which means those worries are gone and you can relax.

GIFTS Multi-talented, Debater, Unbiased

NUMBER 4

CHALLENGES Slapdash, Flighty, Mercurial

(1+6) + (6) = 13 = (1+3) = 4

True wisdom is modest. It arrives quietly, waits until you're ready, then moves on

You

The theme for your birthday is expansiveness. While on one hand this is about exploring the broader world, it's also about discovery. And that occurs when you get away from a familiar setting. Whether it's making local journeys or going further afield, you benefit from being in a different environment and doing things in a new way. You need to be well away from your everyday life.

This form of balance is important for you, because while you love having lots of plans and arrangements, you're sometimes anxious about getting bogged down in them. Geminis thrive on new ideas and activities, so repetition is boring for you. The trick is balancing the two – what you must do, with activities that are about discovering new places and doing things that you've never done before.

Tempting as it is to organise plans based on past experiences, there's a world waiting for you to discover. Stick with the familiar, and you're committing to one destiny, dominated by the past. Take a chance on the unknown, and you'll make breakthroughs that aren't just important, they're as essential as breathing. Once you learn how to step into this new world of the unfamiliar, not only will you be glad you did, but you'll become expert at embracing the unexpected and begin having an enthusiastic affair with destiny itself.

You and others

Dealing with others is part of life and, mostly, fun. But decisions can be tricky. The views of others can be a challenge. You don't think of yourself as being rigid in your thinking. However, this isn't just about plans, it's about getting to know people in a whole new way. That not only deepens your understanding of them, it will also broaden your world.

Health and wellbeing

When life's demanding, you'll stick to a wellbeing regime. However, you thrive on variety, so there's a danger you'll rebel and do nothing. The answer? Avoid a demanding schedule. Instead, loosen up and explore, The more intriguing options you have, the more fun you'll have experimenting and the more you'll explore and enjoy it.

Goals and challenges

While it's easy to reduce life to certain goals and challenges, for you it's really about how you embrace life as a journey of discovery each day. Take that approach. Not only will you learn a lot, you will indeed enjoy every moment of the process.

THIS DAY FOR EVERYONE

Once you've committed to something, you rarely need prompting to take action. On the contrary, you sometimes have to curb your tendency to be single-minded. Still, your feelings about one particular situation or individual have become so intense, you could be regarded as obsessed.

Fewer joys are greater than spending time with somebody you know loves you

JUNE

17

G
\
E
/
M
\
I
/
N
\
I

You

If there's any challenge for you as a June 17th Gemini, it's the conflict between the desire to take it easy and the drive to broaden your horizons, to think about new ideas, to do more and to explore the world that always seems to be calling to you. The settled side and the restless side are both genuine and legitimate parts of your nature. Previously, you've focused on one then the other. You've either been out there in the wider world, discovering things, or you might simply have been talking with those individuals who are more knowledgeable about ideas, people or places than you are.

It doesn't matter where you've been or what you've been thinking, but your mind has been active, if not working overtime. Yet, there have also been periods when you haven't just relaxed, you've totally kicked back. The trick is to learn to combine the two.

This may sound difficult, if not challenging. However, even thinking about it will get your mind going. That's the key. It's to realise that this doesn't relate to anything you've done before. Actually, it's taking everything that you've done and putting those experiences into one glorious package of discovery and adventure. As a Gemini, you were born to do exactly that – to explore, to discuss ideas and, from time to time, to reinvent yourself. That's exactly what you're doing.

You and others

When you need practical help, or your spirits need a boost, you know who to call on. And often the individuals in question will achieve miracles. But, in a bizarre way, others are no help at all, and sometimes undermine your confidence. The problem? Discerning between the two. Find that one person whose clarity is unfailingly accurate. Ask their guidance. End of problem.

Health and wellbeing

There's a tendency for people to say, "When everything is settled, then I'll look after myself." And, often, you're one of those people. Finding a way to look after yourself, a regime that's easy enough to follow and a way of eating that's not too complicated can be very difficult. However, if ever there was an investment to make in yourself now, it's that.

Goals and challenges

This makes it sound as if there's a final goal in life, and once you've achieved that, things will be done. But as long as we're breathing, there will be goals to achieve. What's most important for you is to recognise the joy in the goals you're currently exploring. Once you do that, everything else will be easy.

THIS DAY FOR EVERYONE

You're by no means a control freak. Yet when certain decisions you've made routinely for ages are given to others to deal with, you're unhappy. You may be tempted to battle to restore arrangements as they were before. Don't. You'll soon have other, far more intriguing, activities to think about.

GIFTS Quick-thinking, Adaptable, Traveller

CHALLENGES Scattered, Unsettled, Argumentative

NUMBER 6

(1+8) + (6) = 15 = (1+5) = 6

JUNE

18

G
\
E
/
M
\
I
/
N
\
I

With family and friends, you speak in a kind of shorthand. But a heart-to-heart is vital as well

You

As a Gemini, you were born under one of the cleverest and most versatile signs. You rarely think about this until you're talking to somebody who has no imagination. While usually your inquisitiveness is a gift, it can also mean that when you need to focus or make decisions, you're drawn into exploring other possibilities; some very real and worthwhile.

But, more often than not, pressures on time or practicalities mean you've got to stick with one particular plan. This isn't just annoying, it can be frustrating, especially if you've other ideas. Learn to recognise when it's not about doing more, it's about moving on. For you, remembering that is crucial; it's the difference between struggling or accepting things as they are. Challenging as this is, once you've learnt this knack, you'll also have realized how to sidestep other frequent struggles in your life, all of which have to do with settling on a plan, decision or commitment, acknowledging that and then firmly moving on.

You'll then discover that there's a bridge to the next thing to do, the next plan, project or encounter. The trick is to hurl yourself into whatever is next, knowing that there'll be new discussions and discoveries. And new decisions. Those exciting moments appear regularly. The trick is to be free from the past and ready to embrace the future.

You and others

Friendships can be both tricky and deeply nourishing. Those who you get to know over time become trusted friends, people you talk things over with. Yet sometimes it's vital to chat less and venture out more. You've known certain people for so long that there are no surprises. Balance is key. Sustain long-standing ties while you're exploring new ones.

Health and wellbeing

You don't think of yourself as extreme. This applies to how you eat and look after yourself. In fact, when you're stressed, it's likely you'll embrace a strict routine, when thinking will clarify your mind. Yet if ever there was a time to look after yourself, it's then. Being kind to yourself is the best approach to any challenge.

Goals and challenges

Setting goals is exciting. Meeting them can sometimes be difficult, simply because you set those goals so high that it's unlikely you'll be able to achieve them. Yet you keep trying. That's one of the gifts as a Gemini, your inquisitiveness. You'll take a chance, just for the fun of it, to see what happens. There's no better approach to the new, unfamiliar and exciting than that.

THIS DAY FOR EVERYONE

The time has come to do your sums. And this doesn't just refer to who owes what to whom. It is about the effort you've made on behalf of certain individuals. While some acknowledge what you've done and a few try to return the favour, amazingly, others just seem to take it for granted.

GIFTS Bright, Fluid, Equitable

CHALLENGES Unfocused, Procrastinator, Sporadic

NUMBER 7

$(1+9) + (6) = 16 = (1+6) = 7$

Meditators speak of stillness – and, as every Gemini knows, a quiet mind is bliss

JUNE

19

You

For you, your birthday is all about living many lives. Not just the two lives that are known as the Gemini twins, but also many different worlds, living in many different realms and in some ways, being very different to other people. What's more, these won't necessarily come together, nor do they need to.

In fact, if everyone who knows you came together in a single room and were chatting, each person would describe a different, and often unique, side to your nature. This is both fun, and vital, for you, because it allows you to explore ideas and experiment, as an individual, in a way that's beneficial. But, even more, you'll be discovering things that, otherwise, you wouldn't have encountered.

Experimenting in this way is essential and is, in fact, a theme for your approach to life. It's not about finding the single way to do anything but, rather, learning from every experience and taking chances in the process. This allows you to make the best of your inquisitive nature, the part that thrives on having lots of interesting options to explore.

It's the same with people and activities. The trick is to trust some and recognise that you may have to take a chance on others. You'll be learning from each of them. Most of all, it's about recognising the joy in discovery, because that's what it's all about.

You and others

Spending time with those around you is important. However, you can easily allow their ideas, thoughts or concerns to influence your thinking. Listen and learn, but remember your priority is being true to yourself and your commitments. The process of discovering who you are never stops. But when you're around certain individuals, that process of growth accelerates. Learn to spot those periods.

Health and wellbeing

Are you looking for the secret formula for staying on top of things when you're feeling overwhelmed? You've tried dealing with every detail, and that doesn't work. The trick is to take things a day, or even an hour, at a time. Do what you can. As a quick-minded Gemini, you'll be amazingly relaxed, and actually enjoy every twist and turn.

Goals and challenges

Often when we speak of goals, the focus is on a single, distant, final objective that you have in mind. Yet for you, goals are about actually being able to enjoy what every day offers. That is the most important thing during this particular cycle, and during your entire life.

G
\
E
/
M
\
I
/
N
\
I

It's unlike you to sidestep the responsibility for important decisions. But with the circumstances on which they'd be based shifting, you need time to think and to ask questions. What you learn will make you realise you're not alone in facing changes that are more complex than they seem.

Cancer

Ruler The Moon **Symbol** The Crab
Element Water **Flower** Lily

June 20 – July 21

Cancer The only sign ruled by the Moon, Cancer highlights cycles – both nature's rhythms, especially the oceans and tides, and those in our lives. Its symbol, the crab, is linked to water, as are the sign's flowers – the waterlily and the lotus. Your herbs are aromatic tarragon and verbena, and your tree is the maple. Your jewel, the pearl, not only comes from the sea, it mirrors the Moon's form.

C
/
A
\
N
/
C
\
E
/
R

I'll remember that the Moon shines even on dark nights, and so can I

You

You benefit from the influence of two signs – Gemini, the sign next to yours, and your own sign, Cancer.

This is an unusual blend, because the Gemini part of you is a rather clear-minded air sign, while Cancer side is not only an intuitive water sign, but benefits from the influence of the rulership of the Moon, the heavenly body that has to do with cycles.

And for that reason, your intuition is very strong. You sense when it's time for things to grow, both in nature, but also in individuals. You sense when stillness is important. This balance in yourself means that you're able to be a good friend, both to family and loved ones, but also, if you have a job, to those at work, as well.

You manage to give advice in a way that doesn't seem like advice, but it almost seems more like you're listening to others.

For you personally, however, finding that kind of nurturing is important. That has to do sometimes with family, but often it will be with that special friend who knows what you're thinking and who's able to encourage you to sit quietly and talk with them.

Most of all, it's about recognising the powerful cycles that shape the world around you, and even more importantly, shape your own life.

You and others

The formula here is about giving and receiving. That seems simple, but as you've discovered, when dealing with those around you, all too often you tend to end up doing a lot more giving and much less receiving. The trick is knowing when to stop, and even more, when to ask.

Health and wellbeing

Being a Cancerian, looking after your mood is as important as looking after your body. When you recognise that it's time to stop and rest, it's as significant as what you eat or what you do or the way you exercise. Pausing in this way is an important gift for yourself.

Goals and challenges

While what you do out in the world is important, what goes on within is just as important, and there are times when you wrestle with your right to go after things you dream about or want to achieve. The most important part of the process is to pause and consider what personally is most important to you.

THIS DAY FOR EVERYONE

Obviously, you're not thrilled about admitting you made an unwise decision, especially because this involves a matter where you battled to have things your way. However, the circumstances have changed. Acknowledge that you dislike admitting you got it wrong, apologise, and move on.

GIFTS Inviting, Empathetic, Warm

CHALLENGES Oversensitive, Hypervigilant, Moody

NUMBER 9

(2+1) + (6) = 9

Nature's power to grow, even in unlikely places, will inspire me

JUNE

21

C
/
A
\
N
/
C
\
E
/
R

You

To a certain extent, you tend to feel responsible for others, for their happiness, for whether they're enjoying life. This isn't something you think about. It comes naturally to you, and it's a wonderful quality. However, the challenge is recognising when you feel responsible, when actually, you're meant to be encouraging them to look after their own interests.

And, equally, it's time for you to focus on what you need. In some cases, this is time for yourself. In other cases, it's pursuing something that's important to you, whether it's a hobby or an activity, or simply spending time alone. For you, joy – true joy – comes from within. You are aware of this, but you don't always give yourself the gift of time to share that for yourself, and striking the right balance between what you want to give to others and having enough time for yourself is one of the most important gifts for you.

Once you begin to recognise that, you'll also develop a clearer sense of what you need to do in order to bring joy into your life. You may have a career or activities at home that are rewarding, but the important thing for you is to seek out the single passion that lifts your spirits, something that you look forward to. It may be one thing; it may be a number of things. It may change. But the most important thing is that it's entirely yours.

You and others

You're a natural diplomat, but that isn't always the best way for you to deal with those around you. Being persuasive is one thing, but there are times when either frank discussions or getting others to just talk about their own issues openly is what's most important. That's the big lesson.

Health and wellbeing

When it comes to health and wellbeing, your tendency is to think that you can be either self-indulgent or austere. However, there's something in between that has to do with being able to enjoy each day and find activities that make you happy. It may be a walk. It may be exercising. It may be indulging yourself in eating something, or eating less. Whatever it is, it's finding it that's important.

Goals and challenges

There isn't a single shift that has to do with achievement. It has to do with finding that balance between being happy with what you're achieving and what you're not.

THIS DAY FOR EVERYONE

For ages you've managed to keep one particularly tricky issue under wraps. It hasn't been easy, but you've felt strongly that this was nobody else's business. Now it is and, in fact, you'll need to ensure certain individuals are aware of the full facts, including why you've said nothing until now.

When I'm down, I'll imagine the power of the Sun emerging from behind a cloud

JUNE

22

C
/
A
\
N
/
C
\
E
/
R

You

Your initial instinct when there's something to discuss is to pause and reflect and figure out what you need to say. This might have to do with conversations with others, with your own activities or with your job. And then you think once you've got it all worked out, you'll talk things through. The trick is to recognise that those around you are also on what might be termed a journey, and they, too, are figuring things out. If you spend too much time thinking, you might miss the chance to benefit from what they have to say. What's more, by asking others what they're thinking about and what they're learning, you will all broaden your horizons. This process of discussion is an important one, because it also allows you to remove the burden from your shoulders to figure things out.

For you, finding joy on your own and with others is a journey. It's not something you work out on a single day, but a skill that you'll develop over time, a skill that you become better at as each day passes and a skill that allows you to enjoy what life offers all the more. As a Cancerian and a water sign, life isn't so much about what you have or what you own, or even about your relationships, as much as how you feel each day, and whether, when you wake up in the morning, you're looking forward to what the day holds.

You and others

You're well aware of your role in supporting others, but you're less conscious of the need to allow them to support you. That exchange is an essential part of it. It's almost as important as breathing. Recognise that, and you'll find and sustain that all-important balance.

Health and wellbeing

It would be nice if you could find a single routine that you could stick with, but for you, joint exploration is important. That's a kind of exploration that is about doing things together – and taking advantage of those who have a knack for introducing you to new activities and new pursuits.

Goals and challenges

Sometimes people are encouraged to make a list of things they want to accomplish. However, because you're intuitive by nature, it may well be that you're not fully aware of what's most important until suddenly you're facing that opportunity and, in doing so, know you've found the moment to say yes.

THIS DAY FOR EVERYONE

There's no wrong way to refuse an offer you find unappealing, or which simply doesn't work. If the individual behind the offer takes offence at words, bear in mind they may be playing a game, one in which they'll use guilt to lure you into doing what they want. Politely but firmly ignore them.

If a dream seems unachievable, I'll remember others that seemed just as impossible

You

For you, there's a real appeal to having order in your life, knowing exactly what you're going to be doing on any day, possibly any week, or even a year from now. However, being ruled by the Moon, the heavenly body that is itself constantly changing, means your instincts are telling you that a somewhat rigid way of organising things could be frustrating – and that's true. In fact, you may have discovered that when you try to organise things too much, you just have to reorganise them at the last minute.

Your lesson is, indeed, to understand that cycles exist, in nature, in the world around you and in your own life, and especially in relationships with others – personal relationships, but also out in the world. Once you're able to embrace that, then instead of worrying about things going the way you want, you'll find that you encounter something exciting.

And because both your thinking and your planning is more flexible, you're able to explore that. This then allows you to do more things in a day, in a week and in a month than you would have imagined possible. That flexibility that is the greatest gift you can give to yourself, as a Cancerian and somebody ruled by the Moon, the body in the heavens that teaches us all about those cycles.

You and others

Sometimes you feel like you need to take a significant role in dealing with others. This can be tricky but at times it's useful, because if an individual, family, a friend, or even a colleague is being difficult, you can lead them to what they need to learn. But when it comes to those closest, the most important thing is to speak from the heart.

Health and wellbeing

The idea of seeking a stable way of doing things is wonderful. However, for you, what's most important is to be enthusiastic about what you're persuing. That means changing things around from time to time. This may mean undertaking something new or simply altering the order in which you approach such matters.

Goals and challenges

The word challenge tends to imply a single situation on a single day. However, if you think of those challenges as opportunities, a chance to do something new, to learn something and to challenge yourself in a new way, then instead of worrying about them, you'll plunge into them with joy.

JUNE

23

C
/
A
\
N
/
C
\
E
/
R

THIS DAY FOR EVERYONE

Usually, there's no wrong way to express concern about a matter somebody is struggling with. However, currently, one particular individual is presenting an upbeat façade to the world, and would be upset if they thought you saw through it. What they need, however, is somebody to do a lot of listening.

GIFTS Prudent, Warm-hearted, Sentimental

NUMBER 3

CHALLENGES Nervous, Defensive, Oversensitive

$(2+4) + (6) = 12 = (1+2) = 3$

At those moments when I feel like a vulnerable child, I'll wrap myself in loving warmth

JUNE

24

C / A \ N / C \ E / R

You

There's a part of you that feels that if you can just get things figured out, then everything will be okay. However, being a Cancerian and someone ruled by the Moon, the heavenly body whose cycles are so powerful and so obvious, there's a lesson for you.

And that is that there are periods in life and during the month when it's about growth, when it's about stillness and when it's about rest. While that's something you may understand intellectually, there's a part of you that still feels as if you're always supposed to be doing something.

If you're not pushing yourself to get something done, you're encouraging someone else. And of course, the lesson here – and, in fact, the gift to yourself – is to recognise that you're allowed to stop.

And, just as at the time of the New Moon when there is stillness, stillness in nature, you will also be still. Ironically, during that time of stillness, you'll have time to reflect. There comes great joy in that moment, simply because it allows you to both question what you're doing and to consider your options. You will also be able to consider the idea of broadening your horizons in terms of the people you spend time with, what you're doing or what you're seeking for your own life, in the present and in the future.

You and others

The question for you and others is, are you responsible for the bad mood of those around you? There seem to be certain individuals who think that's the case. And if you allow them to convince you that that's true, then you'll have a problem. This may require taking a tough line, because the fact is, every individual is responsible for their own wellbeing.

Health and wellbeing

Cycles are the subject for you. Of course, being a water sign, that's only natural. Yet you have a tendency to feel that when it comes to your health and wellbeing, you will do better if you have a regime. The important thing is to recognise that deep within you lies a need for cycles. Pay attention to that and make it the basis upon which you make decisions.

Goals and challenges

When it comes to organising your life and your aims, your most important goal isn't what you actually achieve but what you learn in the process. Make that your priority, and everything else will fall into place.

THIS DAY FOR EVERYONE

There's a difference between making tentative plans, which is what this period is all about, and lasting commitments. The problem is, one individual views every arrangement as final. Gently but firmly help them understand that, at the moment, anyway, plans that are flexible will be better all around.

I know I'm connected to nature's powers. Sometimes, I just have to remind myself

JUNE

25

You

There's a secret to being you, and that is to pause and review what you're happy with and what you're not. This is important, not because you're going to get things organised perfectly, which is a powerful instinct you have. But rather, it's to recognise that you'll have fun figuring everything out. There aren't problems that need to be fixed so they're perfect, but rather, being ruled by the Moon, which waxes and wanes every month, you'll realise that certain things develop in cycles, and that while certain elements of your life and activities are quiet, others will be growing.

This doesn't just have to do with you and what you're doing – with your activities, your passions, or your job if you go to one. It also has to do with your relationships with others and ensuring that, at times, they're thriving, but that at other times, you give yourself space. Similarly, you may develop a new hobby and be obsessive about it for a month or even a year, and then decide it's not nearly as interesting and move on.

This isn't just important. It's natural, and if those around you wonder why you're moving on, simply smile at them and say it's because it is indeed the most natural thing for you to do. That capacity to discover new activities and to be passionate about new pursuits is one of life's greatest gifts.

You and others

Life can be enormously rewarding. However, certain individuals around you seem to think that it's your job to make it rewarding for them too. Recognising that this isn't your obligation may be difficult, but you don't have to say it. You simply need to disappear at the appropriate moment.

Health and wellbeing

There are those who regard health and wellbeing – how you eat and how you look after yourself – as a bit of a science. For you, it's a matter of discovering what feels good. That changes and it is not something that you need to discuss with anybody else.

Goals and challenges

Much of the world seems to think that there's one particular goal, and it has to do with achievement and money. While you may be interested in those things, what's most important is to find the challenges that you want to achieve and that are your challenges and what you alone wish to pursue.

C / A \ N / C \ E / R

Few things are more precious than time with loved ones. Now, somebody you care about is putting others first. Before you get hurt or angry, ask what's going on. The odds are good they've an obligation they haven't mentioned. Once they explain, you'll understand what it is they're dealing with.

Good times are fun, but lasting joy comes from an endless well deep within

JUNE

26

C
/
A
\
N
/
C
\
E
/
R

You

Your birthday chart shows how important others are in your life. The individuals around you, whether they are family, friends, colleagues or people you know from the past, are part of your own growth. Their ideas, their activities and, in fact, their complaints, all contribute to your understanding of what makes the world go around. However, it's important to recognise that this doesn't mean that you're responsible for making them happy. But you may end up doing a lot of listening and, as a result, you'll discover things within yourself that you want to explore. And this is the irony of it.

While those around you will play an important part in your life and lead you to think and grow – and of course, certain individuals will bring you great joy – the actual joy will come from the you within you, the person you discover when you're in the midst of all of those individuals or, equally, having escaped from those individuals for a while, this may have to do with the you who's able to take a walk alone.

In every case, as a Cancerian and somebody ruled by the Moon, your life is about cycles, and discovery comes in that way. Just as when plants are growing they'll flower, and then the flowers will fall off and they'll pause. Give yourself the gift of time to pause, as well.

You and others

There are many who say that keeping a routine is an important thing, but from your point of view, keeping your own rhythm is even more important. If you want to share doing things with others, do so, but if they want to stick to that routine and you don't feel like it any more, it's absolutely okay for you to say no.

Health and wellbeing

It's funny how some people think of food as more of a science, where as a Cancerian and somebody who's well aware of their feelings, you well understand that this is as much about your mood. Being able to indulge yourself when you want, choosing to be austere when you want to be, and being able to do whatever you decide at the moment that's right is most important.

Goals and challenges

The trick to understanding the cycle of challenges arising is to recognise that, rather than worrying about them, challenges are to be welcomed. They're an invitation to a variety of growth you might not otherwise experience and may even lead to acquiring one of life's greatest skills or experiencing life's greatest joys.

THIS DAY FOR EVERYONE

Sometimes, you're in a rush. As often, however, it's pride that prevents you from allowing others to deal with certain crucial arrangements. You've no choice but to hand over a range of such matters. And the sooner you talk this over, the more swiftly you can let go. That should win over the doubters.

Although nobody takes lessons in how to love, we all have an endless ability to share it

You

For you, as a Cancerian, being born into a world where achievement is often measured in possessions, in money or in a title, is a paradox. While you may enjoy having good things, you also have a deeper knowledge of what might be termed inner values, that is, those feelings that come with being happy with others but, even more, with being true to yourself.

Of course, if you're living a busy life, despite being a juggling act, it can be joyous. The trick is to manage to find that time that's so important to be yourself, even if you are in the middle of doing exciting things or find yourself distracted by those who you care about. And that is your lesson. It isn't what you have or what you earn. It's the way you own your time and your joy.

That may sound selfish but, intriguingly, when your close friends, family and even colleagues witness you embracing that joy, they will not only be happy for you, but they'll also begin to learn from you – and this is what's best about that. This variety of joy is infectious. It's something that you will share, not just because you talk about it, but because you live it. And this is one of your most important journeys as a Cancerian, to not only experience that joy but, in experiencing it, to share it with others.

You and others

Helping those around you comes naturally to you. When you extend yourself, you don't even think about it. Receiving help from others – their support, their goodwill – is more difficult for you. The lesson? If you understand that accepting is as important as giving, you won't struggle with receiving any more.

Health and wellbeing

Often, regimes are not only boring, they suggest that you're unhappy. Search for a formula that works. The trick is to find something that isn't extreme, is fun and, in fact, that goes with your natural flow.

Goals and challenges

Those around you may have lots of ideas about what you should be doing. If so, thank them very much and ignore them. Their version of advice isn't advice. It's actually somebody trying to impose their will on you. The most important goal that you could possibly follow is a goal of your own.

THIS DAY FOR EVERYONE

Exciting ideas are in the air. While you're eager to explore, others are wary and fear wasting their time or being disappointed. Forget about trying to win over the individuals in question and, if necessary, get involved on your own. Then you can discuss your own experiences.

There is no fee for kindness, yet the joy it gives is endless and timeless

JUNE

28

C
/
A
\
N
/
C
\
E
/
R

You

You love a challenge. A challenge gives you an opportunity to exercise the muscle of your mind, the muscles of your body, but also the muscle of your feelings, of what inspires you. If there's any challenge in this, however, it's that there's a tendency for those around you to measure your success at meeting such challenges in more worldly ways. Whereas for you, it's more about your intuition and what you learn and being able to hone those worldly skills, but also to go within.

The trick, of course, is recognising that not everybody even has an inner world. Those individuals won't understand what you're talking about when you refer to a sense of personal achievement, and still less about inner peace. But for you, as a Cancerian, that combination of achieving what you want in the world around you, and also achieving that inner peace, is one of the things you were born to discover and to do.

While you may not be able to talk to others about it, you can be an example of how to live that way, and that's also important. Often it's not what you say, but it's the peace others recognise in you that becomes something they would like to experience. They may come and sit by you simply to enjoy that peace. If so, you will know that you have achieved your goals.

You and others

There's a temptation to do whatever is necessary to keep others happy. Hopefully, you've already discovered that while theoretically that's easy, it's about the most draining thing you could possibly attempt to do. The secret is an exchange. Do something for them, but then get them to do something for themselves.

Health and wellbeing

There are those around you who will be happy to give you advice about what you should be eating, how much, and when and, equally, how you should be moving your body. However, as a Cancerian, you have the greatest instincts in the world. Pay attention to those, and ignore what others have to say.

Goals and challenges

It's impossible not to discuss your own goals with others. They may offer to analyse things for you, because that's what people consider to be conversation. However, the important thing for you to remember is that by no means do you have to pay attention to that analysis.

THIS DAY FOR EVERYONE

Just when you thought that once-troublesome issues had been dealt with and were in the past, sudden changes have put them at the forefront of everybody's thinking and discussion. Worrying as this seems now, be bold. Speak from the heart. The warm response you receive will amaze you.

Healing occurs when hope meets need in a setting that allows for the miraculous

You

As a Cancerian, you have an instinctive understanding of the difference between learning in the normal way – that is, learning when you go to school – and learning a skill. Whether it's a professional skill or a sport, you just need to get out there and do it. Understanding is another matter, however. That comes from reflection – from sitting, thinking about things, talking to those who you admire – and understanding will also shape what you do and what you learn.

Many people don't realise this, and those you're chatting with – about what you're doing or the possibility of rethinking things, the possibility of pursuing something new – may think that everything they understand will come from taking action instead of this particular variety of reflection that is so important for you as a Cancerian.

The fact is, if they don't understand how important it is, you probably won't be able to teach them, in which case you'll remain friends with them, or perhaps you'll remain a member of their family, but when it comes to reflecting on what you're doing, the rewards you're getting at, what you want to seek more of, they may not be the people to talk to. Gradually, you'll begin to discover those who share this understanding with you, and those individuals will become your true family.

You and others

Discussing what makes you close to someone can itself be a very tricky thing. The most important thing is to analyse whether you feel comfortable with that person and whether you want to see them again. Make that your assessment of who is close.

Health and wellbeing

There are those who are absolutely dedicated to a particular wellbeing regime, whether it's eating or exercising in a particular way. However, they're not you. Being a water sign, you're better off doing what feels good, rather than what someone else says is right.

Goals and challenges

You have an instinctive sense of when it's time to set a new goal and, equally, when it's time to leave something behind you. But what's most important is to recognise those activities that touch your heart. This is because, being a water sign and ruled by the Moon, you understand that more deeply than anybody else.

Once you understand that, while you've an easy-going attitude about the remarkable events taking place, others aren't nearly as comfortable with them, everything will make sense. You'll not only know why certain individuals are determined to do things their way, you'll back off and allow them to do just that.

Those who say there's a right way to love have entirely missed the point

You

As a Cancerian and a water sign, it's important that you note something about your character – your natural instinct is to try to help where you can, to try to fix situations wherever it's possible.

In fact, you can end up putting this first, particularly in circumstances involving others. Of course, the trick is to balance that with the importance of your own life and things you need to do for yourself.

You may tend to put off your own needs, until you recognise the importance of establishing what might be described as a give-and-take ratio. That is, you give – it's important for you. But also, there are times when you must take assistance from others, or times when you're on your own and you put yourself absolutely first.

The irony is that you find that the more you do that – the more you put yourself first – the more you will be celebrated by those around you.

That's simply because in taking this approach, you'll be recognising how important it is that you nurture yourself, and that alone will be the kind of lesson you've been wanting to give those around you.

Even more than that, it will allow you to discover your next set of goals and set you off on that path with enthusiasm.

You and others

Not everyone gets along all the time, and there are moments when there have been tensions with others, if not very difficult situations. The trick to dealing with this is to recognise that there are occasions when you need to disagree with others, and sometimes those disagreements mean saying farewell.

Health and wellbeing

There are types of extreme exercises people get involved in that suit them, and which may suit you. But in this particular case, the kind of extreme health and wellbeing you need to get involved in is doing what's absolutely true to you and nothing else.

Goals and challenges

Every once in a while, somebody comes along and you begin discussing what you want to do. They then give you advice without even asking if you'd like it. You may want to listen to them, but what may be most important is to be so selfish that you will do only what pleases you. There could be no more important goal in life.

THIS DAY FOR EVERYONE

You've hoped to sidestep one particular demanding situation involving an element of your way of living or working. But recent events made it clear you'd have to go along with others' decisions. Worse, there's no room for negotiation. Grim as it seems, don't argue. Ultimately, this will benefit you hugely.

GIFTS Thoughtful, Persistent, Wise

NUMBER 8

CHALLENGES Clinging, Homebound, Apathetic

(0+1) + (7) = 8

Trusting my instincts is easy, until I try to get things right – then they often go wrong

You

Numerologically, he first of every month signifies the number one and new beginnings. In fact, this is all about you discovering your own rhythm. However, it's important to recognise that this isn't about a single rhythm.

It's about your own ups and downs, not in the sense of negativities, but in the sense that there are times when you're bursting with energy, as if there is a spring bubbling inside you, and there are times when you need to be still. These are all important.

In fact, those still moments give you time to rest and reflect. These are mirrored by the seasons and, also, when you're reflecting, new ideas will develop, ideas that might possibly not have grown had you not taken that time for stillness.

The trick, therefore, is to ignore those who are encouraging you to get out and about when that isn't what you want to do. This is important for everybody, but for you, as a Cancerian and somebody who is ruled by the Moon, the planet which has its own cycles, the message is very clear. Pay attention to when you want to be still and do that. Then, when you're stirred by passion to do something, to achieve something, to go somewhere or, in fact, to fall in love with something or somebody, do it, and do it just at the moment you feel is best.

You and others

It seems strange that those around you don't have the same sense of cycles you do, but the fact is they don't. When they want to go along with you, recognise that they may not be following the same rhythm and, if so, simply allow them. Step back and be who you are. Let them be who they are.

Health and wellbeing

There's a single message for you, and that message says: move. Walk, dance, hop, jump rope – whatever it is, feel your body. Feel the muscles in your body, indeed, moving, and not only will you feel that. You'll feel the sheer joy of being alive.

Goals and challenges

Sometimes, challenges are just that, but for you, challenges are about defining the hill you want to climb, and then climbing it. Then having gotten to the top, it's about recognising there are plenty of other hills you could climb and embracing the joy of knowing you can climb each of them.

THIS DAY FOR EVERYONE

Somebody seems determined to reveal flaws in your thinking. While you acknowledge that you can get it wrong, you're confident that in this case everything is accurate. Still, explore what's being said. At minimum, you'll learn something. But the odds are good you'll discover that others are correct.

GIFTS Visionary, Loving, Accommodating   NUMBER 9

CHALLENGES Irritable, Worrier, Over-extending $(0+2) + (7) = 9$

Lively get-togethers are fun but life's joys are found in the least likely of settings

You

Your birthday theme is a balance between your own life and your own stories, and the lives of others and their stories. While you may care a lot about what they are doing – and in fact, in situations where you care about others you'll be thrilled by their activities – by no means does that suggest you need to get involved.

You can be involved – by caring about it – but you and your own interests must come first. As a Cancerian, you tend to feel that in order to show you care, you need to be out there with others and, often, those around you will be delighted if you come, but the fact is, looking after yourself and your own interests is an important part for you as a Cancerian.

Being born under the sign of nurturance, that balance between being interested in and caring about others, but also caring about yourself, is always an important one. It's also one you're always learning, because you're changing, and the world around is changing too, and that balance itself changes.

Perhaps the most important thing to keep in mind is that this isn't selfish. This is also showing those around you that they, too, can live a life that's exciting and full of activities and caring, but also ensures that they, too, are looking after their own best interests. That's the secret.

You and others

There's a single phrase that defines your role when it comes to you and others. It's give and take. That means in both cases the individual in question must recognise what the other is interested in and enjoy that. This always shifts. There is no fixed recipe.

Health and wellbeing

For you, looking after yourself should be part of your routine. It's important. However, doing the same thing week in and week out doesn't qualify. Enjoying life is the best possible routine for your health and wellbeing.

Goals and challenges

It's easy to list what you need to do and what you want more of, but what may be most important for you to do is to note and follow what lifts your spirits and what challenges you in the best possible way. Make that the centre of your goals, and the rest will fall into place perfectly.

THIS DAY FOR EVERYONE

Few things are more upsetting than clashes with those closest over issues that really shouldn't be a problem. Or so you think. Begin delving into the source of those differences. What you learn won't just be surprising. You'll realise a number of matters need to be discussed. And the sooner, the better.

Those who insist there's a right way to give a compliment have missed the point entirely

JULY

You

For you, as a July 3rd Cancerian, discussing life and plans and projects with others can be tricky. This is simply because you'll be talking about what you want to do, and you'll be eager to hear what others have in mind.

The difficulty is that others will want to be helpful and give you advice, except you'll be well aware that what they think is a good idea isn't necessarily going to suit you, and this is where tact comes in.

You may find yourself being drawn into what they're doing, simply because they seem so determined to be helpful and you find it difficult to say no. And this is one of your challenges – to differentiate between those who think that they're offering something wonderful but don't fully understand that you actually function in a very different way than they do. This is because they aren't an intuitive water sign, and you are.

If there's any skill, it's the skill of being able to withdraw from the offers of others who think that if you do what they say, then you will thrive. The secret is, appreciate who they are and help them to appreciate who you are, and your relationship will thrive. And even more than that, you will live out each day appreciating life's joys all the more and, equally, appreciating what they brought into your life.

You and others

Some people are naturally generous, and they have an instinctive sense of what will benefit you. Others are well meaning but just plain selfish. They will organise your life so that they enjoy things, and that's one of your big lessons. Learn to say this single word firmly: no.

Health and wellbeing

The trick with this is to be able to recognise those regimes that make others happy but are depriving you of life's joys. The fact is, you can do what's good for you, but it doesn't need to take away from your everyday joys. It's about making choices that add to your life in every way.

Goals and challenges

It's so easy to be distracted, if not drained, by goals that have made others successful, yet saying, "That's wonderful, but I'm not interested," can be one of the most difficult things in the world, especially for you, a sensitive Cancerian. Practise saying no, just as you might practise playing the piano, and you will benefit for the rest of your life.

03

C
/
A
\
N
/
C
\
E
/
R

Everybody has to deal with issues of some nature, it's just those you're facing now seem both more complex and more frequent than usual. This is mostly because changes, while beneficial in the long term, are chaotic. Be patient. The results will more than justify the disruption you're currently facing.

The problem isn't what unkind people say, it's paying attention to their words

JULY

04

C
/
A
\
N
/
C
\
E
/
R

You

It's said that planning ahead is good, and that's true. However, you have to consider what you're getting involved in – whether it's new territory in terms of activities, in terms of ideas, in terms of the culture you might be in or the people you'll be around. If that's the case, it's almost as if you were learning a new language.

You may indeed actually have to, but it could also mean that you'll need to take time to figure out what's going on. You may feel that you're supposed to be bold and just plunge in, but this particular variety of moving into new territory is about a kind of discovery, and when you recognise that, then you'll actually enjoy looking after yourself.

You'll treat yourself as if you were a very special kind of tourist, moving into a new kind of experience, into a new setting, a new country, a new way of thinking –and once you do that, you'll also begin to enjoy what you're doing.

The trick is to abandon that feeling that you're supposed to figure it out on your own, and instead treat yourself as the very special being that you are, the individual who deserves to be tutored when you're entering new territory and, in being tutored, will become very skilled at living in that setting and living very well, indeed.

You and others

The message for you is to be aware of certain individuals who are what might be termed "chronic complainers". Whatever it is that's going on, they'll find something wrong, and they'll expect those around them, possibly you, to remedy that. The fact is, they're just spoiled, and you and your needs come first.

Health and wellbeing

There seems to be somebody around you who has very strict dos and don'ts for self care. That might work for them, but being ruled by the Moon, the heavenly body that has cycles, that kind of thing isn't your style. In fact, the more you align with your own rhythms, the better.

Goals and challenges

When it comes to goals and challenges, don't let others take over. They may mean well, but they're trying to impose their own interests and values on you. When others try to do that, say thank you then give serious thought to who and what is most important to you.

THIS DAY FOR EVERYONE

The time has come to talk things over. True, with so much going on, the last thing you're in the mood for is in-depth discussion of minor issues. However, those differences aren't nearly as insignificant as they seem, something which will become clear as others reveal why they're concerned.

The formula for ending suffering? Dwell on love until there's no room for anything else

You

You love making plans, because they make life easier, but, at the same time, you hope for the unexpected. You enjoy having to think quickly and come up with new ideas – actually it's your idea of fun.

This is because you have a strong inquisitive side to your nature, and that inquisitive side responds well when you have to take care of sudden twists and turns or perhaps meet people who will help you resolve the surprising developments that have arisen.

Not everyone understands this, which means that there can be those around you who will try to convince you to simply either go with the flow or make more solid plans.

But this is very much your own journey – and if you try to take the advice of those who want to make plans and have you stick to them, then you'll simply be following their theme.

This shows the inquisitive side of your nature as well, the part that thrives on discovery, the part that enjoys those twists and turns and, in fact, recognises that the unexpected allows you to flex a muscle that is unique to you, one that is about embracing the unfamiliar and about discovery – and about the joy of learning something new, ideally every day. Embrace that, and you will be making each day a joy.

You and others

The trick is to do something that seems odd and that is to have two sets of routines. One is for others, and will enable you to go along with what they want, but your own is for those discoveries that make life itself exciting, and those are the adventures.

Health and wellbeing

For you, as a Cancerian, mood is as important as the time of day or what you're doing. Being ruled by the Moon, you have an understanding of the importance of this, but others don't, so don't try to explain. You will never be able to.

Goals and challenges

Beware of borrowing the goals of others. They will be delighted to share them with you, but that doesn't mean it's wise. This is the most important thing for you to discover. You pursuing their goals will make them happy, not you.

Currently, it may seem life is like a chess game, in that you can only move so far, and only under certain circumstances. Frustrating as that is, it's forcing you and others to pause and reflect on your priorities with every step. This prevents you being pressed into making hasty decisions.

Sometimes it's only when a heart is broken that true love can find its way in

JULY

06

C / A \ N / C \ E / R

You

Do you ever wonder why some people seem to make life so difficult – they turn ordinary situations into something unpleasant or pick up on unnecessary challenges? Well, it's not about you. It's about them. The fact is, certain individuals seem to be programmed that way.

The skill for you is to notice that and, unless it happens to be a child who you're raising or a very close friend, to acknowledge that that's just what makes them tick, that's how they look at the world. Then back off and know that you're different, and that by no means should you let them undermine your thinking or your life. This has to do with the individuals around you, but it also has to do with life in general and any setbacks you're facing.

As a Cancerian and a water sign, you can be sensitive and can often turn seemingly unimportant situations into something that has to do with you personally. That may indeed have to do with your mood.

That's one of your greatest lessons – to recognise those moments when the choice lies entirely with you, whether you'll enjoy what life brings you or turn it into a drama. You could even turn those dramas into something exciting and enjoyable. After all, many people go to the theatre to do exactly that. You're able to do it in your own life. And better yet, you're able to direct how the play goes.

You and others

Beware of the stories that others tell you about what they're trying to do for you. While they may have good intentions, putting yourself first is the best way to accomplish what you want in your own time.

Health and wellbeing

It's said that dieting and working out with somebody else is great. However, in certain situations, the individual you have in mind may want you to do things their way, in their routine and eat what they need to eat, as opposed to you looking after your own needs. Think about this and think about it carefully.

Goals and challenges

Making lists about what you want to do is important. However, what's more important is to follow your instincts. As a Cancerian and a water sign, these are powerful, more powerful than those of others, which is the reason that those around you don't necessarily encourage you to listen to what your instincts tell you.

THIS DAY FOR EVERYONE

Admitting you're wrong is no problem. However, certain individuals insist their facts are right. The real problem is that they're looking for a battle and have chosen their topic, which involves you. Say nothing. The individuals in question will soon turn their attention elsewhere.

GIFTS Gentle, Protective, Thoughtful

CHALLENGES Withholding, Avoidant, Indignant

NUMBER 5

$(0+7) + (7) = 14 = (1+4) = 5$

Nobody decides what kindness is. Only the recipient can say, and even then, it changes

You

As a Cancerian, you seek security and stability. Yet at the same time, in life you need new challenges – not just to have things organised but something new to think about. On occasion, this will involve others and their support, which is important.

But what's most significant for you is to put what you need to do and your own objectives first, then get others involved if you feel like it. Most of all, you need to recognise that what you learn from setting your own goals isn't just about life itself, but constitutes an opportunity to review what's worked and what hasn't, and what you want to leave behind you.

As a Cancerian, you have an instinctive understanding of the cycles of nature. You are, after all, ruled by the Moon, the heavenly body which is known for its cycles. Yet sometimes you try to make your life fit into the kind of order that others follow.

Recognising that there are times when, like the Moon, you have more energy, and other times when you need to be still will allow you to use these quiet times to reflect on what you've done, what you're happy about and what you'll want next. Do that, and when it comes time to make major decisions, you'll already know where you stand and what and who is most important – and, even more than that, what brings you joy in life.

You and others

The thing for you is give and take. This is necessary when dealing with others. However, certain individuals are convinced that if you organise things in a way that makes them happy, then everything will work. The secret is to learn to say no – not to debate the rights and wrongs of it, but simply to do what you want to do. Not by arguing, but by just putting one foot in front of the other.

Health and wellbeing

You're sensitive by nature and need a break from the rigours of life every once in a while, including the rigours of eating well. Yet it's important you balance looking after yourself with indulgences. These may have to do with something you eat or something pleasurable, and are as important as the vitamins you take – in fact, in some instances, more important.

Goals and challenges

Because you're creative by nature, sensing what will be rewarding is of great significance. That may mean rethinking your goals as you focus on them. In some cases, these will last a week, in some a month and in some cases they'll last years. But in every case, if that goal comes from the centre of your being, from your heart, then you will achieve it.

JULY

07

C / A \ N / C \ E / R

THIS DAY FOR EVERYONE

You've tried a range of ways to say no and achieved nothing. The fact is that the individual in question pays little attention to what anybody says, and this includes you. Making your point will require the variety of drama that you usually do everything you can to avoid. And nothing less.

Talking somebody out of a bad idea only delays it. Showing them they're loved ends it

JULY

08

C
/
A
\
N
/
C
\
E
/
R

You

As a July 8th birthday, you balance a desire to get out there in the world and do what you want to do. It may be that world is your home, perhaps in business or travel. You are creative by nature and enjoy doing things that are lasting, that bring you pleasure and will benefit others. Yet, at the same time, being a Cancerian and a water sign ruled by the Moon, you have your ups and downs.

When you are experiencing downs, you want either reassurance from others or need to build up your own sense of ego or sense of optimism about what's next. That may involve looking back on what you've done before and the challenges that you've managed to meet. But it may also involve doing something out of character for you, which is to pause and take a break – to walk, to look at the sky, to recognise that it isn't always about doing or not doing, but about being. This is one of the greatest skills for you.

The point of it is to give you the strength to tackle what's next, because as a Cancerian and somebody who is one of the cardinal signs – the signs that begin each season – starting something new is as much a part of your nature as breathing. Find that balance between the need to be still and nurturing yourself to meet that next challenge, and you will have found the most important balance in your life.

You and others

Rituals are an important part of life and often of those around you. Family or friends enjoy them. You always meet on a certain date and do something in particular. But every once in a while, those rituals can turn into a trap. Being able to create your own, often with new friends, is an essential part of your life.

Health and wellbeing

It's said that if you get into a routine, you can keep that for life. But actually it's not true. Times change, you change and what makes you happy changes. But also things can become so routine that you don't even notice what you're doing and you end up getting lazy. Excitement comes from doing something different, learning something with somebody new and challenging yourself in a way that is as exciting as it is rewarding.

Goals and challenges

Planning ahead is important, but often those plans need to be rethought before they become reality. Yet there's a part of you that worries you didn't think about those things first, that you didn't catch the need to make those changes. Observe how a plant develops new leaves or even flowers. So, too, will your challenges develop and grow.

THIS DAY FOR EVERYONE

Planning ahead may be a virtue and make life easier. But with your ruler Mercury retrograde for a few more days, you're better off regarding even the simplest of arrangements as tentative, if not a bit of an experiment. While things may go as expected, the odds are good there'll be several changes.

A smile from the heart can turn a pleasant moment into a profound and lasting bond

You

You tend to swing from gathering people and activities, even sometimes objects, to shedding them. Once you've got too much going in your life, you realise it's important to let go. Still, saying farewells can be very difficult indeed and you may find excuses to put it off.

But this is one of your greatest lessons. It's letting go of certain elements of your life, even habits. That may mean letting relationships go, but it also may have to do with certain goals that once meant a great deal.

The other element of this is to recognise that, being an intuitive water sign, you have what might be termed a rich inner realm, that is, those feelings and perhaps even the mystical side of your nature that senses what's going on in the world around you, in the lives of others and, importantly, in your own life.

Sometimes you keep feelings of that nature to yourself, because you know others won't understand them. But if you have one or two friends or family members who are themselves intuitive and with whom you can talk about those feelings, then it's important to do so.

That's the secret for you. As a Cancerian – and somebody who is on one hand bursting with initiative, and on the other goes deep within – it's not what you do or say, but finding the balance that's important.

You and others

Habits are comfortable – at home, with family members or with friends all make it easy, because you don't have to make decisions. You can do the same thing on the same day or go to the same place. However, that makes things predictable. The secret for you, and one that's important to remind yourself of, is that change is like taking a deep breath and bringing new life into your life and those of others as well.

Health and wellbeing

Often those who get involved in a wellbeing routine, whether it's what you eat or getting out and about, follow it in a way that makes it duller by the day. The trick is to turn it into a joy – and an experiment. That may mean you lose individuals who are committed to that strict regime. If so, that's fine, because you'll have more fun without them.

Goals and challenges

It's hard to measure if you've achieved a goal unless it's something specific – writing a book, say, or getting a degree. So it's essential you set your own goals, not measured by others but those that mean the most to you. You may not discuss them with others, but when you achieve them, your spirits will get a boost like nothing else.

THIS DAY FOR EVERYONE

It's rare, when making plans, that you lavish attention on details. You long ago learnt that because things change, you're better off dealing with such matters at the last minute. Not everyone agrees. Tempting as it is to reassure them, that's unwise. The best strategy is to say nothing.

Sometimes a fierce debate conceals a loving and passionate exchange

You

You often tend to measure your days in what might be called good vibes, that is whether something you're doing lifts your spirits. While that's wonderful and important, not every day brings that kind of thing.

If you measure success by that and are disturbed when it doesn't happen, then you may not recognise what you've achieved in situations that are less easy to deal with – facing people who are difficult, facing obstacles, or perhaps even having to undo something from the past that may have been difficult to contend with.

Whatever it is, the thing for you to recognise is that often the most important achievements occur in the most challenging of circumstances. This by no means indicates anything is bad. It's just simply that it's a big stretch for you.

As a water sign, and somebody who feels more deeply than the other signs, it's vital that you recognise that sometimes those feelings of struggle are an indication of making an effort – kind of as if you were lifting weights to get stronger. Most of all, recognise that often after those struggles come delights. Delights that simply wouldn't have been possible had you not struggled. When you're celebrating in that way, remember that for the next time you face similar obstacles.

You and others

Habits play a big part in your relationship with others. There's a celebration of doing things the same way. But also, that can be limiting, and it can be difficult to say no to certain habits. It may take courage but, bizarrely, once you do make a change, others will agree that it was wise, and you'll all be delighted, because life isn't just about doing things the same way. It's about discovery.

Health and wellbeing

Some habits are good. However, some are unhelpful. Also, some pleasures are appealing. In every case, it isn't how much you enjoy doing something or not. It's about examining where it fits into your life and if it brings you benefit in the here and now. If it doesn't, it's time to say farewell to it.

Goals and challenges

Occasionally, you put off tackling a particular challenge because the time doesn't seem right. But often it's because the situation or people involved are themselves challenging. Take a deep breath, stand firmly on your feet, and note that not only can you meet that challenge, you can overcome it. And, better yet, think about how wonderful you'll feel when you've done it.

THIS DAY FOR EVERYONE

You seem to be caught in one of those tricky situations in which a particular individual will go to any length to avoid taking responsibility for something they did wrong. While this isn't your problem, it is essential you make it clear you had absolutely nothing to do with the matter in question.

When hearts are tender, careless laughter can cause deep wounds

You

Ages ago, you got in the habit of fighting to do what you want. While this is important, many of the things you were fighting for at that time are no longer rewarding. Yet because you battled for them, you're keeping them as part of your life, mostly to remember what you've achieved.

Yet times have moved on and, in fact, the kind of review that was so important for you, has changed. It's not just about finding new battles, but also exciting and rewarding new activities and, possibly, individuals in your life.

Habits are important, and they might be viewed as kind of an arbour that holds up roses in the garden. But in your particular case, those habits can hold you back. The trick is to regard yourself as if you were a plant that bloomed anew each season, and that as you bloom you must choose what you want to be drawn towards, just as a flower is drawn towards the sun.

It may well be that certain activities and goals that were once rewarding actually no longer mean that much. While you're inclined to reach towards others, decide what those are, commit to them, and, within a very short time – months or possibly even weeks – you'll be achieving them.

You and others

Tempting as it is to stick with those you care about, every once in a while you need a break, and that involves doing something with somebody new. It may just be a one-off visit, or it may be someone who will become an important part of your life. But in every case, mixing it up, blending family and friends and those you've known forever with new encounters, will be the tonic you need.

Health and wellbeing

Maybe you're looking for a quick formula for feeling better, or you've heard about one from others, but you've lived in your body for a while and you'll be using it for a while yet. So making it comfortable and happy may also take time. Regard it as if it is a beautiful piece of furniture that needs to be cared for over time. Don't rush into being perfect, enjoy the process of looking after yourself.

Goals and challenges

It's not about whether you've succeeded or not, but by whose values you are judging. Often those around you will have clear ideas about what you should be doing with your life, which may differ from yours. You're number one in your own life, and you need to decide what you regard as success.

JULY

11

C
/
A
\
N
/
C
\
E
/
R

THIS DAY FOR EVERYONE

If it seems that you're running up against people who are either demanding or opinionated, that's no surprise. However, it's worth noting that your views on several matters are equally inflexible. Begin reviewing these, and suddenly discussions with others will go better.

Healing occurs when the power of love outweighs the force of fear

You

Every once in a while, you have a deep conversation with the most important person in your life – yourself – about what you want to do. There may be certain things you'd like to change, goals you'd like to pursue or doubts you're wrestling with.

While you can go round and round with these, there's also the chance to discuss these matters with others. However, that can be as tricky, especially if it's family or close friends you're talking to, each of whom will have their own view about what's in your best interests.

The secret to dealing with all of this is to sit down with yourself and consider what actually brings you joy. True, not everything in life can be joyous and certain situations require plain discipline. Still, the simple act of doing what you need to do is itself joyous.

The trick is to avoid sticking with the old just for the sake of it, or to keep those around you – family, friends or colleagues – happy, but to explore. And in exploring, discovery's an important part of that. Report back to those around you how much you're enjoying it. Instead of seeking their guidance, invite them to join you in that process of discovery.

You'll be turning destiny around. Rather than seeking others' guidance, you'll be giving it to them. Together, you'll move ahead into a far more rewarding chapter.

You and others

There's a secret to dealing with tricky matters. That is to raise them. And the more swiftly you do that, the better. Once you begin, you'll realise that often those issues were on the minds of others, and they're grateful you brought those matters up. Most of all, say exactly what you want. Here, too, others will be grateful for your bold approach.

Health and wellbeing

You have a choice. You can have really big ideas about the way you look after your body, then to do very little simply because it's overwhelming. Or you can do something radical and take things one day at a time. Do that and you'll not only be acting in your own best interests, you'll be setting an example for others as well.

Goals and challenges

You often forget your own achievements, some minor, some major. First, you put them all behind you, then you compare yourself to others. Every once in a while, if not even once a day, it's useful to recall what you've done and enjoy the satisfaction those achievements have brought. Do that – then when you tackle what's next, you'll do so with joy and conviction.

THIS DAY FOR EVERYONE

Having right on your side is reassuring, especially when you're dealing with those who are eager to debate existing plans or priorities. Still, before you challenge others, it would be wise to double-check even seemingly solid facts. Times change, and so you're likely to make several surprising discoveries.

Hearts all swell and know what's needed without a word being spoken

You

As a Cancerian and an intuitive water sign, you go back and forth between your practical side, which thrives on security, and the part that is sometimes described as superstitious, but has an instinct of the rhythms of nature and also a clear sense of the degree to which your own way of looking at things can influence both how they flow and the outcome.

Of course, as you've discovered, it's tricky discussing this approach with certain people, and it's even made you a bit self-conscious. However, if you can blend the two in your activities, in your major goals and in your everyday pursuits, then you'll find you're benefitting from both, and there'll be a new kind of magic in your life. But, even more than that, there'll be a new kind of joy.

You wouldn't have thought that this would have an advantageous effect in practical or financial terms. Yet if you think positively about what you could do, you might be surprised. At the same time, being able to look towards those whose company can be challenging in a more positive light can alter that as well.

The trick, therefore, isn't so much expecting magic, but turning your own mind into the tool that makes magic happen. Try that, and you'll be amazed how much you achieve.

You and others

Particular individuals often withhold their approval until you do things their way. Sometimes that may be a game, but often it's a manipulation as well. The most important thing is to recognise when that occurs, and to make a point of making your own decisions and doing exactly what you please.

Health and wellbeing

Most people speak of changes in the way you eat, or move, or exercise, as a regime. However, there's another approach, and it has to do with the idea of being nice to yourself. Choose to eat in a certain way, and to move in a certain way – one that you enjoy. That's a much better approach than having any regime.

Goals and challenges

The term challenge implies an uphill struggle. However, life is all about cycles – day and night, up and down – and you won't have a goal without a challenge. Bear that in mind, and when challenges arise, you'll view them as climbing a hill, at which point you'll have an amazing view, not just of where you've come from but of what's next. That isn't so much a challenge as it's a goal realised.

Change is in the air. While it's clear things can't remain as they are, you've been hoping you could discuss and deal with certain tricky matters gradually. But, ironically, the disruption caused by those changes will force others to acknowledge, and join you in tackling, the issues you have in mind.

Often we pray to a divine being beyond us, when, in fact, that power lies within

JULY

14

C
/
A
\
N
/
C
\
E
/
R

You

As a Cancerian and a water sign, one of the three signs that are sensitive and highly intuitive, not only do you derive insights from what you sense, but also some of your greatest joys come not so much from physical possessions or achievements, but your feelings.

This by no means indicates that you don't enjoy acquiring things. In fact, many Cancerians are great collectors. It just means that it's important for you to recognise that whatever you're doing, a portion of that activity is based on those feelings.

If there's anything tricky, it's that those around you won't necessarily have the same deep emotions. If you try to discuss them with others, they may look at you blankly because they don't understand. So it's important that while you may be close to certain family or friends, you pick and choose those with whom you discuss these feelings.

It also means that sometimes you'll juggle what you say. In some cases, you'll need to be very frank and deal only with the facts, while with others you can talk about your emotions. It's like speaking two languages. But also it's about being a very special person, because not everybody has the capacity to experience life's deepest joys and its deepest feelings in the way that you do as a Cancerian. That's a precious talent, one to be savoured and enjoyed.

You and others

You may be in a routine or perhaps those around you like to do things the same way. Whatever the case, there's a tendency to stick with the familiar. However, changes allow you to retool things that you didn't realise needed to be rethought, and to make them better, either on your own or along with others.

Health and wellbeing

Your sense of wellbeing has as much to do with the state of your mind and your feelings as with the body you're living in. Instead of focusing only on your physical body, your activities and what you eat, pay close attention to your words and ideas, the way you feed your mind and your feelings. Focus on that and you'll feel terrific every day.

Goals and challenges

You need to assess whether your current goals are actually appropriate for the person you are today. Every so often, it's essential to stop and consider whether what you were once passionate about still means as much to you. This may have to do with life out in the world, or your personal life. Whatever the case, ensure that your goals are something that you actually care about.

THIS DAY FOR EVERYONE

In your efforts to avoid causing offence or seeming overly critical, you've given one particular individual the impression that you've no objection to what they've said or done. But that's not the case. This leaves you little choice but to be frank, and in a way that removes all possibility of doubt.

When the moment is right, an abrupt "No" can be a statement of love

JULY

15

C
/
A
\
N
/
C
\
E
/
R

You

There are many definitions for the word success. On one hand you're a cardinal sign, one of the signs that begin in each season, but also you're an intuitive water sign, so your own definition of success may shift with your mood. The question is, does it have to do with worldly achievement – perhaps making money or being recognised – or is it about living a happy life in which you are content with what you're doing and the people around you?

Ideally it will be both, but times change and life changes, and having these all at once can be tricky. This means that defining success for you has to do with how you feel about yourself and what you're doing – and the joy that you have every day when you wake up.

Compare yourself to others and it's difficult to have that joy. But if, on the other hand, you simply feel the best you can each day, and then reach out and share that feeling with others, whatever the day holds, you'll feel better – and you might even find that those good feelings are contagious.

Even more than that, as someone who is a cardinal sign, it's important that you be bold and take chances – at least every once in a while. It's an important muscle for you to exercise, and the more you do, the more you'll enjoy what, ultimately, you achieve.

You and others

We often get into rituals – with friends, or often with family at certain holidays or times of the year. While that's nice, it can also be dull, if not restrictive. Alter the place or activity or even the people involved a little, and get others to agree with this approach, you will find a new way of doing something that, while a familiar ritual, won't become a trap.

Health and wellbeing

Others may have told you that certain activities are good for you, so you're trying them out instead of doing something you really enjoy. This has to do with how you eat and with how you move. But even more than that, it is about doing things that give your spirit a lift. As a water sign, that latter is far more important and can actually be the foundation of your wellbeing.

Goals and challenges

Everyone has a list of things they want to do. Yours may have been compiled some time ago. But, every once in a while, it's not only vital to review that, it's important to take the metaphorical piece of paper that list is written on, and write a new one. There's no better time to do this than the present.

THIS DAY FOR EVERYONE

On several occasions over the past few weeks, when discussing certain tricky situations, you sidestepped the full facts. While, at the time, it was about sidestepping pointless discussions, you're urged to inform those involve of the details you left out. And do it now, before they discover these for themselves.

GIFTS Welcoming, Loyal, Visionary

NUMBER 5

(1+6) + (7) = 14 = (1+4) = 5

CHALLENGES Cranky, Nervous, Hurts deeply

Remedying problems only repositions them. The solution? Rise above them

JULY

16

C
/
A
\
N
/
C
\
E
/
R

You

Many Cancerians are easy-going by nature, but most find, deep within, standards that come from their childhood. These shape what you want to do or become in life. There is a part of your Cancerian nature that is just plain driven. And in certain areas, you have very clear ideas about how things should work.

However, being ruled by the Moon, you're also sensitive. Your mood fluctuates. It changes depending on what you're doing, what you've experienced and the people you're around. In some cases, certain individuals can undermine your feelings, and you have to be cautious of them. It's the same with joy – certain individuals lift your spirits.

The path, of course, is to create your own mental and emotional climate. Ideally, you will do that, not based on who you're hanging out with, but how you actually manage your mood and your time. There's a trick here, and it's to break a habit a day, to find something that you do well and wisely because you do it and just to stop it as an exercise.

But, even more than that, the other trick is to find a joy a day. That may be more difficult, simply because it's easier to find things that you're unhappy about, and that's the whole point. In finding that joy a day, you will lift your spirits permanently.

You and others

You don't really think of it when you're with certain people, especially if you know them well, but there are rules about what you do, what you enjoy, and what you don't do. In some cases, that's fun. It's the joy of being with somebody you know. But it can also be restrictive. Consider breaking away from those with too many rules and you'll not only find you're able to relax, you're able to have fun in ways you'd forgotten were possible.

Health and wellbeing

Many people think of the regime that comes with wellness as a strict one. That if you stray, then you're doing yourself a disservice. But actually doing something wild and crazy and relaxing and enjoying life may be in your best interests. Think of that. It will be a lot easier and a lot more fun.

Goals and challenges

It's often useful to choose little challenges, then to list and overcome them, than to discover an easy way to surmount what appear to be huge mountains. Achieving certain goals that seem a long way away demands only that first step. The pay off? The joy that comes with doing so.

THIS DAY FOR EVERYONE

After weeks of battling seemingly insurmountable obstacles, you've discovered a fundamental misunderstanding over what you were dealing with. As aggravating as going back to the beginning seems, what you learn will explain what went wrong and, in the process, eliminate that confusion.

Joy can appear in the most unexpected settings, some so surprising you're taken by surprise

You

As a Cancerian, you are on one hand sensitive, but also you're driven. You have a clear sense of what needs to be done, or you do until you talk to other people who have an entirely different agenda. The trick to dealing with this is to acknowledge that they want things done their way, and then very quietly go on and do what you think is most important first.

This doesn't only have to do with tasks. It also has to do with life's joys and, to be honest, who is better at assessing the joys that you'll experience than you? There are those around you who are quite sure they know what's in your best interests. If so, listen to them politely, then change the subject and go back to doing what you want to do. With certain individuals this is easy, but with others, it may seem as if you're almost being secretive or challenging them. If so, those are the ones you want to be particularly aware of, and you also want to be especially conscious to put you and your own interests and your own goals first.

Do that and the happiness you have won't be their happiness, but will be the happiness you've created from your own goals. A happiness that grows with each passing day, knowing that as you add one achievement to the next, you're able to enjoy what you do and who you are all the more.

You and others

Your message has to do with being aware of and cautious about complainers, those who need things done a certain way, those who regard those who don't do things their way to be somehow inferior. This isn't about you. However, they will be superb at making you feel guilty. The trick is to politely ignore them and do exactly what you want.

Health and wellbeing

If there's a secret to feeling well, it isn't following someone's regime or eating the way someone says you should. It's simply to get moving. That may mean getting out and about, or eating in a different way. And it needn't be a tough road. It's about just being sure you enjoy what each day offers.

Goals and challenges

As a Cancerian, you like things that are familiar. You know what you're doing. But there's a part of you that gets bored and needs new things to do. Be aware of the fact that occasionally you'll let something that you're doing slip, just so you have an opportunity to fix it. Here's an idea: you might enjoy life more if you embrace a new activity or pursuit – something you can learn about and a new joy to add to your life.

JULY

17

C
/
A
\
N
/
C
\
E
/
R

THIS DAY FOR EVERYONE

There's little point in arguing with somebody who has already made, and committed to, a decision. Although you don't realise it, that's exactly what you've done, and in a range of situations. Review existing plans, especially those you regard as unchanging. They could be holding you back.

Can you dance with love? Yes, especially when you're alone and your feelings are free

JULY

18

C
/
A
\
N
/
C
\
E
/
R

You

As an industrious Cancerian, you're always aware of what you want to do and your future goals. But it's hard not to be aware of setbacks of certain types, situations that you didn't expect. Or perhaps it's about those who either aren't happy to get involved in changes so will throw obstacles in your path, or who will complain with every step.

Instead of waiting for them to catch onto what you're doing, simply proceed. If they discuss what you're doing, and even complain, then change the subject. Gradually they'll realise that you won't get drawn into in their game of complaining, and they will turn their attention to other individuals.

In your case, the task ahead is not a difficult one. It's to discover new joys – joys that can be achieved easily, joys that don't require the cooperation of those individuals who seem to have fun triggering obstacles or making problems.

This is one of your biggest lessons and challenges. It's to choose your own approach to what you're doing and, in doing so, to programme exactly how it will proceed and the ways in which you're going to sidestep, if not avoid those complainers.

Do that and everything else will flow with an ease that is so thrilling that you may regard it as sheer magic.

You and others

There are two approaches to any situation. The first is to define your objective and take the first step. The second has to do with trying to predict the way those around you respond. If you start worrying about others, you might find future steps complicated. If, on the other hand, you make each step your own, you'll not only achieve more, you'll enjoy it as well.

Health and wellbeing

The theme for this is choosing to look after yourself, to move in a way that is fun, that you want to do, maybe with those around you. This suggests that you do something that is uninteresting, but they're enthusiastic. Give it a try. The secret is the word no, or perhaps no thank you – but definitely the word no.

Goals and challenges

Every once in a while, you begin something, and everything falls into place as if by magic. Then you discuss it and others begin to ask questions – questions that trigger worries. Suddenly the magic is gone. There's a solution, and it's not doing things in a different way. It's deciding who you'll discuss your activities and plans with, and who you won't, then sticking to that decision.

THIS DAY FOR EVERYONE

Having to deal with tedious problems is bad enough. But having to discuss them at length with those who'll insist on going into these matters in detail is the last thing you're in the mood for. Despite that, these need attention. And the longer you wait, the more troublesome they'll become.

Faced with a complainer? Just listen. Often that's all they need – somebody to hear their pain

You

Every once in a while, when you're feeling restless or bored or just want to chat with somebody, you'll talk about what you're doing. In some cases, those you're chatting with will encourage you. In fact, they'll even seem excited. But, from time to time, you'll also encounter somebody who's a critic. They don't even realise it. They think they're being constructive and helpful. However, you end the conversation feeling worried and perhaps even concerned that you need to rethink everything top to bottom. The most important thing to think about is who you're trusting.

This is a big lesson for you. Refuse to allow what might be regarded as toxic thoughts to influence your thinking. Strengthen the voice in your own head, what might be called your wellbeing mantra, your chant, and ensure that what you're thinking about boosts your spirits and also gives you the confidence to pursue what you have in mind – and, equally, to recognise that there are certain individuals who think in a very different way and who you must be careful about, especially when you're fostering a new plan.

It's not that there's anything wrong with them or you, but what it is all about is making choices that give you the best possible beginning to each day of your life and to each plan you're unfolding.

You and others

Now and then, it's important to consider who you trust, who you would ask for support, and to identify those individuals who are fun to know, but don't have your best interests at heart. Recognising that is important. But so is choosing who you spend time with, especially during those precious periods where growth is your priority.

Health and wellbeing

There's a lot of discussion about what to do to be your best – how to eat, the activities you should undertake. But there's another secret, and it's an important one. It's what not to do, that is, how to relax. There's a much greater art to that than there is to getting out and exercising. Give it a try. With experience, the odds are good you'll become an expert.

Goals and challenges

There's a lot said about persistence and about how important it is to stick with what you want to achieve. However, it's more important to pause and first consider whether what you want to achieve is still important to you, or whether there's something else you'd rather put first. Think about that, and it may answer all your questions about how to achieve your current and future goals.

JULY

19

C
/
A
\
N
/
C
\
E
/
R

The last thing you want to do is upset anybody. Yet if you don't raise and discuss a particular minor misunderstanding, it could swiftly turn into a major issue. True, the simple mention of this is likely to ruffle some feathers. Say nothing and the odds are good you'll face serious dramas anyway.

Want a magic wand to remove every obstacle? It's simple. Not caring about those problems

You

You have phases of wanting to keep track of things, to save elements of your life that bring memories that you've collected, things you've picked up here and there. Then, every once in a while, there's a feeling that you need to get rid of it all.

The trick, of course, is to do a little of each. But sometimes, it is about clearing the way, not just of stuff but also feelings, feelings about those possessions.

Even more, you tend to sometimes save up feelings about experiences with others and, on occasion, those feelings will prevent you from spending time with those individuals or even pursuing certain activities. This is key to your awareness of what drives you.

As a Cancerian, you love achieving things. But you're also sensitive enough that you'll tend to avoid situations that have, in the past, been unsettling or even worrying. Notice whether they're associated with a particular experience or an individual who seemed to undermine you.

If so, recognise that by no means should you allow that to stop you. Even more, recognise the joy in pushing past doubts and achieving what you want to. Tackle a small thing every day and a bigger thing once a week, and soon you'll have restored that essential self-confidence.

You and others

There's what might be termed a push-pull between you and certain individuals, often after a conversation with them, you feel less enthusiastic about life. Not everybody is positive. If you are in need of support, think about who you want to spend time with. While not everybody is upbeat by nature, you can pick and choose the moments you spend with those individuals.

Health and wellbeing

For you, the balance between a strict regime and excess is a tricky one. What's important is that you enjoy how you look after yourself, whether it has to do with movement, how you eat or simply how you think. In every case, the priority is making sure that whatever you're doing, you feel better when you pause than when you began. Make that your priority.

Goals and challenges

There are those who set a goal and talk about it constantly. But actually both goals and challenges change. They change over time and they change with what you accomplish. Also, they change as your focus shifts. Check it out. Make sure you're not talking about goals that once meant a lot to you when actually what's important is now very different.

THIS DAY FOR EVERYONE

There are many ways to say no. While you tend to assume others are aware when things aren't going well, and that a request is unlikely to be agreed to, not everybody picks up on such things. That being the case, you may need to be very clear, if not blunt, about your views.

Joy. A short word, yet seemingly beyond reach. Until you embrace it with your heart

You

As someone who is very much Cancerian but also part Leo, you're juggling two very strong elements of your nature. The Cancerian part is nurturing, reflective and sensitive, yet also highly creative and often highly enterprising. But the Leo enthusiasm and zest for life is important too.

However, you can sometimes get so involved in what's fun that you forget about your goals. The trick is to honour both sides. That may seem complicated, and sometimes it will be, but on the other hand you have double the opportunity to enjoy what life offers and double the opportunity to share those joys with others. Even more than that, it gives you the opportunity to be creative in a way that very few benefit from.

By being a sensitive and nurturing Cancerian, you bring that awareness to any relationship in any situation – from family to career.

Yet the Leo side of you enjoys doing something new, and possibly in a slightly theatrical way. Combine those two and your life will be full – full of changes and full of excitement.

But most of all, it will be full of the kind of satisfaction that comes with being both emotionally kind and generous – and creative as well.

You and others

Rather than getting things organised the way some people like to do, it's important that you be spontaneous, that you do something suddenly, that you just head out – perhaps for a run or to do something that lifts your spirits, and at times you get others to join you as well. While there may be those around you who think a routine is best, for you, spontaneity is the name of the game.

Health and wellbeing

Tempting as it is to get involved in some kind of routine, here again the trick is to do what you enjoy, although that itself may change over time. But the more it changes, the more you'll discover and the more you'll enjoy.

Goals and challenges

Setting goals is natural. You don't really think of them that way, especially if it's something you want to do anyway, and that is the point of this. There may be those around you who make the idea of setting goals so complicated that even thinking about it seems boring. Yet with your energy, you're always setting goals, but it's just you move swiftly from thinking about them to action so don't realise that you set those goals – and often don't realise what you've achieved either.

JULY

21

C
/
A
\
N
/
C
\
E
/
R

Unsettling as recent events seemed, you recognise that instead of being reason for concern, they were breakthroughs. True, these weren't in the form you'd anticipated and could take things in an unexpected direction. Be patient. The more you explore and learn, the more optimistic you'll be.

Leo

Ruler The Sun
Element Fire

Symbol The Lion
Flower Marigold

July 22 – August 21

Leo Whatever you're doing, you Leos have style. Being ruled by the Sun, your magnetism comes naturally, and being fire signs, you're usually juggling your busy diary while charming others. However, when you're relaxing, you'll do it with the conviction of your symbol, the lion. Your flower is marigold, your spice, golden saffron and your trees are the heady, scented bay and the olive. Your stone is gold topaz, or simply wearing gold.

L
/
E
\
O

I know I've a talent for brightening others' day, and I enjoy doing it

JULY

22

L
/
E
\
O

You

As a Leo born close to the sign of Cancer, you share the qualities of both signs. On the one hand, you have the fiery enthusiasm of a Leo yet, on the other, you also benefit from the sensitive awareness that comes from Cancer, which is one of the three water signs.

This balance threads through your life. It means you have the theatrical side that is so much part of Leo, but you can also be tender, loving and kind, and aware of what people are struggling with. Sometimes, in fact, your own pride will lift the spirits of others, but it also shapes your decisions, and sometimes, when you realise it's time to do something new, you'll hit the wall hard to make that happen, whether it's learning about something, getting fit, or perhaps pursuing the joy of doing something new.

Yet, also, the vulnerability that comes with the water sign side of your nature is so important. While you can be sensitive to the criticism of others, you can also support those who might be struggling with their own doubts and unsettling feelings. In fact, that balance between the two is one of your most beneficial characteristics as a Leo who lives with a touch of the gentle sign Cancer. That shining light, that sensitivity, is your unique gift, a gift that you give to others and one on which you thrive personally.

You and others

The generosity that is your signature is something that touches almost every situation involving those around you. However, the fire-sign part of you sometimes dominates as well, and you can be impatient, forgetting that not everybody thinks or moves as swiftly as you do.

Health and wellbeing

You are a bit vain. In fact, most Leos are, and it's the reason that those born under your sign tend to look fabulous and be so glamorous. However, you can suffer for your looks. The trick to avoiding this is to turn what you need to do – whether it's how you eat or how you exercise – into something that brings you joy as well.

Goals and challenges

Achieving a goal is one thing, but recognising that you've achieved it and moving onto the next can be rather difficult for you. The solution? When you set out to do something new, begin thinking about what's next. Then also tell yourself when you feel that you've achieved it. You can congratulate yourself and know what you're moving on to.

THIS DAY FOR EVERYONE

The difference between an opinion and a fact may seem clear, but certain matters are so complex that the difference is unclear. Knowing this, for now focus on delving into the details of the situations in question, then consider what you regard as solid facts versus mere opinion. Your conclusions will surprise you.

GIFTS Open-hearted, Chic, Enthusiastic

CHALLENGES Excessive, Inflexible, Petulant

NUMBER 3

(2+3) + (7) = 12 = (1+2) = 3

Giving the kind of compliments that lift others' spirits is a true gift

You

As a Leo, you've a fiery nature. Not only do you think and move swiftly, living an active life is essential – for your sense of health and wellbeing. But, equally, expressing the theatrical side of your Leo nature is vital.

This isn't just about how you move. What you wear – what might be termed your costume – can be remarkably important to you. That may be reflected in what you wear every day, your somewhat dramatic look, and could even lead to collecting beautiful clothing, which then becomes a passion.

It can often also broaden into an interest in beautiful objects – things to wear, and for your home, too. This may lead you to become a connoisseur of a particular item, such as watches, ceramics or even orchids.

It's the same with people. You're drawn to intriguing individuals, then find some a bit boring. The trick to all this, from possessions to people, is to embrace your fire-sign self, the part that needs to feel deeply.

Core to this is deepening the love between you and those closest to you, whether that's your family, loved ones, offspring or friends. Achieve a balance, then those possessions will have a place in your life, while the love of others, which is central to your being as a Leo – and somebody who is ruled by the heart – will take its place at the centre in your life.

You and others

For you, caring about others can turn into a bit of a dance, where you try to do so much for them that you feel you've done enough, and then feel embarrassed by what they do. The trick to all of this is to simply share how much you care, perhaps with words, perhaps with gestures or perhaps through stillness.

Health and wellbeing

For you, joy comes in moving. You may think you've found the perfect thing to do. It may be exercise, it may be dancing – it doesn't matter what. What's important is that you move your muscles in a way that's joyous, that you feel more alive simply because you've done it.

Goals and challenges

It's vital that you remember you always need to have something to aim for. Before you've achieved one goal, you need to line up the next one. And remember, not everyone is like that, so not everyone will understand how important this is to you.

JULY

23

L
/
E
\
O

True, there are times when a careful assessment of plans and their potential outcome isn't just wise, it's vital, but at the moment, you can afford to be more easy-going. In fact, what's best about these arrangement may also be what's least expected. Knowing that, you'll want to explore everything.

GIFTS Charming, Lavish, Artistic

NUMBER 4

CHALLENGES Stubborn, Haughty, Demanding

(2+4) + (7) = 13 = (1+3) = 4

My fire-sign enthusiasm gives me the energy to turn ideas into reality

JULY

24

L
/
E
\
O

You

While you're a fire sign, your theme is renewal. True, the fire-sign side of your nature thrives on taking action and, just as much, getting plans and projects going with others. This involves teamwork. And devising a plan, then turning it into action, is very satisfying for you.

Even more, seeing the enthusiasm and excitement others are experiencing lifts your spirits. This is especially because it's unlikely they'd have come up with these plans, or put them into action, on their own.

Yet, also, once in a while, you need to pause, create some "alone time" and reflect on the influence of those activities on the world around you and, just as much, on your own mood – how they lift your spirits. This variety of reflection may be out of character for you as a fiery Leo, but it's essential for your own wellbeing and will add to your sense of self.

If you don't do this every so often, you'll just keep on going and, in fact, will often end up doing the same thing over and over again, just different versions of it.

However, pause to reflect, and ask yourself whether once-exciting activities, challenges or even alliances are still interesting to you, or whether you should move on. While the joy that comes with being a Leo is yours for good, renew that joy regularly – and you'll renew your zest for life, as well.

You and others

Being close is wonderful, and for you, as a fire sign, that warmth is incredibly important. However, you tend to forget that those around you aren't always as intense as you are. When they back off, it simply means they're backing off, not that they don't care.

Health and wellbeing

The theatrical side of your nature will like to do some kind of fitness routine that is, itself, theatrical. That may have to do with dancing or doing a super climb up a big mountain. However, it's also worth simply taking a walk, ideally with somebody you care about.

Goals and challenges

While it's natural for you to aim high, that's fine. However, the secret is not to rush. Deep down, you know that time and effort pay off, but in certain of your goals, the capacity to be patient, to persist, isn't just important, it's vital. Understanding that is a fundamental truth.

THIS DAY FOR EVERYONE

For ages you've been battling to turn one particular plan or project into reality. Or perhaps it's been the reverse – you've been fighting to see something undone. Whatever the case, sudden insights will raise questions about these matters. Giving serious thought to these insights is essential.

I only notice how joyful I am when I spot others who need a boost

You

As a Leo, you feel responsible for others at an early age. It comes naturally with being ruled by the Sun. You feel your role is to encourage and inspire others. While this is a wonderful characteristic, and can become part of your life later, if you're working with family, it also is important for you to have time for you alone. Not only that, but it's as important, from time to time, to allow others to support you.

Initially, you might be too proud to do this. Leos do have pride, and you could brush off other's efforts. The trick to this is not only to recognise those who can and would like to help you, but to add adventure to your life by learning something new regularly.

This may be difficult at first, because you may feel embarrassed that you don't already know about a particular subject – that Leo ego can sometimes get in the way. Yet if you make a commitment to yourself to learn something new perhaps once every year – a new skill, a new language, something that excites you – you will enjoy life all the more and, quite possibly, draw others into your life. You'll also discover that you are a diligent and enthusiastic student, one who enjoys learning something new with every dawn, and one who feels a tremendous sense of accomplishment when they go to bed at night.

You and others

The support you give to others is wonderful and they benefit from it. However, you can get stuck giving, but not receiving. The trick, of course, is for you to learn to say yes, and to do it nearly every day.

Health and wellbeing

While it's important for you to get out and about, and to feel your muscles moving, at the same time, it's vital you socialise. The best idea for you is to combine the two. Once you're out, doing what you enjoy with those whose company you enjoy, you'll not only do it more often, you'll adore it.

Goals and challenges

While it's healthy for you to always have several challenges that you're chasing, it's also a good idea to edit them from time to time, otherwise you risk never getting any of them done. Saying farewell to some of them, some of which you no longer care about, isn't just wise – you'll be glad you did. It makes space for what's next.

JULY

25

L
/
E
\
O

THIS DAY FOR EVERYONE

Although you've been referred to as headstrong in the past, you've never really understood why. From your perspective, you were doing no more than making the necessary decisions. Bizarre as it seems to you, often others ask permission, and only once it's given will they make the decisions in question.

GIFTS Direct, Sharing, Magnanimous

CHALLENGES Huffy, Uncompromising, Wilful

NUMBER 6

(2+6) + (7) = 15 = (1+5) = 6

Asking for help doesn't come naturally, but when others offer, I accept instantly

JULY

26

L
/
E
\
O

You

You're a fire sign and, therefore, very active, with a mind that works overtime. It's a bit fiery, too. So while you have a busy body, you also have a very busy head, all of which raises the question when to pause and reward yourself, when to rest and relax and when to stop entirely.

That question is an important one, because often you live life at such a pace that you don't even think of stopping. This isn't just about rewarding yourself, or letting others share their pride in you or admire what you've done, but it's also about reviewing what you're doing. The ironic thing is, while you, as a Leo, are probably a high achiever, you're also anxious about looking around you and considering whether somebody else may be doing something better or more interesting than you are.

Rather than envying them, talk to them about it. This is the real challenge for you, to recognise that the world is full of people who are doing different things. And while it's important for you to be proud of what you're pursuing and achieving, and of your life with others, it's also vital that you share that with others and hear what they have to say. Allow those around you, friends, family and loved ones, to be your greatest teachers, and it will deepen the relationship for all of you.

You and others

You wouldn't think that you'd have to learn to enjoy life with those you care about, but as a Leo, and somebody who tends to be out there doing things, it actually is important for you to pause and appreciate how dear certain individuals are to you. This may be family, this may be friends, this may even be colleagues whose company you enjoy. Whoever it is, appreciate them deeply and let them know that you do.

Health and wellbeing

For you, feeling well and looking after yourself may have begun with simply being fit. But your particular variety of Leo nature needs to achieve a balance. This has to do with exercising your mind as much as your activities. This, in turn, may take you into areas such as martial arts or even yoga.

Goals and challenges

Every once in a while, you need to review your goals. You don't think of this because you're so busy achieving them. However, if it seems to be the same goals again and again, it may be time to say farewell to those and to explore, select and embrace a new set. You'll be glad that you did.

THIS DAY FOR EVERYONE

It's not until you encounter somebody who has no interest in being diplomatic that you realise how important diplomacy is. Yet the individual in question responds to forthright situations by nature and, consequently, needs to be spoken to in that manner. Adopt that approach, and everything else will be easy.

Gifts of flowers and candy are exciting; the gift of Leo love can be life-changing

You

Every sign has its style but, as a Leo, your style is distinct. Your pride is important, and sometimes you have a classic style and approach to life – but also, being a fire sign, there's a certain amount of flash that comes with your way of doing things, even if you're very conservative.

But this isn't just about how you come across. This has to do with what might be termed your inner world, your thoughts and your feelings.

You're generous by nature, you're caring, you're creative and you love to help others – your family and friends. While this is all very wonderful and important, there's another part of your nature that needs help.

It's not that you need help in any worrying way. It's just simply that, sometimes, you don't pay enough attention to that inner self, and it becomes restless and temperamental. And for that reason, it's vital that you give as much passion and attention to yourself, and to what brings you joy, as you do to others.

That will change over time, but it will also turn into one of your greatest passions. In fact, the passion that you bring to exploring your inner feelings, the excitement of new ideas and doing things that lift your spirits, won't just benefit you. It will feed back into those who are closest in your life as well.

You and others

As a Leo, you're intense by nature. So your relationships with others, with family and friends, tend to be intense and passionate as well. This isn't necessarily to do with romance, it's just you care deeply. The challenge? Finding that balance between caring and giving others space is an essential one.

Health and wellbeing

You have an instinctive sense of the need to keep moving – that's part of being an energetic fire sign – and, also, you have an instinctive sense of fun. But, amazingly, you don't always connect the two. You need to make the moving, the fitness, the health and the wellbeing fun. That's the secret.

Goals and challenges

Those around you question why you always seem to be seeking a new challenge when you could just relax. They don't realise that, as a fire sign, you thrive on challenges. If they offer you an easier way to do things, thank them, and then pursue your latest challenge your way and with enthusiasm.

JULY

27

L
/
E
**
O

THIS DAY FOR EVERYONE

Only now are you noticing that, in the midst of recent twists and turns, you made all sorts of decisions, but you didn't inform those involved. This wasn't your intention but, rather, things were moving so swiftly that you forgot, which is fine. Still, you've got a lot of talking to do, beginning right now.

I know when I'm right, especially when I believe in somebody

JULY

28

L
/
E
\
O

You

As a Leo and a fire sign, you're aware of your reputation for being somewhat flamboyant. However, at the same time, you rather enjoy a slow pace of living and thinking that seems very atypical of your sign. The reason? It's because you also enjoy spotting the little things in life that are such a pleasure.

In fact, this reflects another of your Leo characteristics, which is the fact that Leo is one of the four fixed signs, the sign in the middle of each season, and so you enjoy stability and can get into a habit.

You work very hard to make elements of your life look and be the way you want yet, every once in a while, that, too, can become boring for the fire-sign part of your nature. It's about finding a balance between these two – the things that you enjoy and the elements of your life you've carefully created and crafted, versus those changes that bring new and important challenges your way. This is a priority for you.

If you review these matters every once in a while – perhaps every six months or so – you'll give yourself the space for those new discoveries. They may be new activities, it may be studying something, it may be getting to know somebody. And in doing that, you'll enrich that wonderful Leo life even beyond the joys you're presently experiencing.

You and others

You like being very close to people and you also like knowing they care about you. However, certain individuals have a tendency to push you to do things that you have no interest in or intention of doing. Tell them you appreciate it, then thank them and very firmly say no.

Health and wellbeing

As you're well aware, you particularly enjoy what might be called a ritual. That ritual may be how you eat, how you work out or how you look after yourself. Whatever it is, you really like it. However, every once in a while, you need to review and change that ritual, otherwise, on one hand, you'll lose the joy in it, and on the other, you may become a teeny bit lazy.

Goals and challenges

You know what you want to achieve – and what you don't want. However, what you don't know is when to pause and consider whether to rethink those things. The trick is to make a date with yourself, perhaps every six months, or even every year, to conduct exactly that variety of review.

THIS DAY FOR EVERYONE

It may seem that certain individuals, or possibly destiny itself, are trying to take over. Certainly, your plans have been disrupted more than once. It may seem you're alone in these struggles, but look around you and you'll soon realise that's not true. Everybody is facing similar difficulties.

GIFTS Lavish, Heartfelt, Spontaneous

CHALLENGES Demanding, Stubborn, Extreme

NUMBER 9

(2+9) + (7) = 18 = (1+8) = 9

Leo confidence gives me a boost, but I often use it to give others a lift too

You

Like your ruler the Sun, you shine with a certain generosity. This comes naturally, and for this reason, you rarely pause and consider how much you're giving or receiving from others. Yet, from time to time, it's important to consider this – not because someone is giving too little or too much, but because it's vital that you find a balance in your own life.

While you're a fire sign, you're also one of the fixed signs of the zodiac, which means you tend to get into habits. Habits of what you do, but also habits involving the people you hang out with. While family is one thing, and learning to live with and love them is important, those that you get to know, friends or even colleagues, are also important.

However, every now and then, it's essential that you review the nature of that relationship and consider whether it still enriches you. It may be that you simply need to have a heart to heart discussion, and that discussion may also be part of your own review about what's working for you and what isn't.

As a Leo and a fire sign, this kind of review may not come naturally. Still, once you begin, you'll realise what a good idea it is and probably decide to make it a regular part of your regime in every area of your life.

You and others

Being the fixed sign that you are, you enjoy settling into things. However, often a certain individual will do you a favour. They'll shake things up for you, encourage you to do something new, to explore – and in doing so, they may trigger a far-reaching and valuable change in your life.

Health and wellbeing

While you're quite rightly proud of yourself, you also get bored with certain disciplines – disciplines that are supposed to keep you healthy and well. Yet you're unsure of what comes next. The trick is to have someone who gets you to try at new things. Sometimes, trying them can be more fun than sticking with them, but you'll find the best approach for you.

Goals and challenges

It's easy for you, as a fire sign, to talk about things you could do. Actually undertaking new challenges, however, can be difficult, especially because you're such a perfectionist. The secret is to become an expert at failure. That way, it doesn't matter whether you do things perfectly or not, you'll learn from absolutely everything.

JULY

29

L
/
E
\
O

THIS DAY FOR EVERYONE

Deep down, you know that giving in to those who insist they need your help usually leads to problems. Still, ignoring those who are struggling isn't easy. If you must do something, set clear limits and stick to them. That allows you to relieve your sense of guilt, yet avoid major dramas.

I have an instinctive knowledge of the way to enjoy life and to love others

JULY

30

L
/
E
\
O

You

Many of those born under Leo thrive on style and drama. However, there are as many, and you may be one of them, who are, in fact, more focused on their creative side, and whose imagination is broad, but who prefer to keep a low profile. These Leos are most comfortable being around those closest to them.

If you are one of these, then the art, the joy and the beauty that comes with being a Leo are important but, equally, so are the kindness, the generosity and the quiet. The quiet that comes with those who are dearest, be it friends or family, or even, occasionally, colleagues with whom you share a vision.

Whatever it is, if you're this variety of Leo, you tend to avoid dramas, but every once in a while, it's important for you to do exactly that. To embrace a certain situation, or perhaps a certain individual, or possibly even a certain goal, with passion.

You may do it quietly, or you may do it so theatrically that you surprise yourself. If so, remember, that you were born under the rulership of the Sun, the brightest object in the sky, it brightens everybody's life and if you're feeling a bit theatrical, not only is it wise, it will also come very naturally to you.

Enjoy it. Who knows? It may become your way of being for the rest of your days.

You and others

If you enjoy being in the shadow of others who are dramatic types, because it's less effort, then it may help you to discover that theatrical side of yourself. True you may not take to the stage, but it could also be that you inspire those around you, from friends to children, to do exactly that.

Health and wellbeing

You can be manically fit, that is, you can do what's in your best interests every day but be so quiet about it, that no one has any idea how much you enjoy what you're doing. If you begin to talk about it, you might even find you're able to persuade others to join you in those pursuits.

Goals and challenges

For you, some of the best goals are the ones that are adopted discreetly, things you do in the background, things that others are unaware that you've done. Yet, every once in a while, it's important for you to share those, not so much because others will admire you, but they might well learn from them.

THIS DAY FOR EVERYONE

It's not that you're overcautious, but in the past you've ignored seemingly unimportant details only to discover later that they were significant. Now, such information is unreliable, or worse, unavailable. This means trusting your intuition, which is far better than you acknowledge, even to yourself.

Some say I'm stubborn; when I allow others to distract me, I'm reminded why

You

It's important that you experiment with your Leo identity. View it as a game with yourself. This is because, as a Leo, a fire sign and somebody ruled by the Sun, you can be very grand. You don't think of it this way, but when you compare yourself to others, you are.

Yet you also have a very simple nature, in the sense that you're uncomplicated. You want a good life, and it's important for you that others around you are happy. And, of course, when changes are essential you hope they'll go smoothly.

However, you also have a stubborn streak, and when you've got things organised, you want them to stay that way. Similarly, you hope that those closest will accept that and not try to change you in the way that some do.

One of your biggest lessons is to recognise that, sometimes, those changes aren't just worthwhile, they are an opportunity to enjoy elements of your life you simply wouldn't have known about were it not for those individuals coming into your life and making the effort to get you to make those changes, which, as you will be aware, isn't always easy.

At the same time, if you practise a new exercise, a simple exercise of saying yes first and then trying things out, next, not only will life become a lot more interesting, but you'll have a lot more fun as well.

You and others

As much as you enjoy those who are already close to you, life is also about broadening your horizons, and that means bringing new individuals into that circle and, occasionally, letting some go as well. It's like having a garden that you need to replant each year.

Health and wellbeing

As you're well aware, you do have a lazy streak, and once things are organised with your health, you tend to stick to the same way of eating and the same fitness routine, until it gets boring and then you begin to slip. Of course, the trick is to find somebody or something that inspires you.

Goals and challenges

On occasion, you complain that life has become a little too predictable, but at the same time, you will often sidestep challenges that appear because they're too much trouble. It's important you face the fact that you can't do that and then complain about life being too predictable.

JULY

31

L
/
E
\
O

GIFTS Noble, Protective, Arty

NUMBER 9

CHALLENGES Unbending, Agitated, Haughty

$(0+1) + (8) = 9$

My instincts are so strong that I trust them – and I am always glad I did

AUGUST

01

L
/
E
\
O

You

Life is full of questions. That's something you can't argue with, but the tricky thing is that, as a Leo and one of the fixed signs of the zodiac, the signs born in the middle of each season, you thrive on stability. You like to know what you're going to eat during the day, you like to know what you're going to wear. You like to go to the same restaurants – and possibly you even go on vacation to the same place.

While that's comforting, every once in a while, it's vital you have a shake-up, and it may well be that those around you are the ones who encourage you to do that. But that may end up with a power struggle, which you, as a Leo, always try to win. The secret is to realise that in allowing them to win, that is, going along with what others want you to do, it's you who's actually winning, because you're the one who will benefit.

The trick is to embrace the unknown and the unfamiliar and change in a way that doesn't come naturally to you. But with a little effort and experimentation, you might not only develop a taste for it, you might realise just how much you like it.

And this could reward you in every way of your life – from the way you feel about yourself to the way you feel about others, and even to the way you feel about getting up in the morning.

You and others

Being one of the more fixed varieties of Leo, sometimes, those around you seem to be determined to disrupt you and your life. They may come across as a bit of a bully. Yet, deep down, you know they have your best interests at heart. Recognise that and let them win.

Health and wellbeing

As a luxury-loving Leo, when it comes to looking after yourself, that is eating well and being fit, you like to be looked after properly. However, you also tend to develop a routine. The secret to this is to make that routine exotic, which means going far away to places that offer you proper Leo luxury.

Goals and challenges

Signing yourself up for a new goal regularly may seem like a crazy idea. But if you put it in your diary, then instead of being worried about what you're doing – and wondering what you could do that's new – you'll look at your diary and realise it's time for you to discover and embrace a new goal.

THIS DAY FOR EVERYONE

Few things are more exasperating than having decided to get all the facts in order, only to discover the actual situation you're dealing with has changed. And, judging by the current set-up, there'll be yet more changes. Knowing that, waste no time on details. For now, focus on the big picture.

GIFTS Eager, Natural, Forthright

CHALLENGES Fixed, Anxious, Headstrong

NUMBER 1

(0+2) + (8) = 10 = (1+0) = 1

For me, as a Leo, my job is bringing joy to others, whatever the time or setting

You

From your point of view, the ideal life is one in which you have things organised and you're able to enjoy what you do. That is, the routine of your day, your activities, those around you, how you dress. All of these things are important to you as a Leo.

Yet, at the same time, every once in a while you become aware that things are a bit too predictable. The fixed sign part of you, the Leo that likes things to remain the same, will think this is how events should be, but then possibly an individual or circumstances will force you to make changes.

And this is where the test is for the fixed-sign side of your life. If you do the minimum, then you probably won't enjoy it and will turn those changes into a battle. If, however, you recognise this as a new way of thinking, living and possibly loving, you'll realise that this is actually a breakthrough – a breakthrough from which you'll benefit.

And, even more than that, you'll realise that, as a fire sign, you need to change things every once in a while, and that the changes you're making now are less than the changes you might want to make regularly, as you live out the days of your life. This is simply because you'll discover that in doing so, you not only make life a lot more interesting, but you'll love life itself all the more.

You and others

The changes that seem to be being forced on you aren't just in your best interests, they're encouraging you to alter your pace with those around you. In doing so, you'll discover new joys with each other, in the present and in the future as well.

Health and wellbeing

Over the years, you've struggled to find the perfect routine, the perfect way of eating – those activities that make you feel wonderful. What has been missing is a lack of variety, but now you have an opportunity to change that.

Goals and challenges

If there's a single phrase that's important for you to keep in mind when it comes to the goals you set – and how you deal with the challenges – it's aiming higher. Often, you will try to minimise changes because you find them unappealing when, actually, embracing them makes them far more exciting.

AUGUST

02

L
/
E
\
O

Clear-cut as the plans being discussed may be, it's worth keeping in mind that even the simplest of arrangements could run foul of the current unsettled mood. Those who you're counting on could be difficult or, alternatively, you may change your mind. Whatever the case, expect a few surprises.

Others view obstacles as problems. I regard them as reason to get seriously creative

AUGUST

03

L
/
E
\
O

You

As a fire sign, you hate wasting time, and so you streamline elements of your day. But then you get stuck in habits that are dull and you find that you want to do not just something new, but something that's exciting. Of course, being ruled by the Sun, that is second nature to you. You aren't about a low-profile approach to anything. But the trick to this is to escape planning and to act with spontaneity and, even more, to act from the heart. This is what others love about you, and when you allow yourself to be truly loving in the way that comes naturally to you, you're not just fun to be around, you're absolutely magical.

The trick to dealing with all of this is not so much even to take chances, but to be totally who you are. As you move into that state of mind and that state of being, you'll regularly find yourself doing things that you didn't expect to do.

Even more, you'll find a new joy, even when you're dealing with what once seemed like burdens, and they will be resolved by what can best be described as your loving Leo nature. A nature that isn't just generous, but is so creative that you can come up with solutions for issues you just thought you'd have to live with – and that even more, you're able to heal once difficult relationships and bring love to every element of your life.

You and others

If there's any element of your life that's about joint efforts and about pioneering with others, it has to do with maximising the love in your life and, as it happens, the love lives of others as well. You have a magic touch. Use it to inspire others. This is one of those contagious conditions that you want to encourage.

Health and wellbeing

Fitness alone is boring, but allowing energy to flow through you is positive. And once you're doing that, then you'll find the kind of thing you need to do. Not only to feel fit, but to radiate the kind of energy that comes naturally to you as a Leo.

Goals and challenges

Embracing certain offers may seem unwise. Still, take a chance. Explore. For you, as a Leo, this not only comes naturally, but it will allow you to spread the excitement that comes with those offers to the people around you.

THIS DAY FOR EVERYONE

By no means are you secretive. However, you've kept certain complex issues to yourself, mostly because explaining the background would take valuable time. While that's true, certain changes demand this variety of frank discussion. Since you've no choice, tell others everything and right away.

There's no denying Leos are stubborn; it's because I must accomplish my goals

You

Born as a fire sign and as a Leo lion, you are powerful. But you have fixed habits and beliefs, beliefs that can actually end up with your own lion's cage, built of habits that you feel uncomfortable letting go of. Habits you complain about, but would regard yourself as weak in relinquishing.

Yet you're bored, and that boredom is a recognition of the need to break free – something that may seem strange until you actually do it. The secret is to begin that process of breaking free in little ways.

Once you start to let go, and discover how to take those steps, then it will be like an explosion, but the wonderful sort that comes with fireworks. Suddenly, you'll see your life working in a completely different way and with each step, you will feel freer and more inspired to walk away from the old way of doing things and to take chances.

This isn't just about making changes in how you lead your life day to day. It's about changes in how you love, how you look after yourself and what you're doing. Nor is it about a single day or a single period, it's about a shift in your point of view about your own life.

It's about leaving elements of the past behind and embracing a future that is, itself, constantly new, fresh and inspiring.

You and others

While usually you're the inspiration for those around you, when it comes to making big changes, sometimes it's important to let others take the lead. They have a different nature and although they aren't Leos, they may be able to teach you a new approach to the changes you're embracing.

Health and wellbeing

While, with good reason, you're proud to be a Leo, it's also vital that you recognise how important it is that you be flexible. This is not merely about your body – that is, from exercise – but you need to be flexible in your mind, in a way that allows you to reinvent yourself.

Goals and challenges

One of your greatest characteristics is that you never give up. However, it can also mean that you get stuck in certain strategies when actually the best thing you could do is let go of all your goals and begin again. The result will be magical.

AUGUST

04

L
/
E
\
O

THIS DAY FOR EVERYONE

Last-minute changes in plans are always a problem, but that's especially the case now, because this means discussing, then rethinking, everything. On the other hand, this will indeed get you thinking, a lot. What you learn and the improvements you make will almost justify the stress you're currently facing.

My creative side is always coming up with ideas. Some are simple, others life-changing

AUGUST

05

L
/
E
\
O

You

Every Leo has a certain pride, and you love looking good. However, you're also getting bored with having to look a particular way that you think other people will like.

This is because it's vital that you get in touch with an important part of your Leo nature, which is the child within. In fact, it's said that the sign Leo actually rules childhood, with that spontaneity children have, that joy of simply being alive and that freedom to play.

You can have that too. All it requires is for you to abandon your ideas about what you think others would appreciate or be impressed by, and instead come closer to that joy.

Ironically, in doing that, then what you do, the way you live and what you wear will be a reflection of a person who's much more comfortable in their skin and much more happy with themselves. Soon, you'll find that by simply being you, you'll begin to inspire others. They will ask you how you discovered this new way to be, and the fact is, it's not just that you'll look better, you'll feel free to do what might be termed "play".

That is, in fact, to play in a way that you never have before and to feel free, along with those around you, inspiring them to discover a whole new way of being. Could there be any better way to live life than that?

You and others

The secret for you is to organise less. That is, have an idea to get together, but don't actually plan. This is part of your new course in joy, in simply allowing things to be – and relaxing and watching what destiny brings your way.

Health and wellbeing

The most important question for you, at any moment, is, are you happy? If you're not happy, then why not? True, many things in life are challenging, but there's a difference between being challenged and responding to that, and being unhappy, which may mean you're actually ignoring that challenge.

Goals and challenges

There's a tendency as a Leo to think that you absolutely have to win. You have to do what you're doing perfectly. However, here's another option, whatever you're doing, decide what you're really committed to is giving things a try and taking your chances. That's what makes life fun.

THIS DAY FOR EVERYONE

When discussing changes, you thought you could stick with existing arrangements and gradually incorporate the two. Now you're in the midst of making those changes, you realise this isn't possible. Don't panic. Just consider whether it's time to say farewell to past arrangements, or to the new ones.

GIFTS Heartfelt, Honest, Delightful

CHALLENGES Proud, Unyielding, Wilful

NUMBER 5

$(0+6) + (8) = 14 = (1+4) = 5$

When others are bored, they do puzzles; when I am, I come up with an amazing plan

You

There's a part of you, as a Leo, that is all about seeking perfection in life.

It's the part of you that wants beauty, that wants a certain glossy presence in your life. But there is another more playful part of you that wants to try things out, and is just as happy to flop, to fail and then to do it all again – in life, in work and in love.

This is an example for others as well, and the more you do this, and the more you make changes in this way, the more joy will show on your face and in your body.

You'll be relaxed, you'll be healthier and not only that, you'll be the you who takes part in those activities and so will inspire others.

That easy going attitude will mean that you'll probably enjoy what you're doing far more, but, gradually, you'll shift from simply looking good to radiating the kind of joy that comes with being ruled by the most powerful body in the heavens, the Sun.

Having been born a Leo, this is your birthright. But it's strange how few of those born under your sign actually embrace the potential to be a true Leo. To not live a glamorous life according to some else's values, but to actually radiate the joy of the Sun within your being – every day, and to become closer to that as every day passes as well.

You and others

As you become more easy-going and free and loving, you'll find it's easier to be more free and loving with others too. You won't complain in your head so much about them, but rather, you'll simply accept them. Better yet, the radiance in your mood will add to your life.

Health and wellbeing

The question isn't what you should do to feel better, but what you truly enjoy doing. The closer you come to that inner sunny core, that personal being of love, the easier it will be for you to decide what's best to do, without even having to think about it.

Goals and challenges

You're determined, you always will be – that's part of being a Leo. But the big question is, will you still want the goal you're going after once you achieve it? This is a question that you will find yourself asking increasingly and one that, eventually, having recognised the answer, you will no longer need to ask.

AUGUST

06

L
/
E
\
O

Nobody would blame you for taking the rather abrupt manner of certain individuals the wrong way. While you'd be justified in thinking they've been rude, the fact is they've had too much to do and not enough time to do it in. For now, say nothing. Within days, they'll make it up to you.

Doubts rarely trouble me, and my confidence enables me to overcome others' doubts

AUGUST

07

L
/
E
\
O

You

You have a natural style and also a determination to do and have everything that you can. However, increasingly you've got questions about your goals. On one hand, you've been seduced by what others do and seeing what they have. Yet, at the same time, you're increasingly aware that the deeper you go within, the less you care about them, and the more you want to learn to laugh and to play and to enjoy who you are.

This is the journey of being born a Leo. While, on one hand, there is a theatrical side to your nature, and a part that really enjoys being admired. Your style emerges naturally from that. However, if you were only your style and nothing more, then it becomes very empty and very hollow.

If, on the other hand, you begin to use the energy of the Sun, which is connected with your deep inner being, and begin to explore it in different ways, you'll discover ways to laugh and to play and to have fun in whatever it is you're doing – whether you're in a job, at home, climbing a mountain or simply relaxing.

The key? It's to move increasingly closer to the essence of your nature, that sunny being within you. And if you're guided by that, then the choices you make will always be ones that don't just suit you, they will add new sunshine to your life.

You and others

If you're still living with a book in your head that tells you what success looks like, then you may not be having a very good time dealing with others. But if, on the other hand, you're easy-going about things and simply do what makes you happy, you'll be amazed how happy others are as well.

Health and wellbeing

There are enough books on health and wellbeing to fill a large library, but that doesn't seem to make people more joyous. The secret? It's to take advantage of your inner Leo child. Do that, and naturally you'll choose to move in a way that makes you feel terrific, and to eat in a way that's good for you. Then there will be absolutely no problem with anything else.

Goals and challenges

There's an odd belief that achievement requires suffering. However, as you live your life as a Leo, and somebody whose inner light is powerful, you'll realise that those challenges simply complicate matters. Instead, you'll approach things with joy and both achieve and love them as well.

THIS DAY FOR EVERYONE

The last thing you're in the mood for is a discussion about the tendency of one individual to be careless in certain matters. Ordinarily, it wouldn't be important but, increasingly, you end up dealing with the details they ignore. If you can disentangle yourself, take over entirely – that's really the only option.

GIFTS Amiable, Fascinating, Chic

CHALLENGES Unbending, Demanding, Excessive

Feeling inspired is great. Spreading that feeling to everybody I meet is even better

You

You have a tendency to get involved in a lot of things with a lot of people. Of course, this comes with being a Leo. Yet, at the same time, that energy tends to be focused on what they want and what excites them. And one of your journeys as Leo is first to discover what excites you, what brings light to your life.

In a world and in a society where there are all kinds of trends about what excites people, being a Leo can be a challenge, because simply discovering what is most important to you as an individual can actually be very difficult – mostly because there are plenty of other people, and forms of media, ready to tell you what you should be enjoying.

This doesn't just have to do with what you do, it has to do with the way you live and your priorities. However, being a Leo, you have what might be termed a big energy, and once you embrace that, in a way that not everyone will fully understand, you'll also begin to realise just how much joy you can live with. And, even more than that, the kind of joy you can bring into the life and experiences of others.

In doing that, you'll discover your true purpose as a Leo, which is not to follow anyone else's plan or anyone else's routine, but instead to be completely and utterly true to yourself.

You and others

Many of those close to you look up to you. You don't really think that until you realise that, often, people will imitate what you're doing. This is all the more important as you move closer to that amazing inner you that is the true Leo within.

Health and wellbeing

There are many complicated routines for good health. However, in your particular case, that routine has to do with one simple thing – a variety of love. Love for earth, for water, for the Sun, for grass, for laughter, for resting. The rest of it is secondary. Once you realise that, you'll also realise the being deep within you is the one who experiences joy, the joy from which all forms of health will come.

Goals and challenges

People will discuss all sorts of formulas for achievement with you, as well as plans to make those achievements. However, the more you realise your nature as a Leo and somebody ruled by the Sun, the more you'll realise how hollow those objectives are, and how much can be achieved being motivated from within.

AUGUST

08

L
/
E
\
O

Life would be a lot easier if, in certain situations, you could talk things through with others, then reach a final decision. But with so much in transition, it's unlikely that even simple decisions will last for long. Regard whatever you organise as an experiment, one from which you're learning each day.

Problems are an invitation to pause and plot a more creative approach to plans

AUGUST

09

L
/
E
\
O

You

As a Leo, somebody ruled by the Sun, and a fire sign, you may feel a burden to inspire. This is probably something you've felt your entire life, but weren't aware of until firstly, you were grown up, and secondly, you became aware that not everybody else cared whether they inspired those around them.

And then, as you've learnt more, you've realised that inspiration isn't about outer achievement alone, although you're very happy to encourage others to do what they want and to achieve a lot. But it's also about a deep link to an inner power. This is something that comes naturally to you as a Leo and somebody ruled by the Sun, but one that you're only getting to know yourself as the years pass. And as you become more familiar with it, you're in a better position to share it with others.

At one point, you thought it was just about being a little bit different, but now, as you live out the days of your life, you realise that, while achieving what you have in mind is important and very gratifying, achieving what is possible for your inner self – that magical being that is who you are – is even more important.

And those achievements will grow each day and add to the joy in your life, when you wake up in the morning and when you go to bed at night.

You and others

There are all sorts of ways of relating to those around you – chatting about things you have done and will be doing – but for you, as a Leo, and someone who carries joy within you, sharing that joy is the most important thing. You can't really plan it, but when you're able to do it, there's nothing better.

Health and wellbeing

Often, when certain individuals are encouraging those around them to look after themselves, to eat well and to work out, they will encourage good habits. While that's appealing to you as a fire sign, it can also be incredibly dull. The best possible approach for you is to be spontaneous – joyously spontaneous.

Goals and challenges

Planning ahead is wise and setting goals is great. However, for you as a fire sign, what's even better is acting spontaneously. When you do that, you may need to alter those goals, but what you'll be doing is taking advantage of the moment.

THIS DAY FOR EVERYONE

You're on the verge of upsetting somebody – and the problem is that you were worried about their seemingly underhand behaviour. Once you trusted them, but now you're not so sure, and this is the problem. Watch them too closely and they'll feel guilty, which will only make things worse.

When challenged by others, I can be fiery. At the same time, I'm devising solutions

You

As a Leo, you're loving, and not only that, you watch out for others as much as you do for yourself. So if they're up to something worrying, you'll do your best to lift their spirits or encourage them to go in the right direction.

However, it's important for you to recognise that while you can encourage them, they're not necessarily a Leo. What you can do, however, is share with them a condition that's called optimism. That is, an infectious condition that means they don't want to be you but, rather, they are determined to become the best version of themselves they can be.

This seems strange to you because, as a Leo, this characteristic is built in to your being. But many others don't have the courage, the conviction or the enthusiasm that you do. If you're able to help others see that, then you can withdraw and busy yourself with your own activities, and watch them thrive, rather as if you were watching a plant grow.

But also, this will allow you freedom to nurture yourself in the same way. Rather than over-planning what you're doing, you'll be spontaneous. Embrace that approach in relationships with others and in your own life, and you'll remember what it is to wake up in the morning full of joy and go to sleep at night delighted with all you've experienced.

You and others

If there's a single phrase that should define your relationship with others, it's "let them take the lead". Once they're doing that, encourage them. If things don't work out, encourage them to find a solution but, most of all, shine enthusiasm on them. It's the best thing you can do.

Health and wellbeing

While there's a great deal to be said for keeping fit, some of those people who do keep fit aren't very happy when they're doing it. So there's another component that's important for you to recognise as well, which is to keep calm. If you do that, along with keeping fit, then you'll have perfect health.

Goals and challenges

If there's anything tricky, it's that once you line up a challenge, you'll stick with it. However, the gift for you is to learn to recognise when you don't care about that challenge any more, and when the world has moved on to embrace something new.

AUGUST

10

L
/
E
\
O

Only days ago, you wouldn't have just objected to last-minute changes in plans – you'd have been irritated that others didn't keep an eye on things. However, recent events have taught you that if you adopt a mellow approach to such matters, you'll easily ignore minor issues that would ordinarily upset you.

Others questioning my plans is irritating. However, their concerns can be informative

AUGUST

11

L
/
E
\
O

You

One of your most attractive characteristics is your joy in watching others thrive. In fact, it always surprises you when others don't feel the same way. While this may apply to family or friends, it can also apply to anyone you know – to colleagues, to neighbours. And while this is important, it's also essential that you're aware your spontaneity and enthusiasm for others must be reflected in your own life.

True, you aren't always as much of a cheerleader for yourself, and, in fact, you can settle into habits that once worked for you, but which no longer do.

The trick is to pay as close attention to the joy in your own life as you do to that in others, and to track down any of those habits that are no longer appropriate and change them.

As you may be aware, as a Leo you're a fire sign, but you're also what's termed a fixed sign. And so you get into habits and don't even realise that they're holding you back. Sometimes, events in the form of circumstances, and possibly situations involving others, will jolt you out of those habits and, bizarrely, you'll fight them.

The lesson? It's to let go completely – and to plunge into something new. As wary as you are of those changes initially, once you make them, you'll wonder why you hesitated even for a moment.

You and others

Certain individuals around you have a habit of asking questions about what you're doing and where you're going. And, even worse, they ask why. That may annoy you. However, these individuals are true friends, because they're actually asking you to think about whether you care about what you're doing.

Health and wellbeing

As a Leo, you were probably born with an interest in looking good. It's part of being a Leo, so it's likely you do what is necessary to ensure the outside is in good shape. The trick, however, is to make sure the inside is also thriving – and that doesn't just have to do with your muscles. It has to do with your heart.

Goals and challenges

The idea of regularly changing your plans is unappealing to you as someone who likes to know what you're doing. Yet the fire-sign part of your nature needs regular new challenges, small and large. The irony is, if you make those new challenges part of your routine, then you'll benefit doubly.

THIS DAY FOR EVERYONE

When you learn breakthroughs are coming, of course you're delighted. Yet the form and direction they take may not seem remotely welcome. Still, explore it. You'll soon realise this isn't about reorganising existing arrangements, but about creating something new and exciting.

GIFTS Protective, Lavish, Creative

CHALLENGES Lethargic, Petulant, Anxious

NUMBER 2

(1+2) + (8) = 11 = (1+1) = 2

When I say yes to a plan or idea, that releases powers that can make magic happen

You

As a Leo and a fire sign, you have a wonderful ability to care for others. In fact, you feel responsible for ensuring that they're happy and for providing for their wellbeing.

While this is fantastic, it also means that sometimes you can take over, and other people don't get a chance to develop their own instincts for making good choices.

Finding that balance is difficult, because of course you hate to see them fail. However, you have learnt a lot from things not working out – and they will too.

This is one of the greatest lessons for you, to recognise those moments when it's important for you to encourage others and be there, yet recognise when it's important for you to stand on the sidelines.

But this doesn't just have to do with others. It has to do with you too, and with making changes in your own habits, your own way of thinking and your own activities.

There are things you have intended to do differently for ages but have never got around to, simply because the part of it that needs a boost always seems to be taking a break at the moment when you need encouragement the most.

And that's the secret for you. It's to encourage yourself, when necessary, as much as you do others.

You and others

The trick when dealing with others is to know that moment when it's time to hand over the reins and let them go on their way. Then you can celebrate with them as they succeed, inspired by you.

Health and wellbeing

The formula for health and wellbeing for you challenges a part of your nature that settles into a plan. And that's the part that's associated not so much with being a Leo, but with being a fixed sign. Despite that, if you make a point of changing what you do and how you look after yourself regularly, you'll not only be more enthusiastic, you'll feel better as well.

Goals and challenges

While you, as a Leo, love to succeed – and every Leo thrives on success – there's another part of you that actually enjoys a bit of drama. Allow yourself that. Create challenges for yourself so you'll feel that success is well-earned – then you'll enjoy it all the more.

AUGUST

12

L
/
E
\
O

You knew you'd have to draw the line with one particularly uptight individual, but you've put off saying anything, mostly because you dreaded any confrontation. At this point, however, you'd rather deal with that than face even one more day of their negative attitude and unruly behaviour.

GIFTS Forthright, Magnanimous, Arty

CHALLENGES Exacting, Headstrong, Stubborn

NUMBER 3

$(1+3) + (8) = 12 = (1+2) = 3$

Helping others is a joy. While usually they know about it, just as often they don't

AUGUST

13

L / E \ O

You

As a Leo ruled by the Sun, you tap into your own source of inner energy and light. You don't think about this until you encounter situations where others seem so needy. You've spent time with them, and after you leave them, you feel you are drained.

Yet you kind of believe you're superhuman. While, in a way you are, balancing this is important. Giving to others is essential, but at the same time it's also essential that you teach them to create their own light and life.

That may sound unkind, and many Leos dislike the idea of not being generous. It's natural to you. Yet, sometimes, in holding back, you force those who are possibly just too lazy to get their own act together, and that's the greatest gift you can give to them.

While you, as a Leo, are naturally full of enthusiasm, not everybody is and, occasionally, they need a serious kick to get them going. Do that, and instead of shining that light on them, you'll teach them to create their own light. Perhaps it's won't shine quite as bright as yours, but it's one that's bright enough to add to the world.

And it will enable you to stand side by side and enjoy each other's company, and the company of those around you. From friends and family to loved ones – knowing that you're all contributing to the world.

You and others

You enjoy your gang – those people whose company you thrive on. But at the same time, they can be dull and demanding. The trick is to find a new group, a group who don't just enjoy your company but who also challenge and encourage you.

Health and wellbeing

There's a bit of you that has the feeling that looking after your wellbeing is a chore. One of the greatest gifts you can give yourself is to turn it into something that's not only beneficial but fun. In fact, maybe you'll get a group together who do what turns life into a joy.

Goals and challenges

It's easy to get caught up in being successful, but according to others' values. For you, as a proud Leo, success is complicated. It includes many things, and this, in part, is sharing what you achieve with others. Do that and the rest will come naturally.

THIS DAY FOR EVERYONE

You recently agreed to last-minute changes in long-standing plans. While it was annoying and upsetting, circumstances shifted and there was nobody to blame. Actually, with so much in transition, you're urged to adopt a flexible attitude towards sudden changes – it will make life a lot easier.

GIFTS Charming, Open-hearted, Charitable

CHALLENGES Self-centred, Excessive, Proud

NUMBER 4

(1+4) + (8) = 13 = (1+3) = 4

I'm strong but also easily hurt; fortunately those closest spot it, because I never admit it

You

Once of the greatest benefits of being a Leo is what could be called your lustrous nature. There's a beauty that comes with your energy. It's not just glamorous – although most Leos are – but, actually, it's a side of your nature that inspires others without you actually realising that you're doing it.

A smile from you – some encouragement to do something – will set others off, rushing after things that simply wouldn't previously have crossed their minds.

This variety of generosity is wonderful and, occasionally, people will ask why you do so much for others.

The fact is, you don't even think about it. And actually, if you do, you realise that, by nature, this feeds back to you. If you do something for someone else, it always comes back in some way. It's a contagious situation called joy, in which what you do adds to the lives of others –and they, in turn, then add to the lives of others still.

But, even more than that, it means that those around you, whether it's family or friends, colleagues or even neighbours, all simply feel better about themselves and about their lives. Which means that the time you spend with them isn't about helping lift them up, but about all of you enjoying who you are all the more, every day.

You and others

Talk is important – getting others to talk about things, and also you talking about what you intend to do. However, as a fire sign, you will understand that doing – taking action – is best. And if that means you need to go off and do what you need to do, leaving others behind, not only is it essential, but you'll also teach them the importance of taking action themselves.

Health and wellbeing

While a workout is OK, being a Leo, and somebody who has joy in your life, playing a game, getting out and about and having fun is even better. Why? Because you'll not only get moving but you'll move the most important part of your being, which is your heart.

Goals and challenges

There are two kinds of goals. There are material goals, goals in the world, the kinds of goals recognised by people in business. And then there are goals that have to do with climbing mountains: metaphorical mountains or real mountains. And those are the goals that, once achieved, mean the most of all.

AUGUST

14

L
/
E
\
O

THIS DAY FOR EVERYONE

Is life a bit dull? That's no surprise, mostly because the issues you're facing are almost entirely based on practical matters and so allow for little in the way of creative solutions. And worse, there's no battling these. However, the sooner you get these dealt with, the more swiftly they'll become history.

GIFTS Spontaneous, Natural, Generous

CHALLENGES Uncompromising, Static, Agitated

NUMBER 5

(1+5) + (8) = 14 = (1+4) = 5

My capacity to love others unconditionally is one of my superpowers

AUGUST

15

L
/
E
\
O

You

You may be a fire sign, but every once in a while, you run into individuals who draw you into debates that have to do with yes or no, right or wrong, more or less – all of which drive you crazy. But because they seem so determined to talk about things in that way, you get involved.

Of course, the trick is to stop and to do something that is quite natural for you as a fire sign – to simply plunge in and see what works. That may upset others, but by that point, you'll actually begin the process of teaching them something.

It's something that's also important for every Leo to do, because your enthusiasm for life involves exactly this kind of what might be termed "daredevil behaviour" – that is, taking chances.

This will enable you also to break the habit of trying to please others, which you sometimes do, and instead be the best you that you can be – somebody who's full of life and who brings that vitality to any setting or situation. Once you've done that, then you'll wonder why you allowed those individuals and their very narrow ideas about how things could work to distract you. And that may be the biggest lesson of all, one that you'll learn again and again, and one that you'll benefit from every time you learn it.

You and others

Notice how those closest to you, whether they are family or colleagues or friends, live their lives and make it clear that, while you're delighted for them to live life the way they want to, you approach life in a very different way, one that is as spontaneous as it is joyous.

Health and wellbeing

There are many ideas about what looks good. A sleek body, glowing skin. But actually, what looks best on anybody is being relaxed and moving in a way that shows you're at one with yourself and with your body, that you're glowing with vitality. There's nothing better than that.

Goals and challenges

Every Leo has their goals. You don't really think about it, you simply have them and act on them. However, those around you may be challenging you to explain those goals. If so, simply change the subject. It's by far the best solution.

THIS DAY FOR EVERYONE

Few things are as annoying as facing last-minute changes in plans that you struggled to organise in the first place. But the more you learn, the more you'll realise these changes aren't just wise, but could eliminate problems that have been a source of concern for you and others. Now, you needn't worry.

Often, disagreeing with others is pointless, but when it matters, it's crucial

You

The Leo energy, the Sun energy, that is naturally within you is strong and powerful. However, sometimes you can get so involved in what you're doing, and so determined to achieve what you have in mind that you actually lose yourself in those pursuits. The trick is to catch that compulsive drive and stop it before it takes over and, in fact, exhausts you.

There's also another side of your nature, one that you visit less frequently because it's not as dramatic, but one which is important for you, simply because it's that part of you that helps you understand why you truly want to do what you do. It's what might be termed the quiet, reflective side of your nature.

It's warm and quiet and most of all, when you're there, you know instinctively what and who is important to you, what you want to embrace next – and, equally, what you want to leave behind.

Even more than that, it's in these still moments that you gain joy from life itself and from being who you are. And while, as a Leo, you'll always have that expansive side – that very special kind of Leo lustre that is part of your nature – your quiet side is what makes life worth living, and the more you are aligned with that, the more wonderful your life will be, each and every day.

You and others

While you can pursue your own goals solo, there are certain instances when you'll need a team, when you'll need their knowledge or their ideas or enthusiasm. Whatever the case, do exactly that. Create that balance, so you support them and they support you.

Health and wellbeing

Usually, this is described in terms of how well you look, and the success of a new regime has to do with that. Are you slim and glowing? Actually, this has as much to do with your inner world and feeling wonderful within.

Goals and challenges

There are all sorts of achievements within your grasp and, in fact, as a Leo you're likely to do whatever you choose. However, there's one achievement that can be unreachable for most but which is important for you – and that is inner peace.

AUGUST

16

L
/
E
\
O

Sometimes, minor disagreements are no more than that. However, those you have now could expose long-standing and unresolved issues. You've been ignoring these because you had no idea how to deal with them. Now, suddenly, there's a way. While this is inconvenient, you must still take advantage of it.

GIFTS Altruistic, Entertaining, Lavish

NUMBER 7

CHALLENGES Anxious, Headstrong, Haughty

(1+7) + (8) = 16 = (1+6) = 7

I never listen to those who tell me their way of doing things. It won't work – I'm not them

AUGUST

17

L
/
E
\
O

You

There are two sides to your nature, firstly as a Leo, a fire sign, and secondly, someone who is born with the Sun as your ruler.

One part of your nature is driven – the one who gets up in the morning and can't wait to do something, and thinks, having done that, "What's next?".

And the other can be exquisitely lazy and will kick back and really enjoy doing nothing. But there's a part in the middle that needs to come out, too. And it's a part that has to do with a child-like joy in discovery.

There's a certain fear that if you don't keep doing what you're good at, then you'll descend into boredom. But the fact is, that intuitive part of you enjoys doing things in new ways.

True, this would mean breaking certain habits and doing things differently. However, the compensation for that is a single thing, and it's a three-letter word: joy.

It's about moving into new territory and doing things in new ways – and it's rewarding simply because you're doing it, not because of your own success or the success that others recognise.

Not only that, once you get good at this, that variety of joy can become a habit, and it will be something that you not only love to have as part of each day. It will be something you're able to create every day as well.

You and others

If you're a typical Leo, you probably have a gang, a gang of friends, some of whom you've been around for a long time. But it's time for you to add new people to this gang. Those who won't encourage you to do the same thing because they like it, but will encourage you to break patterns and do new things.

Health and wellbeing

As you know well, your habits are very strong, and once you get into one, it's hard to break it. The trick is to create a habit that makes space for you to feel well, no matter what you do, to eat well and, most of all, to think and rest well.

Goals and challenges

If you're ready to break through, to leave certain elements of the past behind, it's time for you to get what might be called a good coach. This may be an individual, but could also be embracing a side of your nature that often inspires other people. Now, it's time to inspire yourself.

THIS DAY FOR EVERYONE

There's a fine line between a sudden breakthrough and an exciting but unwelcome surprise. And in one particular situation, you're experiencing both. The trick to all of this is to forget about planning ahead and instead to take each day and each hour as they come. It will make life a lot easier.

GIFTS Creative, Charismatic, Commanding

CHALLENGES Impatient, Irascible, Rigid

NUMBER 8

(1+8) + (8) = 17 = (1+7) = 8

Fun can be planned, but the best moments are as unexpected as they are thrilling

You

As a Leo and a fire sign, for you action is like breathing. However, every once in a while, you need to stop and take a different kind of breath, the kind of breath that stimulates you and, also, that helps you break patterns.

As a Leo, you can get so involved in doing – doing what you're good at and doing more of it – that you don't stop to consider whether it's just repetitive and if it's time for you to break patterns, to do things in a new way, to develop new habits.

If there's any difficulty with this, it's that being what's termed a fixed sign, one of the fixed signs of the zodiac, you occasionally have trouble coming up with that new pattern, and this will actually encourage you to do something else, which is seek guidance or help from another.

Normally, you're the one who's advising and supporting those around you, but in this particular case and, in fact, every once in a while in your life, it's essential that you recognise that you need that little boost from somebody. Perhaps it's a sharper kick that's important, to break those habits and to discover the new world that is ready to open up before you. A world that will open up only if you begin to do things differently, and, more than that, to see possibilities in different ways and look at life from a different angle.

You and others

In this particular case, the trick is to learn the degree to which you tend to lead the way. And, even more, it's about the importance of letting go of that. Why? So you can allow others not only to shine their light, but to shine their light for you.

Health and wellbeing

The standard combination of eating well and living well is an important one. However, for you to feel truly well, it's another component that's essential. In fact, it's even more important, and that is, joy. Joy in life, joy when you wake up in the morning and joy when you go to sleep at night.

Goals and challenges

Oddly, your biggest challenge isn't facing challenges, it's knowing who you can rely on when you need guidance. Being the one who others come to, you're not always aware who you need to go to. This may be one of your biggest challenges of all.

AUGUST

18

L
/
E
\
O

One of those difficult periods, during which single problems seem to have no solution, is what you're facing. The trick to dealing with these is to walk away, possibly for a few days. Once you have some distance, you'll recognise there's an entirely different approach, one that works perfectly.

Last-minute ideas, plans and passions can turn an ordinary day into a glittering event

AUGUST

19

L
/
E
****
O

You

As a Leo and a fire sign, you have a talent for living life well – and not only do you manage to look great and live abundantly, you also manage to accumulate the good things that come from a life well lived, from memories to gifts from others.

And while this collection of both experiences and objects can be rewarding, at the same time, there's a sense that you're carrying around baggage.

You know this isn't the most important thing in life, except you can't quite define what is. That's partly because you're living in a time during which people think so much about possessions and objects and clothes that they forget about the core meaning to life – your inner world, your feelings. This could be your feelings for others but, even more, it's about your feelings for yourself, and that part of your nature that also reaches for something higher and more compelling.

And this is part of your challenge, as a Leo who, on the one hand, has lived and is living an exciting life, but who, on the other, also recognises that there must be something deeper, perhaps something that's less easily defined. Make that your goal, make that awareness your journey, and not only will you learn a lot each day, but you will enrich your life in a way that objects never could.

You and others

As you begin to carefully choose those with whom you spend time, you'll also begin to realise that, while some people are merely a distraction, others add to your life in ways that you're only beginning to understand. And that may make them some of the most important people in your life.

Health and wellbeing

While you can focus on life's celebrations, you can also do something different. You can take another approach to your wellbeing and make every day a party, a wellbeing party – one during which you do things that will make you feel better at the end of the day than you did at the beginning of it.

Goals and challenges

Tempting as it is to stick to certain personal goals and achievements, which are important, the trick is to find a balance between those and the individuals with whom you're pursuing those goals, or possibly even who are challenging you. In every case, recognise how much you're benefitting from them.

 THIS DAY FOR EVERYONE

If ever there was a time when it's essential to be cautious of those who are manipulative or who never think of others, it's now. True, they aren't always easy to spot. Still, if you think back to other individuals who've had those traits, you'll find it easier to recognise those who are similar in the here and now.

Letting others take the lead isn't easy; however, certain individuals' ideas are magic

You

As a Leo, you're creative by nature and, of course, as a fire sign, you enjoy making things happen. However, if you do too much, you won't just exhaust yourself, often those around you benefit more than you do from your generosity of spirit and creativity.

From your perspective, life is very much about using that enthusiasm, and in all sorts of ways. This isn't just about creating a happy life for yourself and others. Nor is it about creating success in your work, although this can be a vital expression of your zest for life.

However, there's another variety of success that's essential. And this is the variety that lives within you and is lasting. On one hand, it has to do with being able to enjoy each day, to feel thrilled when you get up in the morning, on the other, it's also about feeling contented when you go to bed at night.

As a Leo, you were born with a generous spirit – so generous that you sometimes neglect your own interests. The trick is to think a little less about the happiness of others. You may thrive on your ability to create that joy for those around you, and the more the better. Yet, as you go through the day, it's essential you feel joy simply for being alive.

That is one of your greatest gifts as a Leo. When you achieve that, the rest of those joys will be a bonus.

You and others

The trick to enjoying the world around you is to go from finding friends who are all about having a good time to finding the friends who recognise how important it is to enjoy life's precious moments – and to ensure that they happen every day.

Health and wellbeing

Tempting as it is to find exercises you can do quickly, you're urged to become obsessed with something that makes you feel excited, whether it's a sport, whether it's yoga, or even if it's fishing. Whatever it is, if it brings you joy, make that your priority.

Goals and challenges

The question for you is a simple one. Are you bored? If you are, then it's time for you to completely rethink things. That may seem odd, but if you aren't making the best of events, it's time to change them.

AUGUST

20

L
/
E
\
O

THIS DAY FOR EVERYONE

Only days ago, you were battling with certain individuals about details that seemed important. Now, looking back, you're beginning to realise you were sidestepping the real issue. Deep down, you know what it is. The challenge is raising it. Once you do, everything else will be easy.

GIFTS Creative, Noble, Enthusiastic

CHALLENGES Headstrong, Exacting, Unbending

NUMBER 2

(2+1) + (8) = 11 = (1+1) = 2

True joy is about the right moment, the right people and, most of all, love

AUGUST

21

L
/
E
\
O

You

For you, the idea of getting into good habits is wonderful, and once you know what you're meant to be doing to look after yourself – to live well, and to manage your life well – then you know that you're doing the best you can. Or so it seems, because there'll always be a part of your nature that feels that there's something better.

To a certain extent, this is due to the influence of your neighbouring sign, Virgo, which is a little bit of your own being and has some bearing on your character. But, mostly, it's about departing from the belief that if you can get your habits fixed perfectly, you'll be happy. Eventually you'll realise that the thing that will bring you the greatest joy is living a life that's about discovery, about little discoveries every day, and also about major discoveries every once in a while.

While it's true that sometimes these can be disruptive, each of them will add to your life in a wonderful way. They're like a variety of intellectual or even spiritual vitamins.

Whatever the direction that you take, the minute you begin to programme that variety of exploration and the resulting discoveries into your life, it will take on a new lustre. And every day you'll wake up with a new enthusiasm about what will be coming your way over the next 24 hours.

You and others

If you view life as something to get on with in an orderly fashion, then you might not like this idea, but if, on the other hand, you view it as a celebration, a party, then you'll know exactly what to do next.

Health and wellbeing

There are two approaches to your health and well-being. There's listening to what others say you should be doing and eating. And then, there's actually feeling your own body, feeling your own muscles and feeling whether you're on top of the world. Pay attention to that, and you'll know exactly what's in your best interests.

Goals and challenges

While it's simple to set goals and stick with them, the most important thing is to keep those goals growing and changing. It's as if you have a very enthusiastic plant growing and you have to send it in the right direction. Live a life that's as full of enthusiasm and you'll enjoy every minute of it.

THIS DAY FOR EVERYONE

You're beginning to recognise that, instead of being reason for concern, recent unsettling events were actually breakthroughs. True, they weren't in the form you anticipated, and they could take things in an unexpected direction. Be patient. The more you explore and learn, the more optimistic you'll be.

Ruler Mercury
Element Earth

Symbol The Maiden
Flower Buttercup

Virgo

August 22 – September 21

Virgo As a Virgo, you combine an earthy sensuality with the sharp cleverness of your ruler, Mercury. The pleasure you derive in beauty, nature, living and eating well is genuine, yet being the sign of early autumn, you've an instinctive awareness of the wise use of resources. Your flower is forget-me-not, your spice, aromatic cardamom and the mighty oak and the hazel are your trees. Your jewels have earthy colours, from topaz to sardonyx.

V
/
I
\
R
/
G
\
O

There's a joy to having the facts, acting on them, and being confident of the result

You

As a clear-minded Virgo, you know exactly what you want to do. However, because you were born right next to the rather fiery sign of Leo, which is ruled by the Sun, there's a part of you that doesn't mind a little flurry of energy, a little excitement when you walk into the room.

This can be confusing, but on the other hand, it allows you to have a much more exciting life than other Virgos. And, in fact, the secret to this is to note the part of you that likes to figure out the correct way to do things. Then, you also need to recognise times when you not only want to ignore it, but actually would benefit from doing that, and allowing your Leo side to take over a bit.

And, eventually, you'll find a balance between the two. The Leo side is always about fun and joy, and isn't nearly as responsible as the Virgo side. Yet, when you combine the two, you'll not only enjoy life more, but you'll also share that joy, a very logical and ordered joy, with those around you, and it becomes a kind of infectious variety of fun.

Not only that, you'll also bring a sense of joy to some of the more orderly Virgo elements of your day and your life. You might even find yourself taking chances that previously you never would have considered.

You and others

Your instinct is to help people at any time. If there's something they need to learn to do, or just simply learn something new, you'll be there. However, the trick is often to stand back and let them learn for themselves, and then congratulate them when they do it.

Health and wellbeing

As a Virgo, you can come up with a plan and obsess about it and do it precisely every day. However, the secret is to borrow a little energy from your Leo side and to turn that plan into something thrilling.

Goals and challenges

One of your skills is your ability to set very clear goals – but there's one important goal you need to include, and that is the one that involves getting things wrong. While there are many things you can learn perfectly right away, the things you get wrong several times always turn out to be the most instructive.

AUGUST

22

V
/
I
\
R
/
G
\
O

THIS DAY FOR EVERYONE

When you think somebody is mistaken, you'll say so, and without hesitation. But now, and in several situations, certain individuals are being bizarrely touchy. It's a tricky time for them. Tempting as it is to ask what's wrong, you'd regret it. Busy yourself elsewhere until they're in a better mood.

GIFTS Precise, Methodical, Analytical

NUMBER 4

CHALLENGES Judgemental, Demanding, Suspicious

$(2+3) + (8) = 13 = (1+3) = 4$

Beauty appears in many forms. However, acts of kindness have their own unique beauty

AUGUST

23

V
/
I
\
R
/
G
\
O

You

You have a strong instinct, an instinct that tells you what's in your best interests. But then you'll make a list, and convert that instinct into a list that is very much in order, yet seems to ignore what's actually most important.

The secret? Be spontaneous. Yes, by all means make that list, and know that everything is on there, but at the same time, if something comes to mind, do it. Plunge in, take a chance and, even more than that, take joy in the outcome – even if it isn't quite what you'd expected.

Begin to walk away from the idea of things being good or bad or right or wrong and, rather, simply view them as a life experience.

As a Virgo, once you learn to do that, instead of worrying about getting things right, you will live in the moment on your own or around others and, whatever the outcome, you won't look back. In fact, you'll be anticipating yet more adventures. These will arise in part from plans you've made, but other adventures will appear as a result of an unexpected discussion, something you spotted or an encounter with somebody else.

They are the kinds of things that will increasingly become part of your everyday life and your everyday thinking, and the kinds of activities that will add to your life in ways you wouldn't have thought possible.

You and others

Tempting as it is to talk about how things went last week, yesterday or even a short while ago, avoid it. Reviewing such matters with those around you means you're living in the past, and the only time you can really have a good time is in the here and now.

Health and wellbeing

As a Virgo, you have a strong instinct for looking after your body, but the trick – not only to looking after it but to enjoying every day – is to glory in the miracle that is your body, that it breathes, that it grows and, most of all, that it's you.

Goals and challenges

We're all taught to set ourselves goals. However, perhaps the most important one you can set is a list of goals to have fun. Once you've done that, turn your attention to all those practical necessities. They may look very different.

THIS DAY FOR EVERYONE

By no means are you overly sentimental, yet you seem determined to hang onto certain arrangements. You may hope they'll spring back to life. Not only is that unlikely, but the more time and effort you invest in them, the less you'll have for the new developments currently coming your way.

Doing things right, initially, isn't just wise. It sets the tone for a plan, project – or romance

You

As a Virgo and an earth sign, you sense quality in the world around you – in food, and especially in objects. Not just objects of value, but from the simple beauty of a flower to something on a table at home.

What's more, you're interested in the object's story and its background, and will discuss these with others, and you enjoy learning about them as well.

This is one of the wonderful things about being a Virgo. You can appreciate what you encounter while not necessarily wanting it to be part of your life. But there are times when something, perhaps an object or even an activity, wakes you up. You feel delighted, and you want to learn more.

This is when it's important for you to take action. Don't waste any time thinking about whether it's in your best interests. Simply plunge into it in a way that you, as a Virgo, might not ordinarily do.

This act of responding to what you care about is itself important. While you may stay involved in that particular study or activity for the rest of your life, it may also only last a month, but whatever the case, you'll have learnt something important.

And that is how to overcome your often very sensible mind and instead follow your rather spectacular passions.

You and others

Acknowledging that while you may like people, and even be related to them, yet won't always agree with them is difficult. But the minute you recognise that – instead of trying to figure out a way you can share that common value – you don't agree at all, it's okay.

Health and wellbeing

At some point, somebody must have told you that you're always supposed to maintain an even mood. It's something that's very common with Virgos, and here's the newsflash; you don't need to feel the same. In fact, you'll have ups and downs, and that's not only normal, you'll learn a lot from them.

Goals and challenges

Being a Virgo, you probably have a list of goals, and you may even have a list of challenges that you want to overcome. However, make sure that list is in pencil, maybe literally, or possibly, metaphorically, in the sense that those goals and those challenges will change every day.

AUGUST

24

V
/
I
\
R
/
G
\
O

Tempting as it is to offer advice to certain individuals who are complaining, it would be unwise. Saying nothing may seem uncaring, but the fact is that they actually enjoy the drama, so have no intention of making an effort to improve on things. That would end the pleasure they get from complaining.

Simple joys can bring the greatest pleasures, from a quiet chat to a joyous event

AUGUST

25

V
/
I
\
R
/
G
\
O

You

Most young Virgos, even those who haven't yet gone to school, have an instinct to analyse things. They make lists, possibly in their heads, or they'll organise their toys. This analysis is as natural to you as breathing. Next comes making plans. That's the point at which you can write things down, then turn plans into action.

All of that works well. However, there's another part that's important, and it's allowing the unexpected event, the surprising idea, even an invitation that takes you into new territory, to become part of your life. To learn from experience, you need to allow the uninvited into your life. This may seem worrying because, of course, you like things organised – but you will learn from it.

First of all, it will teach you to become more inquisitive if something you don't know about appears. Then, you'll begin to explore, and either you'll discover that actually you find it quite boring, or – and this is more likely – it will become part of that process of broadening your horizons.

Equally, it will have to do with meeting people you wouldn't otherwise have met, or having opportunities that you wouldn't have encountered. But most of all – and this is what's most important – it will teach you to experience life's joys in many ways.

You and others

There's a trick to listening to others when they speak, and it's to listen with interest, not with the part of your brain that's so good at analysing what they're saying switched on. Turn that off and simply listen, and enjoy what they say for exactly that, their words.

Health and wellbeing

Being a Virgo, you don't always love paradoxes, but here's an important one for you. You want a perfect routine for looking after yourself and the way you eat, but the fact is, that perfect routine needs to change and to change regularly. The more often you change it, the more perfect it will be.

Goals and challenges

This is a very old saying, but it's one that's particularly appropriate for you – and that is: that failure is a far better teacher than success. For you, as a Virgo, you try very hard to organise things and get them right. Yet recognising that you might actually fail could be a treat.

THIS DAY FOR EVERYONE

There are minor disagreements that occur in all sorts of settings which come and go swiftly. But what's arisen recently – and will continue to be a topic of serious discussion over the coming days – may seem overwhelming, at least initially. Still, talk this over. The more you do, the more you'll learn.

Living with others' mistakes is annoying, as they'll do it again. Explain the changes needed

You

As a Virgo, your instinct is to work hard to figure out your day and the order in which you'll do things – and, equally, the week, and the month, and the year, even several years ahead. This comes naturally to you, so much so that you don't even think about doing it.

Yet, at the same time, life often dishes out unexpected events, which means that you need to rethink those plans. Again, this is something you have become accustomed to, and when you're doing that, you try to get it just right as well. In fact, you try to plan ahead simply because you're adjusting plans that change, and that's the key for you.

It's to recognise that even the most carefully made plans will change, because life itself changes, and instead of working so hard to get everything organised in detail, which you tend to do, you'll give yourself a wonderful gift – and that is the gift of spontaneity. To be willing to do things suddenly. In fact, you might even start doing things suddenly without needing to be prompted by others.

You could just change your mind and call someone and suggest you go some place you've never been before. Whatever it is, whatever you do and whoever it's with, make that gift of spontaneity to yourself and your life will go from one that's organised to one that is full of joy.

You and others

While, harmony is nice, so is being able to work together with even difficult individuals. There's an important secret to making the best of others, and that is to offer mutual support. For you to support others, and for them to support you. Then you'll know that in doing so, you're helping each other be the best you can be.

Health and wellbeing

As an earth sign, you tend to think the condition of your body has to do with what you eat and how you move and how you look after it. And while that's important, it's also vital to recognise how much your mood has to do with how you feel. Sometimes, if you can lift your mood, you'll feel a whole lot better.

Goals and challenges

Planning ahead is a virtue, it's true, but one of the most important plans that you can make, is to plan ahead to fail. That may sound strange, but if you allow yourself to take chances where you might fail, the odds are good that your successes will be spectacular.

AUGUST

26

V
/
I
\
R
/
G
\
O

Teamwork is essential, in both your personal life and activities out in the world. Yet one or two individuals are driving you crazy. Ignoring their antics won't be easy, but it's better than trying to get them in line. Besides, those individuals will soon calm down, actually before you'd have expected it.

It's better to do something right once, than plunge in while short of facts

AUGUST

27

V
/
I
\
R
/
G
\
O

You

There's a difference between a drive to have things well done – to have what you might call Virgo perfection, which is something you'll always have on your mind – and living a real life.

And in that life, the line between things being done adequately and perfection is unclear, and in fact, not only that, it allows you to view yourself and your life as what might be termed a work in progress.

That is, rather like a plant growing, it too can shift. If you move it into the light, it will shift; if you trim it, it will grow differently. In your case, also, it's about where you shine the light on your own life, and the direction in which you are growing.

Tempting as it is to stick with what worked before, you – just like that plant – will grow better if you put yourself in a different setting and in a different light.

And yet you're in a position where you can also do something that the plant can't do, and that is try out new things regularly and throw caution to the wind.

Take chances in a way that you, as a cautious Virgo, might not ordinarily do, and not only will you grow as well as a plant that has been given a lot of fertiliser, you'll enjoy every day of that process of discovery as well.

You and others

There's a secret to having a good time, and that isn't figuring out what would be fun, but to seek out those individuals who are what might be termed renegades –the ones who do something unexpected and have a great time doing it. You'll learn a lot from them.

Health and wellbeing

There's also a secret to feeling really well, and that is to learn to feel your vitality. If it's low or isn't there, don't think that the answer is to take more vitamins. It's about restoring your energy and actually pausing to rest in a way that you don't often do.

Goals and challenges

Many Virgos have a list of goals as long as their arm. Here's a suggestion. Make a very short list – say just three – then deal with those goals before you take on the next ones. You'll be amazed how easy and fun it is.

THIS DAY FOR EVERYONE

Nobody would blame you for worrying when somebody close is keeping pivotal facts to themselves. However, it would be unwise to judge, no matter how convincing what you've learnt appears to be. There are other facts of which you're unaware. When these surface, it will change everything.

GIFTS Meticulous, Diligent, Natural carer

CHALLENGES Distrustful, Self-pitying, Fussy

NUMBER 9

(2+8) + (8) = 18 = (1+8) = 9

Sometimes a kind word or gentle touch isn't just helpful, it can change another's life

You

As a Virgo, you like to make plans, and you prefer those plans to be well thought out. In fact, you are perfect at planning. However, when it comes to actually living your life, those plans don't always work – and that's because life itself is unruly.

Your big lesson is to learn to make those plans more like life and, in a way, that means not being quite so specific, but leaving yourself room to grow.

If you make plans that are too detailed, and then try to stick to them rigidly, firstly, things won't go as you expect. But secondly, you'll see something else going on that has nothing to do with those plans and if you decide to pursue that instead, you'll feel you're not following the plans that you should be.

There is joy in imperfection, including plans that don't work out, and there's joy in new beginnings and discovery, and that's what this is all about.

There's even joy in getting things wrong – and that's something that you, as a Virgo, find very difficult to accept. Yet, as you'll discover in love and life, the more you experiment, the more you'll come to understand.

Yes, you may hit a few hard walls in the process, but what you learn will teach you to enjoy that, and to enjoy what each day brings you, whether it's what you planned or not.

You and others

There's a single rule that will make it much easier to get along with others, and that is to ban two words – right and wrong – when talking about what you've done, and talking about what they've done. It's amazing how much more pleasant conversations will be when you make that single, simple change.

Health and wellbeing

While it's important that you eat well and that you get enough sleep, there's another issue that it's also vital to be aware of, and that is how exhausting feeling guilty can be. As a Virgo, it's something you often experience, and it's a feeling that does you absolutely no good.

Goals and challenges

The idea of getting things organised is appealing, and that has to do with listing your goals. However, what's most important is to write them in pencil. The more frequently you revise them, the more fun life will be.

AUGUST

28

V
/
I
\
R
/
G
\
O

Debating versus arguing is rarely clear; the objective, getting things right, always is

AUGUST

29

V
/
I
\
R
/
G
\
O

You

The line between things being just okay and them being perfect is very clear to you, and it always puzzles you, as an organised Virgo who pays close attention to the smallest detail, that others don't notice.

The fact is, they may well also want the best, but they don't discriminate as clearly as you do about an ideal which you'll figure out in your mind. And, often, you'll do the necessary footwork to make things happen. Yet, every once in a while, it's vital for you to recognise that compromise isn't just necessary – it's actually by far the best approach to making things happen.

On the one hand, this means you have to be willing to listen to what others have to say and, in fact, to go along with their ideas – even when you don't necessarily think they are wise. But it also means taking chances on either new or untried activities, or even taking what may seem like unprecedented risks.

Initially, you may worry about this, but, gradually, you'll soon discover the good fun that comes with venturing into new and potentially risky territory, and the success that comes with it. Enough that – you'll wonder why you waited so long before plunging into activities that are as exciting as they are risky. Make a habit of it, and life will be a lot more fun.

You and others

While it's wonderful to hang out with people who think like you do, ensure there's always at least one individual who could be regarded as a troublemaker in your circle. That's the person who's going to take you new places, and even more importantly, come up with inspiring and exciting ideas.

Health and wellbeing

Everybody loves feeling great. However, it's important that you enjoy both the ups and the downs in your life, physically and even when you're a bit low emotionally. Why? Because every time you have a down, you'll appreciate the ups all the more.

Goals and challenges

People admire those who aim high, and you have a habit of doing that. However, if you aim too high, then you'll be so focused on that distant goal that you may not notice ones that are closer, and actually far more exciting.

THIS DAY FOR EVERYONE

It's worth considering the fact that while some decisions can be made once and will last forever, others must be regarded as tentative. This means that, for now, things are settled. Yet, at the same time, you'll have the freedom to explore the rather intriguing ideas and offers coming your way.

Experience proves the high cost of compromise, while caution always pays off

You

You're probably aware that, as a Virgo, you're a bit of a perfectionist, and you can also be impatient, which means that you line up very specific goals, and then want things to happen right away.

The funny thing is that often they do, which proves that if you're demanding enough of yourself and of the world, then things will happen. But it also means that, firstly, you don't have much fun and, secondly, that you can miss out on the things you'll learn about, the people you'll encounter and the exciting developments that come about because of mistakes, because you've gone in entirely the wrong direction. And, at the same time, you'll have learnt a lot and maybe met some very interesting people along the way.

In fact, it's those adventures that a very precise Virgo often misses, simply because you're so busy getting things right. This isn't just about life or places you go, it has to do with the people you hang out with and who you care about. It may well be that if you're a little more laid-back, you'll find it easier to get along with family members and, equally, you'll find you have more fun with those closest.

In fact, if you're a little more easy-going, you might even have a lot more pleasure from what the days in your life, and the companions in your life, have to offer.

You and others

Simply deciding that life is going to have joy in it, wherever you are and whatever you're doing, may seem pretty radical. But if you begin talking about it with those closest to you, they might join in and, in fact, you might find yourselves all having a wonderful time.

Health and wellbeing

The idea of seeking fun when you're having a workout, whether it's running or being at the gym, may seem strange, but it is possible to do that. It's possible, in fact, to turn looking after yourself into a party. That's the secret.

Goals and challenges

As an idealist, often you'll set yourself goals that could be described as astronomically high. While this can be inspiring, it's also overwhelming. There is something to be said for setting your goals very low and achieving a lot of them.

AUGUST

30

V
/
I
\
R
/
G
\
O

THIS DAY FOR EVERYONE

There's a difference between things going wonderfully, which they will be over the coming weeks, and events being what you'd planned. Ironically, what's least expected could turn out best in the long run. Knowing that, explore absolutely every idea and offer that comes your way. You won't regret it.

The instinct for kindness is natural to all Virgos but, bizarrely, many are taught it's weak

AUGUST

31

V
/
I
\
R
/
G
\
O

You

You're very clear about your own style, your own objectives, and your priorities, and often, you simply do what you do.

Yet, there are situations where you find you have to explain a lot of detail to others, and if that process of explanation goes into justifying them, or even seeking their approval, then it's important that you stop and think about whether it matters.

If you need the cooperation of certain individuals, fine, but if you are in a position where suddenly you find that you're trying to get their approval, then it's important to take a deep breath and change the subject.

It might even be a good time to find something else pressing that you need to go and attend to. Then you can choose to spend time with that individual later.

This process of not just embracing new challenges and adventures but also celebrating them – and celebrating the chance you're taking – is a vital one for you as a Virgo.

It's very important for you to achieve what you want in whatever area of life, whether it's your job if you have one, your physical well-being, your creativity or just the quality of life. But in every case, the most important individual you can please is you, and that's something that you and you alone can make decisions about.

You and others

It's important to recognise that those around you, whether friends or family or colleagues, are all very, very different. And while you're close to some emotionally, others you aren't. With some, you may have fun doing things but you can't really have a chat. Recognise that, and you'll be much less aggravated.

Health and wellbeing

As a Virgo, you can very easily analyse something and divide it up, and it's true, feeling well can have to do with your body, with your mood, with your spirit. But actually, each of them is the same, because they all influence each other.

Goals and challenges

Make a list of what you want to do, but when you make that list, make sure to leave spaces on it for new ideas. What arises unexpectedly, and on occasion out of the blue, may be far more important than those goals you've spent a lot more time thinking about.

THIS DAY FOR EVERYONE

Some disappointments are a mere nuisance, but one you're about to face could seem a disaster. While ordinarily, you'd respond swiftly to a situation of this nature, do some serious investigation first. Once you discover just how timely those changes are, you'll exchange feelings of panic for relief.

Often, what's best varies with the time and place; rarely is there only one right moment

You

When you're busy making plans – whether it's in your own life, whether it involves how you live or your life out in the world, and even whether it's around you – you'll consider everything, and you'll do your best to ensure that those plans unfold as you intend.

However, it's important to recognise that plans are rather like breathing. They change as your circumstances change. If you're sitting in a chair, you breathe slowly, whereas if you're walking or running up a steep hill, your breath becomes quite different.

In the same way, it's vital you recognise that those plans will be easy at times, then difficult, then challenging, and then perhaps they'll change entirely. When you are prepared for that, you'll see them as an adventure, instead of something that's supposed to be perfectly organised. And, equally, you'll feel more comfortable about sharing them with others, and allowing others to get involved, where ordinarily, you might be hesitant, because you have no idea what they'll do.

While that's true, certain individuals can be tricky, and others will come up with ideas you'd never pursue. That may be the point of it. The more you explore because of the people in your life, the more fun you'll have simply being alive, whether it has to do with plans, or every day.

You and others

One of the things that surprises you as a Virgo, and somebody who tries to be true to yourself all the time, is how different certain people can be at different times. Almost as if they were different individuals. Not only is this interesting, you may have more sides to you than you realise as well.

Health and wellbeing

There's a great deal of talk about the importance of sleeping well, if you're sleeping in the right kind of bed, and whether or not you're having dreams. But there's another part of you that also needs to rest, and that's your mind. You don't need to go to bed to rest your mind, you simply need to prevent it running around and stirring things up.

Goals and challenges

When you're setting goals, it's important to think about what you want to do. But probably what's even more important is that you write those goals down in pencil. What you learn in the process of trying to achieve them is far more important than what you'll think about when you're beginning that list.

SEPTEMBER

01

V
/
I
\
R
/
G
\
O

GIFTS Good planner, Lucid, Precise

CHALLENGES Particular, Sceptical, Wary

NUMBER 2

$(0+2) + (9) = 11 = (1+1) = 2$

Those complaining need instructions. Those suffering need kindness

SEPTEMBER

02

V
/
I
\
R
/
G
\
O

You

As a Virgo, you learn in a lot of ways. You learn by research, you learn by talking to people, you learn by being observant. But, most of all, we all learn by discussing things. The reason is that those around you, people you know, or experts, will have had experience in what you're doing. This is particularly important for you to bear in mind, because you always have a lot of projects going on. And while you can do your own research, talking to others will not only bring you new information, you'll also develop a fresh perspective.

But also, ironically, when planning gets dull, when it's boring or when it's just taking too long, it may be that others can help you on your way. And there's another kind of information they can offer, and that is when it's time to stop and abandon that plan, because things simply aren't working.

You might not be willing to do that on your own, but allowing those around you to both inspire you and guide you is one of the most important lessons for you.

As a Virgo, you can often be very determined. So determined, in fact, that you refuse to acknowledge when, clearly something won't work, and instead turn your attention to something that might work a lot better.

You and others

The most important thing for you to remember about relationships, whether it's family, your friends or colleagues, or even neighbours, is that everyone is there to teach everybody else. You're teaching others, but they also are teaching you things. Many of which are very important indeed.

Health and wellbeing

These days, there's a tremendous emphasis on figuring out the right kind of physical activity to pursue and the right kind of diet to follow. However, perhaps the most important message for you is to learn when to stop. To simply stop. Stop thinking, stop doing and rest.

Goals and challenges

Aiming high comes naturally to you. You don't even think of it that way until you compare notes with other people. However, it is important for you to pause and review what you're doing often, too often. It may be that it's time for you to change your goals.

THIS DAY FOR EVERYONE

It would seem that while problems cause dissension, everybody would agree that there are golden opportunities to be taken advantage of. Unfortunately, that's not the case. In fact, if you are to make the best of what comes your way, you may need to compromise, at least in the short term.

GIFTS Health-aware, Stickler, Considerate

CHALLENGES Over-concerned, Idiosyncratic, Fussy

NUMBER 3

(0+3) + (9) = 12 = (1+2) = 3

Beware of those who insist their advice is vital. Their guidance may be more ego than fact

You

As an earth sign, you're practical, and your ideas are very clear but, as you well know, not everybody around you is quite as practical. And, in fact, they'll often come up with ideas that are so wild, you can't even believe they've thought of them.

Yet, at the same time, the more you chat with them, and the more you explore their ideas, you realise that although some of what they have in mind is pretty far out, on the other hand some of the ideas that they have to share are fascinating, if not a very real gift – simply because it's something you never would have thought of yourself.

And this is the important point about expanding your activities. Not figuring it out yourself, but allowing space for those around you – family, friends, colleagues, or even neighbours – to add something exciting to your life. To allow them to bring something new.

This process of exchanging ideas is something people talk about a lot. But, as a Virgo, often you will allow others' ideas to influence your own. In this particular case, the lesson for you is to actually learn to accept others' ideas. To embrace them and, in some cases, to embrace their point of view with enthusiasm as well. It will enhance your life, whatever you're doing, and it will add to your happiness for the rest of your days.

You and others

Being a Virgo, and somebody who has a clear sense of what works and what doesn't, you'll often be in the role of teacher, imparting information to others. Yet, at the same time, often they'll have things to show you. The most important thing you can do? It's to listen.

Health and wellbeing

There are lots of way to feel good, and in fact sometimes when you don't feel so great, you'll find that you're suddenly healed, not by having the right thing to eat, or the right medication, but by great company. That's one of the most important ways to look after yourself.

Goals and challenges

Every once in a while, you need new goals. You need a new hill to climb. However, finding that hill is a skill, and it may involve asking the guidance of others in a way you wouldn't usually do. So, possibly, the guidance and the new skill may come together.

SEPTEMBER

03

V
/
I
\
R
/
G
\
O

Being disappointed by others is no surprise; disappointing myself is a worrying shock

SEPTEMBER

04

V
/
I
\
R
/
G
\
O

You

There's little more challenging to you than imposing order on chaos. You run into this frequently, and as a Virgo, you often wonder how others can cope with being in such unruly, unsettling situations.

However, as you'll often discover, what seems unruly actually is a setting that allows people to think in a new way, and in a way that sometimes you don't allow for yourself.

It is so random, and so chaotic, that sheer chance, unexpected developments or an idea that comes out of the blue, opens everybody's mind to a new way of doing things, including yours. In fact, you might find this so inspiring that you'll alter the way you organise your life, or how you live at home, so that you can be more easy-going.

There have been times when your high standards have overshadowed life's joys, or even prevented you taking chances. If you can embrace a little of that chaos, then you'll take chances – not only in what you're doing, but perhaps in certain relationships, or even in life's joys.

Each step that you take in this direction clarifies in your mind the fact that you have the capacity to have a good time. And it points the way to taking more chances. Not the kind that are risky, but the kind that will lead to the sort of joys you're developing a taste for.

You and others

It's only on occasion that you realise the people around you don't share your drive, whether it's to get things done, or to achieve a certain quality. And then there is the fact that even if you talk to them about it, they won't care. Let them be who they are, and enjoy who you are.

Health and wellbeing

There are a number of ways to improve on a difficult situation. One is analysing it, another is talking things through. But perhaps the most important one, and the one that occurs to you least frequently, is to simply get away, to create a little space between you and the issue in question.

Goals and challenges

The thing that's most challenging for you is to recognise that sometimes, the best thing to do with a problem is to either back off from it, or to give it up entirely. At minimum, take a break. It will change everything.

THIS DAY FOR EVERYONE

Recently, you were upset by sudden developments. Since then you've learnt a lot, much of which has both surprised and delighted you. Remember this when other dramatic developments arise over the coming weeks, and instead of battling them, focus on exploring what they offer.

Kindness takes minutes and costs nothing. Yet others treat it as if it were gold

You

As a Virgo, you tend to want a single plan, and to focus on one thing at a time. Yet, as you've discovered, because you're inquisitive by nature – and you enjoy learning about what other people are doing – you tend to turn that single plan you had in mind into a variety of activities, some of which involve others, some of which you're sharing with them and a few that are merely about you giving advice.

However, what happens is that the plan fills your day, and your mind, and can become overwhelming unless you do something that is very difficult for you as a Virgo and, that is, care very little about the outcome.

To you, doing things perfectly is a passion. Yet in some cases, they actually aren't yours to deal with, while in others, if you stop worrying about the outcome being perfect, then you'll simply do what you can each day. And what will happen as a result is that you'll enjoy what you accomplish on that day.

Then, when the day is over, you'll be able to relax, instead of fretting about what will happen next. This is one of the greatest skills for you as a Virgo, and someone who hurls yourself into life, to learn. It's not just to take a deep breath, but to truly relax. And to find the right people you can enjoy downtime with as well – those individuals you might regard as your relaxation gurus.

You and others

In certain situations, you have to tolerate people, whoever they are. But in others, you have a choice – and one of the most important choices you can make is to get away from those who moan and groan as much as possible. They don't belong in your life.

Health and wellbeing

Every once in a while, you think it's a good idea to ramp up your physical activities, to eat strictly, to get out and perhaps go for a run, or to work out a lot. Actually, often what's best is to adopt a regime that's a bit more gentle, and be kind to yourself.

Goals and challenges

For you, setting half-goals may seem a real compromise. However if you do that, you'll soon realise it gives you the option to alter those goals, and to include new ones. And, even more than that, it's to explore in a way that is as helpful as it is delightful.

SEPTEMBER

05

V
/
I
\
R
/
G
\
O

Life often brings surprises, yet those you remember best are the ones that were challenging. Yet the surprises coming your way now will be memorable for other reasons. While you may be short of reassuring facts to begin with, once you get involved you'll recognise just how promising they are.

GIFTS Logical, Sensible, Nutrition-aware

CHALLENGES Obsessive, Judgemental, Cynical

NUMBER 6

(0+6) + (9) = 15 = (1+5) = 6

To a Virgo, indulgence must be earned. Once it is, those luxuries will be the finest

SEPTEMBER

06

V
/
I
\
R
/
G
\
O

You

As a Virgo, you were born knowing what's best in any setting. That may sound like an extreme statement, but it's true. Even from your youngest days, you had an instinct about what was appropriate, what was wise to do. About how a room should look. About who was trustworthy, and who wasn't. About who was good fun, and who might not be.

And you still have that, but what's tricky for you is being in situations where other people not only are unaware of such matters, but actually don't care. Tempting as it is to give them advice, the trick is not to offer it.

This may seem unwise and uncaring, because if you suggest something, you might help them avoid problems. But the fact is, they might rather enjoy the idea of running into difficulties and then having to solve them, because they aren't Virgos. And in your case, it's also important that you have a few things you can devote yourself to that satisfy your need for beauty and perfection in life.

This may have to do with activities on your own, or it could involve others. It may have to do with something new. Or it may even have to do with keeping an eye open for an encounter with an individual, or a place, that will give you an opportunity to exercise that muscle of perfection in a way that gratifies you. This is so important.

You and others

There have been times when you have been critical of others, and it seemed important that they should know about that. But, as the years have passed, you have begun to understand that not only was it unimportant for you to say anything, but actually the individuals in question had no intention of making any changes.

Health and wellbeing

Tempting as it is to get a routine going that you know is in your best interests, it's more important to take chances – and even more than that, to find something that isn't just good for you, but that you adore, that makes you feel like a million dollars.

Goals and challenges

It's important that you set your own goals. It may seem obvious, but sometimes you allow those around you to influence your thinking. You then set goals that you think will impress them. Make sure those goals are a part of your heart and your mind, and then everything else will go well.

THIS DAY FOR EVERYONE

Never say never, as the saying goes – and rarely was such advice more apt than now. In the past, you may have said there were certain things you wouldn't consider, or even certain individuals you'd do anything to avoid. But that was then. Times have changed – and so have you.

GIFTS Neat, Coherent, Hard-working

CHALLENGES Wary, Self-critical, Suspicious

NUMBER 7

$(0+7) + (9) = 16 = (1+6) = 7$

There is no more powerful passion than one that's been tested by time and reflection

You

If you could live life on your own – if you had your own little planet, or had your own island to live on – it would be much easier. Because then you could make the plans you need to make without having to deal with others.

But, as you have learnt, not everybody is a Virgo, and you do have to deal with others, which means that you face questions that are unsettling, shake-ups in plans you've made and individuals whose priorities are very different from yours.

All of which means that turning a plan into action can be difficult. Yet, at the same time, you're aware that those individuals have an amazing touch when it comes to making things happen, and in life itself, and it's something that you rather envy.

That touch has to do with spontaneity, something you as a Virgo don't always allow to emerge from your character. And this is a big lesson for you. It's to let those unexpected events, surprise invitations or developments you didn't foresee become a part of your life.

They will broaden your horizons, and bring a kind of joy that you might not know how to manage, at least initially. But it's something that you, being a clever Virgo, and someone who's very good at learning, can pick up. You will have to allow those who are very good at doing joy teach you.

You and others

Not surprisingly, when you are organising things with others, you're tempted to take the lead. However, the fact is not everybody around you is interested in the same things as you, or in the same amount of detail. The trick is to compromise. Take turns.

Health and wellbeing

There's a tendency to think that health and wellbeing has entirely to do with how you eat and how you look after yourself. But it's also about learning different skills – about adding new activities to your thinking, and exercising your mind as well.

Goals and challenges

The trick to making the best of the twists and turns that occur frequently in your life is to recognise that each is an opportunity – not simply to learn something, but to thrive on the process of making your brain cells work harder.

SEPTEMBER

07

V
/
I
\
R
/
G
\
O

GIFTS Natural carer, Virtuous, Diligent

CHALLENGES Sceptical, Demanding, Over-concerned

NUMBER 8

(0+8) + (9) = 17 = (1+7) = 8

Accepting that somebody doesn't care they cause problems isn't easy, but brings peace

S E P T E M B E R

08

V
/
I
\
R
/
G
\
O

You

You don't normally think of it, but when you're making plans – whether they are social plans, whether it's something that has to do with your job, if you have one, or family matters, or when you're organising things – you'll focus on the practicalities. In fact, it's a pleasure for you, and you're good at it.

However, as you will discover, the more people who are involved in those plans, the more ideas there are, and your vision of what's possible – and what's best – may be watered down by their contributions. Tempting as it is to encourage others to do what you know is best, instead try something very difficult for you – stand back and listen to what they have to say, perhaps even go along with it.

This is something you'll have experienced in the past, and will again in the future. But when you're ready to embrace the fact that it's not so much that others know better, but they may have an idea that works better in that particular situation, then you'll be more relaxed about letting them take over.

This also means that perhaps you will have more free time to pursue what's important for you on your own, or with those whose approach is more suited to you. And that's the big lesson in this. To allow others to take over, and then to go off and do what you enjoy.

You and others

Frequently you inspire others, but sometimes they also inspire you, which can be a bit of a surprise for you, because often you know your thinking is clearer. However, the special something that others have is a variety of hope that you occasionally find hard to achieve.

Health and wellbeing

While your wellbeing has a lot to do with your physical body, and even your mood, another thing that's important is your sense of hope about the future. And that's something that can't be rushed – it needs to be developed slowly. Kind of like doing exercise. The more you work on it, the more you'll benefit from it.

Goals and challenges

Setting small goals may seem to be awfully modest, but as you do, and as you achieve them, you'll realise how wise it is. Because then you'll have much more to celebrate, and each goal you achieve will help you shape the next ones.

THIS DAY FOR EVERYONE

Sudden changes are unsettling, and could upset others. Still, there's no question that these are in everybody's best interests. Knowing that, discuss recent developments, not with the objective of keeping everybody happy, but rather with the intention of defusing issues before they turn into problems.

GIFTS Detailed, Perfectionist, Eloquent

NUMBER 9

CHALLENGES Workaholic, Fussy, Worrier

(0+9) + (9) = 18 = (1+8) = 9

It's tempting to speak frankly. But, ages ago, I learnt others aren't always ready for the truth

You

One of the most important skills for you, as a Virgo, is learning to let go. As you well know, you work hard at getting things organised, and coming up with a perfect vision of what's possible. The perfect plan. The perfect solution for a problem. And often, you'll be involved with rescuing individuals who are struggling, helping them sort out their lives.

All of this is important and, in some cases, it may be your job as well. There's a skill that needs to be used to deal with all of them, and that is the skill that comes with saying, 'That's enough.'

It may mean that you've done everything you can, or it may mean that you need to hand over those tasks to somebody else. Yet there's a part of you that finds it very difficult to let go, a certain pride in finishing things, and that's your big lesson. To indeed let go.

However, there's also another reason – and that is when you let go of one thing, quite naturally, the next thing will appear. And that thing that appears will fit in with the skills you've learnt recently.

Adopt that approach, and instead of clinging to what you want to finish, you will say farewell to it, knowing that something wonderful, and something that is perfectly suited to you, is coming your way – probably within the blink of an eye.

You and others

You're modest – perhaps too modest. It's important that you learn how powerful you can be when you need to be. This isn't about explaining what you have in mind, or getting others to do what you think. It's simply a matter of stating the truth.

Health and wellbeing

It's very possible for you to feel guilty, even when you're looking after yourself. Why? Probably because the regime that you have in mind is almost impossible to attain. The trick is to be a little more forgiving, and a little more easy-going on yourself.

Goals and challenges

As a Virgo, and somebody who likes to organise things, you know very well how much you like a list. Yet it's vital that you recognise that the goals in your life will change. Every year, every month, every week and, in fact, every day.

SEPTEMBER

09

V
/
I
\
R
/
G
\
O

Although you're likely to be short of facts about recent developments, that shouldn't keep you from taking action on what you do know. If others say you'll need to organise plans beforehand, thank them politely, but ignore them. With things moving this swiftly, you'll need to think and act fast.

GIFTS Clear-headed, Attentive, Industrious

CHALLENGES Severe, Doubting, Critical

NUMBER 1

(1+0) + (9) = 10 = (1+0) = 1

The joy of anything perfectly done is rare and wonderful. The mystery? So few recognise it

SEPTEMBER

10

V
/
I
\
R
/
G
\
O

You

This may seem an obvious statement, but you've been you your whole life, which means that clear and crisp mind of yours, that observant nature, has been looking at things from the time you were very tiny.

In fact, many Virgo children are amazing at being able to sort out elements of the world around them, long before others. So you've grown up watching the world around you. The trouble is, sometimes nowadays those observations turn into a concern that things aren't being done right.

And this is where it's vital to recognise that, at times, others will want your guidance. But, equally, there are other times when they won't, so it's important to ask. And if others don't realise you could help them, then quietly back off and do something else.

This is very difficult for you, because you really care. But in doing so, you're also using a different portion of your nature, which is actually looking after your own interests, and ensuring that what you're dwelling on is something that is rewarding for you, and is appreciated by those around you. That is one of the most important lessons for you. Often, you've helped those who are ungrateful. Now is the time, not only to share your thoughts and gifts with those who are grateful, but to recognise how valuable your company is.

You and others

Often you're the one who's a guide for others, but there's a big lesson here, and that is to recognise that those around you have ideas and advice to offer you that isn't just good. It could be valuable, if not life-changing.

Health and wellbeing

Of all the difficulties you may face in life, boredom is, for you, the worst. This means it's vital for you to have fascinating activities and challenges around you. At home, that means people you can spend time with and, most of all, that you ensure you have adventures of your own.

Goals and challenges

If you don't have any challenges around at the moment, it's important for you to create a few. In fact, you might always want to have some handy. Things you'd like to do, physical challenges, puzzles you intend to solve, or perhaps even something you plan to paint. Whatever it is, make sure you have it ready.

THIS DAY FOR EVERYONE

As much as you enjoy learning about changes in the world around you and those reshaping the lives of others, you're less enthusiastic about changes in your own life. Yet judging by recent planetary activity, they're unavoidable. Explore what's arisen. You need only learn a bit more, and you'll be thrilled.

To you, a minor but vital correction is just that. Others neither understand why, nor care

You

As a Virgo, you love it when life is in order. It makes you feel like everything is balanced. However, you've also learnt that if things are too organised, and events are too predictable, then even you get bored. In fact, occasionally, you'll let something go or change something, just so you'll have a new challenge.

However, on occasion, it's important for you to broaden your horizons. Take yourself into new territory, where you're dealing with situations or people about which you know little. You don't even know whether you're getting it right or wrong. But that's the whole point of learning in this way.

Also, it's about using a different part of your character, which is inquisitiveness. While you've always been interested in what's going on around you, this variety of learning has to do with an entirely different part of your mind and your spirit: the part that is totally about discovery.

Ironically, many Virgos avoid this because they're anxious about the fear that they won't be able to learn.

On the contrary. Not only will you learn a lot, each day you'll discover new facts. But, even more, you'll discover a new passion in your life – about living, about learning and about how exciting it is to discover something new each and every day.

You and others

Teamwork. It's an interesting word, because often it's useful, if not vital. But it can also be a problem, and hold you back. The issue? It's trusting others. Discovering that alone is one of life's most important insights.

Health and wellbeing

Learning to spot when you're feeling overwhelmed is difficult, because often you're so busy figuring things out, you don't even realise if you're stressed or tired. The trick? It's to take a deep breath every once in a while. And if that feels like an effort, maybe it's time to take a break.

Goals and challenges

It seems natural for you to want to seek the perfect plan or the perfect goal. However, in certain situations, not only is that difficult, it simply doesn't exist. Acknowledging that is the greatest gift you can give yourself, because it turns the situation in question into one of life's most important adventures.

SEPTEMBER

11

V
/
I
\
R
/
G
\
O

Being told you're about to be disillusioned may not sound like good news, but when you think about it, you're trading a fantasy, one that's likely to be disappointing, for real facts. If you're facing any challenge, it's narrowing down your range of options and deciding what you'll do.

Those simple moments when the food is good and the company better are sheer joy

SEPTEMBER

12

VIRGO

V
/
I
\
R
/
G
\
O

You

Every once in a while, you find yourself in a situation where things are so complicated that you know you need to find a solution, and you're seeking the perfect plan. But then you realise that, probably, nothing will work unless you simply allow things to fall apart as they are, then deal with the complaints.

This runs counter to your nature as a Virgo. Yet what it does is it takes you to the deepest core strength, the strongest part of your nature, and allows you to let go of something that isn't working to make space for new ideas. And to experiment and possibly to have to learn something new.

All of this is wonderful – you'll feel better the minute you decide it's the best option. And this is the hard part for you, as a Virgo. This doesn't just have to do with activities, it may have to do with close alliances – with looking after yourself, with a personal crisis.

Whatever the case, this process of discovering what's new isn't just important. It will take you on a journey of exploration beyond anything you've done before. Because previously, you have been in control of situations, but this is about tangling with destiny. It's about allowing destiny to become your teacher in ways that you wouldn't have considered possible, but that you will find amazingly informative.

You and others

Normally those around you look to you to organise things. So when they see you letting things fall apart, they wonder. Actually, you may have the kind of discussion you've never had before with others, in which you learn how to cope with what looks like disaster, but is actually an opportunity in disguise.

Health and wellbeing

There are some situations for which there's a particular remedy. In the situations you will face, the remedy has to do with a single thing. Deep breaths. There's nothing more powerful when it comes to wellbeing.

Goals and challenges

There's nothing better, when you're dealing with goals and challenges, than to simply allow things to unfold, to stand back and let destiny take over. This is more of an art than figuring out a plan. The trick is to know when to step in. That may not be when you expect – and this is the greatest skill of all.

THIS DAY FOR EVERYONE

If you were told you were a creature of habit, you'd probably disagree. Yet you're battling necessary changes in elements of your daily routines. What's more, you're aware how much of a benefit these could be. Consider the possibility that those habits are more dominant than you care to admit.

The greatest Virgo lesson? Spotting those who don't care about getting things right

You

Being an earth sign and ruled by the clever planet Mercury, you're well aware of what works and what doesn't. But those around you aren't – and that's really part of the problem.

When things are going wrong, you're usually the one who points out not only that things need to be done, but also what the solution is. However, clever as you are, there are certain situations where, firstly, things may actually need to fall apart and, secondly, the solution may be you dealing with something else entirely.

It may well be that there's some other area of your life that needs attention, but you've always been so busy with other things, you haven't dealt with that.

This, therefore, is your lesson. It is why you're very good at dealing with certain kinds of crises, yet you're not quite as good at spotting unworkable situations in your own life. Every once in a while, you get a handwritten invitation to deal with.

If you learn to identify those, then you'll also add a skill, which is being able to learn from them and deal with them. The trick is to willingly ask others' advice, even if that feels uncomfortable. That, too, will change your relationship with those individuals from what was tension to a closeness you'd never have anticipated possible.

You and others

Often you take on the role of advisor, which comes naturally with being a Virgo. Yet, every once in a while, it's essential that you not only listen to others' advice, but also that you seek it. It's an important lesson and one that will prove incredibly valuable.

Health and wellbeing

Typically, you rather like a rigid regime. It's because it's well defined and you know where you stand. But every once in a while it's important that you relax. Not so much spoil yourself, as simply live day by day, free of duties and obligations.

Goals and challenges

The single message for you is to set flexible goals. As a Virgo, you like to know where you stand, so you tend to measure your goals by both achievement and the time they'll take. Sometimes you need to give yourself a break, and simply have an idea of what you'd like to achieve – nothing more.

SEPTEMBER

13

V
/
I
\
R
/
G
\
O

GIFTS Orderly, Sensible, Lucid

CHALLENGES Judgemental, Exacting, Finicky

NUMBER 5

$(1+4) + (9) = 14 = (1+4) = 5$

Doing things right seems simple. But you've learnt that others' views differ from yours

SEPTEMBER

14

V
/
I
\
R
/
G
\
O

You

Every once in a while, others come to you for insights or advice about the circumstances they're dealing with.

This is so natural to you that you don't really think about it. Being a Virgo, you have an instinctive ability to analyse situations and view the issues others need to deal with in a way that they don't. However, every so often, you too need to pause, take a breath and consider what's going on.

And that's exactly the case now. Just as you would encourage others to look at things from a different angle, it's essential that you stop. It may not be that you want to ask others for help, but rather that you simply want to pause for long enough that you begin to realise what it is you don't know, what you need to learn or what you need to explore, in your own way.

And in doing that you need to alter your habits, your way of looking at life and even your way of thinking.

Others may tell you that, but as a Virgo you need to figure it out for yourself. And when you do that, you'll have broken a habit of self-sufficiency that often served you but has also restricted you. It will also open your mind and, quite possibly your heart, to experiences beyond anything you would have imagined possible only a short while ago.

You and others

Often, you have a tendency to expect others around you to stay as they are. Partly because they can be rather stubborn. Yet you may notice that they're changing, they're evolving, possibly along with you. In fact, you can share the experience together.

Health and wellbeing

You don't think of yourself as being extreme. However, when it comes to your health, you can be extremely good to yourself, in the sense that you can be very rigorous about what you'll allow yourself to eat and the fitness you're doing. Try relaxing instead.

Goals and challenges

Once you make a commitment, it's a steady one – and you keep your word. That's also the case with the personal goals you set. It's worth reminding yourself, however, that as the world around you changes, you change too – and you can revise your goals as well.

THIS DAY FOR EVERYONE

Sometimes, even the simplest of plans take ages to organise. While that's been the case recently, now and over the coming days things will move with astonishing swiftness. Bear in mind, however, that you'd best have all the details beforehand – because you'll have no opportunity afterwards.

The sheer joy of well-organised luxury may not be lasting, but the memory will be

You

As a Virgo and an earth sign, you're logical – you know that. However, you sometimes forget that others aren't particularly logical, and, more than that, they don't have your appreciation for style, for doing things well, for quality and for beauty.

And the fact is that as much as you may try to explain this to them, it seems they don't care – they actually aren't interested.

They may be interested in other things – in sports or music – but the quality that's so important to you simply doesn't matter to them. This also means, therefore, that if there are certain tasks you may undertake together, it's important that you make space for them.

It's also important that you leave certain things to them – allow them to get on with their good ideas, and focus on what it is you want to do. That seems obvious, but often you feel that it's important you share those tasks.

The trick is simply to do what you need to do and leave them to their own ideas or pursuits without even discussing it. Again, for you as a Virgo, that may seem difficult, but simply allowing people to do what they do naturally will make life a lot easier.

The more skilled you become at that, the easier it will be to live with those individuals with whom there used to be constant tension, if not arguments.

You and others

Tempting as it is to discuss certain situations, there's a secret to making changes and avoiding difficulties and that is, don't explain. Simply make those changes quietly. The odds are good that others won't even notice.

Health and wellbeing

There are times when we all like to work up a sweat, but there are other ways to feel well, too, and in your particular case a little crazy wildness is a good idea. That could mean doing something like dancing off all those excess calories and having a lot of fun at the same time.

Goals and challenges

Every once in a while, you feel it's important to explain to others what you have on your mind and your priorities. The fact is, they don't understand, and they don't care, either. This may sound cruel. But they live in a very different world from yours. Accept that and the rest will be easy.

SEPTEMBER

15

V
/
I
\
R
/
G
\
O

GIFTS Tasteful, Stickler, Natural carer

CHALLENGES Obsessive, Condemning, Exacting

NUMBER 7

$(1+6) + (9) = 16 = (1+6) = 7$

The minute you discover a mistake, you'll remedy it. Puzzlingly, others don't even care

SEPTEMBER

16

VIRGO

You

Some Virgos decide from a very young age what works best in life for them. Whether it's about what works at home, what works out in the world, what works in love – they stick with that philosophy their whole life.

But other Virgos, you included, are inquisitive by nature and regularly change their approach to such matters.

You change your rules simply because every time you do this, you learn something new. And what you learn will then go on to enrich your life.

While you understand this, others don't, and if you're asked by somebody to explain, you're urged not to. Just say that the changes you're making were an idea you had and you'll probably have many more.

And then quietly go off and think more. Because, for you, this process of exploring options is like taking the best kind of vitamins – it's very special. It allows you to be more like yourself than others.

While all Virgos share some characteristics, certain particular Virgos, you included, have a talent for examining life and making the best from it and making every twist and turn count.

Enjoy that, even though sometimes others won't understand why. But it doesn't matter because you're the one who is making the best of every one of those twists and turns.

You and others

Ordinarily, as a Virgo and somebody ruled by Mercury, you'd happily talk things over with others. However, there are moments, and you'll recognise them, when it's best to say less and to simply stick with looking a bit vague about the reasons you made certain decisions.

Health and wellbeing

What's important for you is to recognise that while there's lots of things you can do that are good for you, such as eating certain ways and doing certain types of activity, what brings you joy is quite another matter. Make sure that this shapes what you do. Good health will result.

Goals and challenges

Being told you need to be wary of other people's thinking may seem strange, but the fact is others' standards are very strict and suit them. If they start giving advice, thank them and ignore them – that's the only solution.

THIS DAY FOR EVERYONE

Urgent as certain decisions seem, don't let anyone corner you into committing to something you're not sure about. The problem isn't a lack of options but rather, too many. Explore and experiment. Just ensure others know that that's the approach you're taking and that you'll finalise plans later.

Joy is those golden moments when everybody seems to understand what's needed

You

As a practical earth sign, and as a Virgo, you always know what needs to be done. And when you know there are things that need to be dealt with, you'll also take action – often without discussing things with others.

Yet there are certain situations where you have no choice. And this is where it can get tricky, unless you recognise something. And that is the fact that, while you know what needs to be done, those around you don't necessarily need to hear the details.

In fact, if there is any secret to dealing with this, it's to avoid pointless discussions and debates. Begin to explain and others will quite naturally ask questions. They may even challenge you, even though they don't know what they're talking about.

The trick, therefore, as with so many of these things, is to do what needs to be done and do it all at once, and to keep very quiet about it. If you need support of any kind, find an expert, don't ask someone who is around who is part of your life, your work or your family. Once you become accustomed to taking this approach, life will be much easier.

In fact, you'll find that you're able to relax and enjoy life with those whose company you take greatest pleasure in because they, too, are able to deal with things swiftly, easily – and without drama.

You and others

You may not be aware of this, but you can seem on top of everything, gliding through. Yet, every once in a while, you have a crisis. Ask others for help, but only ask those who are knowledgeable and capable of giving you a hand.

Health and wellbeing

Shouldering everybody's burdens is typical of you – and it's completely unrealistic as well. The trick is to have a joint effort. This doesn't come naturally, and, of course, the most important thing is to ensure that those who are by your side are as capable and as experienced as you are.

Goals and challenges

When you're planning ahead, it's important to anticipate challenges. That may sound a bit negative. But you'll realise that if you line up those who can help you, they'll be there for you all the time – and that could even be when things are going well.

SEPTEMBER

17

V
/
I
\
R
/
G
\
O

It doesn't matter whether the issues in question are personal or involve others, they're unsettling and therefore not easy to discuss. Despite that, the time has come to raise them. It won't be easy, but once you do you'll notice how grateful others are that you had the courage to bring them up.

GIFTS Hard-working, Analytical, Fastidious

CHALLENGES Disdainful, Worrier, Particular

NUMBER 9

$(1+8) + (9) = 18 = (1+8) = 9$

Trust seems simple, so universal. Yet what you expect is entirely different from others

SEPTEMBER

18

V
/
I
\
R
/
G
\
O

You

Ever since you were a very young Virgo, you have been aware of endings and beginnings. That is, endings and beginning in the world around you from the time you could be aware of seasons, but also the endings and beginnings of tasks. Firstly with the grown-ups around you, and then as you began to do things on your own, you realised that everything starts and then comes to an end.

This is wonderful for you because, as a Virgo, and somebody who appreciates order in life, this knowledge is crucial.

In fact, being able to observe this in nature has allowed you to develop the kind of relationship that is so important for you as an earth sign with events like this.

Another side of this has to do with developing what might be described as another muscle of your character – it has to do with being loving and creative. It also has to do with allowing yourself to express those feelings. Whether it's through perhaps cooking for others or doing things for others. Whether it's doing something on your own. In every case those activities nourish your spirit and are a variety of vitamins that are far better than anything you can get out of a bottle. Most of all, enjoy this quality. It's a very special one, and one that comes with being a Virgo.

You and others

You would like to tidy things up with others but there are times when it's important to leave arrangements open-ended – not to say much, not to do much, but to simply watch what happens. In waiting and watching, you will learn a great deal.

Health and wellbeing

When you're feeling stressed, you tend to seek a regime to follow. It may have to do with something you eat, or something that you do, exercise or even something like yoga. While that's good, the most important thing that you can do, being someone who understands nature, is spend time in it, even if it's simply watching a sunset.

Goals and challenges

It's important that you set clear goals for yourself, that are very specific for you as a Virgo. Yet, at the same time, it's important you keep your heart and mind open for the unexpected, because what's least expected could be exciting – even life-changing.

 THIS DAY FOR EVERYONE

Exciting as recent ideas or offers were, they're taking you into unfamiliar territory. As much as you enjoy new experiences, you prefer to undertake them when it's convenient. Now, however, events have made the decision about timing for you, so simply go with the flow. You'll be glad you did.

GIFTS Precise, Organised, Nutrition-aware

CHALLENGES Suspicious, Finicky, Hypervigilant

NUMBER 1

$(1+9) + (9) = 19 = (1+9) = 10$
$= (1+0) = 1$

Sharing life with others is an adventure. Nature's joys are simpler and more reliable

You

The Virgo earth-sign side of your nature enjoys analysing things. It's something you're good at, and it's also something that makes you feel that you understand what's going on. And, to a certain degree, that you're in control.

However, it's also important that you do two things. Firstly, that you learn from experience and, secondly, that you borrow a little of the energy you get from Gemini, the sign that shares the rulership of Mercury with you. And Geminis can come up with a dozen ideas before breakfast.

It's not that you're going to take advantage of those ideas, it's just simply realising that, despite the way you feel, you could do all kinds of things and that there are many options, some of which could be unexpectedly exciting and a few even bizarre.

That, then, will make it easier for you to sit back and relax and let things unfold without you worrying about the outcome, which is the biggest lesson for you.

Because, as you've experienced in the past and soon forgotten, it's what happens at the last minute that can be most important and least expected.

Take that approach and, instead of worrying, you will indeed pause and enjoy what nature has to offer you, knowing that something spectacular is coming your way.

You and others

Your capacity to analyse almost anything is a gift. In fact, others often benefit from it, so they will want you to come along and offer advice. While that's okay when it comes to others, it's also important that you say the minimum about what's on your mind. You know why.

Health and wellbeing

Someone tells you that when you're stressed, you need to get out and about and do a bit of sweating. While there are times that this is true, there are also times when you, in particular, benefit most from not doing. That is, from sitting and being quiet and reflective.

Goals and challenges

When you set a goal, you tend to stick with it, simply because it means a lot to you and, as a Virgo, you will have thought it through. However, it's important that you realise that not only it is okay to rethink goals, actually, often, it's a very good idea.

SEPTEMBER

19

V
/
I
\
R
/
G
\
O

GIFTS Fastidious, Methodical, Tidy

CHALLENGES Fretting, Finicky, Difficult

NUMBER 2

_(2+0) + (9) = 11 = (1+1) = 2_

When you explain plans to certain people, they soon forget. Instead, write them down

SEPTEMBER

20

V
/
I
\
R
/
G
\
O

You

Going through life, as a Virgo, you learn a lot. You learn from experience, you learn from what you discuss. But, also, as you move through life you tend to attract objects – you tend to buy things and to collect things, and each one of them adds enjoyment to your life.

In some cases, a single object will develop into a genuine collection. This might be anything from seashells to some variety of ceramics or, indeed, sports cars – whatever it is that you might be interested in.

However it's also important that, from time to time, you shed both the thoughts that are connected to that collection and maybe that collection itself.

That isn't to say you shouldn't have things around you that you enjoy. Rather that sometimes it's beneficial to consider whether the time and energy you invested in collecting something is part of the past and, perhaps, there is a new future waiting for you.

The simple thought of considering that alone frees you. And for you, as someone who works so hard to make life perfect, that is in itself freeing.

Give yourself the gift of considering the possibility of letting go – of both elements of your past and of physical memories, souvenirs, keepsakes, collections – and you'll find you feel much freer and happier.

You and others

It's useful to recognise that while you may enjoy the company of a lot of people, you actually relax with very few of them. If you need time to chill, time to enjoy yourself, make sure that it's those individuals that you decide to be with.

Health and wellbeing

There's something to be said about having ambitious plans for looking after yourself. But there are also times when keeping things simple is more important. That may mean simple movement, simple ways of eating – or even simple rest and relaxation.

Goals and challenges

As you well know, you have in the past been, and may even be at the moment, distracted by certain obsessions, things you want to do or other desires, ideas or concerns. The lesson isn't dealing with those obsessions, it's learning how to still your mind. That's one of life's greatest challenges and most rewarding accomplishments.

THIS DAY FOR EVERYONE

As much as you enjoy talking over intriguing ideas, ensure others understand that you're doing no more than exploring possibilities. Certain individuals will mistake your enthusiasm for serious interest. Explain that as clearly as you can and you'll avoid misunderstandings, if not hurt feelings, later.

You expect so much from yourself, there's no room for more perfection in your life

You

As an earth sign you're very good at handling practical matters. But being ruled by lively Mercury, you're also an ideas person and can sometimes get so involved in those ideas, those things that you want to do, that you'll focus on that alone and completely forget about the practical side.

The challenge here is to embrace that practical side as well, so you have the time and, when necessary, the money, to pursue ideas that excite you. This is about juggling in a way that you don't usually have to, because in many areas of your life you have what might be described as a golden touch.

You're able to do whatever you do and figure it out well. But there are also certain moments when twists and turns in life force you to look at things from a different angle. Initially, you may struggle, but then you'll begin to see what can only be described as a golden sunrise.

This may be literal, but probably it's a new way of looking at things, one that will be the answer to many of the difficulties you've been struggling with.

Remember that sunrise when similar difficulties arise, and you'll realise that it isn't about analysis, but about allowing your intuition to guide you. That is the answer now and it often will be in the future as well.

You and others

You have a gift, a knack for spotting the skills that others have, sometimes ones they're unaware of. Take advantage of their abilities in the most positive way – ask them to help you, but encourage them to develop those skills as well.

Health and wellbeing

You may not be excited about getting involved in any kind of regime that has to do with eating or fitness, and that's fine. There are wonderful ways to do what you need to do that are called walking, getting out and about, taking deep breaths. All of those are perfect.

Goals and challenges

Often, you'll stop short of polishing off a plan or project just because you like the idea of continuing to work on it. There's a secret, and that's to have several tasks underway at once, each of which is contributing to your life.

SEPTEMBER

21

V
/
I
\
R
/
G
\
O

Libra

September 22 – October 21

Libra Being ruled by Venus, the goddess of elegance, beauty and love, you, as a Libra, have an instinctive style and talent for making others – everybody you meet – feel special. This talent often becomes your career, and those personal links develop into a lifelong passion. Your flower is the rose, your herbs are pungent mint and sorrel and ash and poplar are your trees. Jade, in its infinite shades, is your stone.

L
I
B
R
A

It's possible to say no so charmingly that others don't realise they've been refused

L
\
I
/
B
\
R
\
A

22

SEPTEMBER

You

Born on the 22nd, you are at the very beginning of the sign of Libra. Some would call this the cusp, but actually it's more about the beginning of a cycle and, at the same time, a change in the rhythm of life. Autumn begins in the northern hemisphere, and spring in the southern hemisphere. But, just as much, it's about embracing an entirely new vibe.

It's about leaving the painstaking, earthy Virgo behind you and embracing Libra's expansive nature. As an air sign, you're all about ideas – about the past, the present and the future. Beyond that, it's the perspective that comes with having the scales as your symbol. You will always be seeking balance, in life, with others and in the world around you.

Of course, this brings with it a challenge, and that's the discovery that, however close you are to others, they won't necessarily think the same way you do. You're always confident in creating that accord, and always understand others. Yet nobody, even a twin, is the same as you. However, there's a joy in that, too. The unending exploration of what makes another person think – what makes them tick – and most of all, of the differences between you.

Once you learn to enjoy that, and become skilled at the process, everything else will make sense. In fact, every day you spend around those closest to you will be a joy.

You and others

There are many different languages in the world, and many ways of looking at things, but the most important language to learn is that spoken by those closest to you, whatever their role in your life – whether they're family, friends, neighbours or colleagues. While their words and ideas may differ from yours, the message from the heart will be similar.

Health and wellbeing

The formulas for both looking and feeling your best are infinite and seem to increase every year. Equally, there are innumerable diets and routines that promise to hone your shape and wellbeing. However, being ruled by Venus, the planet of balance, if you follow that Venusian instinct about what's best for you, you'll always do exactly the right thing.

Goals and challenges

Your greatest goal isn't achievement in the world, although that matters to you. It's quite a different one, and it has to do with finding the balance of happiness. This is something very few find, but if anybody ever could, it's you, being born on the first day of Libra.

THIS DAY FOR EVERYONE

The last thing you're in the mood to do is discuss troublesome problems again. What you don't realise, however, is that with things moving so swiftly, these are rapidly being transformed from being a nuisance into events as welcome as they are unexpected. The sooner you get involved, the better.

I can stand up for myself without worrying what others think

L
\
I
/
B
\
R
\
A

23

SEPTEMBER

You

We all go through it, that mission of being on the lookout for a single way of dealing with each day, of dealing with others and, once that elusive goal has been achieved, trying to maintain it. However, with each breath, life changes, and whether you're dealing with someone close to you – a family member or partner, or possibly a dear friend or colleague – each breath alters that relationship with the individual in question.

Still, as a Libra, you cling to the idea that if you can just figure out that formula, you'll be able to achieve the balance symbolised by the scales. Better yet, you hope that you'll be able to maintain it forever – and that is your lesson. You're ruled by Venus, which, on one hand, signifies harmony and balance. But you must also remember that Venus is the ruler of earthy Taurus, the sign that's all about what's practical and what works.

If you borrow a little energy from practical Taurus, you'll stop worrying quite so much about figuring things out and will, instead, focus on the joys of the moment. And, even more than that, you'll allow yourself to enjoy pleasures of many varieties you'd worry about if you were in Libra mode, and will instead embrace them wholeheartedly, as a Taurus would. Learn to combine the two and you'll benefit now and in the future.

You and others

The idea of taking chances in relationships is unappealing to most Libras. And, even worse, the idea of allowing things to go wrong, then possibly explode, is really unappealing. Yet once you allow that to happen, and get through one or two explosions, you'll realise that often those bring you closer than your efforts at harmony would ever have achieved.

Health and wellbeing

Most Libras have a luxury-loving streak. Even if you don't, there's a part of you that really doesn't like the idea of austerity. Yet, every once in a while, you may embrace a routine, a diet or some form of health regime that is tough. The trick, of course, is to be a Libra, and to find the balance between the two.

Goals and challenges

From the time a child is very young, they're asked what they want to be when they grow up – as if any child would know. However, as an adult, you may still wonder what you want to do. The answer is not to wrestle with possibilities, but to reach out, to take chances, to have experiences. There's no better way of learning what you enjoy than by doing it.

If ever there was a time to do a lot of listening, it's now. While you've plenty to say about plans currently in place and changes others are suggesting, there's a lot going on behind the scenes and some of those developments could change things overnight. Knowing that, avoid unnecessary discussions.

Often, winning others over requires charm blended with persistence

L
\
I
/
B
\
R
\
A

24
SEPTEMBER

You

As a Libra, you think carefully about things. Yet this thought process can go through many chapters, each focusing on a different element of a particular plan or passion. This achieved, then the air-sign part of you, the part that enjoys exploring options, begins to wonder if you couldn't improve on that perfection. You may think this to yourself or, equally, you may discuss various ideas with others. Or you may begin to worry.

You're actually enjoying this back and forth debate. This may have to do with something today, or next week, or it may be a different, and distant, concept. Whatever it is, this process is core to you, as a Libra. It's about the deepest side of your nature. But, also, you put pressure on yourself, on relationships and on your activities out in the world – pressure to change and to become more perfect – and solely because of the ideas that are spinning around in your head.

Actually, the most important relationship you have isn't with those around you, it's with those ideas. When, instead of struggling with them, you are able to rein them in – to become their master, instead of wrestling with their ups and downs – they will become your servant. Achieve that, and you'll be able to enjoy your own life, what you do and your relationships with those around you all the more.

You and others

There's a secret to being happy with others, and that's to shift from worrying about them and wondering what a smile means, to simply enjoy the moment. But, most of all, it's about savouring the preciousness of the time you spend with those closest to you, from friends and family to loved ones. Each one of those minutes is a gift.

Health and wellbeing

There are many kinds of health and many kinds of wellbeing, and you can, in fact, whip your body into a perfect shape. But if there's tension on your face, it's a whole different matter. The solution? It's to find joy in life. Do that, and that tension from your face will go, and you'll glow – whatever the shape and size of your body.

Goals and challenges

Others will often interfere with your plans and make suggestions, because they want to be involved. But what's most important is to do what you want to, whatever others say. You may worry about finding a balance – that's the nature of your sign – but in the case of achieving your goals, you come first.

THIS DAY FOR EVERYONE

This is one of those rare periods during which the mood is about turning even complex ideas into plans that aren't just practical, but that everybody is happy about. Knowing this, don't just focus on what's most important or pressing, but also think about those that will shape your future.

If I didn't get what I wanted, it's OK to revisit the issue – and be tougher

L
\
I
/
B
\
R
\
A

You

It's easy to lose track of what you're doing, and even to lose track of your objectives. As a Libra, the sign of balance, and the sign that is powerfully linked to others, it's easy to do this. What's more, it's also easy to be drawn into the behaviour of your opposite sign, Aries, which is ruled by Mars, the planet of individuality, ego and energy, and which can sometimes be so self-involved that Aries folk forget about others entirely.

While this is something that doesn't come naturally to you, it's worth borrowing that Aries self-absorption from time to time. This is about developing a skill, one that's important for you. It's about recognising the balance between you and others – whether you're chatting about something, whether you're silent, whether you're out playing or whether you're working together on a project.

Firstly, note what you're talking about and, equally, who's in charge of the conversation. Then think about what you actually want to achieve, discuss or learn. Finally, recognise that at no time will this exchange of ideas, or any other, ever be perfect.

That's the point of it, and that's part of your journey having being born under the sign of the scales – it's understanding that things are always changing. Once you embrace those changes, you'll enjoy every minute of it.

You and others

As a perfectionist in your relationships, you analyse and often discuss tensions with those closest. While certain individuals tell you not to let things bother you, others advise staging a confrontation. However, this isn't the way you think. You want harmony. And that comes from accepting relationships the way they are.

Health and wellbeing

You sometimes take others' minor comments too much to heart. While they may be actually asking about you, it's possible they're thinking about themselves. Yet the most important person in the world is you – and how much you're able to love yourself.

Goals and challenges

As a Libra ruled by balance, you have a tendency to shift your goals from day to day, at least in your mind. Yet it's important to be flexible and willing to rethink those goals when an opportunity appears. There are times when, to your own surprise, you've simply refused to entertain changes simply because you struggle so much to make plans, but life is like breathing. You must continue to breathe, and you must continue to make plans.

25
SEPTEMBER

Sharing others' joys is wonderful, but having different interests is great, too

L
\
I
/
B
\
R
\
A

Ω

26

SEPTEMBER

You

As a Libra, you have a well-earned reputation for being a charmer. Yet, deep down, within every Libra, lies a troublemaker – a part of your nature you may be aware of, and one that can provoke clashes. Some you battle within yourself, but some are with others, even those with whom you're friendly and comfortable.

There are all sorts of reasons this occurs. Sometimes it's because things are a little dull. However, you'll also use this technique – sometimes unwittingly – to provoke others, to wake them up and get them talking about things they need to discuss, possibly about you and them, but, at times, the focus is on them as individuals and their issues, often those they refuse even to acknowledge.

This is a skill, but as a Libra, it's difficult for you to acknowledge this provocative side of your nature. If it's mentioned, you may deny that you ever provoke anybody. Yet the fact is that many Libras are powerful negotiators, because they know exactly how to throw others off-balance. Whether it's in the realms of law or in government, in counselling or at home, even with friends, it's a valuable asset. But it's made all the more worthwhile by not only acknowledging it, but embracing it as well. Do that, and you will not only understand yourself better, you will appreciate who you are all the more.

You and others

A good debate is always healthy, but actually engaging in one isn't just important. Doing so reminds you of the questions you have, of what's most significant to you and what you admire in others. Most of all, it's about the zest that comes from standing up to those around you.

Health and wellbeing

There are all kinds of workouts. There's a workout in the gym. There's a brisk walk. But there's another kind of workout, and that has to do with being willing to stand up to others. Not that you'll be boxing with them, but in standing up to them, you'll be using the muscle of the mind – a very powerful muscle in your life and in your world.

Goals and challenges

As somebody who is acutely aware of the need to create balance in your life, putting yourself and your interests first can be difficult. In fact, you may even feel you must explain why you're doing it to others. Actually, those closest know how important that is, and they may even have been encouraging you to do exactly that. Put yourself first, and not only will you enjoy it, they will be delighted as well.

THIS DAY FOR EVERYONE

When you took a tough line with one tricky individual, you feared they'd only become more troublesome, but bizarrely, they're calmer and their attitude is far more cooperative. If you're thinking that all they needed was for somebody to draw the line, that's true. The fact is, you did them a favour.

Seeing others happy is heartwarming; being happy with them is even better

L
\
I
/
B
\
R
\
A

You

One of the difficulties of being an idealistic Libra is that, from time to time, you can be fooled by what appears to be the sincere friendship of others. Of course, this isn't necessarily a friend – it may be anybody from a family member to a colleague. Whoever they are, they seem to be trying very hard to make things easy, and instead of being difficult, as others often are, they're easy-going, and understanding. It may even seem they're seducing you into having a relationship with them that you've always hoped for. They are.

And once that trusting friendship has been achieved, they'll turn the tables. Unsurprisingly, this shocks you. Yet it's important to remember that while you, as a Libra, value harmony, not everyone shares those values. And certain individuals regard the ups and downs of relationships as fun, and will trigger excitement and challenges by misbehaving.

How can this be dealt with? Do nothing. Don't respond. Learn from it. And, as important, recognise them for what they are. They'll never change. Instead, busy yourself with those whose company you enjoy, then return to those individuals in question, knowing they will turn around, as they always do. Just as each day the sun rises and sets, certain individuals will behave in certain ways. Understand that, and life will be a lot easier.

You and others

Deep down, you have a conviction that the perfect balance exists in life, and that once it's achieved, you can relax and enjoy relationships with others. But in almost every case, there is a give and take that's very much a part of life. If you achieve that balance, enjoy it, but realise that the rest of the world will probably still need to indulge in those ups and downs.

Health and wellbeing

You tend to swing between not looking after yourself at all and following an healthy regime. But for you, balance is the most important thing, as is the pleasure that comes with self-care. If you can find a way of eating and looking after yourself that gives you pleasure, the rest will be easy.

Goals and challenges

As a Libra, you'll often set goals in relationships – you'll either be influenced by what others are doing, or listen to their advice. This can be risky, because those around you could change, while you'll be stuck with their advice. The solution? It's doing what's most challenging yet essential. And that is putting yourself and your own interests first.

27

SEPTEMBER

THIS DAY FOR EVERYONE

Out of character as saying yes to an offer that's come from out of the blue may be, your instincts are telling you that this is as good as it seems. Better yet, what you learn and experience – and possibly who you meet – will add to your life, and in ways beyond anything you can currently conceive of.

Even the most difficult individuals will always respond to charm

L
\
I
/
B
\
R
\
A

28
SEPTEMBER

You

As a Libra, you're often seduced by the side of your nature that's ruled by Venus, the planet of balance, charm and grace. And you believe that if you can manage to organise things in such a way that your own life and the lives of those around you are harmonious, then things will run smoothly and plans fall into place. While that might actually be the case for a little while, with the world around you changing, as it does, and with individuals changing, as they do, that balance is unlikely to last for long.

And this takes us to the symbol for your sign – the scales. They are designed to shift, a reflection of the way the world shifts. There's day and there's night, and then there are the seasons. And as those shifts take place, they influence the people in the world. So, quite naturally, you need to shift as well. This means that, instead of the eternal balance that you're always seeking as a lasting goal, there's a secret. And that is to recognise that contrast is key – in your own life, in relationships and in the world around you.

When you're able to embrace that, then instead of struggling to ensure things are perfect, you'll enjoy every contrast, from those that occur suddenly to those you expect, between day and night, between winter and summer. Whatever their nature, you'll embrace them wholeheartedly.

You and others

There's a secret to living happily with those around you, and it's to discover the joy in the dramas between you and others – even the joy in the clashes. Once you embrace those, then instead of worrying when someone's upset, you'll treat it as if you were at an opera, where people turn dramas into beautiful music.

Health and wellbeing

While one side of your nature thrives on a routine, whether exercise or eating, there's another side that enjoys change, so much so that if you're too strict, you'll rebel. There's a trick to dealing with this, and that is to go for contrast in each – a week doing one then a week doing another, a day doing one then another, even one type of meal then the next.

Goals and challenges

As important as having a single challenge can be, you also need smaller challenges for each day and week, and a few that are long-term. It may seem strange, but if you come up with a range of challenges that will keep you busy, instead of complaining about life's twists and turns, you'll actually learn to savour them.

THIS DAY FOR EVERYONE

For weeks you've sensed that you'd soon have to alter or rethink certain elements of your life. While these once flowed without a hitch, problems are more frequent, so much so that you'd rather wrestle with the necessary changes and deal with them now than wonder what will go wrong next.

Don't justify your dreams to others. State them simply, no more

Ω

L
\
I
/
B
\
R
\
A

You

Every Libra is familiar with having arguments in their head. A debate about something you might be doing shortly, or did in the past. This type of inner discussion is something that's all too familiar to any Libra, and it can be exhausting, especially because often what you're thinking has absolutely nothing to do with the life you're living or what you'll actually be doing that particular day.

It's a variety of distraction for you, as an air sign – that is, something that occupies you and prevents you from brooding too much, or thinking about things that are dull or, perhaps, issues that you've been avoiding because you have no idea how to deal with them. The most important thing to learn from this, however, is that it's all part of being an air sign, one of the three signs associated with the mind, ideas and imagination. The issue is whether you'll go into what might be described as "air-sign overdrive" and allow your mind to spin out of control. If so, you will miss out on a lot of life's joys. Simply recognising this is a huge victory. Learning to sideline that chatter is even more important. Do that, and instead of facing the challenge of ignoring the ongoing inner chatter, you'll be enjoying each day's precious moments, and the resulting golden twists and turns.

You and others

If you're uptight, if your mind is in overdrive, then put off the discussion you have in mind. Wait until you're calmer. Similarly, if it seems that others are looking for a battle, here too, back off. You have a choice, and achieving some kind of accord comes more swiftly when both of you are in the right mood.

Health and wellbeing

There are many kinds of addictions. We hear lots about sugar and caffeine, substances that overstimulate your mind. But as an air sign, be cautious about the unending and pointless mental chatter. The secret? Busy yourself with other, compelling interests. That will change everything.

Goals and challenges

Everybody asks what you're planning, but often, it's important to think what you're going to do today – to develop what might be called mini goals. A lot of them might be tiny personal aims, yet they're still an accomplishment. Very rarely have there been more worthwhile goals, and very rarely will you have had a greater sense of achievement in accomplishing them.

29

S
E
P
T
E
M
B
E
R

THIS DAY FOR EVERYONE

Somebody has been telling tales, saying things that aren't actually lies, but which have little to do with the truth. They assume that, because these aren't clear-cut falsehoods, they'll get away with it. You're urged to point out that you're aware of these, and you've no intention of putting up with them.

Confrontation only fuels battles, while silent strength defeats them

L
\
I
/
B
\
R
\
A

30

SEPTEMBER

You

The phrase "Be true to yourself" is about an ideal – and it's an appealing one. However, for most human beings, it really isn't possible. For you it's actually a challenge. It's simply because, of course, as a Libra, you are often swayed by others. There's what you have on your mind, yet others could have an entire agenda that's very different from yours. You'll try hard, not only to understand what they want and their demands, but to go more deeply – your hope being to achieve greater insights about their thinking and views.

Your challenge is acknowledging that they live in an entirely different world, and that as much as you would like to share those feelings, you're unlikely to fully understand them. In some cases, with certain individuals – no matter how much of a Libra you are – their ideas will be as foreign to you as if they were speaking another language.

This is the secret of being born a Libra, and under the rulership of the scales. That balance swings back and forth, but you wouldn't have anything to balance if you weren't dealing with individuals who live in a different world, have a different way of thinking and a different set of values and ideas. Once you understand them, not only will you no longer battle being mystified by what makes them tick, you'll actually enjoy the process of coming to terms with that.

You and others

There are many tales – songs, novels, plays – about the swings in close relationships. However, there is a joy in this. For you, as a Libra, discovering that joy is part of the point of dealing with those around you. Once you do that, there may be a little less drama in your life, but there will be a lot more harmony and a lot more sweetness.

Health and wellbeing

You don't think of yourself as a perfectionist, yet when it comes to eating or working out, you are. While some may appeal for a while, there's another option. It's to forget about doing it "right", and simply go for what works in the moment. And when the time comes to make changes, you'll do so without regrets.

Goals and challenges

You have a tendency to obsess over the perfect outcome and how to achieve it. Of course, this isn't unusual. Yet you tend to base your own feelings on the reaction of others. Here's the secret: make what you feel and what you care about most important. Base your goals on that and that alone.

THIS DAY FOR EVERYONE

Only days ago, others were on edge about changes. You were cautious about both questions you asked and suggestions you made. However, not only has the tide turned, but things are falling into place almost magically. A lot of this is a result of the sudden unsettling yet amazingly productive changes.

Ignoring those who are unkind or rude is more powerful than confronting them

01

You

As an air sign, you benefit from the capacity to be amazingly logical, However, you are also sometimes subject to feeling something that is entirely illogical, and that is guilt. This is often the result of a conflict, a sense that you should be doing something other than what you're currently doing – even if you're being entirely responsible or, quite simply, enjoying life for what it offers you.

So the issue isn't what you're doing, but what your mind insists you should be doing, even if it's not possible or realistic. That's what makes this complex issue tough to spot. It's that you're worrying so much about others that you don't pause to think whether those feelings make sense. And that's what is most important. While, it's true, you're an air sign and therefore incredibly logical, there's a part of your nature, particularly when it comes to alliances with others – with loved ones, with family and with partners – where your sense of loyalty to them overrides your logic. Most of all, you feel that if you can make them happy, then everything else will be great.

The lesson now is to recognise those commitments; the sense that you have to deal with your own guilt about others not being happy, and your responsibility to make them happy. In both cases, it's entirely up to them. And for you, life's joys are entirely up to you.

You and others

Following on from the issue of guilt, here's what's important for you to recognise: you don't need to help those around you to be happy. Let them look after themselves. Your job is to be true to yourself. The more real you are, the more authentic you are, the more passionate you are about life itself, the closer you will be to those who matter most.

Health and wellbeing

There are certain individuals who are by nature excessive, and who plunge into things. For you, as an air sign, balance is essential. If you're hanging out with somebody who overdoes it, the biggest gift you can give to yourself is to stop – even if they carry on. Tell them you'll join them later, then take a deep breath and appreciate who you are.

Goals and challenges

These days, the custom is to talk about what you've done, about your successes and disappointments and, equally, your plans for the future. Everybody discusses their goals with others. However, be selective who you talk to. Certain individuals have an ability to undermine the strongest convictions. Learn when to stop. You'll be glad you did.

It's time for a frank discussion with somebody you're close to. So close, you wouldn't think this is necessary. The problem is, that closeness can mean you assume they agree to changes or new plans, when in fact they don't. Talk these through now. The longer you wait, the more complicated it will be.

Standing my ground with those who are impossible requires persistence

L
\
I
/
B
\
R
\
A

02

OCTOBER

You

The subject of making changes is a tricky one for Libras. Not just changes in your own life, but changes in the lives of others – and the fact that, as a Libra, you think all such things through, and in depth. You'll discuss various options in your own life, what others are thinking about, and then, often, discuss them further. As an air sign, while logic is important, that won't keep you from having the same discussion several times.

The trick is to recognise that, as important as these ideas are for you as an air sign, ultimately, if you're going to make changes in the world around you and what you do and think, you need to commit to those changes.

The perfectionist side of your nature wants to get things totally organised, so there'll be no anxiety about this. But, of course, with each day, with each hour, changes arise anyway.

When you recognise that, when you embrace the fact that life, and your world, are constantly changing, not only will such matters no longer worry you, you'll realise this is all about learning something new and important. It's that we all came here to experience what life offers and to grow and change because of that. But also, because it's about what you're learning, you can never get things wrong. If there's a secret, it's to plunge in and learn from those experiences.

You and others

Simply recognise that life is a game of choices; the choices you make, the choices that others make and sometimes the choices you make together. It's difficult because you get so lost in that game. Yet that's the fun of it. However, sometimes it's important to back off, and recognise that you're playing a game. Do that and, instead of worrying about winning, you'll enjoy the process.

Health and wellbeing

Yes, there's eating well, and yes, there is going to the gym. But there's a better way to deal with health problems, and that is to take a deep breath, then take another. As a Libra, you often forget to breathe when you're worried. Try it. It's an easy way to deal with tension.

Goals and challenges

In most of Western culture, there is a win/lose story. That is, the person who wins gets what they want, and the person who loses doesn't get much of anything. Yet there's a better approach, and that's about tackling things together, as a team. That way, everybody wins, and nobody can lose.

THIS DAY FOR EVERYONE

The past few days have been demanding, if not just plain exhausting. Still, looking back on what you've faced up to – and have mostly managed to deal with – you should have a sense of accomplishment. Better yet, the decisions you've made will last longer than you imagined possible.

Complaining is satisfying but achieves little, while charm can do wonders

L
\
I
/
B
\
R
\
A

You

The word commitment is an important one for you as a Libra because, of course, as an air sign, getting things figured out is vital. It may have to do with life, with love, with goals, with work – or with how you live with a passion.

Whatever the case, that commitment requires a lot of thought and a lot of discussion or, at least, so you think.

However, there's an easier way to deal with this, and that might be termed very "un-Libra". It's a way that has more to do with ignoring discussions with others – and ignoring gathering the facts – and feeling what goes on deep within when you think about a certain activity, a certain pursuit or a certain individual. It may have to do with, indeed, what you're going to do for a living if you work. It may have to do with a certain relationship. Or, it may have to do with what brings you joy or love.

The key is to feel what's going on within, and instead of debating what will happen should you take action on it, simply take that first step without turning it into a major plan. Then take the next step, and the step after that and the one after that, and so on.

Instead of wasting time, effort and quite a lot of energy on debating, you will learn from life itself.

You and others

There is a solution for tensions with others, and it's to talk. Not about what's on your mind, or about an idea or a solution, but to let that talk wander, let it take on its own life. Do that and you'll soon discover why it matters so much that you achieve an accord with the individual in question, and then achieving that accord will be easy.

Health and wellbeing

We all know what we should and shouldn't eat, and how we should exercise. But there's not much about how to eliminate anxiety. And, as a Libra, this is important, because it influences so much else – when your mind rampages, or focuses on worry, The secret is simple. It's to decide where you'll allow your mind to go.

Goals and challenges

The trick here isn't to figure out a formula, but to question whose goals you're following. Are they yours, or are they somebody else's? If they are somebody else's, the next step is to get rid of them and to figure out what you care about most. Do that and everything else will fall into place as if by magic.

03

OCTOBER

After a tricky couple of weeks in which you've had to compromise, not always willingly, suddenly things are coming together. This isn't just an improvement. It's worth revisiting certain of these recent tricky matters and discussing the possibility that arrangements could be reviewed.

GIFTS *Elegant, Committed, Agreeable*

CHALLENGES *Irrational, Diffident, Unavailable*

NUMBER 5

(0+4) + (1+0) = 5

Those who think they've a right to be rude can be trained to behave

L
\
I
/
B
\
R
\
A

04

OCTOBER

You

The words yes, no and maybe are unhealthy for you. Of course, you can't stop using them. Yet they come into conversations with others where you're trying to figure something out, and while you're trying to achieve a firm yes or a possible no, others keep saying maybe, which drives you crazy. For some Libras, this kind of debate isn't just important, it's actually a part of your life. It may even be something you do for a living.

At the same time, you often come across those who seem to make a career out of complaining – not a professional career, but who do it very frequently – and when they complain not only about you, but about the world around you, it's hard to tell them you just want to back off.

Yet that's what you need to do. You may not say those words but, as a Libra, your obligation to yourself is to be aware of what you are putting into your body and your mind. While you may eat well, if you hang out too much with those who are constantly doing the yes/no/maybe routine, it is like eating a variety of toxic food.

Once you back off, you're doing yourself a favour by putting yourself and your interests first, which for you is always a challenge. Do that. Not only will you feel a lot better, you can pat yourself on the back for having done it.

You and others

Sometimes, it's difficult to acknowledge how others really are, but this is an important point for you. Certain individuals are argumentative while others are actually bullies. Once you know that, you'll also realise how important it is to draw the line with them. The healthiest thing in the world you can do is to politely say, "I've got to be somewhere else," and leave.

Health and wellbeing

Tension can be a problem for a lot of people, but ironically, for you, it can be a hint that you're hanging out in a situation that isn't in your best interests. If you're feeling uptight, if you can't sleep, if you're restless, think not so much about your body, but about our mind. It may well be that you need to go on a diet, but a diet that cuts out certain people rather than certain foods.

Goals and challenges

As a Libra, you're a planner by nature. But what if you just plunged into something, not only without a plan, but without any rules at all? What if you simply just see what happens? For some Libras, it's a wild and crazy idea, but for you, it will be incredibly helpful.

THIS DAY FOR EVERYONE

Pivotal decisions are pressing. Although your views may seem clear, mostly because they involve matters you've dealt with in the past, so thought about in depth, there's more. These are more recent events, some of which seemed important at the time, but have actually changed everything.

It's possible to confront somebody without them knowing it

L
\
I
/
B
\
R
\
A

You

Your ruling planet, Venus, is the planet of beauty and of balance but, interestingly, not of joy. So when you're trying to create that perfect life, you won't always naturally assess what can and will bring you joy. Also, when you're with others, you won't always think about who lifts your spirits and who leaves you feeling empty. You may notice that certain individuals make you feel uncomfortable, but you can't quite pinpoint why. That's because you focus on keeping things flowing, ensuring everybody is happy with what's taking place and the company of others.

While, obviously, this is crucial, it's not so much because you need to do something right away. Rather, it's about recognising that, despite your best efforts, certain situations, and individuals, will be tricky. You need to ensure you're providing yourself with backup, in the form of people and circumstances that bring you joy. Whatever it is, ensure it will boost your spirits. This could range from activities you love or things you do in nature, such as being with animals.

This will provide a variety of emotional vitamins that are very important for you as a Libra, and someone who is sensitive and generous by nature. Make this change, and should those joyless situations arise, you'll be able to deal with them.

You and others

It's easy to fall into a conversation comparing things: comparing your day, comparing your vacation, comparing a meal you had, and also comparing your life. There are those who, no matter what you say, will always top what you've done, until you begin to feel that, somehow, you're a bit of a failure. That has nothing to do with you and everything to do with them. By no means is their life joyous. They just enjoy making others feel unhappy.

Health and wellbeing

There is a trend these days for those who are looking after themselves to live a fairly austere life. That is, to give up one thing or another because it's good for you. While that may be the case, less is not more. In certain situations, a little more may be what's needed. For you, ruled by Venus, indulgences aren't just worthwhile, they are valuable.

Goals and challenges

Have you been battling to achieve certain goals but getting nowhere? Don't alter what you're doing. Instead, pause and think whether, (a) you really care about them, and (b) whether actually there's something else you'd rather be doing. There may be other things that are dearer to your heart.

05

OCTOBER

THIS DAY FOR EVERYONE

It's clear that one particular individual is trying to use guilt to corner you into doing something that you'd otherwise refuse outright. While you're usually tactful about such matters, you're tempted to confront them. Don't. They'll never admit to what they're doing.

I have every right to say a firm no to unreasonable demands

L
\
I
/
B
\
R
\
A

Ω

06

OCTOBER

You

As a Libra, and somebody ruled by the gracious planet Venus, being in the midst of those who are unhappy – people who are combative or even those who just simply can't seem to get on with things – is difficult. This is because you want the best for everybody, and if you see someone struggling, you feel you must help in some way. It's natural for you.

However, it's vital that you recognise there are certain individuals and certain situations where others' problems are theirs and theirs alone to deal with. Their difficulties and even their pain are not your responsibility.

Acknowledging this is a challenge, because you have a need to look after others, to show interest in them and do what you do can. So putting your own interests first isn't just out of character – it makes you feel uncomfortable, if not plain selfish. However, there are times when it's vital to recognise that your values and needs come first. This variety of Libra balance can be one of the most challenging for you to spot and understand.

This is especially the case when you're around people who are addicted to their own dramas. You know that about certain individuals, yet you're still drawn to them. The secret to dealing with all of them is to tell them you're sorry they're struggling, then say you've got an appointment elsewhere.

You and others

At times, it seems as if your role in the lives of others, and theirs in yours, is fixed. In some cases, if it's family or somebody you work with, it is. In others, it's negotiable. In fact, in certain relationships that might be termed toxic, it's essential you negotiate. In many cases, make changes before the day is over.

Health and wellbeing

There are many ways to recover from life's difficulties, but perhaps the most important one is to have a good time. That may seem unwise, especially if you're around people who are struggling, but the best therapy for you is to duck out of those situations and do something that lifts your spirits and makes you feel glad to be alive. If you have to go back to others' problems, you'll return to them in a much more positive mood.

Goals and challenges

It's very easy for those around you to change the past according to what suits them, and they begin to include you in their story. Saying, "No, that's not what happened at all," may sound argumentative, but in certain situations, it's not only wise, it's essential.

THIS DAY FOR EVERYONE

Somebody seems to have either determined to do things their way or, alternatively, ignored important facts, yet they intend to proceed with their plans. That would be no problem, but inevitably what they do will have an impact on you. This means getting involved. You really have no alternative.

GIFTS Devoted, Fair, Understanding

CHALLENGES Ambiguous, Fluctuating, Elusive

NUMBER 8

(0+7) + (1+0) = 8

Facing impossible people? You can help them learn to be agreeable

L
\
I
/
B
\
R
\
A

You

Are you finding that you're diving into the past? It's easy to do, especially when those around you seem determined to remind you of certain experiences. Chatting with others about them is one thing, yet those discussions often dwell more on what they're are going through than what you have in common.

And this is often a tricky moment for you, as somebody who truly cares about others, but who wants to ensure those relationships are balanced. That is, you're interested in their concerns, yet you want to make sure you get equal time. The trick is to listen to what they have to say, but only so much. Then pause, and broaden it out from you and them to, possibly, a shared experience.

The point is to politely draw a line. You may even need to break away for a while. This isn't about escaping but, rather, allowing you to shift the power in the situation – and the power over your own mind. That is, what's influencing your thoughts as a result of those conversations. As a Libra, you're sympathetic by nature and you want others to be comfortable. But what's most important, particularly in circumstances of this nature, is that you look after your own wellbeing – and not just in terms of your physical wellbeing. This means making very sure that what you're doing and saying is in your best interests.

You and others

You're urged to listen to what others are thinking about so you can begin to organise your thoughts into a clear vision of what you want. It may seem strange to say, but you can't have a dream come true if you don't know what that dream is. This is about exploring that dream, its nature, its promise and its power in your life – for now and the future.

Health and wellbeing

By no means are you rigid in your thinking. Yet, every once in a while, you'll discover that you're so caught up in certain activities, from practices and ways of eating, it doesn't occur to you to do something different. And, as an air sign, it's vital that every once in a while, you shake things up. Not only will you benefit from it, you'll have a good time doing it.

Goals and challenges

The focus is on your dreams. Not plans, dreams that, as you've become more practical, have vanished. Now it's time to revive them. When asked what you're planning, talk about those dreams. Gradually, what you do, the people you encounter and sheer luck will conspire to make them a reality.

07

OCTOBER

Only days ago, you were complaining about having to rethink plans that took a lot of time, thought and seemingly endless debate. Consequently, once they were settled, it was your intention they would stay that way, but events have forced you to make changes. These were timely, if not essential.

GIFTS Compromising, Diplomatic, Rational

NUMBER 9

CHALLENGES Hesitant, Uncertain, Unapproachable

$(0+8) + (1+0) = 9$

Ongoing calm is the result of dealing with issues when they arise

L
\
I
/
B
\
R
\
A

08

OCTOBER

You

Theoretically, as a Libra, you have a capacity for calm, to stand back and observe what's going on in your life, as well as in the lives of those around you and in your world. Yet, at the same time, that Libra part of you can get drawn into the dramas of others, to such an extent that, before you know it, they become your own. Then, you go from being contented with life to dealing with those ups and downs.

Of course, because these dramas are in others' lives, you can't control them. They can begin to undermine your wellbeing. Spotting this isn't easy. And it's tricky, because you think that if you care about others, surely you will care about their feelings. Yet, in some cases, that cool reserve you can cultivate as an air sign is crucial. True you can add some pizzazz to discussions by getting enthusiastic. But that doesn't mean you need to be swept up in their dramas.

This then leaves you time to enjoy what's going on in your own life. Of course, it may be that there are certain things you've been trying to avoid, so others' dramas give you an excuse. If so, tackle those things you've been trying to avoid, get them dealt with, boost your spirits with that sense of accomplishment and then when you returned to others' dramas, it's amazing. They might not seem quite as important after all.

You and others

On occasion, you realise certain individuals aren't good company, but, rather, they are a duty. They're family, business or an obligation. You've no choice. But that doesn't mean it can't be interesting. You just need to ensure they contribute as much as you do to the proceedings.

Health and wellbeing

Nowadays, there's a lot of talk about what you eat, the nature of your diet and exercise. However, your emotional diet is mentioned far less frequently. For you as an air sign, what you put into your mind is just as important as what you put into your body. If you're feeling upset, tired or unwell, maybe it's time for you to look at your emotional diet, in particular who you're hanging out with and who you are letting undermine your spirits.

Goals and challenges

There are lots of good causes in the world. Often it's important to give them a hand, but it's equally important to consider the nature of those causes and how involved you'll get in them. If it isn't your passion and if it isn't your job, then it isn't your top priority.

THIS DAY FOR EVERYONE

If ever there is a time to believe in yourself and what you wanted to do, have or achieve, it's now. Similarly, the tide has turned in your favour, which means sudden and possibly totally unexpected events could turn what are promising ideas into an arrangement far better than you'd imagined possible.

Don't allow those who are negative about life to influence your expectations

L
\
I
/
B
\
R
\
A

09

OCTOBER

You

It's difficult for you to admit, but certain individuals aren't just tricky, they're actually deceptive and will happily take advantage of you. Of course, the problem is that you don't always recognise that. This has happened in the past and it could happen again. In fact, it happens frequently enough that it's important that you recognise these individuals and, once you do, distance yourself from them.

This is the tricky part because, as a Libra, you prefer to believe the best in others. While that's admirable, it's worth taking a hint from the sign next to yours, Scorpio, which can be somewhat suspicious, and recognise that if somebody seems not to be trustworthy, this may be because that's actually the case.

This, too, will teach you not only about those you can trust, but will also allow you to enjoy the company of those you care about and with whom trust has been built over a long period of time, which for you, as a Libra, is one of the most valuable varieties of relationships there are.

Tempting as it is to invest time in dealing with those tricky individuals who are actually manipulative, if not just plain challenging, they should be a sideline. Make those who you can trust and who care about you the main course for your day, for your week and for your life.

You and others

As you begin to study certain individuals and notice their rather tricky nature, you'll also notice how they're adept at changing the rules; how it's OK if they cut things off at the last minute, or even lie to you. Is this how you would behave with someone else? And if you permit it from others, then think about why you spent any time with them at all.

Health and wellbeing

There are many ways to feed yourself. Obviously there's the food you eat and the air you breathe. But, the emotions around you also feed and influence you. This is especially important for you as somebody who's often very tolerant of tricky individuals. They can be exciting but, as you know, they can be toxic and undermine your wellbeing. The solution? Be alert, and put your interests first.

Goals and challenges

You're very accommodating with others, but every once in a while you need to draw a clear line in situations or relationships. It may have to do with activities in your working life, and that clear line is to say what you're willing to accept and what you aren't. If you can make changes, do. If you can't, then get yourself out of the situation in question.

THIS DAY FOR EVERYONE

There are many ways to say the single word "No', and it can have as many meanings. At the moment, it's more about being hesitant than a firm refusal or, at least, that's how you feel. Ensure others understand that, or they'll walk away disappointed and might never come back.

I can simply ignore those who are being moody or temperamental

L
\
I
/
B
\
R
\
A

10

OCTOBER

You

Every Libra has experienced somebody – a friend or family member – expressing concerns about a particular situation or individual in your life. And, worse, saying they think the individual may be taking advantage of you, or that the situation is risky. As a Libra, you'll probably say "Thanks for telling me," and brush it off. Yet, deep down, you've sensed thing weren't right, but hoped you were wrong. However, there's a part of your Libra nature that enjoys imbalance and taking a risk. It's perhaps because being ruled by the scales, if life is too balanced, it becomes predictable, if not just plain dull. This is why you're drawn to dramatic individuals.

However, there's a difference between those who are experiencing dramas and those who have their own interests at heart and enjoy undermining the circumstances of others. That could well be the case. It has been in the past, and it could be again.

The trick now is to think carefully about whether this person reminds you of someone in the past who, in some way, harmed you. That may sound extreme, because you got over it – but would you want it to happen again? If not, the answer is simple: very quietly walk away from that situation and spend time with those you know you can trust, at least for a while.

You and others

As an air sign, you have a quick mind and you're brilliant at analysing situations, but there are those where over-analysis confuses things. The answer? It's to trust your instincts. They will tell you whether what you're doing, is in your best interests.

Health and wellbeing

There are all sorts of solutions for not feeling well. Some say take vitamins, some say have a drink but, actually, for you as an air sign, one of the best remedies is to take a walk. It doesn't need to be a long walk, and it doesn't need to be in the country. Its goal? To allow you to breathe fresh air. The fact is it's not just the air. It's being away from all those things that are a source of concern.

Goals and challenges

Everybody's told to make a list of what they want to do, and it's not a bad idea. However, sometimes goals stay on that list for so long, you end up being discouraged. The secret is to make the list in pencil so you can erase those goals that no longer mean anything to you and put new ones in and without even caring about saying farewell to them.

THIS DAY FOR EVERYONE

You're by no means fixed in your thinking. On the contrary, you're inquisitive about others and the world around you. Yet you assume certain elements of the past are unchanging, and that's not the case. These aren't just in transition. The outcome of those changes could lead to a timely rethink.

GIFTS Friendly, Uniting, Dedicated

NUMBER 3

CHALLENGES Testy, Uninterested, Fluctuating

$(1+1) + (1+0) = 3$

Just as others have a right to demand what they want, I have a right to ignore them

L
\
I
/
B
\
R
\
A

11

OCTOBER

You

If you're into astrology, as a Libra you'll be aware that Venus is your ruling planet, and its influence means you value harmony in both yourself and your relationships. You may be aware that it is also said to rule the sign Taurus, the earth sign, the second sign of the zodiac, which accents what you earn, what you own and the practical side of life.

Actually, many Libras benefit from a great sense of practicality and manage to live a life that is both profitable and beautiful.

However, the earthy side of your nature can sometimes take over and that Taurean stubborn streak – as opposed to the usual kind of negotiation that comes naturally to you as a Libra – means you'll get stuck into a particular ideal, objective or point of view. And as a result, relationships can turn from easy-going exchanges into challenges.

Think about this. If there's a situation of this nature, it may seem that sidestepping clashes is a compromise, but it's actually an important lesson for you.

That lesson is one about discovering why you were born as a Libra and what there is to learn from the skills that come by being a clever air sign, and an air sign whose symbol is the scales, which has to do with balancing things wisely and fairly.

You and others

As a Libra, you love a peaceable situation, but when necessary you're good at standing up for yourself. Except there are moments when it's wise to back off. Remember that, and use the art of compromise to gain a powerful advantage.

Health and wellbeing

Being ruled by Venus, you have an indulgent side. The Libra side of your nature knows that sometimes that's appropriate. You also have an instinct about when enough is enough, but there are moments when you cross that line and too much seems like a very good idea.

Goals and challenges

There's an old saying about choosing your battles, and it's an important one for you as a Libra, because very often your battles will be behind the scenes. It's almost as if they are a fencing match as elegant as it is brutal. Every once in a while, however, it's important to fight another kind of battle, and that is simply saying no. That may be even more powerful.

While charm wins over almost everybody, certain individuals need a firmer approach

L
\
I
/
B
\
R
\
A

12

OCTOBER

You

The question is, have you ever regretted going along with others' ideas or demands? This is always a bit of a push-pull for those born under the sign of Libra, because on one hand, you know very much what you think, but on the other hand, you are a team player.

It's like a game for you – rather like tennis, or even politics, where you have to work with others. It's interesting to note that many Libra politicians use this ploy. They'll get involved, but then they will do something that you may do naturally – that is, say the minimum and watch what's going on.

This is something you can do, and in certain situations, it's something you're encouraged to do – to watch, to learn, to understand about the situation and the individuals involved before you commit.

True, you may be under pressure from others to speak up. This has happened in the past, and it's likely to happen again. The skill is in figuring out the right thing to say. The skill is being able to stand back long enough from the situation, first to decide what your own priorities are, and then to ensure that you know enough about the situations and the people involved to decide what's in your best interests. Do that and not only will you be making a wise move, you will be making the most of the situation in question.

You and others

There's an old phrase that says to keep those close, close to you; to trust them and them alone. However, every once in a while, you venture into new territory, getting acquainted with individuals who have some kind of exotic charm and they become your fascination, your priority. Think carefully, because, at times, that charm can be somewhat undermining.

Health and wellbeing

The message for you is to relax. That may seem easy to do, but as an air sign, while you may appear to be relaxing – that is, not moving around much – at the same time your mind is working overtime. Being able to slow down mentally is quite a challenge, but it's an important one and it's one that, for you, as a Libra, can be a source of discovery and joy.

Goals and challenges

In standing up for others who need help, you're standing up for something you believe in. You needn't make an issue of it. Just quietly express your views, knowing that you're speaking not only for others, but for yourself.

THIS DAY FOR EVERYONE

It's tempting to stand your ground against somebody who has been pushy and in ways that make you uncomfortable. While their manner may make you uncomfortable, their intentions are good, and once you overcome that irritation, you'll realise that actually, they're very good company.

GIFTS Steady, Understanding, Doting

CHALLENGES Scheming, Obscure, Standoffish

NUMBER 5

(1+3) + (1+0) = 5

I refuse to listen when others complain that I'm not making them happy

L
\
I
/
B
\
R
\
A

You

As a Libra, you were born under the sign that symbolises harmony. But at the same time, you can get so caught up in disharmony, if not clashes, that you forget about that harmony, and those clashes, those difficulties, those facts that just don't fit together, can become almost an obsession.

Even more, there are certain individuals who thrive on that and they may draw you into a kind of relationship that is powerful for you, for the Libra side of your nature, yet is ultimately undermining.

You like the passion. However, the more you learn, the more you will realise that this variety of passion actually serves others, not you. More than that, it throws you off balance. Yet disentangling yourself can be difficult, simply because you worry that you'll upset others, which is a very Libra concern. The solution to this, whether it's a minor issue or something more major – or even something that you've committed to – is to simply walk away.

You can give an explanation if you want – or not. Those who you're walking away from will fully understand why you are doing that. And, even more than that, they'll respect you for looking after your interests. That, alone, is the most important thing – deciding what's good for you and acting in that manner.

You and others

As a rational Libra, there is a part of you that can be sensible, but you can also be so swept away by feelings about a situation or an individual that you take things too much to heart and don't even pause to think about the rational side of that commitment. The lesson is to think first, and commit later.

Health and wellbeing

If you're being advised to eat differently, to exercise differently, to sleep differently, that's probably good, but actually there's one thing that you can do, particularly if you're stressed. That is to breathe – and to breathe deeply. Do that and you'll be amazed how much better you feel about what's going on in your life.

Goals and challenges

Every once in a while, it's important to pause and consider whether what you're putting first is actually your own interests. While there's nothing wrong with supporting those around you, consider whether their dramas are truly worthwhile. This may seem cruel, but acknowledging it will free you to focus on something that is worth your while.

13

OCTOBER

THIS DAY FOR EVERYONE

On rare occasions, an idea or offer appears almost magically. While there's no question that it's worth pursuing, it would involve a serious change, not only in some element of your life, but also in your attitude about one particular activity or pursuit. Still it's worth overcoming those objections.

There are many ways to raise contentious issues; some seem like a compliment

L
\
I
/
B
\
R
\
A

14

OCTOBER

You

When those around you ask for your help or assistance, you'll usually extend it right away, and then pause and think about whether there's something you can really do that's helpful. Ironically, certain individuals are so good at drawing you in that, before you even know it, you're part of what might be termed their mission when, actually, what they're doing is entirely for their own interests and not only won't help others, it may even be undermining them.

The trick for you, as a Libra, is to stop and question this. Not only that – and this is the difficult part – but to walk away from the situation without discussing it with the individuals in question. That may seem dishonest, but it's actually the only way to deal with this. Once you've learnt it, it's a vital skill to make part of your life.

While relationships are important, individuals who are manipulative in that way must be recognised – and dealt with in precisely that manner. This, then, is about doing something that is essential for you, which is putting yourself first.

It sounds very new-age to say it's about loving yourself, but it is exactly that. It may take a while for you to recognise that walking away from situations is about loving yourself, but if ever that were the case, it is now.

You and others

The message for you is to choose your friends carefully. That may sound silly, but as you know, in the past, you have aligned with certain individuals who seem friendly or who you feel you're able to help, only to discover that they are in some way devouring your time, your money or endangering your heart. Recognising that can be challenging, but it is one of the most important gifts of all.

Health and wellbeing

It's very chic these days to follow a rather strict regime. However, for you, as a Libra and somebody ruled by Venus, the planet of beauty, the message is to eat wisely and well. You need treats, and your Libra nature that craves balance will tell you exactly how much of those treats you need and when.

Goals and challenges

For some people, no matter how much you do for them, it isn't enough. Help them, give them money or support or make introductions, and they'll want more but show no gratitude. The trick? Do nothing. Say a silent thank you to them for teaching you an important lesson. Then quietly but firmly walk away.

THIS DAY FOR EVERYONE

Facts may be facts, but this is one of those times during which twists and turns and circumstances will raise questions about both existing arrangements and the plans you're making. Bear in mind that the changes you're facing are ongoing, which means that any decisions must be flexible.

GIFTS Amiable, Diplomatic, Dedicated

NUMBER 7

CHALLENGES Unavailable, Manipulative, Touchy

(1+5) + (1+0) = 7

Certain individuals are intimidating, but you can outwit them with kindness

L
\
I
/
B
\
R
\
A

15

OCTOBER

You

Certain individuals live their lives in their own self-created castle and they think that you should feel honoured if they decide to share their fantasy existence with you. Be wary of this, though, because this fantasy, this game, is very seductive. For you, as a Libra, as an air sign and somebody who's imaginative, you can be drawn into their fantasy world, while gradually they make it a real world, and even begin to exercise some control over you.

This variety of seduction is appealing to your Libra nature, partly because perhaps it allows you to escape from certain rather dull and more mundane situations you're facing in your everyday life.

Yet if you can manage to take a look at this castle of theirs and think, "That's a romantic vision, but my everyday life offers me rewards of a more lasting nature," then you'll be able to look at them and say, "Thank you for those insights. However, I'm going over here to my everyday dilemmas, and my everyday joys and my everyday friends. And I'm going to appreciate them all the more because of the rather toxic fantasies you've just exposed me to."

And then, as you live out your days and your weeks, you'll be very thankful for having had that brief but illuminating adventure.

You and others

The theme for you is to learn who is fortunate and who is trustworthy. That may seem strange, but actually those individuals who are trustworthy and fortunate don't always advertise it, they just live a life that may be very simple, but happy. Notice that and spend time with those individuals. This is a variety of contagion that is a welcome one.

Health and wellbeing

Doubt is an important emotion. Sometimes people are criticised for it because it makes them hesitant, but often that hesitation is an invitation to explore, to gather information, and sometimes if you do, then you'll proceed. But in other situations, that doubt is telling you that you need to learn something. It may be that it's either time to back off or possibly even time to say a firm no.

Goals and challenges

We all have to deal with challenges, to face what is often an uphill climb, but in every case, doing it is an achievement. The important thing for you is to recognise that and not allow others to pretend that what you achieve is in any way due to their inspiration. What you've done is 100% yours alone.

GIFTS Constant. Rational, Agreeable

CHALLENGES Ambivalent, Distant, Wishy-washy

While joy comes in many forms, being happy with my own company is best

L
\
I
/
B
\
R
\
A

16

OCTOBER

You

As a Libra, as you well know, you're ruled by balance, the symbol of the scales, and while it looks static when you see a picture, by nature it swings. That is, the balance is never stable.

Yet, at the same time, you tend to feel that if you can just get things organised, they will indeed be unchanging. That not only is impossible, it actually means that you struggle with something that is preventing you from venturing into new territory and from taking chances in a way that won't just be interesting, but will add to your life.

This belief is preventing you from taking advantage of the swings that are part of being a Libra. It's preventing you from taking advantage of meeting new people and doing things that may be a little bit risky, but which will benefit you. And as you do these things, you'll be meeting new people and adding to your experience.

As an air sign, sometimes you figure things out in your head, but you don't always connect up the experiences you've had with what you've envisioned.

This process of plunging into things carefully but still taking chances will lead to experiences that, in every case, will not only add to your life, but they will add to perhaps your passions, your joy and possibly even to your wallet.

You and others

One of the most important lessons for you is to note those around you who seem to enjoy life's shifts. While many will complain about even a minor change, others will detail the twists and turns in their own life and how they're benefitting from them with enthusiasm. Make these individuals your best friends, if not your colleagues or your partners.

Health and wellbeing

Tempting as it is to search for a regime that you'll follow, it can be difficult for you as an easily distracted air sign. The actual point of looking after yourself is to be flexible. In fact, it could be said that any regime is unhealthy, because it means you're not aware of what you're doing. If you're learning something new, then not only will it be interesting, you'll be broadening your horizons in every way.

Goals and challenges

For you, it's good to rethink things regularly, because it may be that you could do something better. You could add something to it, or it may be there's actually something else you should be doing. Those rethinks aren't just a good idea, they add a new vitality to your life, to your plans and to your future.

THIS DAY FOR EVERYONE

Some disagreements blow in like a fierce storm, but are resolved swiftly and then forgotten. Those you're currently facing – and there could be several – will seem unimportant, but as the time passes and you learn more, you'll realise just how vital it is you deal with them soon and in depth.

GIFTS Uniting, Thoughtful, Congenial

NUMBER 9

CHALLENGES Detached, Hesitant, Meddling

(1+7) + (1+0) = 9

Others don't have to agree with my feelings

L
\
I
/
B
\
R
\
A

17

OCTOBER

You

One of your lessons in life needs to be borrowed from the sign next to yours, Virgo, which is all about practicality and being down to earth. Of course, some of this is a bit dull for you as a Libra, because as an air sign, you're very thoughtful and, in fact, a bit of a visionary. Yet, every once in a while, it's important to borrow two components of Virgo's nature.

One is their perfectionism and the other is their practicality. If you borrow these, then, when you run into difficulties or you can't seem to weigh up whether something is worth pursuing, you'll use that method of examining things that may be dull and rather overly practical from your point of view, but it will also enable you to make plans that are based on simple, rather uninteresting, yet solid facts. And once you do that, then you won't actually have to think too much more about it.

Borrowing these characteristics will then give you a new freedom to fly in a way that is wonderful for you as a Libra, because in doing that, you have created a firm foundation for what you're thinking about.

This may seem strange to you – and feel a bit odd, and possibly even a bit boring – until you realise just how much you've accomplished. It's a skill that, once learnt, will serve you well and in many settings.

You and others

Getting things organised is great and – while by no means as a Libra are you fixed in your habits – when something works, you dislike having to rethink things. Yet the message for you is to embrace change with enthusiasm, by borrowing some of the practicality of your neighbouring sign Virgo. Once you do, you'll discover how much you can achieve with ease.

Health and wellbeing

The outer world is very much a theme for you when it has to do with your physical wellbeing and how you'll benefit. But when you combine this with the inner world of your ideas as well as your more spiritual side, you'll find that you have a full circle, a globe, which is glowing with activities both satisfying and worthwhile.

Goals and challenges

It's important that you consider whose goals you're pursuing, because, as a Libra, it's easy to get caught up with other's objectives and even their passions. You understand them and you may even want to support them. Yet the question is, what's happening to your own passions? Every once in a while, you need to review whose passions are number one.

I find that giving love is actually easier than receiving it

L
\
I
/
B
\
R
\
A

18

OCTOBER

You

Every once in a while it's easy to get caught in a vision of life that's all about how-to goals. That is, how to plant a garden, how to cook. There are rules about all of this, and while those are reassuring, for you as a Libra they can actually be restrictive.

It's true that certain plants benefit from pruning, and obviously certain meals benefit from being cooked in a particular way, but when it comes to your life, it's vital to ignore those rules and trust another part of your nature. This has to do with the wisdom that comes with being a Libra and someone ruled by Venus, the planet of beauty and charm, and also of abundance.

This means ignoring those rules and trusting what your heart and your soul say and, even more, trusting your instincts and moving past those formulas.

Once you do that, the odds are good that you'll spot something that inspires you, or recognise what you're already doing is amazing, yet you've been ignoring because it doesn't seem exciting enough – because all those things you've been hearing about seem more promising. But they're promising for other people, whereas for you the trick is to spot what lifts your spirits, then commit to it with a wholeheartedness that allows you to turn those ideas into miracles.

You and others

As a clever Libra you're good at figuring things out, but there are certain individuals whose charisma enables them to seduce people into following them, just because they're so exciting. That may be the case, but what appeals to you personally is more important every passing day.

Health and wellbeing

When you feel full of energy and optimism, if others begin to prescribe things for you because they think you should have a different variety of energy, thank them very much. Then follow what your own heart, soul and body tells you. There's no better reference for what's in your best interests than you and you alone.

Goals and challenges

We all talk about what we're doing, about what excites us and about our plans, but when did you last think whether what you're passionate about still matters to you? When did you last dismiss something that seemed rather exciting because you were so bound up in passions from the past? There's no one answer, but these are questions that need to be asked regularly – and dealt with in depth.

THIS DAY FOR EVERYONE

There's a fine line between sidestepping troublesome issues and being dishonest. Obviously, you'd prefer to avoid clashes. However, consider this – the insights that result from talking over those tricky situations frankly will more than justify the risk of having to live through and deal with a few dramas.

Whether its personal or anonymous, kindness can be life-changing

You

For you, as a Libra, the idea of making a final plan is very appealing. There are two reasons for this. Firstly, as you will know, you have a tendency to debate certain ideas back and forth, sometimes for a very long time, until suddenly it all falls into place. But at the same time, you want things to be right. You hate it if you set out to achieve a goal, then discover that you forgot something.

However, there's another approach. That is to make final plans, but to make them with the knowledge that, with each day, life changes. In fact, with each breath you change, so the idea of anything being final is bizarre.

If you understand that, then you'll also understand that with each breath you alter your chemistry. The world you're living in and what you're doing, and your ideas and even your mind, evolve moment to moment.

So this idea of things being final may not make sense. Instead think of the best option for the moment. Even more than that, this allows you to explore what comes your way so that if you do have some sort of final plan, that doesn't mean you can't explore something else. In fact, that final plan and your new plan may even meet and turn into something amazing. Take that approach and you will make the best of each month, each day, each week and each hour.

You and others

Relationships are important to you, and while you can focus on achieving an accord, it's also important that you recognise the people in your world are different. So, inevitably, the links with each of them will differ as well, and that is your lesson: to realise that while some alliances will be very proper, others will be rather rock'n'roll.

Health and wellbeing

The debate about what to eat has become a bit of a trend – it's something that becomes a conversation when no one else has anything else to talk about. Yet it's also important because you will listen to others' advice and take it, where actually what's best to do is what you feel is right on the day.

Goals and challenges

Every once in a while, people want to talk about the biggest goal and the most potential in any situation. While that's appealing to you, you also have a sense of proportion, and while biggest is impressive, it's not always best. You don't need to discuss this with others. When deciding what you're going to do with your life, ensure that goal suits you perfectly.

19

OCTOBER

What began as a minor misunderstanding has turned into a seriously complicated mix-up. Tempting as it is to talk issues through now and all at once, it's not that simple. The actual problems go back a long way and will require considerable time and patience to untangle and put to rest.

Mother Nature deserves our love, big time

L
\
I
/
B
\
R
\
A

20

OCTOBER

You

Discussing ideas and plans with others is important, but at the same time it can be confusing. As a Libra and an air sign, what seems your best plan one day isn't the next. Yet, if you chat with others, they'll say, "Oh, but before you said...", and then you'll have to explain to them why changes occurred.

The answer to this is to tell others the absolute minimum. As a Libra, you're not secretive by nature, but if there's a plan you're working on that hasn't yet been dealt with, you might want to think carefully about who you mention it to, especially those individuals who are asking because they're interested.

This is very much about Venus, which isn't just the planet of relationships but also has to do with the wise use of your resources. In every case, pause and think about whether those plans, or even those passions, are worth discussing with others, and whether you actually care about what they have to say.

Once you're looking at your life from that angle, then you'll begin to realise how important your own values, your own vision and your own passions are. And, in doing that, instead of even caring what other people have to say, you will care most of all about those passions being lit up by your conviction that you're doing the right thing.

You and others

From time to time, everybody clashes with those around them, where someone complains about what they're doing, and you think you could do it better. If so, offer to do it. Similarly, if they try to tell you how to do things, let them give it a try. This will reveal the difference between discussion and reality.

Health and wellbeing

The discussion here is about a perfect formula – a perfect way to eat, to exercise, or even to live. Many Libras like to figure that out and stick with it forever. However, you're encouraged to try something new. Trying something out won't just be interesting, you'll learn a lot about yourself as well.

Goals and challenges

The question is, why would you get involved in a challenge that doesn't interest you? Simply because you'll learn from it. If everything you do is fascinating, then it's going to be a repeat performance of the past. Accepting a challenge or going someplace you're not interested in may not work out and you may want to escape right away, which is just fine. But when you do escape, you will escape with the knowledge of the experiences you've had.

THIS DAY FOR EVERYONE

For ages you've sidestepped even acknowledging certain misunderstandings, mostly because you knew paying attention to them would lead to lengthy discussions, but now you've no choice. Unappealing as the idea of talking things through is, once you've begun, it will be a huge relief.

GIFTS Dedicated, Giving, Elegant

NUMBER 4

CHALLENGES Uncommunicative, Elusive, Uneven

$(2+1) + (1+0) = 4$

Anonymous love is love at its most genuine

21

OCTOBER

You

For you, Libra, as somebody who is right next to the sign of Scorpio, you share a bit of that science, depth and focus and, in fact, that tendency for obsession that Scorpios have.

As a Libra, when you obsess about something, it's all in your head, because, of course, you're an air sign. But the Scorpio variety of obsession is deeper and more persistent, and also one that, when you're committed to it, is hard to get rid of.

But then on the other hand, what you learn when you're dealing with this kind of deeper, darker approach to life will be incredibly informative for you. And this is your challenge. It's to enjoy both sides of your nature, even if one seems a bit strange, odd or overwhelming, but then it's rather like encountering an amazing scent, or having a meal that's so fragrant, that the aroma alone it is exciting.

What you're learning now, from yourself and from sharing both sides of your nature – the rather careful, measured Libra side and the passionate, possibly even overwhelming Scorpio side – won't just enhance your life and increase your wisdom, it will also enhance every day, getting up in the morning, in the middle of the day and in the evening – and every hour you spend doing what you love with those you love.

You and others

As a Libra, you like to agree with others or absolutely disagree. The idea of having a sort of a truce is very strange to you. That's because you're ruled by balance – the scales. Yet this part of your nature is important, because it understands not balance but simple passion, and the more you experience that passion, the more exciting life will be.

Health and wellbeing

There are lots of formulas for health and lots of diets to follow and exercise to do. Yet there's a whole other variety of treatment for health that comes from simple joy. That is, from knowing life's stories, and from breathing it in, whether it's from nature or a connection with something divine that has touched you. The more you are linked to that joy, the better.

Goals and challenges

You have a tendency to worry that if you get something wrong, then it's really a problem. But life is a big experiment, and if you take chances – ordering something you've never eaten before, falling in love with somebody new – it's an experiment. And the experiment itself is bound to be profitable.

Certain individuals seem to be in a rush to turn the plans being discussed into action. While you're eager to get things going, your instincts are – correctly – telling you you're short of facts. If you must discuss how things will be organised, do so, but stop short of any kind of solid commitment.

Scorpio

Ruler Pluto
Element Water

Symbol The Scorpion
Flower Rhododendron

October 22 – November 20

Scorpio Compelling by nature and style, as a Scorpio – whose symbol is your namesake, the scorpion – you beguile with your mystery as much as by what you say or do. Whatever your chosen field, your insights will be unique and your capacity for intimacy compelling – perhaps influenced by your ruler, Pluto, who reigns in the underworld. Your flower is rhododendron, your spices are peppers and your plant, blackthorn. The mysterious opal mirrors your alluring secrets.

Sometimes listening but saying nothing is the best option

S
/
C
\
O
/
R
\
P
\
I
\
O

22

OCTOBER

You

If there's any theme for your birthday, it can be summed up in the phrase "endings and beginnings". That's because your birthday continues winding up of one season – that is summer in the northern hemisphere and winter in the southern hemisphere – and the move into another – the emergence of autumn in the northern hemisphere and spring in the southern hemisphere.

But it's also about a battle between the ruler of the previous sign, Libra, which is Venus, and your own ruling planet, Pluto, or, indeed, Mars. In every case, this is about contrasts.

Still, as a Scorpio, you prefer to live life with grace and clarity. When these challenges arise, you'll tend to stick with the familiar rather than allow unsettling changes to confuse things. However, as you'll increasingly realise, often those changes aren't mere changes. They're breakthroughs that are taking you in new directions. That's very much the theme for your birthday.

While the fixed sign side of your nature is a mark of stability – and it means you know what you can expect and what others will expect from you – the greatest expectation at the moment is your willingness to begin to explore, even if it means venturing into unfamiliar territory. Once you do, you'll not only know why, you'll be glad that you did.

You and others

There have often been times in the past when you've tried to avoid the ups and downs of life. Yet as you've lived more, you've found those ups are exciting, while the downs help you understand the nature of your deepest feelings far better than you ever imagined possible, so much that you may even begin to embrace them.

Health and wellbeing

An affection for a healthy regime is great because whether it's how you eat or a form of exercise, it means you're looking after yourself. Yet, if it's a compulsion there's a problem – you haven't included joy. Find a way to add that and not only will you feel and look great, you will blossom in your heart.

Goals and challenges

The question is whether it's worth setting higher goals and taking a risk that things won't work out. If you're in doubt, think back to when you faced a similar dilemma and went for it. You took a chance. And not only did you do well, you did better than you expected and had the bonus of experiencing a tremendous feeling of victory. Take chances now and you'll have the same benefits.

THIS DAY FOR EVERYONE

You've been battling with certain individuals about what seemed to be important details. Now, looking back, you're beginning to realise that you were sidestepping the real issue. Deep down, you know what it is. The challenge is raising it. Once you do, everything else will be easy.

GIFTS Magnetic, Scrupulous, Trustworthy

CHALLENGES Paranoid, Extreme, Bitter

NUMBER 6

(2+3) + (1+0) = 6

Being true to others can involve love, or loyalty, or both

S
/
C
\
O
/
R
\
P
\
I
\
O

23

OCTOBER

You

As a Scorpio, you admire those who are able to focus on their goals and to stick to that. It's something you value. You're embarrassed by those who plunge into something without planning and, as a result, suffer – or at least from your point of view they do.

Yet, as you've discovered watching those individuals, while they're floundering around and experimenting and making mistakes, they learn a lot. They learn things you wouldn't have learnt had you been following the careful path. When you hang out with them, you learn things that benefit you, too.

In a way, you're both of these. One part of you wants to focus on a direct goal and achieve that without being distracted. Yet another part of you, the part that's an intuitive water sign, recognises that the more willing you are to be what might be termed seduced into trying something new and to venturing into unfamiliar territory – whether it's personal, involving relationships, or your activities out in the world – the more you'll learn and the more you'll benefit from what you're doing.

Allowing yourself to grow in this way is one of the biggest challenges for you as a Scorpio. And as you actually begin to thrive as a green plant does in a garden, it will be one of your greatest joys.

You and others

All relationships – with family, friends or even colleagues – involve a balance between people who are quite simply different, with a range of ideas of how things could be done. Your tendency is to correct them, so they'll do things the way you know works. However, often they ignore you and have a better way of doing things than you've ever envisaged.

Health and wellbeing

You used to dislike eating certain foods because of their texture or flavour. Now, you're beginning to realise that times have changed, you've changed or perhaps even that food has changed. Similarly, there are elements of your life that you said you would never enjoy. And now you find yourself doing them and having a fabulous time.

Goals and challenges

There are a number of phrases that could follow the words, "I've always wanted to…", but haven't, because you've found various excuses. This is the golden moment for you. The minute you transform those excuses into an opportunity, your life will become far more exciting today and each and every day.

One of life's skills is predicting the future based on the past

S
/
C
\
O
/
R
\
P
\
I
\
O

24

OCTOBER

You

There are those who say that, as a Scorpio, you argue when changes are suggested. From your point of view, when you manage the conversation, if not manipulate it, it's because you know what you're willing to do and what you're not. When others suggest things you have no intention of doing, you will simply but politely change the subject.

However, what they're suggesting may be interesting – partly because you simply never paid attention to it before, or because their enthusiasm about those activities or ideas is contagious, and you're beginning to wonder if instead of sticking to your own views, you might actually benefit from trying things out.

This is a turning point for any Scorpio, and it's one that you will encounter again and again. Because Scorpio is what is termed a fixed sign, you are a creature of habit. Once you get into a habit, budging is difficult.

This is why these breakthroughs are so important. They allow you not just to make changes, but to make discoveries – discoveries about the world around you, about the people around you and, probably most importantly, discoveries about yourself. You'll embrace a new perspective on life and its possibilities – but, most of all, about what you personally can achieve now and in the future.

You and others

For you, micromanaging seems normal – watching what's going on and, if you see things veering in what appears to be the wrong direction, pulling them back. However, as you're increasingly aware, that means doing things in the same old way again and again. And not only are you getting a little bit bored, you're realising that there is a wide world of adventurous experiences waiting for you.

Health and wellbeing

The idea of a regime is appealing, especially when it comes to looking after yourself – how you eat, when you get up, when you exercise, and, even to a certain extent, what you think. However, it doesn't give you a lot of freedom. The more you realise you can have fun if you take chances and venture into new territory, the less appealing that regime will be and the more appealing an adventurous life becomes.

Goals and challenges

You like to know where you stand. However, with the world and the people around you changing, it may be better to be a little less clear about your plans and a little more inquisitive, especially when the unexpected arises. It could be that what is least expected today becomes your best friend tomorrow.

THIS DAY FOR EVERYONE

Nobody would blame you for telling a particular individual how much of a nuisance their last-minute changes to plans are for you. Before you say anything, however, do a little investigation. You may well discover those changes weren't their fault and they're as unhappy about them as you are.

GIFTS Conscientious, Deep, Powerful

CHALLENGES Fanatical, Ruthless, Crushing

NUMBER 8

(2+5) + (1+0) = 8

Accepting others' shortcomings isn't easy, but accepting my own is another matter

S
/
C
\
O
/
R
\
P
\
I
\
O

25

OCTOBER

You

As a Scorpio, you have a tender heart. You're a water sign, and water signs are more sensitive than others. Of course, you are ruled by the powerful Pluto, so you have a great deal of focus. Yet there are many Scorpios who work in areas that require tenderness – from being involved in fashion to actors, artists and writers. Whether famous or not, a large portion of their nature is involved not in following some objective achievement, but in expressing something more artistic.

That's true of you too, and it's an essential part of your nature. It's also vital to your relationships with others. It may be that not everyone understands this, which is what's tricky because, of course, not everyone else is a water sign. And even those who are water signs don't always understand the importance of this soft side of life and of your nature.

However, the more you understand it and the more you share it and discuss it with others, the deeper this will become. Not only will it become an important part of your life, it's something that will become an increasingly important in the lives of those around you. In that sense, you'll not only be improving your own existence, you'll be improving the existence and wellbeing of others and, even to a certain extent, the world.

You and others

Being open and vulnerable about feelings can have a cost. In certain situations, others will be grumpy or difficult, and you might regret bringing things up. That is, until the individual in question begins to tell you how much what you said to them meant, and you'll realise there are few things more powerful than talking about your feelings.

Health and wellbeing

We're all told stories in childhood about what's good for you and what isn't. Yet there are certain things you decide as an adult you don't like. The time has come for you to dump all of those stories and decide what feels good to you, in terms of both what to eat and what to do, and to benefit from the joy that comes with making those choices.

Goals and challenges

There are two kinds of goalposts that can be put up when it comes to goals and challenges. The kind you see in the playing field are planted firmly on the ground. They are the sort that many people live with. However, as an intuitive water sign, it's important to be aware that you could move your own goalposts, so what's most important to you, whatever you do and achieve, brings you joy.

THIS DAY FOR EVERYONE

Sometimes obstacles are just difficult situations that need to be overcome. But what you're currently facing is an invitation to delve into and learn about an increasingly tricky matter. While the actual process might be challenging, what you discover will more than justify the effort required.

Often others misinterpret my silence as agreement, but that isn't so.

S
/
C
\
O
/
R
\
P
\
I
\
O

26

OCTOBER

You

For you as a Scorpio, the line between what is private and spoken – that is, what you don't discuss and what you talk about easily – is very clear, or at least it's clear to you. However, that line actually moves from day to day and even from subject to subject and mood to mood. Yet, at the same time, if you're feeling uptight or concerned, a part of you gets very grumpy and asks, "Why would I talk about that to anybody else?"

There are those around you, though – it may be a family member, it may be a close friend, or it may be somebody you trust – who you will reveal more to than anybody else. Gradually, as a Scorpio, one of your journeys is being able to discuss these matters more openly with family and with friends, so they understand you better, but also so that you can begin to realise how long they've known and understood everything anyway.

This is the key to being a Scorpio among those who love you. While you think that you're hiding deep, dark secrets that nobody understands, the fact is they do. They're just being patient with you, because they've known you weren't ready to talk about things. The more swiftly you begin to discuss both concerns and your heartfelt passions, the more swiftly you will be able to enjoy time with those closest to you.

You and others

There are many different kinds of intimacy with others – not so much physical intimacy, although that's important – but how much you trust certain individuals. Just as the Moon goes from the sliver of the New Moon to the Full Moon and back to the sliver of the New Moon, so, too, your feelings of trust evolve.

Health and wellbeing

These days, there's constant discussion about what's good for you foodwise. But how do you truly know what's good for you? Well, as a Scorpio and someone who's highly intuitive, you can probably ask your body how it feels when you eat something. That will tell you far more than anyone else ever could.

Goals and challenges

Setting goals and acting on them is important. There will be those who tell you that the minute you're clear about a goal it's important to act on it, yet a part of you as a Scorpio and a fixed sign tends to wait. Then sometimes you wait too long and the moment has passed. How do you know? The best answer is to ask yourself whether you'd regret not plunging in right now. Usually that will result in you taking action right away.

THIS DAY FOR EVERYONE

Unsettling as recent events seemed at the time, you're beginning to recognise that they were breakthroughs. True, these weren't in the form you've anticipated and could take things in worryingly unexpected directions. Be patient. The more you explore and learn, the more optimistic you'll be.

Loving myself means being true to my desires, despite others' demands

♏

You

You were born at the season of the year, if you're in the northern hemisphere, which is autumn, and if you're in the southern hemisphere, during spring. In both cases, it's a time when the natural world is making changes. For you as a Scorpio this is important, because you often feel responsible for organising things. Yet when you observe nature, if you have a garden, or even if you're in the grocery store just looking at what's available, you'll realise that nature itself changes, and changes what it offers. In the same way, you, too, are a creature of change.

You don't think of yourself that way. In fact, many Scorpios work hard to be consistent. But, as a water sign, you are an individual with tides – tides of passion and tides of enthusiasm. Returning to that symbol of nature is not just about nature itself, but about what you take from it, how you eat and what you enjoy.

When you walk in nature, each of these changes are important because the more aware you are of the way that the natural world around you evolves, the easier it will be for you to deal with the changes that come into your life; changes that might be unsettling initially, but which are beginning a new cycle, one that will ultimately bring you joy in new experiences and discovery.

You and others

As a Scorpio who tends to be rather private, the idea of discussing doubts is unappealing. True, if there's someone you trust, you may do that. However, the more you talk about these feelings, the more you realise these doubts and worries are actually very normal indeed.

Health and wellbeing

Getting out and about and doing something to feel good is wonderful. As a Scorpio and a fixed sign, you'll tend to stick with one thing until you get really good at it. While this is tempting, it's also a fantastic exercise of another sort to try something else, and then to try something else after that, in order to exercise the muscle of growth, development and discovery.

Goals and challenges

In the past you dismissed certain objectives because you weren't quite sure you could achieve them and, as a Scorpio, you hate the idea of failing. Now, however, you've become inquisitive enough that these seem less worrying. Not only are they possible, but the potential for learning how to do them is more accessible. Take a chance and give them a try.

27

OCTOBER

Somebody has decided to point the blame for certain problems in your direction. Tempting as it is to hope everybody's well aware of the facts, you're urged to stand your ground. Mostly, this is about making it clear to the individual in question that you won't tolerate any such manoeuvres.

Generosity comes from the heart, not the bank account

S
/
C
\
O
/
R
\
P
\
I
\
O

28
OCTOBER

You

For you, as a Scorpio, the difficulty of hanging out with others is that there are things you want to share only with certain individuals. When those around you are asking questions, you will sidestep them, because you feel that either it's none of their business, or they won't understand where you're coming from.

Actually, is they probably would understand. It's just that you are so careful about who you share things with that you don't want to let them know what's happening. Part of your journey as a Scorpio is to respect the sensitivity that's so much a part of your nature, but also to share the part that is very perceptive with those who will appreciate that.

Gradually, you'll acquire a new viewpoint. It will remove many of those barriers to sharing things with others, but will also teach you to do something you never would have expected to be able to do with others, and that's have a laugh – about the ironies of life, and about how concerned you were about being open. After that, you will find that there's an entirely new way of relating.

You may have to do it again and again in different ways with different individuals, but each time you do this, you'll recognise that it's a skill you've acquired and one that brings you a new richness, intimacy and friendship that you hadn't previously thought possible.

You and others

The question is, how much do you want to tell others? You don't realise how secretive you are until certain individuals ask perfectly ordinary questions that you regard as probing. If you're uncomfortable, discuss it with them . You'll soon realise the reason they're asking is they simply want to know more about you.

Health and wellbeing

There many formulas for health and wellbeing, most have to do with what you eat and the vitamins you take and even the order in which you take them. It's true, feeling well is a skill. Once, people simply aged and slowed down. But nowadays it's about how you feel each day. For you, those feelings of wellbeing are perhaps the most important varieties of vitamins you could take.

Goals and challenges

Every once in a while, you probably make a list of your goals. If you don't actually put pen to paper, as a Scorpio, they will be very much in mind. However, it's important to recognise that some of your goals may be relics from the past. So before you begin to write down goals for the future, let these go.

THIS DAY FOR EVERYONE

While you're easy-going about most situations, there are a few you have strong feelings about. Tempting as it is to take a strong stance, at least explore what's come up or what others are suggesting. At minimum, you'll learn something, but what rises could prove to be unexpectedly exciting.

Little is more rewarding than changing another's life, but discreetly

S / C \ O / R \ P \ I \ O

You

Every so often, you face a situation in which you realise you've completely lost your perspective and can't figure out what to do with certain tricky individuals. Then you realise the issue is your desire for control. In fact, as a Scorpio, you were born under the sign that is perhaps the most analytical. Also, being ruled by the planet Pluto, which wants all the facts, you feel that if you can just learn enough, you will have control.

However, the irony is that the more you delve into life, the more you realise that no matter how many facts you gather, circumstances themselves will reshape the situations you're dealing with. But not only that, they will reshape your priorities too. This doesn't just have to do with those rather tricky situations. It has to do with life itself and with those you care about, with close relationships, with your passions, your personal passions and passions involving others.

Once you recognise that, in many cases, you have very little control, you can set a goal or objective. But then you need to yield to it.

You'll also find a new joy in being alive. With every breath, instead of worrying about things going your way, you'll simply enjoy the fact that you're breathing – because you're living out yet another day, a day that's full of promise.

You and others

Every so often, you struggle with a situation simply because you want the other individual to do what you want. The problem is that you haven't discussed it openly with them. While those born under the sign of Scorpio are brilliant at manipulating others – and can convince those around them to do what they want –often it's far easier if you simply ask.

Health and wellbeing

Many Scorpios have a physical health routine and a diet that they follow closely, often for years. However, you are always changing and evolving, and even though you believe you are being true to yourself, that is, to the values you keep, every cell is being replaced over time and so, too, must that perfect formula.

Goals and challenges

It's appealing to have a single clear goal. But why would you do that? The fact is, there's a big world out there waiting for you to play with it, waiting for you to come and try out new things. The first step is the most challenging one. After you've taken it, the world will embrace you with plenty of unexpected opportunities.

29

OCTOBER

Few things are more disheartening than having resolved tricky issues, only to have something similar spring up from nowhere. However, you're in a period that's about dealing with these measures one by one. Tedious as that seems, each that you tackle will add insights that will make the next easier.

GIFTS Insightful, Dedicated, Determined   NUMBER 4

CHALLENGES Apprehensive, Unapproachable, Hurtful   *(3+0) + (1+0) = 4*

I will always review every option before going back to the familiar

S
/
C
\
O
/
R
\
P
\
I
\
O

30

OCTOBER

You

One of the things you may or may not be aware of as a Scorpio, is that in 1930, the ruling planet for your sign changed. For most of history, Scorpio has been said to be ruled by the planet Mars, the planet of action, the athlete, the warrior. Then Pluto was discovered, and it became the ruler of Scorpio.

Now, as a planet it's been demoted, but it's still considered to be the ruler of your sign. And Pluto adds a different colour to being a Scorpio, because it's the planet of secrets. Not just secrets as in things that aren't said, but also the kind of secrets that give you power. The Roman god Pluto was considered to be the ruler of the underworld. He knew what no other being could, whether they were a god or a human. Having that complex mythical background, you, of all the 12 signs, have probably the most rewarding journey of self-discovery, but also one in which you go deep within to understand yourself and the world, more than anybody else.

This freedom to explore is important. At times, others won't necessarily understand what you're experiencing, but a few will have a bit of Scorpio in their nature. And when you begin to talk about the depths of awareness that are so much a part of the journey that comes with being a Scorpio, you will find you have a kindred spirit,

You and others

As a Scorpio, you have a greater understanding of others than most. Remember this, because when others complain about situations where you see a solution immediately, you'll have to explain it slowly to them. This will give you compassion, but it will also give you a depth of perception very few benefit from,

Health and wellbeing

As much as you would like to be given a single formula about how you eat and look after yourself, it isn't that simple. Times change, you change and even your body changes. Once you recognise that, as an inquisitive and perceptive Scorpio, you'll enjoy the process of discovery that each of those changes takes you on.

Goals and challenges

Every once in a while it's worth reviewing your goals. Of course, circumstances change, but also, what you've learnt and what excites you is changing. And the more swiftly you grow, the more swiftly those intriguing developments will change. You have the gift of inquisitiveness when it comes to setting those goals, so not only will you discover a lot, you'll enjoy the actual process of discovery as well.

THIS DAY FOR EVERYONE

Ordinarily, when facing an obstacle you'll confront the situation. Only if that doesn't work will you ask for advice. Now, with Mercury accenting questions, you'll find that you're missing vital details. The more swiftly you seek the guidance of others, the faster you'll get things back on track.

Being willing to admit when I've missed something important isn't just wise, it's vital

S
/
C
\
O
/
R
\
P
\
I
\
O

You

The fact that your birthday is on Halloween, or All Hallows Eve, the day before the Day of the Spirits, means that you benefit from an awareness of the two worlds, of the everyday world – something most Scorpios are good at handling – but also the world, not merely of spirits in the Halloween sense, but our inner world, our own spirit, our own nature. And finding a balance between this is so important, especially because we're in a period during which there's an emphasis on the practical and scientific side of life. Your co-ruler is Mars, the planet of action.

You dislike hanging around too long and hearing people talk when you could simply go out and gather facts. All of these sides of your nature come together to turn into someone who is inquisitive, and who enjoys discovery, it's you. These discoveries aren't necessarily about the world around you, though you could go travelling. They're also about what make us tick as human beings, what make us feel what we feel, what bring us both anxiety and joy.

For many Scorpios, that's an important part of your life and journey. And especially for someone born on October 31st. Recognise that privilege and how much you've learnt from it. Not only will you be fascinated by each day, you will enjoy it as well.

You and others

While you benefit from a fascination with the complexity of life, not everyone does. Certain individuals, even those you're close to are unwilling to talk about those ideas, and are sometimes even spooked by them, while others enjoy going on and on about it. It won't be easy to guess who are the ones you want to talk to most, and who are the others you'll leave for times when you're chatting about everyday matters.

Health and wellbeing

As a Scorpio, you are strong, but as a water sign, you can be influenced by the mood of others and your own moods. So it's important to look after yourself physically, but also to undertake activities such as yoga or perhaps one of the Chinese martial arts that builds your energy, wellbeing and resilience.

Goals and challenges

It's rare anybody thinks what they're doing is in the hands of the gods. And it isn't necessarily literal. But sometimes it's worth declaring what you'd like to do, standing back, and seeing what the gods deliver to you. For you, as a Scorpio, who's usually out there making things happen, standing back and seeing what comes your way could be exciting.

31

OCTOBER

THIS DAY FOR EVERYONE

For ages, you've worked hard to turn one particularly promising idea into a plan and hopefully a lasting arrangement, but not only are things not going well, the plans are falling apart. Don't worry. Let them go. Something is already on the horizon that will be far less of a struggle.

I've learnt how dangerous saying "I'll try" is. Either commit or forget it

You

Being born on November 1st, particularly in the northern hemisphere, means you're looking at matters of light and dark – in the world around you, the shorter days and the longer nights. But also, there is light and dark in the terms of your own nature. As a Scorpio, and somebody ruled by the planet Pluto, part of you understands that elements of life either can't be explained, or you need to step back and allow the power of nature to take over.

Yet, at the same time, another part of you wants to ensure that things go in the direction you want, and this is part of the battle of being a Scorpio. At the same time, however, it's crucial for you to stand back and recognise that often what you regard as ideal may not be in the best interests of you or the world around you, those who you care about, or perhaps a project. It may be that you are being taken on a journey of discovery. What you encounter, or learn, as a result of that journey will benefit you in wonderful ways, will broaden your horizons and may even help explore the dark. You'll realise that by allowing yourself to be taken on that path through the darkness, you'll reach a different kind of light. And that light will be the kind that will illuminate your life, now and over the years to come.

You and others

People say you're perceptive and, increasingly, you realise how true that is; that there are certain things you notice that others don't. And that capacity to spot more than others means that often you will not only be explaining things to certain individuals, but you will become their defender or their guide.

Health and wellbeing

There's part of you that believes if you can figure out what you should do – that is, how you should eat and how you should work out – everything will be fine. However, ups and downs are normal, just as there is day and night. Your energy will have its own surges and times when you need to be still. The most important thing is to honour those cycles.

Goals and challenges

Your goals are almost set in stone, because that's your nature. Has it ever occurred to you that if those goals aren't working out, or in fact, if the circumstances in which they're set are shifting, it's fine to change them, even to change them in midstream, or to dump them? Give that some thought because, every once in a while, it will be the best possible strategy.

THIS DAY FOR EVERYONE

Sometimes mistakes are a nuisance, but often they're minor, and dealing with them requires little thought. While those you're currently facing are more complex, what you learn in the process of untangling them will answer questions or allow you to delve into issues you've been wrestling with for ages.

Truth is absolute. But that doesn't mean I have to tell everybody everything

You

As a Scorpio, you have a tender side. You're a water sign, and of all the water signs – Cancer, Scorpio, and Pisces – you are perhaps the most perceptive. This gives you a nature that is able to notice much more than others. And in fact, many of those born under your sign use elements of it. They may be artists. They may be performers. They may write. While some do it professionally, others do it simply as a way to use that intuitive part of your nature. But also, it's a part that relates deeply to others, to those who also have a deeper and more intuitive side. You also connect with those who have no idea about their own feelings, and you can become a friend, a guide and, in some cases, a sort of guru to those individuals.

But even more important is exercising what might be termed your imaginative or your creative muscle, which is allowing that part of you that is a visionary grow, so you can experience it deeply. Not just in helping others, although that can be very rewarding, but to do it in a way that is yours and yours alone.

If it involves creating something, perfect. If it involves others, also perfect. But the point of this is to recognise that, whether it's on your own or with others, it's a very personal journey which is dictated not only by your needs, but your joys.

You and others

There's a question that it's vital you ask – and that is, who do you trust? Also, which individuals do you trust with your feelings? Sometimes, you may feel a connection with somebody, but that doesn't mean they should be honoured with the trust of your deepest feelings. Think carefully.

Health and wellbeing

These days, we pay attention to what we eat, and to exercise. But not as much attention is paid to the kind of thoughts we put into our minds. Or the kind of spiritual energy we hang out with. There tends to be an emphasis on science, yet the less material, more intuitive side of you as a Scorpio is just as important, and one that is essential you pay attention to.

Goals and challenges

Have the goals and challenges you're facing truly been chosen by you, or are they the result of the thinking of others? It may well be that those individuals have your best interests at heart and also are highly intuitive, or it could be that they're simply telling you to do what they would have done. This is an important question, one for you to reflect on now and to think about often in the future.

02

NOVEMBER

S
/
C
\
O
/
R
\
P
\
I
\
O

Being lovingly faithful to others is important; being faithful to myself is essential

03

NOVEMBER

You

There are two sides to every Scorpio. Basically, there's the focused Scorpio, who is ruled by Pluto and tries to be invulnerable. They may even be a fighter in whatever arena they're in, as the influence of your original ruling planet, Mars, the warrior, comes in. You'll stand up for whatever it is you feel is important.

Yet there is a more vulnerable side to your nature. And even if you are one of those warrior types, there's a portion that is sensitive and intuitive, that understands what those who are not as strong as you are facing. And at times you may feel that vulnerability.

This is the important thing for you to understand, because when you allow yourself to feel that vulnerability, you are incorporating it into your own being, which means that you'll understand others better. Also, when you're close to somebody, it makes them feel comfortable, because they are aware that you know and understand how vulnerable they are.

It may sound strange that the stronger you are, the more vulnerable you're able to be. But this is one of the great paradoxes of being a Scorpio, and a water sign, in a period during which force is so overwhelmingly favoured. The deeper you go, and the more you understand yourself, the stronger you'll be.

You and others

Not everybody understands sensitivity of any kind. And because many people learn to focus on their mind over their feelings, they may not even know if they're happy or not. Be aware of that, and if you're talking to somebody who seems to have absolutely no idea what they're feeling, make a careful decision about how much you'll discuss with them.

Health and wellbeing

Physical wellbeing has to do with having a strong body and eating well. But it's also about having a regime that builds up your sense of balance, that is, your inner being, what some might call your spine. There are many Eastern kinds of training, from yoga to Chinese martial arts, that help, and if you choose one, you'll realise how vital it is for someone of your nature.

Goals and challenges

In a culture where everyone's encouraged to do their best, it can be as important to aim low. As a Scorpio, this may seem strange, but giving yourself the gift of having not too much pressure – at least at certain times of your life – also gives you an opportunity to decide whether what you're pursuing is what you really want to achieve.

THIS DAY FOR EVERYONE

Others are saying you're being stubborn. But from your point of view, certain changes are unrealistic. This is one of those tricky times when it's a matter of sticking with what you believe is best, or relying on those you trust. In this case, go for the latter. Others really do know better than you.

GIFTS Perceptive, Loyal, Passionate

CHALLENGES Compulsive, Forbidding, Suspicious

NUMBER 6

(0+4) + (1+1) = 6

Sometimes silence is a greater kindness than speaking my mind

S
/
C
\
O
/
R
\
P
\
I
\
O

04

NOVEMBER

You

These days, everybody's encouraged to plan ahead. And, in fact, it's a good idea, especially for impulsive types – maybe the fire signs: Aries, Leo and Sagittarius. But for somebody who already thinks things through, and who also will consider a plan carefully, make it and then stick with it, being told that you need to plan ahead is unnecessary. If anything, what you need is the strength and the courage to change plans when things aren't working. And that can be very challenging indeed. In fact, you can spend so much time debating changes that the opportunity to make those changes vanishes.

And this is where it's important that you do something that is difficult for you, which is putting yourself first. One of your excuses for not changing plans is that it will be unsettling for those around you.

However, changes of the sort you often make are a great gift for you and others, simply because, instead of being impulsive, you will have thought everything through so carefully that you and others will benefit from that journey.

In fact, if you recognise that, when the idea of making those changes arise, you're not only encouraged to explore it, you're encouraged to say yes first, and then to think of the details later.

You and others

When it comes to making changes, those around you are well aware that you will think them through. They will often wait for you to make decisions, so they can benefit from your wisdom. You may not realise how important this is. Your capacity to analyse things, and to be visionary at the same time, is an extraordinary gift.

Health and wellbeing

You have a capacity to be too disciplined, and life can become a bit joyless, because looking after yourself becomes a strict regime. This becomes a pain to others, who would love to do something spontaneous but, because you're following your regime, you can't. The trick? It's to take a break from time to time. You can go back to it if you decide to.

Goals and challenges

Thinking about how to overcome obstacles is important for you, but if you spend too much time thinking about it, you may never do it. Simply plunge into something new in a way that might could be considered to be "un-Scorpio". Then, not only will those obstacles vanish, you'll find yourself involved in something as exciting as it is thrilling.

GIFTS Observant, Discerning, Private

CHALLENGES Dominating, Fretful, Unapproachable

NUMBER 7

$(0+5) + (1+1) = 7$

Those who truly know what love is won't try to change us

You

It's rare that you're unaware of what's going on. If so, it's probably because you're ending one cycle and beginning another. This is something you don't often sense, because as a Scorpio, and one of the fixed signs of the zodiac – those in the middle of each season – once you're into a plan, you're really into it. And you can tend to have tunnel vision.

Yet every once in a while, there is a need for things to change. A new cycle is beginning. And the trick for you is to recognise the presence of that new cycle. Not so that you can plunge into it, but so you can begin to make adjustments from the old plan and explore the new one, and the world involved.

When you're able to do that, not only will you begin to enjoy this process of change and discovery, but it will also be helpful, and might even be fun. Better than that, you'll get other people involved. And knowing that you're sharing this process, you will learn together and figure out ways to let go of the past.

This has to do with every area of your life. As much as you would like to think of yourself as being a fixed sign, as living a stable life and having very little change, everybody is in the midst of a cycle of change constantly. The more you recognise that process, and the more you involve yourself with it, the more you'll enjoy it.

You and others

Certain individuals are team players. And once you know who those individuals are, they will be your best friends when it comes to the changes that flow through life – something that you, as a Scorpio, don't always recognise. Make them your affiliates, your coaches, and often your best friends. Do that and, as you approach those changes, you'll not only survive them, but you'll enjoy them.

Health and wellbeing

While you may try to eat right, and do some kind of physical movement, at times, it's even more important to stop. Not as in lying around on the sofa and watching television. It means stilling your mind, and simply being – staring out at a sunrise or sunset, breathing the air, and allowing life to come to you.

Goals and challenges

In this modern world, we're taught to think of things in a very scientific way, and that when they're organised, events will proceed as they are intended to. However, life is based on cycles, and if you look at the heavens and, certainly, the cycle of the Moon, you'll realise the more you honour those cycles, the easier life will be.

THIS DAY FOR EVERYONE

Some time ago, you sidestepped even mentioning certain facts or issues, mostly because they're of little significance. But circumstances have changed, and now these matters are of considerable importance. Waste no time figuring out an explanation. Just inform those who need to know right away.

GIFTS Enigmatic, Probing, Powerful

CHALLENGES Crushing, Neurotic, Injurious

The heart's moods are infinite – but the committed heart never wavers

S
/
C
\
O
/
R
\
P
\
I
\
O

You

One of your greatest gifts as a Scorpio is your capacity to take joy from what others are experiencing and how they're developing. In some cases, you'll be doing that together, which is even better. And this draws you closer, which is something that's important for you, as a sensitive and intuitive water sign.

However, it's also important to recognise that closeness won't last, not because there's anything wrong, but because each of you, and each individual in the world, in fact, lives at their own unique rhythm.

There will, however, be other forms of closeness, because when you respect that rhythm, you are able to enjoy watching others grow at their own rate. You're able to observe yourself, and enjoy the rate at which you're developing. You're also learning about different varieties of closeness, and the different varieties of trust that come with this process of growth and development.

Sometimes it really is all about what you're doing. Sometimes it has to do with an emotional or even a romantic connection. But in every case, it's about doing something that is little discussed or noticed in the world today. And that is, honouring the rhythm of life for each of us as human beings. We're all unique, and we all care deeply, and we all connect, but we all do so at our own pace.

You and others

That ideal of being close to somebody, and feeling everything together, is very romantic. And it's peppered throughout poetry, movies and plays. Yet it is an ideal, and it's an unlikely one. Even twins, born with the same genetic programming, live life at a different pace, simply because they have individual brains. And this is what keeps things interesting, because if you could predict what everyone would do all the time life would be fairly dull.

Health and wellbeing

Vitamins and food are important. However, what is often forgotten is your mood. This is important because it influences how you digest food. If you're in a bad mood or uptight, you don't digest things as well. Your state of mind is important. Pay attention to that, whatever you're eating. Your efforts will pay off.

Goals and challenges

The question is whether what you're doing will be rewarding. Are you sure what you're aiming for will make you happy? Of course, you can't always tell, but does the assumption of others that you'll enjoy something make you believe that you will? There is nothing that proves that will be the case. Your reaction is 100% up to you.

06

NOVEMBER

THIS DAY FOR EVERYONE

Tedious as discussing tricky issues in detail may be, you really have no choice. Once you begin reviewing the actual situation, you'll realise that, first, you need to update your own facts. This could so alter your perspective that you'll rethink your views and, in turn, what you have to say to others.

GIFTS Seductive, Deep, Intuitive

CHALLENGES Vicious, Hostile, Apprehensive

NUMBER 9

$(0+7) + (1+1) = 9$

Putting myself and my interests first may be wise, but can confuse others

You

Passion is very much part of your nature as a Scorpio. That passion, of course, has to do with individuals, but it's also about your approach to life in general. You may notice that those around you rarely care much at all. That passion seems unique to you and possibly those who aren't Scorpios, who have a bit of your sign in their nature. This influences things like relationships, or creative pursuits, yet it also it has to do with your everyday life.

You can be passionate about a job, a particular kind of exercise, about learning to cook or garden. It's essential for you, but not everybody feels that way. And the most important thing for you to recognise is that if somebody seems a bit lukewarm about something yet shows interest, they may be interested in their way. Just because they're not showing the passion that you do, it may simply be because they're a different person. And the more you learn about them, the better you'll understand what makes them tick.

This journey of understanding how others are may seem a crazy one, but at the same time, you will learn what might be termed the human language. That is, how to deal with those whose way of living is very different, yet who bring something wonderful to life – just like you do.

You and others

An important way to learn about life is to learn from your experiences. And hopefully you will have learnt from them and won't repeat them. Instead you may want to take chances with people and in situations that are completely unfamiliar and an adventure – yet will, for sure, prove to be an education.

Health and wellbeing

Many people take how they live, eat and exercise very seriously. And it's a good idea to know what nourishes you. But there's another approach to this. And that is to do things for fun, especially when it comes to exercise. You can adopt some kind of dancing that is so bizarre that it can only be a laugh.

Goals and challenges

When you run across something that brings up memories – of difficulties or challenges, of things didn't work out that well – it should highlight what you shouldn't do again. But there's something to be aware of – that is, the past. Circumstances have changed and so have you. And maybe what didn't work then would work now, because the fact is, the world has changed – and you've learnt a lot.

THIS DAY FOR EVERYONE

While the issues you're dealing with may be significant, there's also a funny side to them. And viewing what you're facing with irony or even humour won't just boost your spirits, it could also bring an entirely fresh and unexpected approach – one that's helpful to the matters in question.

GIFTS Sharp, Scrupulous, Fervent

CHALLENGES Fanatical, Grudging, Distrustful

NUMBER 1

(0+8) + (1+1) = 10 = (1+0) = 1

Circumstances may shift gradually, but loyalty remains unchanged for life

S
/
C
\
O
/
R
\
P
\
I
\
O

08

NOVEMBER

You

As a Scorpio, you pride yourself on being a logical individual. And it's true. Many Scorpios are. In fact, sometimes you're so logical that you rely on the past to assess the present, even though circumstances have changed. With the world around you changing, your viewpoint changing and the individuals you'll be talking things over with changing their viewpoint too, basing decisions on discussions alone could actually be unwise.

So, if you're making a decision what do you base it on? As an intuitive water sign ruled by Pluto, the planet of truth and vision, you may be better off relying on your intuition, at least initially. Then, once your perspective is clear, you can discuss your ideas with others, even those who tend to dominate the decision-making process. Approach these exchanges with reshuffled plans. When you're shuffling cards, the point is to mix them up. This is important because, when organising changes, you could unwittingly create a new version of what you've done before.

However, it's time for you to approach certain elements of your life in a very different manner than in the past. Your aim? To achieve a balance between sticking with what you know and exploring ways to make changes when it seems you've no options. You'll be amazed by what you discover.

You and others

Look around and you'll recognise the world itself is changing so much that sticking with what's familiar will only complicate matters. Instead, take a chance on something quite new and you'll benefit, far more than you imagined possible. But then that's the point. This is all about discovering something new.

Health and wellbeing

You know what works for you and stick with it. Once, that was wise. But the world's changing and you're changing, more than you realise. This means being more flexible in your way of living and even thinking. That allows you to ride out the dramatic changes reshaping your world. Better yet, you won't just accommodate those changes, you'll enjoy them.

Goals and challenges

Success is measured in different ways. From family and friends to colleagues or an employer, and then your personal take, the range is huge. However, it has to do with whether you're enjoying life and whether you are headed in the right direction. Ask those questions and changes will be easy to make.

S
/
C
\
O
/
R
\
P
\
I
\
O

09

NOVEMBER

Friendship is wonderful, family are crucial and a trusted beloved is like gold

You

Here's a question: is joy earned? Is it magic? As a water sign, you tend to think that feelings just happen. Yet, at the same time, as a Scorpio who reflects deeply on things, you realise that those feelings, those moods, have a lot to do with what you do and even how you eat. They also have to do with how you organise your life. That is, your job, if you go to one, and how you plan your day. But another component is those who you spend time with and if those individuals support you.

Of course, we can't always be around people who are great fun or supportive. Yet you can make a point of spending more time with those who think the world of you, and so boost your spirits that it balances out the influence of those who are less positive. But what may be most important in a period of growth is realising that what worked in the past may not work in the present or the future. And that journey is very much part of this period of discovery. What's more, this isn't just about you. Ideally, those around you will be equally aware of their own challenges, and are looking after their own wellbeing. If so, then discuss your experiences with them and share the ups and downs of your journey. Of course, it's different for everyone. But we can all learn from each other – and add to each other's journeys the wisdom of our own.

You and others

It may seem a strange question, but who do you trust? Think about this. Generally, family members come as they are, some trustworthy or supportive, and others not. However, there are also your friends. Consider, whether they're more trustworthy; you've chosen them, so they should be. This awareness is important for everybody, but especially for you as a Scorpio.

Health and wellbeing

The big question is why do you eat? Well, of course, you're hungry, but there are other reasons. Sometimes, you're peckish or, possibly, it's a celebration. Aim to combine those feelings when you eat and you'll turn a meal, even a quick one, into a joyous experience, often to be shared – and the more you'll enjoy every single meal you have.

Goals and challenges

As a Scorpio, you're one of the stable, fixed signs of the zodiac. You have a gift for sticking with things. While this is an asset, you'll sometimes struggle to find a new approach to challenges. But you don't always spot this. Add inquisitiveness to your armoury of insights, and even the greatest obstacles will be easier to deal with.

THIS DAY FOR EVERYONE

The last thing you're in the mood for is a lengthy discussion about an already complicated issue. Much as you're dreading this, the individual in question has realised they've got their facts wrong, but they're too proud to admit it. Be patient. Gradually, the truth will emerge, along with a timely apology.

GIFTS Sensuous, Devoted, Committed

CHALLENGES Compulsive, Covetous, Threatening

NUMBER 3

(1+0) + (1+1) = 3

Chatting with those you trust isn't just wonderful, it's a divine gift

You

As a Scorpio, you have very clear thoughts about circumstances and certain individuals, but you won't always express your concerns, simply because it seems pointless. It doesn't help. It will confuse things. And, unless you've good reason to put your foot down about certain matters, you may shrug your shoulders or make a comment but no more. However, once in a while, you actually need to stand your ground. And it's not so much because you need to have your way but, rather, talking about what matters and standing your ground is important for you as an individual. It forces you to review your priorities.

It's likely that the last time you thought about such matters, life was different. Since then, you've grown and changed. Not only that, but in talking this over with those who are very different from you, you'll be forced to rethink your own views so you can express this in a way others will understand.

And for you as a Scorpio and a water sign, someone who is as intuitive as you are intellectual, this isn't just about communicating with others. It will also help you rediscover who you are now. We all grow and change. Take advantage of discussions of this nature, of both having to stand your ground and challenge others, mostly for the sheer joy of what you discover in the process.

You and others

Every once in a while, it's worth considering whether conversations with others are mere chats or something you can learn from. Certain individuals have a wonderful way of posing a question that results in conversations that enrich everybody concerned – and these individuals are worth keeping in your life.

Health and wellbeing

Occasionally, it's worth rethinking your daily regime, including how you look after yourself and how you eat. The big question is, are you responding to your own need to do things differently or it is others' influence? As a Scorpio, you tend to settle into routines, so often changes are the result of others' encouragement. If so, bravo!

Goals, and challenges

Changes are normal, they're like breathing. Yet you often put them off. As a Scorpio, you're a fixed sign, so sometimes avoid making changes, simply because you can't imagine how they'll work. The secret? Chat with those who encourage you to explore. They'll give you the necessary boost to take the next steps.

10

NOVEMBER

Tempting as it is to give advice to somebody who struggling, keep your thoughts to yourself, at least for now. Things aren't the way they seem and despite your good intentions, you could complicate matters. If you must say something, express your support. This will do wonders to boost their spirits.

You may recognise a special bond with another instantly, but often it takes time

S / C / O / R / P / I / O

11

NOVEMBER

You

Here's something to think about: is winning always good? There's an emphasis on it, on getting what you want. But sometimes challenges are about what we can learn.

Whether they're temporary or more lasting, the big question is, what would winning look like? Is it about doing what you want? What seems your best option today may be no more than doing more of what's familiar. As a Scorpio, and somebody who experiences powerful changes from time to time, the battle you're facing may be about moving on from familiar circumstances, shedding an old skin and becoming a new person.

What's tricky is that you won't necessarily know what that new life is like, at least initially. For you, as someone who tends to be a bit of a control freak, the unfamiliar can be difficult. If so, you probably know people who have the same characteristic; ask them to support you in this process. They won't tell you what to do, but will remind you when you're in the midst of it, that – as with the caterpillar becoming a butterfly – you too will turn into a new being, but one you can't yet imagine.

Once that's clear, every other step of this process will be important. And the reason it's important is this won't happen only once in this life – it will happen again and again, yet every time that process will be joyous.

You and others

During periods of transition, do you stick with the familiar, or battle what's out there, despite it being in your best interests. While you're probably aware you prefer to stick with what you know, sometimes simply having the courage to break away from the familiar is a vital first step. The rest will follow.

Health and wellbeing

There are many ways of looking after yourself at different times in life. Often, when challenged, Scorpios will choose the toughest approach. However, if ever there was a time to be gentle with yourself, it's now. Allow those around you to support you, and you'll find life has as many unexpected beauties as challenges.

Goals and challenges

Every once in a while, a problem appears that seems a repeat of past challenges. Maybe it is. Consider that possibility first, then explore further. And, more important, seek guidance from those who know you well and have stood by you during similar dramas in the past. They'll be amazingly helpful.

THIS DAY FOR EVERYONE

There are many ways to say 'No'. While you tend to assume others are aware when things aren't going well, and that a request is unlikely to be agreed to, not everybody picks up on such things. That being the case, you may need to be very clear, if not blunt, about your views.

Being true to yourself seems simple, but Scorpios know how complex it can be

You

Your theme is the difference between intuition and suspicion. As a Scorpio, and an intuitive water sign, questions of this nature come naturally to you. Yet being ruled by Pluto, the planet of secrets, your intuition can easily drift into suspicious feelings, and you could find yourself wrestling with shadowy worries about situations you're aware of, but about which you're also short of facts.

One of your charms is your intensity. Yet these days, we're encouraged to trust facts over feelings, so you may have been ignoring that inner wisdom, possibly for ages.

However, if you base decisions solely on facts, you'll sense you've missed something important. The trick is to analyse what's come your way in factual terms, while also assessing your emotional reaction to those offers. And this takes us back to the power of those feelings and distinguishing between your true intuition and suspicions that rouse questions or, at times, worries.

The trick? Analyse this yourself. But, also, seek out the truth in its most basic form, in discussions with those you've always trusted. Remind yourself of that feeling of clarity. Then make it part of your everyday thinking, and soon those shadowy doubts will vanish, having given way to the clarity that comes with knowing, and living with, the truth full-time.

You and others

Wondering where you stand with others? Think about what they say, the actual words. Most give this little thought. But for you, as a Scorpio, it's vital. On occasion, it's worth thinking about whether those you're spending a lot of time with are just good company or whether they're speaking from the heart and will be there when you need support.

Health and wellbeing

Now and then, it's important to indulge yourself. And during challenging times, a treat is therapeutic. What's more, knowing it's a treat means that you are looking after yourself in very special ways. Some believe being fit involves depriving yourself. While discipline is wise, spoiling yourself can be as important.

Goals and challenges

Thinking things through is vital, but what's even more important sometimes is to take action, just to get the ball rolling. What you do may be impulsive or unwise, but it will get you chatting with others and exploring ideas, some of which never crossed your mind. From that point onward, you'll learn from and enjoy every step.

12

NOVEMBER

S
/
C
\
O
/
R
\
P
\
I
\
O

Others may joke about truth, but for Scorpios honesty is a personal matter

You

Some people think luck means winning the lottery. Well, that may be the case, but not everyone who wins a lottery is happy. For you, one particular question will come up in a lot of different forms: what is luck?

And because there's a focus on luck in your birthday chart, it's essential to think about what that will look like. Especially because for you, as a Scorpio and somebody who gets into your routine, luck could often mean making changes in your day-to-day life, in your activities and close relationships and even in your thinking.

Notice how that's explained. It's not about making those changes, but simply seeing the circumstances you're in from a different perspective, which means that you may decide something is better than you imagined – and that other things that you had envisioned as being thrilling actually should be given second place.

It's also about perhaps accepting a bigger picture in certain activities that you've assumed wouldn't be rewarding. But most of all, it's about allowing those events to unfold in their own time. You can become addicted to worry and you can over-plan. And when you do, that means that it's difficult to be spontaneous – and that's the most important lesson of all for you.

You and others

The single big question is who to trust. If someone says what you want to hear, they may be helpful, especially if you're seeking breakthroughs. Those who encourage you to ask questions and to venture into new territory, especially if it's unfamiliar – and especially if those individuals challenge your thinking – are probably the ones you'll want to listen to.

Health and wellbeing

Many people believe that certain foods are lucky, and that's a wonderful tradition. But other varieties of foods are lucky simply because they do wonders for you. They nourish you in other ways, and add to your wellbeing. These are always good for you, but especially during periods of transition. The more balanced you feel, the easier it will be to embrace the unknown.

Goals and challenges

If you want a motto for periods of change and growth, it's "be bold". While, as a courageous Scorpio, you'll stand your ground, this has to do with breakthroughs, learning something new, venturing into new territory. The more prepared you are to take what seem to be chances, the more swiftly you'll begin to enjoy, and profit from, those changes.

THIS DAY FOR EVERYONE

Having to deal with tedious problems is bad enough, but having to discuss them at length with those who insist on going into these matters in details is the last thing you're in the mood for. Despite that, these need attention, and the longer you wait the more troublesome they'll become.

Generosity is always admirable, but it's at its best when carried out in secret

S
/
C
\
O
/
R
\
P
\
I
\
O

14

NOVEMBER

You

For you, the theme is inner peace. That may sound very spiritual, but actually it's not, because for many people, and especially many Scorpios, the chatter you hear in your brain prevents you from finding peace, simply because you're discussing plans and weighing up what will work and what won't, and what you think of other people.

While there is peace spoken of in many forms of spirituality, that single variety of peace has to do with being able to sidestep, if not silence, the chatter. But silencing that noise is also important because it appears that there will be certain decisions you have to make, and if you allow that chatter to influence your intuition – which is very powerful for you as a Scorpio – then you could miss the hints, the ideas that come with following that intuition, to call a particular individual to go to a particular place.

But, also, this will enable you to find a joy in each day, and in other's happiness, in a way that you may not usually do.

This is important – because in exploring what others are happy with, it will give you an example of the kind of world you could be creating for yourself simply by following your intuition over logic, and by using that hard-won inner peace to make decisions.

You and others

During times of transition, it's usual to ask those you trust for advice. However, you need to actually listen to what they have to say. As a Scorpio, you tend to argue with others simply because you'd rather stick with what's familiar. But if you're truly interested in change, listening to that advice is a gift.

Health and wellbeing

There are a number of special formulas, and no single one works better than another, but what is important is that you take it slowly during periods of transition. This is no time for a harsh routine. Treat yourself with love and with a kind of gentleness that encourages you to take a step into the future.

Goals and challenges

There's a single phrase that you should think about, and that is, "all forms of change bring chaos". If you're moving into a new home, it's chaotic. If you're changing elements of your life, it's chaotic. Even if you're going on a much-desired trip, it will still trigger a certain amount of chaos. As a Scorpio and a fixed sign, you like things to stay as they are and you may actually bemoan that chaos. Actually, when you're experiencing that chaos, it's an indication you're making progress.

THIS DAY FOR EVERYONE

Long ago, you learnt there's little point in arguing with something that's already agreed and committed to a decision. Although you don't realise that's exactly what you've done in a range of situations, review existing plans, especially those you regard as unchanging. They could be holding you back.

True love exists in many ways; at its most powerful, it's unspoken

S / C / O / R / P / I / O

15 NOVEMBER

You

For you, as a Scorpio, living with unanswered questions can be difficult, especially because as somebody ruled by Pluto, the planet of truth, you want answers – and reliable facts. However, with the foundation that situations are based on shifting, and the push and pull of life for many individuals, the kind of guarantees you want are unlikely.

Yet there is a different kind of truth – one that you're learning about. It's a truth that steps outside of the plans you have in mind and, in fact, outside of what is normally termed as a battle to get things done. Instead it forces you to simply look at life from a different angle and to consider what will work in this moment, and the next moment and then the one after that.

This approach is very different, because it doesn't involve planning. In fact, it's rather like living out each day, unable to guess what the weather will be like tomorrow, or next week, or in a couple of months – but to be in the present. That's a philosophical approach to life, but in your particular case, once you even begin to think about it, still less try to master it, you'll discover that the more easy-going you are about decision-making, the easier it will be to be drawn to the right activity in this hour, in this date, tomorrow – and over the coming months and even years.

You and others

If you're living in this unusual world – in which you're not so much trying to make decisions as to do what seems right in the moment – then you're also redefining what achievement means. If you're no longer worrying about succeeding, a challenge becomes an exciting exercise, one from which you will benefit in wonderful ways – not least for the sheer joy of what you have learnt.

Health and wellbeing

Everybody seeks a routine that will make them feel young and healthy. But what will make you feel best during times of transition are those which are adaptable, they accommodate the air and the energy moving through you. The more flexible you are in what you do and the way you look after yourself, the more fun you'll have.

Goals and challenges

Planning ahead is a virtue. But being able to accept what comes your way is a joy, and choosing unpredictability is a superb and rare approach to life. Once you've done that, once you've stopped telling others what you're planning and stopped planning yourself, then whatever arises will be a delightful surprise.

THIS DAY FOR EVERYONE

After battling seemingly insurmountable objects, you've discovered the issue wasn't the situation, but a fundamental misunderstanding of what you were dealing with. Going back to the beginning is aggravating, but what you learn will explain what went wrong, and eliminate that confusion.

Some regard saying you'd do anything for a loved one as extreme, but not to Scorpio

S
/
C
\
O
/
/
R
\
P
\
I
\
O

You

As a Scorpio and a water sign, part of you very much wants to be generous with others. Yet another part of you is careful, simply because you know that kind of generosity can often end in unfortunate situations of people being ungrateful or expecting more. However, there is a balance in this, and the real trick is to actually discuss the matter with others.

As a Scorpio, you'd normally think this kind of thing through, decide what's in everyone's best interest and then put those plans into action. However, the trick is to talk things over, even though you may suspect that not everybody would make decisions as wise as you hope. This may well be the case, but this is part of the point and part of what's important for you. The sooner you get others involved in those decisions, and in making those plans, the more swiftly they will begin to bear a certain responsibility and take that off your shoulders, which is an important thing.

But, even more than that, it will show a growing trust with others, something that is very difficult for you to achieve as a cautious and occasionally suspicious Scorpio.

Take this approach, discussing things stage by stage, including those matters that worry you. Talk about them openly and you will be amazed how worthwhile and often loving those exchanges are.

You and others

The phrase you'll want to use with others is simple: what do you think? As a Scorpio, you often tend to think things through first and then tell others your opinion. In this case, you're encouraged to ask for others' views. You may not always agree with it, but that's the point. This will get you talking and that isn't just important. It will be incredibly helpful.

Health and wellbeing

For you, the best approach to feeling terrific is to step away from what you've done before and to try something new. That may be the last thing you're in the mood for. Yet if ever there was a time to try new things and break old habits, it's now.

Goals and challenges

There are some things you've said you'd never do. Most Scorpios have this sort of sacred list. And now is the time to begin to do some of those things anyway, because it's essential to burst through those concepts and beliefs about things that either were once unacceptable or which actually you're afraid of doing. In every case, the simple act of saying you'll do them will change things and, in some cases, actually doing them will prove to be miraculous.

16

NOVEMBER

On several occasions, when discussing certain tricky situations, you've sidestepped the full facts. While at the time, it was about avoiding pointless discussions, you're urged to inform those involved of the details you left out, and do it now before they discover those matters for themselves.

S
/
C
\
O
/
R
\
P
\
I
\
O

17

NOVEMBER

A Scorpio commitment isn't just for real, it outlasts everything life can deal you

You

Ordinarily, you're setting goals for the future. You think both in the short and long term, which might seem sensible. However, with the world changing so swiftly, this may not be the best approach. Of course, as a Scorpio, and somebody who dislikes unnecessary changes, you may think in those terms so you can avoid seemingly disruptive changes.

But this is a period during which the structure of many elements of the world around you, and in your own life, are changing, so the more flexible your approach, the better. That means making plans in the short term may not be ideal. It also means being willing to explore in ways that would seem unwise, if not just plain crazy, at other times. With things shifting in so many ways, the more you explore them, even if just for the fun of it, the better off you'll be.

This variety of inquisitiveness doesn't necessarily come naturally to you as a Scorpio. Yet you indulge in it, and the broader your vision for the future, the better equipped you'll be to deal with the unexpected twists and turns that are coming your way.

Inevitably, these aren't just for you, but for the world around you. In fact, if there's one single approach you want to embrace now, it's and approach that may be very out of character – and that is, being easy-going.

You and others

During this period of change, when questions arise and you may be drawn down unfamiliar avenues, if ever there was a time to listen to what others have to say and their ideas, it's now. While you seek trustworthy people and pay attention to their ideas, take advantage of the ears and eyes of those around you, and you may spot something you'd otherwise miss.

Health and wellbeing

While a routine is reassuring especially during periods of change, altering various elements of it is advisable. Shaking things up actually reprogrammes your brain, so when those changes arise, you are ready to make the best of them.

Goals and challenges

Setting new goals is worth doing from time to time. But setting goals that are so far out that you can't believe you're even thinking of them, is something entirely different, and that's very much the theme. Because you know exactly what you do well and what you dislike, rethinking goals may seem unwise. Yet make a point of doing one new thing every day, and add something unlikely to your list of goals. Then you'll not only make the best of this period, you'll enjoy it.

THIS DAY FOR EVERYONE

In your efforts to avoid crossing the fence or seeming to be critical, you've given one particular individual the impression that you've no objection to what they've said or done. That's not the case. This leaves you little choice but to be frank, and in a way that removes all possibility of doubt.

GIFTS Scrupulous, Penetrating, Masterful

CHALLENGES Apprehensive, Venomous, Hurtful

NUMBER 2

(1+8) + (1+1) = 11 = (1+1) = 2

Scorpio love for family, friends or partners may be unspoken but is unshakeable

S
/
C
\
O
/
R
\
P
\
I
\
O

18

NOVEMBER

You

As you'll notice, you're in a period during which you have a choice. You can fix, that is deal with, minor difficulties as they arise, with situations that you're unhappy with, which are inconvenient or which others are finding difficult. Or you can take another approach, one that will be far more disruptive in the short term, but which will probably work a lot better in the long run, and that's to stand back, look at the big picture and see where changes are necessary.

Here again, as a Scorpio, you'll tend to look at details and then, if necessary, the big picture. But because this is a period during which the way a lot of the world works, and the way we think, is shifting, the more willing you are to let go of reassuring realities and to take chances on doing things in a very new way – in a new setting, altering your routine or your schedule, or even the world in which you live and work – the better off you'll be.

Again, that may seem crazy and wild. However, it may also be that opportunities come your way, or it could be that you devise something that will enable you to do things in that entirely new manner. This combination is the trick. It's the most important way and the most efficient way to deal with this period of change.

You and others

Sometimes others will encourage change, or you'll have an idea, or circumstances will corner you into it. Take that first step. Don't wait until the final moment when you're pushed, but recognise that the more swiftly you get involved in that process of change, the better advantage you'll take of it – and the more you'll enjoy it.

Health and wellbeing

Sometimes battling for something is good exercise. It focuses the mind. But there are times when the battle leads to tension, and that's no good. In fact, if there's anything that you want right now, it's not tension, which limits intuition. It is the serenity that comes with allowing change to come to you.

Goals and challenges

This is out of character, but for you to pause and simply allow events to unfold isn't weak, it's wise. The reason for this is some of what's arising is so unfamiliar that even you, as a canny Scorpio, wouldn't recognise it. Yet if you borrow the point of view of the sign next to you, Sagittarius, which has a capacity to not only spot but enjoy sudden changes, you'll recognise those, embrace them and make the best of them, all within nanoseconds.

THIS DAY FOR EVERYONE

Change is in the air. While it's clear things can't remain as they are, you've began hoping you could discuss and deal with certain tricky matters gradually but, ironically, the disruption caused by these changes will force others to acknowledge and join you in tackling the issues you have in mind.

There are many ways of sharing life's most precious moments; Scorpios are experts

S
/
C
\
O
/
R
\
P
\
I
\
O

19
NOVEMBER

You

If you notice that what you once regarded as a welcome surprise has become annoying, you'll realise just how much you and the world around you are changing. The fact is, those treats are now boring and predictable. Yet, at the same time, you're wondering what will surprise you, and this is where it's tricky. Why? Because those surprises are appearing, yet you still regard them as difficulties. That's because the world is changing in a way that is requiring you as a stable Scorpio to view elements of your life from a very different angle.

However, if you can find that different angle, you'll be able to see many of those elements from a fresh perspective, and instead of wrestling with them, that perspective will allow you to move ahead. Yes, it will require a certain amount of faith, and it may seem that you're taking chances, but it's a lot better than struggling with each of those changes.

You'll still have the opportunity to say no if you want to, but the more swiftly you get involved with these unusual circumstances, the better off you'll be. The trick is to realise that, as an intuitive water sign, there's a part of you that already trusts this kind of thing. It's just your old habits of control are holding you back. Recognise that and you'll also recognise how powerful that intuitive side of your nature is.

You and others

The question is, how often do you brush off offers or ideas that are intriguing, but you just can't imagine how they'll fit? Yet the sooner you say yes and get involved in exploring them, the better off you'll be. It's important now, but even more so as you live out the coming days, week, months and years.

Health and wellbeing

As a fixed sign of the zodiac, you like your pleasures. In fact, you like certain pleasures regularly, and the same way. However, with the world around you changing, it's time for you to change your habits, sometimes because it's good for you, but also because certain things you once enjoyed won't be like they used to be. While you could struggle to find the same products, foods and activities, you could also plunge in and try something new, and you could do it deliberately.

Goals and challenges

When was the last time you intentionally altered your goals and embraced new challenges? Future events ahead will encourage you to do things in a new way, but the sooner you realise that those occasionally unwelcome challenges are going to make your life more interesting and more rewarding, the better off you'll be.

THIS DAY FOR EVERYONE

Having right on your side is reassuring, especially when you're dealing with those you're eager to debate with about existing plans or priorities. Still, before you challenge anybody, double-check even seemingly solid facts. Times have changed – and you're likely to make surprising discoveries.

The deep feelings that make others weep lead to a Scorpio's emotional core

You

Because this day is related both to Scorpio and to the sign Sagittarius, we're talking about dealing with both energies, and if ever there was an unusual pairing, it's this one. While the Scorpio is a reflective and sensitive water sign, Sagittarius is an expansive and impulsive fire sign. However, if you can learn to benefit from the two of them, the breadth of ideas that come with Sagittarius's inquisitive side and the reflective nature of Scorpio, you will benefit in many wonderful ways. In fact, this will be terrific, not just for you but for those around you, for the excitement that you will bring to the lives of everybody, from friends and family to colleagues.

But not only that, instead of worrying about how things will go – and the details that are so much a part of the Scorpio life – you'll also find that you're able to enjoy things in ways that you never understood or expected. By exploring this spontaneous side of your nature, you'll also begin to embrace a part of your own being that's always been there, but which you may have held back because your Scorpio side wanted to make very sure that you were in control of everything. But, of course, what you're discovering is that there's more than one way of controlling things, and sometimes that spontaneous Sagittarius approach is the best way to live life.

You and others

The idea of being multiple personalities is something that is not unusual in the zodiac – take Gemini, which is the twins in one sign. Embrace both sides of your nature – the impulsive fire side and the reflective Scorpio – and you'll enjoy life all the more.

Health and wellbeing

There are lots of approaches to looking after yourself, as many as there are signs of the zodiac. But in your case, creating a menu of activities that accommodates the breadth of your character will be an adventure and one that allows you to experiment. Perhaps the most important commitment you'll want to make is to continue to explore, because this kind of exploration is like taking vitamins.

Goals and challenges

To have your approach to making goals change may seem strange, yet this balance between your internal nature as a Scorpio and the need to expand, and expand constantly, will make life so much more exciting that you will wonder why you didn't think of it before. When you embrace that expansive side of your nature, you will find that every day is much brighter.

S / C \ O / R \ P \ I \ O

20

NOVEMBER

Sagittarius

Ruler Jupiter
Element Fire

Symbol The Archer
Flower Dandelion

November 21 – December 20

Sagittarius Being half horse, half human – and what's more, an archer – it's no surprise you Sagittarians are restless. The third fire sign, you thrive on new ideas, action and challenges, and suffer when life is too predictable. While you're risk-takers, you've an instinctive sense that comes from your ruling planet, the fortunate Jupiter. Dandelion is your flower, sharp cinnamon is your herb and the yew is your tree. Your stone is gilt topaz.

S
A
G
I
T
T
A
R
I
U
S

GIFTS Vivacious, Eager, Articulate

CHALLENGES Restless, Rash, Clumsy

NUMBER 5

(2+1) + (1+1) = 5

Nothing's better than waking up brimming with energy

You

You were born at the beginning of the sign of Sagittarius, so have to find a balance between the influence of the sign before yours, Scorpio, and its tendency to be reflective and secretive, and your own expansive nature, which is constantly shifting and exploring.

You're always growing and developing in a way that benefits you, because the inquisitive side of your nature finds delving into complex, if not puzzling, questions worthwhile and rewarding. That process of exploration leads to setting goals and exploring ideas, as well as considering how you'll look after your own interests. What you learn as a result of that Scorpio tendency to delve into facts and to gather information. And information that's reliable is very helpful indeed.

The Sagittarius side of your nature is always inquisitive, and needs to expand and grow. Consequently, when you're learning about something or, indeed, somebody, you enjoy and benefit from asking questions.

And then you begin to look at medium-term and long-range plans. This is a secret for you. If you take advantage of that short time you took exploring the very careful side of your nature, then – when you begin to turn those plans into lasting arrangements, and possibly even lifelong plans – you'll be sure you're doing the right thing.

You and others

You're an energetic fire sign, but at the same time, you have a strong need for not only the stimulation of others' company, but also the ideas they bring your way. What you discuss with those around you, everyone from friends and family to colleagues, will add to your life enormously.

Health and wellbeing

The Sagittarius side of you prefers to eat quickly and have something that's tasty but that you can also move on from. However, there's another part of you that enjoys a dish you can delve into and learn about. If you manage to add that to your diet once a week, you'll be glad you did.

Goals and challenges

As a fire sign, you always need new goals. However, some of your goals and objectives are important enough that they'll become a foundation for years – if not your whole life. Find a balance between those two and you'll also find lasting satisfaction.

THIS DAY FOR EVERYONE

The last thing you want is to disappoint anybody, yet sudden changes in circumstances mean you can't do what you've promised and deal with more recent obligations. Explain that to those who you're worried about upsetting. Not only will they understand, they'll do what they can to help.

GIFTS Expansive, Lively, Inquisitive

CHALLENGES Impatient, Explosive, Fickle

NUMBER 6

(2+2) + (1+1) = 6

The world's full of amazing places and people, and I love discovering them

You

As a Sagittarius, you're restless. And this is, in fact, one of your most profitable characteristics, in the sense that between being ruled by the expansive Jupiter and being a fire sign, you're always interested in what's going on around you and, even more, you're eager to learn and, when it suits you, take part.

That interest ensures you meet new people, and take advantage of opportunities to visit new places, that you broaden your horizons, which, in turn, leads to new ideas and, potentially, new pursuits. However, this can be distracting. In fact, the challenge is to sustain what you have that works in your life – in your relationships, in your habits and out in the world – yet, at the same time, to include these intriguing developments. This is because being somebody who's ruled by Jupiter, the planet of growth, ideas and discovery, both via study and travel, it's vital that you always have something new to discover and learn about.

It may involve actual ideas that you study. It may involve getting to know people. It could mean going places, anywhere from school to travel. In every case, this will add to your life.

As a Sagittarius, those experiences you encounter and what you learn won't just be interesting, they will contribute to your daily existence and to the rest of your life.

You and others

Most Sagittarians are sociable anyway. But for you, it's especially important that you are around people who you can chat with and bounce ideas off. In doing this you'll learn a lot, as their views will add to your knowledge.

Health and wellbeing

One of the advantages of being a Sagittarius is you're full of vital energy. This comes with being ruled by the planet Jupiter. But it also means that you can actually forget to eat or not eat enough or at the right time, and end up being exhausted despite that natural energy. The secret? The challenge of maintaining balance in all things.

Goals and challenges

There's a phrase, moving the goalposts – which speaks to the idea of almost reaching a particular goal, then setting entirely new – and often very distant – ones. This is very common to those born under the sign of Sagittarius and is something to be cautious of.

22

NOVEMBER

THIS DAY FOR EVERYONE

The events coming your way will be exciting, but the odds are good that they'll trigger the stubborn side of your nature. Bear this in mind and, when you're becoming exasperated, instead of digging your heels in ask others to explain what they have in mind. That will change everything, and soon.

23

GIFTS Quick-thinking, Exuberant, Mirthful

CHALLENGES Erratic, Reckless, Disparaging

NUMBER 7

(2+3) + (1+1) = 7

Exploring new places brings a special kind of excitement

You

While you've a strong physical nature and need to be out and about, whether on a walk or involved in sports, there's no denying the power of the philosophical side of your nature. This is the side that asks questions about everything – about what works, what's wise, what's kind and, equally, what isn't. It is associated with your ruling planet, Jupiter, and explains the element of your nature that can get lost both in considering what's best to do in the here and now, and future plans.

Moreover, you'll spend hours considering what you can learn more about. While that interest in the world around you is important, don't allow that inquisitiveness to keep you from focusing on something and, possibly, allowing it to become a real passion. This has nothing to do with age. It's a challenge for Sagittarians of any age, because too much focus can mean excluding other activities, when you are by nature restless.

So the issue isn't what you're focusing on, but finding a balance between your central core enthusiasms and your other activities. You might even ask someone to give you some pointers in identifying your priorities and organising them. That won't just be helpful in the here and now, that individual could be helpful over the years to come and add to your life.

You and others

Because your thinking moves swiftly and you connect strongly with people, when you're spending time with those who think equally swiftly it's a tremendous connection. Yet, at the same time, there are those who interest you, but who simply think and move more slowly. The trick is to understand that and to adjust your own pace in accordance with theirs.

Health and wellbeing

Looking after yourself – that is, eating wisely and moving in a way that's useful for you – can be easy. However, you get distracted. Probably the best approach is to choose the easiest thing to do, which includes eating simple but nourishing foods and doing something as simple as taking regular walks.

Goals and challenges

Some of the signs near you, particularly Capricorn, tend to over-analyse everything, but you don't. At the same time, it's important to rethink recent events. Maybe not as frequently as your neighbouring signs, but if you put it in your diary to review what you've done say, a couple of times a year, you'll be glad you did.

THIS DAY FOR EVERYONE

Unsettling as sudden changes may be, what's coming your way now and over the next week isn't just exciting. Those events could be the answer to persistent problems. However, they won't seem that promising when they arise. Make a point of exploring everything. You'll be amazed by what works out.

GIFTS Buoyant, Spirited, Daring

CHALLENGES Fidgety, Outspoken, Disapproving

NUMBER 8

(2+4) + (1+1) = 8

The best challenge is both physical and requires learning something new

You

You don't think of it until you're making plans with others and realise how cautious they are – about even the simplest of things – but the fact is, you're a natural optimist. While that makes life easy for you, you've a knack for overcoming the obstacles that would stop others in their tracks. However, not only are certain individuals cautious, even when things are going well, they seem to find something to complain about. Obviously, you can sidestep their negative comments, making plans that involve them isn't easy, and they can be difficult to talk to, whatever the nature of the conversation.

It doesn't matter if you've known them for a long time – they might even be family. What's most puzzling is that, despite their tendency to complain, they're often helpful and supportive. The trick to dealing with those who seem to find the downside of almost anything is to let them comment and to let them moan, and also to ensure that you have enough kindred spirits around you, those who are optimistic in the way you are, so you can also chat with them.

Having both types of people in your life means you'll not only benefit from the balance and the wisdom they bring. Their ideas could broaden your own thinking and either encourage you to achieve more, or prevent you from taking action you'll later regret.

You and others

There are clusters of many kinds. Sometimes, if you allow yourself to be intrigued by those who don't really make much sense, they'll add a lot to your life. In fact, they may make life more exciting than those who you know better yet who are predictable.

Health and wellbeing

Having a regime that makes you fit is wonderful. But if it's something you don't really enjoy, and will drop, then it's not a good idea. The trick is to find something that works for you as a restless Sagittarius, that's probably varied but also gives you plenty of time to do other things.

Goals and challenges

Taking chances and exploring, the world is essential for you as an inquisitive Sagittarius. Yet also it's essential that you think twice about what you get involved in, particularly if those arrangements are long-term. Make that your policy and you won't regret it later.

24

NOVEMBER

In some situations fast action is vital, but in at least one, you're urged to wait until you have the clarity, in terms of both hard facts and your own feelings, that comes with certain moments. If you do that, then you will be sure to explore your options and avoid lasting decisions.

GIFTS Courageous, Wide-ranging, Ebullient

CHALLENGES Judgemental, Flustered, Volatile

NUMBER 9

(2+5) + (1+1) = 9

Sometimes the only cure for feeling down is a bad comedy movie

You

As a Sagittarius and a fire sign, you really enjoy discussions, especially if they're enthusiastic – if not actually heated. Keep in mind, however, that what you enjoy and regard as being an enthusiastic exchange of ideas might seem to more timid souls – and probably those who aren't fire signs – to be a battle, one that somebody will win and have the final word.

The real problem is that you don't take these exchanges to heart. All three fire signs, Aries, Leo and Sagittarius, enjoy lively conversations. However, if others are loud or trying to prove something, to you or to others, including quieter types, consider whether it would be better to chat about something less combative. At the time, that might seem weak. But, when things are calmer, you'll realise you would have just been drawn into that particular issue when there's so much else to explore and discuss.

Better than that, once you understand this, you'll master the art of recognising when there's more to be said, when there's something to discuss that you'll learn from or when you'll learn about others from their ideas, views and passions. And, especially, when it's time to change the subject and move on to something else that's as interesting, but less controversial.

You and others

As a fire sign, you're a quick thinker, which means often you'll dominate discussions, This is not because you're trying to take control – you just come up with more ideas. However, there are those with whom you have a strong connection and get together often. If those individuals are slower thinkers, you may need to do exactly that – to take over to ensure that you cover everything that's on your mind.

Health and wellbeing

Are you feeling tired? As a Sagittarius and a fire sign, sometimes you don't notice fatigue until you're completely exhausted. One of the most important components for you is to recognise when you need to rest. Rather than thinking it a waste of time, see it as an investment in your wellbeing.

Goals and challenges

Everybody tells you to list your goals, and usually it's a good idea. However, as you do, make two columns. One for a list of activities and goals that excite you, and the other for those that seem worthy but dull. If you want to do something from that dull column, think three times before you commit to it.

THIS DAY FOR EVERYONE

Recently, when discussing plans, you sidestepped certain details. You weren't being careless or, as some suggest, secretive. It's just that you knew things would change. If others are concerned, explain slowly and in detail. Otherwise, they'll continue to assume that you were being careless.

Fighting for what or who I believe in isn't a battle, it's an honour

You

You probably don't think of yourself as being complex or demanding. But you are. This isn't in the sense that you demand things from others, but you're so full of ideas and activities and hopes and enthusiasms, and the accompanying requirements, that it's vital you think carefully about your priorities.

But, also, you talk things over with others, both those closest and those whose advice you trust. This ensures you've somebody to bounce your ideas off. However, it's also about them knowing enough to give you useful advice. If you don't do this, if you don't outline your hopes and plans, you may overwhelm yourself and leap in to making solid plans without thinking things through.

So this isn't just about an update, but a worthwhile discussion with those who are able to ask worthwhile questions and guide you. They may be colleagues, family or loved ones or trusted friends.

While organising yourself in this way may seem overwhelming, it leads to something unusual for you. And that's having arranged both your thinking and plans well enough in advance that you, and others, can consider what you want to achieve and, even better, can relax. This may not come naturally but, as you'll discover, it's a good habit for you, as an inquisitive Sagittarius, to develop.

You and others

As you move through elements of your life, or activities or interests, it's important to bring some friends from the past, but also to acquire new companions that have to do with what you're pursuing at the moment. Not only will you learn from them, you'll be able to chat about what you're exploring and enjoy that all the more as well.

Health and wellbeing

As a Sagittarius, you're inquisitive. This includes new fads that have to do with the way you eat to how you exercise. While it's worth exploring what arises, also recognise that unless food or a particular kind of exercise is your passion, keeping it simple is probably the best choice for you.

Goals and challenges

Nobody works harder than you at achieving what is important. However, you also can have a short attention span, which means that if you haven't achieved that goal swiftly enough, you'll move on to something else. Think twice before you allow that to happen, particularly if those goals are very dear to your heart.

26

NOVEMBER

S
/
A
\
G
/
I
\
T
\
T
\
A
/
R
\
I
/
U
\
S

Nothing beats waking up knowing I'll be doing something I've never done before

You

Often you'll jot down ideas of what you want to do. While, of course, almost everyone keeps some sort of list of plans and goals, and will add to them from time to time, in your case, those lists are often scribbled down here and there on bits of paper, some of which you discover six months later in a pocket.

However, when you're comparing notes with those around you, you sometimes feel that, despite your enthusiasm, you're missing something. The fact is, as a Sagittarius and somebody ruled by the expansive Jupiter, you're inquisitive by nature, and whatever you're doing or wherever you are, you'll also be exploring. For you, it's like breathing. But this can mean many Sagittarians don't have a single goal, or perhaps it reshapes itself over the months and years. This unique part of your nature is what enables you to do something that is extraordinary.

Even better, you manage to shift those goals and redefine them while adding to your current vision. While others may advise you to stick to certain objectives or plans, deep down you know while that may work for them, it isn't your thing. For you, the more inquisitive you are and the more willing you are to rethink your goals, even frequently, the more likely you are to achieve them and possibly achieve far more than you imagined possible.

You and others

Understandably, you're fascinated by those who focus on one thing and one thing only. While you'll chat with them, at the same time you wonder what else they do and find them a bit obsessive. It's an important lesson in how wonderful your own inquisitive way of living and thinking is.

Health and wellbeing

Are you feeling grumpy, on edge and ready to bite someone's head off? It may not be your temper. Perhaps it's something really simple. First, are you hungry? Or, it may be that you're tired, and you need to go to bed early and get some rest.

Goals and challenges

Certain individuals are determined to give others advice. In your case, they are advising you to stick with a single focus or a single goal. The fact is, they're not Sagittarians and they don't know what makes you tick. Thank them – and then ignore them.

27
NOVEMBER

THIS DAY FOR EVERYONE

By no means are you antisocial or secretive. Yet Mercury, the planet of ideas, is accenting the parts of your chart that have to do with talking things over with others. It will become clear that you've sidestepped certain matters. While they're not crucial, the sooner you raise them the better.

The best remedy for feeling down is being in nature

You

You have a talent for bringing new ideas and excitement to the lives of others. But then they move on and do their own thing. For you, however, the question is, who brings excitement into your life? While, mostly, you do it yourself, you don't even think of it or wonder how it happens.

This is because you're inquisitive by nature. As a fire sign, you're restless and you thrive on learning, so you're always looking for new things to do, experience and explore. You like learning for the sake of it, doing what might be described as exercising your brain. If there's any problem, it's that once you've found something interesting, you'll still be on the lookout for something else, even while you're absorbed with your current pursuit.

This is the lesson for you. It's finding that balance between sticking with what you enjoy, and giving yourself time to continue to explore and discover, in the way that not only comes naturally to you as a Sagittarius, but that is also one of your greatest virtues.

The fact that you're interested in others and in the world around you adds to your life, but often that interest adds to the lives of others as well. In some cases, you may turn that interest into something lasting. Whether or not you do, it will always have enhanced the lives of those you've encountered.

You and others

Those around you are often seeking that individual who will change their lives. As a fire sign, you tend to be the one who does that not just for yourself, but for others as well. Recognise that your role in life is to be you, and also on occasion to add enormously to the lives of others.

Health and wellbeing

It's important to recognise that the fire-sign part of your nature means you're almost always in perpetual motion, which means that when you're realising dreams or doing things with others, you won't stop and can get exhausted. The trick is to realise that you can conjure up dreams from a seated position.

Goals and challenges

As a Sagittarius you're spontaneous, and often you'll discover something you want to do, simply because it pops into your mind. Yet, occasionally, you need to sit down and review your life. Consider what should go, what's lacking and what's the ideal opportunity you want to come your way.

28

NOVEMBER

GIFTS   Effervescent, Witty, Brave

CHALLENGES   Wild, Stormy, Demeaning

NUMBER 4

(2+9) + (1+1) = 13 = (1+3) = 4

Curiosity is one of life's greatest gifts; with it, no day is ever dull

You

One of your greatest assets, as a Sagittarius, is your sense of humour. You can see what's funny in all sorts of settings, often in those that other people ignore or even sometimes complain about. Spotting this is one thing, but the trick is to find a way to mix this unique perception with the practical side of life. If you need to make money, if you're starting a new project or if you need to figure things out, you'll want to blend your inborn enthusiasm with those practical needs.

While, initially, this may seem strange, once you begin discussing it with others, you'll find that they, too, have interest in what you're doing. They love the idea of breaking away from the dull side of life, and they may well have other ideas or even be in a position to support you. But this isn't just about your sense of humour. You can make this a part of your approach to doing anything new and, in fact, to living life.

Ordinarily, you rely on yourself to achieve your goals, and enjoy hanging out with those who are fun. Yet, every once in a while, it's useful to pause and consider who could be helpful and perhaps even ask for that help. That will be a new and unusual approach to life for you. But it will also be a skill that will benefit you in many, often magical, ways.

You and others

The fire-sign part of your nature says life should be a party. This is natural to fire signs, but particularly Sagittarians. Also, you don't mind a large proportion of drama in the middle of it all. However, it's important that you hang out with people who support you emotionally, as well as back your goals.

Health and wellbeing

Every once in a while, you realise that you're overdoing it, that you're juggling far too much. While you're able to do that, the question is whether you actually have the energy to do it at the moment? Or is some of what you're juggling sufficiently unimportant that you can actually put it off till later.

Goals and challenges

As a fire sign, you don't mind sudden changes. In fact, they keep life interesting. If you did everything alone, that would be fine. However, those around you aren't the same, and many of them are not only uncomfortable with sudden changes, they're also anxious. The most important thing to keep in mind is the more you talk over, the easier it will be.

29

NOVEMBER

THIS DAY FOR EVERYONE

It's true, you're often reluctant to make changes others insist on if you can't understand what you'll get out of them, or why you should bother at all. But the fact is, you have no choice. The situation in question involves others as much as it does you – and they're eager to take things to the next stage.

In my low moments, I recall the last real challenge I faced

You

Sometimes you need to take a break – for yourself, and from yourself and some of your habits. The fact is, you're always busy, really busy, often distracted and sometimes late.

This is the Sagittarian side of your nature. The part that enjoys picking up on, trying out and adding activities and pursuits to each passing day. But it's also worth recognising that it's good to have time for friends, to do what you enjoy, to explore or, sometimes, just to relax or even be still.

But if you keep adding to the list of things you're doing, and intend to do, this not only gets difficult, but can be overwhelming. The only one who can decide how to use your time is you. Those around you may make suggestions. But, as you well know, you'll often ignore them.

The question is, how can you deal with this? Ideally, you'll pause, at the beginning or end of the day, and think about what you could let go of, and you'll make that decision before you actually begin.

Certain things you put first don't really matter, while others are important yet are pushed aside, because they don't seem quite as urgent. Do a frequent mini-review and instead of rushing from one thing to the next, you'll be able to enjoy every element of your day and of your life.

You and others

As a passionate fire sign, you're always moving and you attract people to you. Yet, every once in a while, you also need to allow those who are around you to add to your life, by taking you to places that will enhance your existence, by exposing you to interesting people and perhaps by simply spoiling you.

Health and wellbeing

Feeling fit is important for you as a fire sign and a Sagittarius. However, you have a tendency to get involved in a fitness regime that is as complicated as it is boring. Variety is essential for you. If you don't have that, it's time you made it a part of your regime.

Goals and challenges

Writing down your goals seems dull, especially for someone who would rather be out doing things. However, even if you just jot those things down, you'll remember them. You may later find a note in a pocket, but when you look at it, it will remind you of what you really wanted to do.

S / A \ G / I \ T \ T \ A / R \ I / U \ S

30

NOVEMBER

THIS DAY FOR EVERYONE

You may have thought certain plans were settled. Since then, however, events have made it clear that you must reassess them. As much of a nuisance as it seems, once you begin, you'll realise how much circumstances have changed – and how much your own plans need a rethink.

GIFTS   Humorous, Eloquent, Wise

CHALLENGES   Ruffled, Nervy, Condescending

NUMBER 4

(0+1) + (1+2) = 4

Even if I have no idea how to do something, I'll give it a try

You

Many think of the pursuit of fun as something that's all about childhood. But for you, as a fire sign and particularly as someone ruled by the expansive and playful planet, Jupiter, it's natural to want to turn whatever you're doing – even something rather serious – into fun.

You'll want to bring joy into whatever you're experiencing. You may even want to get those around you, those individuals who are usually grumpy, to enjoy things and to have a good time as well. In some cases, this requires planning, but in others it's simply a matter of the attitude or the people you get involved, or perhaps the places you go, or what you have in mind.

While others might choose a rather dark or difficult or dull setting, you'll find somewhere that is itself an invitation to have a good time. And, as much, it's about spontaneity, taking advantage of the moment.

The point of this is to refuse to let those who regard themselves as practical and, therefore, dull, to overshadow your natural joy in life, whatever the nature of the setting or the relationship – whether it's personal, romantic, or has to do with your life in the world or job. Ensure that whatever you're doing at least gives you the opportunity not just to succeed, but to have a really good time doing it.

You and others

There are two kinds of people: the people you know because they're family or colleagues or even neighbours – they may be fun, or not. But then there's another group of people too; they're pals. They too could be family or neighbours. But those individuals add to your life. They add enthusiasm, they add support and, most of all, they add magic.

Health and wellbeing

For you, as an energetic fire sign, nothing feels better than challenging your body, discovering just how far you can push it before you're exhausted. But unless you're an athlete, that's not always wise or possible. However, what you can do is feel your muscles move and the energy you use with every step, especially if you've some stairs to climb.

Goals and challenges

Everybody knows somebody who's sensible. For you, as a Sagittarius and a resilient fire sign, the sensible people may seem to be speaking a foreign language, simply because you tend to rate what you do on its potential for achievement and excitement, not how sensible it is. Listen to those feelings within, not to those very cautious individuals.

THIS DAY FOR EVERYONE

In their enthusiasm to tell you about certain new ideas they think you'd like, one particular individual could be over-enthusiastic. They may even seem to be bullying you. Yet what they have in mind could be in your best interests. You won't know until you do a little exploration.

GIFTS Athletic, Amusing, Energetic

CHALLENGES Capricious, Disparaging, Irresponsible

NUMBER 5

$(0+2) + (1+2) = 5$

I swear I'll learn something new each day; it doesn't last, but it's fun

You

It's very much your nature, as one of the three fire signs – Aries, Leo and Sagittarius – to feel excited about your day, your week and even your life. The fire signs are all about enthusiasm and a contagious zest for life.

That excitement comes as naturally to you as breathing, in that you don't really think about it. However, it's worth being aware that certain individuals not only don't understand it, they take a negative view of this upbeat approach to life. Of course, they don't think of it that way – they think they're being sensible. Getting along with them? There's a trick. It's to listen to them, and occasionally to take advantage of the advice they give.

However, you may not want to get too close to them, but instead ensure that those you're close to in your life are like you – upbeat, optimistic and eager to explore new things. Create balance in your life between those sensible individuals and those who share your natural eagerness and you'll be able to make the best of your own enthusiasm.

That way, when you're about to do something that might be a little risky, you'll be able to talk to somebody who will help you balance that and ensure that you achieve exactly what you hope for – in whatever activity you're doing, but also in your life.

You and others

Many people enjoy spending time with friends who go back a long way, sometimes childhood friends, people from school or even from the old neighbourhood. While they're wonderful, it's also important that you have friends who are linked with who you are at the moment, and who will support your natural enthusiasm. Whatever it is you decide to do, you'll be sure they'll back you up.

Health and wellbeing

For most Sagittarians, sticking to any kind of regime is difficult, but being ruled by the inquisitive Jupiter means you're always interested in learning something new. Make that the core of your wellbeing regime, and you'll be fascinated by your options.

Goals and challenges

The trick is to blend your life – to combine elements of the past and the present, and to use that to make decisions about your goals. Usually, as a fire sign, you'll leap into that activity first and make decisions later. It's worth pausing before you start, even if for a few minutes.

02

DECEMBER

Not everybody understands that change is essential to Sagittarians

You

Everybody knows certain people who are very good at giving advice. The trouble is, the advice they give isn't actually of benefit to you. Rather, their intention is to alter your approach to life so you'll be of more benefit to them, so that you'll be more like them, as individuals.

They don't actually think about, or have any interest in, what personally makes you tick. This is one of the most important things for you to remember, especially if somebody makes you feel uncomfortable. If they say they're trying to give you a hand or guide you, but have a very different character – if they aren't a fire sign, like you are as a Sagittarius – they are unlikely to view life the way you do. So while their guidance may be well meaning, it could actually complicate matters. The trick? It's to thank them for their advice, then ignore them.

In fact, even more than that, thank them, and then spend a little time with someone else who is an enthusiastic fire sign. Do that, and whatever element of your life that you're exploring, you'll find that having a chat with somebody who boosts your spirits and who agrees with your viewpoint of life will, itself, clarify your thinking. That, in turn, will give you that extra boost that allows you to take the next step to turning a potential dream into a reality.

You and others

As a Sagittarius, you rarely stop to assess whether people have some agenda or a story when they're talking to you. But there are certain individuals who are called rescuers, who try to help people and fix them, except their way of fixing them is to do things the way they would. Be aware of them.

Health and wellbeing

From time to time, people don't feel well physically. Also, everyone has dark moments when things don't seem that promising. There can be several reasons: it may be that you're simply tired and you need to eat, you need a rest or a meal. In every case, think about how to improve on your physical wellbeing first.

Goals and challenges

Long-term goals are important, but they're often tough for Sagittarians, simply because as a fire sign, you're a bit impatient about seeing progress. The secret? Make a list about the stages needed to achieve that goal. And then, as you progress towards it, you can mark off those achievements and measure how far you've come.

THIS DAY FOR EVERYONE

There are many ways to agree to plans, but at the moment, you're being rushed into arrangements you still question. Say exactly that. The fact is, things are still in transition, and you will be tinkering with whatever is arranged over the weeks, if not the months, to come.

GIFTS Intelligent, Droll, Dynamic

CHALLENGES Censorious, Wayward, Erratic

NUMBER 7

(0+4) + (1+2) = 7

Discovering an unwelcome commitment is an adventure in disguise

You

You probably never think of it, but it's vital to be aware of the power of your nature as a sunny fire sign. While you share this warmth with your fellow fire signs, Aries and Leo, yours is different – and distinctive – because it's expansive. You have a unique enthusiasm for life. You approach each day with your own unique joy. You inspire others. Your warmth makes them feel that so much is possible, including things they wouldn't regard as being within reach if they weren't around you and viewing life from your perspective.

What's more, this viewpoint is a bit like taking vitamins. Those who hang out with you begin to absorb your enthusiasm. However, it's vital to recognise that this goes both ways, and you need to hang out with people who lift your own spirits. It may be that you don't think of it, but if you spend time with those who are habitually negative, you feel as if you've lost your bounce. Ironically, while you may take vitamins and try to eat well, do you notice how you're nourishing your mood?

Are you hanging out with people who encourage you to believe in yourself? Many Sagittarians don't, because you have a natural resilience and feel that those who encourage you are somehow imposing themselves on you. Reflect on this, because you not only deserve a boost, you'd benefit from it.

You and others

Every once in a while, it's important that you get what might be termed an injection of new people in your life. Not just family or friends, who are rather inescapable, but those individuals who you hang out with just for fun, just for a laugh or to be inspired. Keep that variety going and you'll recognise how much you benefit from it.

Health and wellbeing

There are many varieties of health and many reasons for wellbeing. While you will certainly benefit from looking after yourself, eating well, perhaps taking vitamins and exercising, for you as a fire sign achieving a goal may give you the biggest boost of all.

Goals and challenges

Every once in a while, it's useful to have a new challenge. However, it's also important for you to write down that challenge. Why? Because as a fire sign you move on swiftly, and once you've dealt with one issue, you'll already have the next one in mind. If you have written it down and can mark it off as done, then you'll be well aware you've achieved it and can move on to the next with a sense of accomplishment.

04

DECEMBER

THIS DAY FOR EVERYONE

For ages, you've been trying to win one particularly stubborn individual over to plans you know they'd enjoy. The problem is that they aren't just being stubborn – they won't even listen to what you have to say. Back off, then get them to ask about your ideas. It will require patience, but it will also work.

GIFTS Lively, Debater, Fluent

CHALLENGES Undependable, Reckless, Clumsy

NUMBER 8

(0+5) + (1+2) = 8

I can't resist saying yes to challenges, often before I know what they are

You

Fire-sign enthusiasm is contagious. It's a wonderful quality, and those who are around you benefit from your inquisitiveness and zest for life. But the question is, do you?

Sometimes you're moving on so quickly from one particular activity, plan or passion to another, from the people and goals central to your life, that you don't actually stop to think about what you've accomplished. If you don't make a note of what you've done or those encounters – which busy Sagittarians rarely do – you may not recognise or recall who you've met, what you've accomplished or, indeed, what you have learnt in the process of achieving those goals.

This isn't just important in terms of boosting your spirits – it's worthwhile knowing what you've accomplished. What's more, when it's time to evaluate the past and consider the skills you've added and what you've done, and assess their influence on your goals, it's worth pausing to consider exactly such matters. You enjoy learning for the fun of it. But maybe it's time to focus on adding a skill. Ask a few questions. Explore. The resulting insights could lead to a rethink of your plans, or even to a new vision of what's next. It isn't just about what you've learnt. It's also about what you might want to embrace over the coming weeks, months, and the long-term future.

You and others

As a Sagittarius, and someone who chats a lot about what you're up to, often those around you will show up to be helpful. But the question is, do those connections remain? Or do they come, learn from what you're doing and take off again? It's worth thinking about.

Health and wellbeing

When you're doing a lot, you'll often prop yourself up in certain ways. For Sagittarius, and somebody ruled by Jupiter, caffeine and sugar can't do the trick, which is fine. What's most important is to be aware of what you're wanting next week and next month too.

Goals and challenges

Every once in a while, you need a new challenge, partly because achieving it is the best thing possible for a Sagittarius. However, it's also important to pause and consider whether the challenge that you are pursuing is very similar to the past, or something entirely new and exciting.

05

DECEMBER

THIS DAY FOR EVERYONE

If you've already talked about what you'd like to do and hoped to achieve, and are running out of enthusiasm, then it's time to change the subject. In fact, judging by the rather tricky current planetary activity, you're better off sidelining those plans and savouring each day for the pleasure it offers.

GIFTS Candid, Buoyant, Sporty

CHALLENGES Curt, Rebellious, Jumpy

NUMBER 9

(0+6) + (1+2) = 9

Joy is discovering a new way of thinking, living, speaking or even eating

You

As a fire sign and as a Sagittarius, your sunny, optimistic nature is what draws people to you. Because of this, being a Sagittarius can be great fun. You think and move swiftly, dealing with life's practicalities as they arise, usually without mentioning it. However, this can also mean that you're so self-sufficient that you don't even notice when others want to lend a hand and, still less, don't stop to enjoy the way certain individuals want to spoil you or what they're offering – attention, support, exciting invitations. What's more, you also either don't notice or brush off the give and take that's part of most close relationships. This isn't just about practical matters. It's about someone wanting to spend time with you, wanting to indulge you simply by paying attention to you.

Unless you give thought to your reaction, it can alter the balance in that particular relationship and, to an extent, all of them. In fact, many Sagittarians feel uncomfortable, because it's as if you suddenly owe something to those who are being generous to you.

The fact is, you give so much to them, and to everybody, in so many ways and every day, that what those individuals are doing for you, or giving to you, is only balancing the equation. Keep that in mind, and when that lovely and loving energy comes your way, you'll not only enjoy it, you'll embrace it.

You and others

For you, saying yes to offer seems strange, simply because you're the one who's usually making things happen. However, when others offer you support, it's important to say yes, because that will lead to valuable discussions and even bring you closer in ways you couldn't have imagined possible.

Health and wellbeing

While you can go off and do something that will make you fit on your own, how about making it a game? How about making it playful? How about enjoying it? That's one of the most important things for you as a Sagittarius, to turn even things that are good for you into fun.

Goals and challenges

As someone who thinks and moves swiftly, the idea of sitting down and making a list, even a grocery list, is difficult for you. Yet if you list your goals, and read that list fairly often, you'll be aware of how much you've accomplished and realise what a joy it is to make that effort – and see that effort pay off.

06

DECEMBER

THIS DAY FOR EVERYONE

Long ago, you learnt to live with and, in some cases, to agree to disagree with certain individuals. But if you're going to take certain complex plans to the next stage, you've no choice but to find a way to deal with those issues – and in detail. It won't be easy, but it is vital.

GIFTS Vibrant, Bold, Jokey

CHALLENGES Rash, Charged, Madcap

The toughest physical challenges can be mastered. Loving another is another matter

You

Having been born an optimist, you don't really think about whether certain people or certain situations could be risky, or even undermine you. When you notice that you're struggling, you generally just try different solutions, do more, consider options and work harder.

However, when tricky situations arise, it's worth pausing to consider exactly what's happening, and who's behind them. While it may be the case that these can't be avoided, you'll simply muster that time, energy, effort or persistence and, possibly, facts necessary to deal with the matter in question.

This approach means you'll be prepared for what's next. Still, there've been times when those situations involved individuals who were in some way taking advantage of you. Being an optimist, you refused to recognise the facts, which could mean they had time to create serious problems. We're all here to learn from such experiences, and to spot troublemakers before they can do any damage.

That's your lesson, even in minor situations. It could involve family, friends or colleagues who leave what should be their tasks for you to deal with. The more conscious you are, the more swiftly you can discuss the matter or make your own decision about what to do. Clear this up, and you'll free yourself for those joys that are so important for you.

You and others

Out of character as it may be, you're encouraged to allow those around you, friends, colleagues or even family, to take the lead. This is isn't natural for you, but it will be helpful. Why? Simply because the way they approach things will be very different from the way you do, and you might learn a lot.

Health and wellbeing

There are all sorts of approaches to wellbeing – healthy diet and all varieties of exercise. But here's the secret, one that's especially important for you as a Sagittarius: it's to walk, just to walk. And as you walk, breathe, take deep breaths. Do both of those, and you'll be amazed how much you benefit from it.

Goals and challenges

It's hard to believe that you actually need new goals from time to time, but in a way you do. It's like vitamins. This encourages you to get excited, to focus on the future, to make new plans and, most of all, to develop a new passion and enthusiasm for life.

THIS DAY FOR EVERYONE

Sooner or later, you'll need to take a tough line with somebody who's difficult on the best of days. While it's understandable that you're putting off addressing the issues in question, they won't vanish. You may, in fact, be better off tackling things in stages. Slowly but surely, you'll get there.

Some adore routine; the challenge for a Sagittarius is living with such individuals

You

Being ruled by the expansive planet Jupiter, you thrive on anything new. Where others are hesitant about undertaking new plans or challenges, you can't wait. You enjoy visiting new places, meeting new people and delving into the unfamiliar. This is very much part of your nature as a Sagittarius, and somebody for whom Jupiter is a strong player. However, it also means that you need to find the right balance between your existing arrangements, especially those that are long-standing, and any tempting new activities.

This can be tricky. It's not that one is better than another, but in your enthusiasm to learn about what's just come your way, you can easily neglect elements of the past, whether it's habits or activities that are worth your while, or even certain individuals.

Finding that balance isn't just important, it's essential, because the more you have in your life – the more you're juggling – the more significant certain elements of the past will be. They offer stability – certain relationships that are a valuable part of your life. Make achieving that balance one of your goals – an ongoing goal – and instead of feeling that you always need to catch up, as you create your schedule you'll balance those elements that form a basis for your life with the present and the excitement the future holds.

You and others

It's easy to get bored with the same thing. Yet in order to achieve certain goals, that's exactly what you need. The trick to dealing with this is to do other things that aren't just flexible, they are also changeable. Find that balance and achieve those goals, and you'll have a good time, and quite possibly learn a lot in the process.

Health and wellbeing

Everybody knows that eating well and sleeping well is important. However, as a Sagittarius, you're always bargaining with destiny, feeling that if you can fit a little more into each day, then it'll be fine. It is, in the short term, but it's also important to recognise that your body, like a car, needs fuel, and it needs it regularly.

Goals and challenges

A question that's important to ask is, what have you won recently? That may sound strange and, in fact, that's the point. Often you won't even think of what you've achieved. You don't stop to notice. But if you do, you'll be excited about it and might even give yourself a valuable pat on the back.

08

DECEMBER

THIS DAY FOR EVERYONE

Tempting as it is to sidestep dull facts, and even more tedious rules and regulations, these really can't be ignored. It may seem as if you've got away with it, but things are likely to catch up with you within a week or so. Invest time in dealing with these now, before they become any more complicated.

09

DECEMBER

GIFTS   Eager, Ebullient, Wide-ranging

CHALLENGES   Restless, Nervy, Capricious

NUMBER 3

(0+9) + (1+2) = 12 = (1+2) = 3

Trusting nature is one thing; trusting a human being is quite another matter

You

The impatient fire-sign side of your nature loves fast action, and struggles when you're stuck dealing with life's duties and dull details. While these often slow you down, and are frustrating, if not aggravating, you also learn a lot from them. In fact, they serve a purpose. While you prefer to move swiftly from one activity or obligation to the next, these painstaking matters – whatever their nature, personal, work-related or otherwise – all slow your pace and force you to examine what you're doing, learning or achieving.

The fact is, if you weren't cornered into this variety of review, you'd be unaware what you've done. True, you're sometimes forced to keep track anyway. As a result, when you need to list your achievements to get a job or a licence, for example, the details are handy.

That alone is an amazing payoff. Better yet, those insights may help you streamline tedious tasks. While this type of organisation doesn't come naturally to you, once you begin doing it, you'll find it enables you to enjoy things that you used to ignore, simply because they seemed such a nuisance. This is the trick to being a fire sign and enjoying life's luxuries. Instead of rushing through tasks, take time to do them and appreciate how sensual the achievement of those tasks is, and how sensual the rest of life can be as well,

You and others

Sometimes the best links in your life are formed with very different types of people, people who ordinarily you wouldn't get along with. But then, this is no surprise. If you've dealt only with those who are exactly like you, you'd already know them. The trick is to let each of those companions teach you something – about the world and, even more, about yourself.

Health and wellbeing

Because most Sagittarians are chronically short of time, the idea of so-called fast food is very appealing. Except as you know, it often isn't that good for you and can get very boring. But the trick is to make nutritious, delicious and good fast food. It can be done.

Goals and challenges

It's important to set up your own challenges. You would think that's obvious, but sometimes you'll allow those around you, an organisation or certain individuals, to tell you what to do, and it's easier to let them figure it out. Except, as you'll soon discover, you will have streamlined the way to achieve those goals in ways others would never have thought of.

THIS DAY FOR EVERYONE

It's said that you should never go to bed without settling differences. Yet, as is the case now, if you want to at least express hope you're reaching accord with others, even saying that might be challenging. But when you wake up in the morning, you'll be glad you did.

A day without at least a small risk is like a day without sunshine

You

The word spontaneity could be described as a keyword for all those born under the fire signs – that's you, as a Sagittarius, and also Aries and Leo. You all think and move swiftly. Not only does it come naturally, you enjoy it. Yet, as you're aware, not everyone in the world around you – from family or friends to colleagues, if you work – understands or, in fact, appreciates it.

There's a trick to learning to deal with those who think and act more slowly, and it is to take advantage, in the nicest possible way, of their slower pace.

These individuals, especially those born under the earth signs – Taurus, Virgo and Capricorn – think and move slowly, but are also thorough, and both enjoy and are superb at taking care of the variety of details that you find extremely dull. The problem? In your haste, you often forget to ask for help.

This is not simply about appreciating others. It's about giving those you know a chance to do what they're good at, and for you to focus on what you're best at and enjoy.

That way, you'll also avoid the complaints that come with you attempting to deal with the kind of details that others enjoy, and the compliments that come with your ability to make magic happen, in a way that the other signs simply aren't able to achieve.

You and others

As you know, there are certain individuals who are allies, that is, your friends, who will be beside you, who will, as some people say, "have your back" when you're doing something that's tricky. Or perhaps they will be the earth sign you need, who will help guide you. Whatever you do, trust these individuals.

Health and wellbeing

As a fire sign, you can get wound up from time to time – so wound up that you don't even realise you're exhausted. The lesson is to stop, even if you don't feel tired. It won't be until you do actually stop and take a couple of deep breaths that you realise that your irritated mood is nothing but sheer fatigue.

Goals and challenges

Everybody has to set goals – even you do when you're at your most rushed. It's just that those around you tend to set goals that are more detailed than yours. Talking them over may drive you crazy, but it's better to do it at the outset than to try to do it when you're already well into those activities.

10

DECEMBER

THIS DAY FOR EVERYONE

Sometimes, discussions are about an exchange of ideas. At the moment, however, it would seem that your main role in several such discussions is as a listener. Tempting as it is to offer advice, it's not really wanted or, in fact, helpful. The individual in question needs to talk and talk and talk.

11

DECEMBER

GIFTS Persuasive, Heroic, Frank

CHALLENGES Demeaning, Defiant, Fiery

NUMBER 5

(1+1) + (1+2) = 5

Understand others' beliefs isn't easy, but trying to learn about them is fascinating

You

As a Sagittarius, and somebody ruled by the inquisitive, philosophically inclined planet Jupiter, you're fascinated by those who talk about new, unfamiliar or intriguing ways of looking at life. This ranges from how life works here on earth, to those who discuss ways of thinking, or even realms, that extend beyond our everyday world. They fascinate you, and in some cases, you're drawn into exploring their ideas or even teachings.

This can be tricky for you, because while you can be drawn to those who set themselves up as gurus who give advice, you don't necessarily question their ideas. It's simply that their ideas so intrigue you, you could turn plans into action and, possibly, commitments, without much thought. However, it's important to pause, and ask a few questions.

While some may have worthwhile ideas and good suggestions, others may be demanding or possessive. You may even battle with them. While that may be complicated, and while those individuals who set themselves up as authorities can be as irritating as they are fascinating, the experience is worth your time.

With every encounter you can broaden your horizons and discover interesting ideas or people. Yet while you think of yourself as being inquisitive, you have a stubborn streak, and you could well be facing it here.

You and others

You don't think of yourself as having any particular characteristics because you are simply true to yourself. Yet certain individuals find your passionate nature, your intensity and the fact that you are entirely who you are, attractive and charming. Take advantage of this, in the sense of recognising how much you add to the lives of others.

Health and wellbeing

As somebody who is an inspiration to others and full of energy, every once in a while you have to remember to look after yourself, to look after your body and your energy level. Maybe this has to do with pausing and taking a rest, perhaps with eating a little differently, or even with letting those who care so much about you spoil you in the way they'd like.

Goals and challenges

Every once in a while you need to rethink what you're doing – not just your objectives, but how you're approaching them. If you do that, it may be that certain simple changes will prevent you complicating matters that would require more serious changes along the line.

THIS DAY FOR EVERYONE

The last thing you're in the mood for is disappointing people and leaving situations undone. But certain individuals have ignored your cautious advice and are blaming you for their problems. Explain firmly where you stand, then withdraw from discussions. There really is nothing more to say.

GIFTS Forthright, Droll, Fluent

CHALLENGES Blunt, Wacky, Capricious

NUMBER 6

(1+2) + (1+2) = 6

The best adventure is as challenging as it is unexpected

You

You sometimes think the best gift you could possibly have is some free time – time to relax, time to do what you want, time to ponder. But, despite those dreams, it seems you always have too much to do. Yet you also tend to refuse offers of help from those around you, some of whom really enjoy doing exactly that kind of thing. They're not only able to impose order on life's tedious practicalities, they'll happily organise you, then deal with those matters so you don't have to do.

Yet you say no. Why? Usually, the reason is that you feel explaining what needs to be done would take too much time. But the truth is that you're impatient. Others can probably figure out how to deal with any such matters and with what you're doing – and probably better than you.

That may be a shock. However, at the same time, it will create an entirely new relationship. Firstly, with time. You'll have more of it. But it will also alter your relationship with those individuals who you've simply dismissed as being unable to handle things as well as you. Yet they can, actually, do better than you. This recognition of their abilities will change your relationship as well. They'll know you appreciate them and trust them with those tasks. Even more than that, you'll now be able to speak as equals as well.

You and others

Recognising that some individuals have the same joy as you you do at being spontaneous and as acting swiftly is a great gift. You'll want to thank them for what they offer, but also you want to recognise who you can trust with those pressing tasks.

Health and wellbeing

For you as a Sagittarius, in particular, clearing out your space is as important as exercise. Getting rid of excess stuff, which you look at and which depletes your energy, is as important as doing actual exercise.

Goals and challenges

One of your biggest challenges is keeping track of what you've done. While you may keep a diary, actually noting your achievements is a lot more difficult. But how will you remember what you achieved if you don't at least make a note, or save a souvenir, that will remind you of those achievements?

S / A \ G / I \ T \ T \ A / R \ I / U \ S

12

DECEMBER

There is no tidy way to make sudden and, in some cases, dramatic changes in long-standing arrangements. Others may complain that they, too, are being influenced by the changes triggered by this current cycle. Unsettling as these are, there's no arguing the fact that things must move on.

GIFTS Silver-tongued, Hearty, Coherent

CHALLENGES Curt, Fidgety, Disapproving

NUMBER 7

(1+3) + (1+2) = 7

Love is a joy and a challenge; understanding others is an endless puzzle

You

As an expansive fire sign and a Sagittarius, you hate regretting what you didn't do, so you try to fit everything you can into any day, any week any month or even any year. While this means you're able to get an amazing amount done, you can become overwhelmed, if not driven crazy, by tasks and obligations that pile up. Worse, those obligations are even more overwhelming because you set them for yourself. Of course, when you did you were confident that you had time to fit those tasks in, along with everything else.

The trick? Borrow a characteristic from your neighbouring sign, Capricorn, which is a practical earth sign. That may seem dull to you, as a fire sign. Yet the exhaustion you feel and the disappointment you experience when you've no time to do what you intend, or to do it properly, isn't worth it.

This is important because your life's about making new friends and meeting people. And if you don't have time to spend with them, then you won't get to know them and deepen that early acquaintanceship into something lasting. A slower pace probably won't come naturally to you, as a fire sign and as a Sagittarius, but once you learn that skill, and employ it from time to time, it will add enormously to your life, day by day, week by week and month by month.

You and others

Core to your life are family and friends, people you have been with a long time. But ironically, when you meet new people and don't have time to get to know them, it's difficult to have that feeling of closeness, of trust and intimacy. Regard the time you spend with them as an investment in friendships and in your future.

Health and wellbeing

Sometimes you get so involved in what you're doing that you regard even going to sleep as a failure. While you're not conscious of that, it does happen and it means you're unable to enjoy all of life because you're exhausted. The trick, of course, is to fall asleep before you collapse in a heap.

Goals and challenges

You set your own pace, you set your own goals, but sometimes you don't realise that because you're in such a hurry, it seems like destiny has done it for you. The trick, and the magic, for you is to realise that you've created those goals – and you can set the pace for them.

13

DECEMBER

THIS DAY FOR EVERYONE

There's a difference between a possible solution for a problem – and you have lots of those – and the kind of solution you can be sure will last. At the moment, nothing quite fits. While others are impatient, your instincts are telling you it's vital that you wait until more worthwhile ideas surface.

There are physical challenges, but those of an emotional nature are something else

You

Often, when you're making a plan or promising something to others, in your enthusiasm you'll say that you can achieve far more than, realistically, you know is possible. But you've done it in the past, although it may have exhausted you and taken far longer than you thought. And because of that, you'll think that you can do it again.

However, you've another option. You could pause and simply take a different approach. This involves thinking about what needs to be done, the time those activities and obligations will take, and the hours in the day, and viewing them from an entirely different angle. But it's also about doing something that's completely out of character. That is asking for the support and help of others. Both of these are very much against your nature as an impulsive, independent fire sign.

Yet you live in a world of people who not only like you, but will also be happy to help and, better yet, to learn from you. They'd be excited to spend time with you. This won't come naturally to you because, despite being sociable, you're sure it's easier to do everything yourself. However, not only will these individuals lend a hand, but you'll find you're able to get more out of each day and to deepen those relationships in ways you've hoped for, but not yet achieved.

You and others

Even if you're not particularly into astrology, you sense your fire-sign nature, the speed at which you think and the way in which you tend to override the activities of those who don't move as swiftly. Even if they may be more skilled at certain activities than you are, think carefully before you do it again.

Health and wellbeing

Often, it's important that you pause before you begin doing something, and think about whether you actually have the energy to do it, or would benefit from someone else's support, guidance, or perhaps even handing it over to another individual. This won't come naturally, at least at first. But the payoff for making those changes will be huge, if not lifelong.

Goals and challenges

You have a stubborn streak. You don't think of it that way, because you're always enthusiastic about new ideas. But there are certain activities, certain relationships and even certain things you simply don't consider because, long ago, you decided it wasn't your thing. If ever there was a time to consider allowing those to be your thing, it's now.

14

DECEMBER

GIFTS Inquisitive, Honest, Spirited

CHALLENGES Probing, Clumsy, Abrupt

NUMBER 9

(1+5) + (1+2) = 9

Laughter is said to cure even the darkest moods. It certainly works for me

You

The fire-sign motto, especially for you as a Sagittarius, is that life is meant to be fun.

Whatever you're doing – household chores, or your job or even seriously challenging tasks – can be a joy, as long as you approach them in the right way. And that is, in the lively fire-sign manner.

While at times that's true, you can also act so swiftly that you forget about important details and unwittingly complicate matters. The problem is that if you moved at a slower pace, you'd be able to deal with them right away. And if you ignore them entirely, you'll end up having to go back over things, which is, of course, even worse. Yet still, the optimistic side of your fire-sign nature says that life at its best is lived at a swift pace, even if that means ignoring details.

The trick is to find a balance between the two – to occasionally adopt that jet-fuelled approach to living when it doesn't matter, but also, when it's necessary, to take time to deal with details, most of which will come up sooner or later.

Equally, focus on spending time with those you care about most, those individuals whose company brings you joy. Find the balance between these every day, and not only will you get as much done as you can, you will enjoy the day itself all the more.

You and others

You may think you know who brings you joy, and which activities lift your spirits. But sometimes you don't stop to try new ones, simply because you're so busy with the old ones. The message from the heavens is to try something new regularly, if not every week.

Health and wellbeing

There are two kinds of pushing. There's pushing to make yourself healthy and strong, and there's pushing to get everything done, which means you never get enough done, and you're always exhausted because you're trying to catch up. Give some thought to this approach – to your diary and your schedule.

Goals and challenges

As you well know, you hate rules and regulations. Yet, every once in a while, situations demand them, either because it's part of them, or occasionally for someone's safety or wellbeing. Whatever the case, choose your battles. You could fight them, or you could simply accept them and move on.

15

DECEMBER

THIS DAY FOR EVERYONE

The planetary activity ahead won't just be exciting. Much of what's coming your way could turn into something worthwhile and often of a long-term nature. However, that won't be clear at the time, which means you owe it to yourself to explore everything, including what seems unappealing.

When others question me, it's not through distrust but genuine curiosity

You

As a Sagittarius, you're not only sociable, you're genuinely interested in others, so frequently face the challenge that comes with the desire to chat with those you meet, and hear what they're up to, while always aware that you've things to do. That awareness that you've dozens of things to complete before the end of the day is one thing. But if the person you're talking to isn't a Sagittarius, their conversational style will be more relaxed than yours. When the topic wanders from one thing to another, you'll get increasingly uptight.

The trick? Set aside time to have a good chat, enough that you can exchange ideas and then move on. This may mean juggling your schedule, but that way, you'll only have to do it once.

For you, life as a Sagittarius can mean always rushing on to whatever is next – from appointments to work. But it applies as much to simply hanging out with others.

Whatever the case, the trick is to do whatever it is that you need to do, and allow enough time for doing it without cutting it short, which is your tendency as a Sagittarius, and somebody who's always juggling several things at once. When you achieve this skill – and it is, indeed, a very great skill – not only will you be able to enjoy life, it will be being the best that any Sagittarian can be.

You and others

Those who know you will understand the pace at which you live – and others will learn. But those who care most about you will help you to remember that haste doesn't always achieve the most.

Health and wellbeing

Deep down, you have a feeling that you can outdo the rest of the world and outdo everybody else, whether it has to do with being creative, whether it has to do with what you fit into a day, or what you accomplish in a lifetime. The fact is, even as a Sagittarius, you have your vulnerable points, one of which is the need to stop and assess what you can do.

Goals and challenges

There are two rules for you to remember. One is that it's okay to take on too much. The second is that it's okay to cut back. That is, when you realise that you literally can't do what you took on as the day began. It's all right to say that either you'll do it tomorrow, or perhaps you won't do it at all.

16

DECEMBER

Admitting you're wrong is no problem. However, certain individuals insist their facts are right and that you must be wrong. The real problem is that they're looking for a battle and have chosen their topic, which involves you. Say nothing. The individual will soon turn their attention elsewhere.

The best questions can't be answered in a day

You

Being ruled by the planet Jupiter – the planet of growth, expansion, and just plain good fortune – is a real gift. Your life is full of amazing people, and wonderful things come your way. Despite that, you're often impatient, to the extent that you'll agree to offers without checking the facts, possibly because you're overly eager or don't have the time to ask questions – or you simply hope everything will work out.

While this hasty approach to various elements of life, and planning, is typical for you, as a Sagittarius, it's a habit, not an unchanging destiny. You can learn to examine the practical side of things – matters such as timing, finances, is there the support you need? Of course, if you wait long enough, you can do that in a hurry too. And you probably did, in the past, possibly more than once.

Or you can begin to approach being a Sagittarius differently. Instead of putting off details until the last minute, which has almost become a habit in your life, you can take one of your best assets, which is your enthusiasm, and share it with others. Ask them to join you in figuring out how to make the best of certain plans, projects or passions, and then to help you turn that into reality.

It may not be your usual approach, but it will be easier – and a lot more fun.

You and others

You already know how important it is to keep old friends in your life. Also, you have a strong instinct about making new ones. When someone's exciting, you'll draw them closer to you. However, what you don't do is edit those individuals. That is, recognise that as new friends come into your life, it's time to let go of old ones. You might still see them out of habit but actually it's time to say farewell.

Health and wellbeing

The ups and downs you face as a Sagittarius can be stressful, and you're resilient. However, it's easier if – instead of draining your energy, as you do with those ups and downs – you find a new balance. Some of that will include trusting those around you with some of the more stressful of those activities,

Goals and challenges

You thrive on challenges, not because you want problems, but because it's a kind of exercise for you. It's like doing a puzzle, but a life puzzle. It's important to recognise that if you have too many challenges going at any one time, you can't do any of them well. The solution? Pick and choose carefully.

THIS DAY FOR EVERYONE

There's a difference between making tentative plans, which is what this period is all about, and lasting commitments. The problem is, one particular individual views arrangements as final. Gently but firmly help them understand that plans that are flexible will be better all around.

Walking faster than I have to makes me feel really alive

You

Considering what you're planning isn't just important, it's vital. You know that, but also you'd rather plunge in then think about your plans while you're actually organising things.

You take this approach because you're convinced that if you're in the middle of things, you can react swiftly and base plans on recent experience. While that makes sense from one perspective, you're urged to pause regularly and think about what you're organising – and for two reasons.

Firstly, if you're exhausted or overwhelmed, you can become moody or irritable without really knowing why, and your decisions are unlikely to be wise or sensible. Secondly, if you pause or, alternatively, do something that is very out of character and make a list, or even ask others for some guidance or assistance, then you can turn those seemingly overwhelming tasks into something that isn't just manageable, but fun.

In fact, if you take things in stages, you can turn what would otherwise have been a crisis into something creative. This approach may be out of character, and it may seem as if you're compromising. However, shifting from that sense of being overwhelmed, which can be a Sagittarian signature, to a sense of pacing – as if you were doing a dance – isn't just a good idea, it can be a thing of beauty.

You and others

Some people are just good company, and a few very special people seem to magnetically attract good luck. They have the ability to spot something exciting, and even more than that, to bring all the pieces together and turn those exciting concepts into a part of a life that you share with them. Draw them close to you.

Health and wellbeing

The concept of resting seems very dull and dreary to you. In fact, it almost feels like a compromise. However, for you, as a Sagittarius and a fire sign, and somebody who tends to live life full steam ahead, simple rest is like taking very powerful vitamins.

Goals and challenges

Every once in a while, you need a new challenge to get you going. This is very much part of your nature. However, there's a secret to this. And that secret is to select that new challenge very carefully.

18

DECEMBER

Few things are more precious than time with loved ones. Now somebody you care about is putting others first. Before you get hurt or angry, ask what's going on. The odds are that they have obligations they haven't mentioned. Once they explain, you'll understand exactly what it is they're dealing with.

GIFTS Courageous, Outspoken, Vibrant

CHALLENGES Reckless, Audacious, Unstable

NUMBER 4

(1+9) + (1+2) = 13 = (1+3) = 4

Joy lives both in life's quiet moments and at its most uproarious parties

You

As a Sagittarius, and somebody who's a life enthusiast, you'll often decide to figure out the perfect plan for the day, the perfect way to do something, the perfect long-term goal or, even, the perfect life plan. While this is very true to your nature as an idealistic Sagittarian, the problem is that you can get addicted to that pursuit of perfection when, often, what life brings your way isn't quite like that.

This means you've no choice but to start with what you have, or are facing, in the here and now, then do the best you can. If you're being idealistic, that may seem a compromise. However, if you simply decide to begin with your current situation and take each step as it comes, you'll find you will experience all sorts of unexpected delights.

You'll be able to go more deeply into certain situations that, otherwise, you'd have given up on. Equally, you'll take time to chat with the people involved – not just about solutions but, instead, about possibilities. And that, in turn, could lead you to a very different path than the one you had in mind when you determined to make things perfect – your way.

This doesn't just have to do with your life, your activities, but also your relationships, even your feelings about yourself. The more flexible you are, the more easy-going you are, the more fun you'll have being you.

You and others

Very often you're the one who takes the lead. Being an enthusiastic fire sign, this comes naturally to you. But there are other individuals who are either clearer or perhaps are themselves guides in some way. If they arrive in your life, listen to them. Even if it doesn't come naturally at first, you will soon be glad you did.

Health and wellbeing

It's terrific to look after yourself, but as a Sagittarius you can have too much of a good thing – and that is the case if you look after yourself too well, by following an obsessive eating regime or exercising too much. Being moderate doesn't come naturally to you. But in this particular case, it's vital.

Goals and challenges

You don't always think things through before you take on a goal or face a challenge. Some would be concerned, if not critical, about that. But often the only way you can learn about what you're dealing with is when you're actually in the middle of it. In many cases, this is exactly the reason why it's better to learn about those challenges as you are moving ahead and dealing with them immediately.

THIS DAY FOR EVERYONE

Usually, there's no wrong way to express concern about a matter somebody is struggling with. However, one particular individual is presenting an upbeat façade to the world, and would be very upset if they thought you saw through it. What they will need, however, is somebody to talk to and to trust.

A badly told but funny joke is better than taking life too seriously

You

Your date forms a bridge between the fire and passion of your Sagittarian nature and the cautious, thorough Capricorn. As you're undoubtedly aware, it's an interesting blend to live with. When you understand the difference between the two, they achieve an ongoing balance, and life takes on a new order, but not the kind that extinguishes your fiery passion.

Rather, those feelings are more measured, so instead of being overwhelmed, you manage to get things done and dealt with.

It's an amazing combination, one that enables you to find a power and intelligence that you can use in ways you wouldn't have believed possible. The trick to all of this is to recognise that the growth and development that's part of being alive never stops. If you think of yourself as a project, one you're still working on, it won't be about getting things just right on any one particular day. Instead, it will be about continuing to explore your nature, to discover your inner world, and the wider world beyond.

You'll discover how your mind works,your intuition, and the creative side of your nature, and bring them all together in a way that allows you to make the best of each day, each relationship and what the next day offers. Take that approach, and you will make the best of being the person you are.

You and others

The best way to be inspired by the two sides of your nature is to hang out with equally multi-talented, expansive people. They don't need to be the same. But there are certain individuals who have a gift for doing a number of things at once. Spend time with them, and it will teach you how to use your gift better.

Health and wellbeing

Knowing when you're doing things perfectly is great. But knowing when you're doing a bit too much is even more important. It's easy to glide into what might be termed perfection overdrive, but it's important to look after yourself rather than becoming exhausted.

Goals and challenges

Everybody needs new goals, but it's best not to take them up all at once. Line them up and make a list – even though that doesn't sound very exciting. If, when you're finishing one, you know you can tackle the next one, you'll be all the more excited about what you're finishing.

20

DECEMBER

Capricorn

Ruler Saturn
Element Earth

Symbol The Goat
Flower Pansy

December 21 – January 19

Capricorn As a practical earth sign whose symbol is the horned goat, you can achieve the impossible, in the form of ascending a mountain or attaining an ambition. Being ruled by hardy Saturn, you're discreet about your many kindnesses, but glory in your tough exterior. Your flower is the pansy, your plants are hemp and ivy and your trees, elm and yew. Your stones are symbolic of winter's dark days – black pearls, black diamonds and jet.

C
A
P
R
I
C
O
R
N

GIFTS Ambitious, Vigilant, Respectful

CHALLENGES Disciplinarian, Pedantic, Mean

NUMBER 6

(2+1) + (1+2) = 6

I'll explore ways to blend – and benefit from – my fiery practicality

You

Being a December 21st Capricorn, you balance the sign just before yours – Sagittarius, a fire sign – with the far more earthy Capricorn. That fiery side is restless and both enjoys and thrives on facing challenges. This is the part of your nature that becomes easily bored, as well.

However, the earth-sign part – the Capricorn side – is not only able to focus on whatever you're facing, but, due to your inborn discipline, also has a remarkable ability to stick with a battle. You will amaze others by what you achieve simply by employing that Capricorn focus.

Yet, every once in a while, you'll experience the restlessness that is part of your Sagittarian side. While, initially, you'll try to chase it away, once you're conscious of it and, even more, how you can benefit from it, you'll realise what an asset it is.

Each side of your nature brings the other amazingly useful skills and perceptions, and when you blend the two, you'll find that not only do you have a greater capacity to adapt to unexpected changes, you'll benefit as much from the joy that is very much a part of your Sagittarian nature, as you will from the stability that comes with being a Capricorn.

The more aware of them you are, the more you'll enjoy what each sign adds to your life.

You and others

It's true, you're generous by nature and you will support friends and family and, equally, the world, in ways that are as appropriate as, often, they're unanticipated. However, there's a part of you that's very discreet about this, and prefers to keep those gifts a secret. Do so but, also, realise that if you do it openly, you'll inspire others.

Health and wellbeing

As an earth sign, you have an instinctive understanding about the importance of keeping fit, and will work hard to do this. However, there's a side of your nature that you tend to neglect, and that has to do with the part that's affected by stress. Allow it to take over, and it can undermine you. Underdoing it? You can begin with simply breathing.

Goals and challenges

Normally, as a Capricorn, you have endless goals for the week, for the month, for the year and for your life – and you don't need any more of them. What those goals need is an edit. Do that regularly, and not only will you recognise how much you've done, but you'll be clearer about what comes next.

THIS DAY FOR EVERYONE

Ordinarily, what begins as a dispute can end up with a constructive outcome. But what you're facing now could have as much to do with a fundamental misunderstanding of your objectives and others'. Make discussing and untangling any such issues your priority, and those tensions could vanish.

Each day's surprise could become tomorrow's opportunities

C
/
A
\
P
/
R
\
I
/
C
\
O
/
R
\
N

22

DECEMBER

You

The joys of the physical world are a part of what comes with being a Capricorn. As an earth sign, you're aware of nature around you in all its forms, from its majesty to an understanding of how things grow. You're conscious of the elements that are an everyday part of our lives, from water to light, the air and energy, and how these, plus sunlight, create our world.

While you try to incorporate these into your life, you are sometimes distracted by everyday duties and obligations to others. That's why it's easy to lose that appreciation for the world around you and, in fact, for something larger than yourself. When that happens, you can lose access to that joy. And you'll feel that loss, but won't always realise what it is, or why. Yet it's important for every person, and especially for you as an earth sign.

There's a trick to dealing with it. Firstly, it's to notice it, and then secondly, to realise that whatever you're doing, you can reconnect with that power.

You don't need to go anywhere. The simple act of pausing and thinking how amazing it is that you are you, and that you're living the life you're living at the moment, is the best place to start. And it's the best way to recover that joy – and, in fact, to begin to feel that joy wrap its arms around you.

You and others

As a Capricorn, you've a knack for helping those around you, except sometimes your instincts correctly tell you that those individuals need to help themselves. The trick is to inspire them. This may be more difficult than you anticipate, but, once you do it, you'll have given them the greatest gift of all.

Health and wellbeing

You may not feel yourself influenced by fads. However, when it comes to the shape of your body, it's really easy – simply because, while there are some things you can change, there are others you can't. The solution? It's to love yourself and love yourself unreservedly, whatever shape you are.

Goals and challenges

It's important to be aware that, as an earth sign, you will inevitably set worldly goals and they're easy to measure. Goals that have to do with your own self and your feelings, however, are much less easy to measure, but you'll feel much better when you've achieved them.

THIS DAY FOR EVERYONE

Sometimes the only way to make a point with certain difficult individuals is to become seriously angry with them. You've had to do this before, and you realise that when you pretend to be angry, it works just as well, but at less cost to your emotional equilibrium.

Any challenge is an adventure, if I choose to make it one

C
/
A
\
P
/
R
\
I
/
C
\
O
/
R
\
N

You

When living your everyday life, you're thinking about what needs to be done and that's pretty much it.

However, you'll also have a broader sense of the influence of your actions on those around you, from family and friends to the wider world. Personally, you know exactly what needs to be done, each day, week, month and, probably, year.

Yet, as an earth sign, you've a powerful connection with nature itself, from spotting a plant growing to looking up at the sky, although often without realising it.

What's more, you're drawn to those who inspire you to focus more on this side of life, often to balance out your drive to get things done. The trick? It's to recognise that achieving that balance is itself an adventure.

That is, juggling your own obligations to others and to work, if you go to a job, but also fulfilling life's joys. It's about blending these into your everyday life.

Part of the fun is figuring it out. It's an adventure – sometimes on your own or, just as often, with others. Just like in fairy tales, it helps if you believe miracles are possible.

That may sound like pure fantasy, but the best way to find out how it works is to try it. And for you, as someone born on December 23rd, that is one of your challenges.

You and others

There are all sorts of people you can spend time with. Of course, some you have a duty to be with, while others are a joy, such as family and friends. But one very important type of person is the one who breaks your habits, who keeps you from doing the same old thing and who takes you into new and exciting territory.

Health and wellbeing

Usually, you're a guide for others. You have initiative and you think things through. However, there are certain individuals who have taken the lead. Let them set an example. What you learn about eating and living well from them won't just be helpful, on occasion, it could be life-changing.

Goals and challenges

There's a part of you that wants life to be organised and, once it is, feels like you can be relieved. However, it's vital that you recognise that nothing is ever static, and life's about the new and, often, unexpected. It's because what's least expected and most disruptive often brings the greatest gifts.

THIS DAY FOR EVERYONE

The principle of being truthful is vital to you and you try not to lie about anything at all. Yet it seems the only way to avoid getting involved in activities you dread. Unappealing as this seems, you'll soon realise how beneficial those activities will be. If you can't say an enthusiastic yes, just don't say no.

I can stick to plans, or view them simply as a jumping-off point

You

You are quite rightly proud of your drive as a Capricorn. However, you've probably noticed that it's easy to confuse those worldly goals with your more personal goals and ideals, and other achievements you have in mind. Those are the kind that you know others will acknowledge, possibly certain individuals you'd like to impress.

Defining this drive is part of your journey. Others may have helpful ideas about the best approach to take, and while you'll listen to their suggestions, it's vital you rewrite these suggestions so they suit you. In some cases, it may mean doing something a little differently than others suggest. But, just as often, it will be about discovering something that isn't merely different – it is entirely separate from anything anyone around you, including you, would have conceived of.

It's about a breakthrough. True, in some cases, it may seem you're rebelling. But there's another way of looking at it, and that's there's a plan for you, one that's taking you in new and often completely unexpected directions.

And, better yet, simply by exploring it, you'll learn something new, exciting and magical. This new path enables you to make the best of the earth-sign side of your nature, but also allows you to see what the heavens offer you, and that's where the excitement comes in.

You and others

Sometimes, as a Capricorn, you'll want to associate with those you look up to so they'll inspire you. But, if you're feeling anxious, you rather enjoy being around those who haven't done as well as you simply because they'll boost your ego. Of course, the secret is to seek out equals who will draw you forward with them.

Health and wellbeing

You can do all you can to keep yourself in good shape, eating properly and working out. However, there's still one thing that can undermine you if you don't pay attention to it and that is, quite simply, stress. The remedy? You could do fancy meditation and all of that, but simply taking a walk and a few deep breaths is a good start.

Goals and challenges

While people often write lists of what needs to be done, perhaps the most important thing for you to do is simply to stop and think about what isn't working. That isn't losing the game, it's actually being creative – and just when it's important.

C
/
A
\
P
/
R
\
I
/
C
\
O
/
R
\
N

24

DECEMBER

THIS DAY FOR EVERYONE

You need a break. You've been under considerable pressure for weeks, and while you've handled it well, some of it will continue for longer. The trick is to recognise this won't last forever and to balance the pressure with doing something you enjoy each and every day.

Plans based on experience chain you to the past; create each day anew

C
/
A
\
P
/
R
\
I
/
C
\
O
/
R
\
N

25

DECEMBER

You

While you're probably aware that your symbols is the Capricorn goat, you may have seen another – not just the goat, but a creature that's half goat, half fish.

This is one of the most ancient of astrological symbols and dates back to Babylonia, thousands of years ago, yet it's still sometimes used today. The fact that it combine these two creatures reflects an intriguing combination in your character.

While you're best known for the practical, earthy goat side, the fish incorporates the more intuitive, flexible part of your nature. This is intriguing, because while it survives very well on land, it can also move into the sea and swim through the tides of life. If you think about this when you're facing difficulties, instead of trying to figure everything out, as an earth sign would, you may begin to rely on your intuition more.

It's balancing the fundamental toughness of Capricorn with the sensitivity that you may not realise you had, or even regarded as weak. The trick to all of this, of course, is to embrace both parts of your nature and to realise that each has a powerful role. The more you understand each part, the more you'll take advantage of it and the more you'll be able to enjoy who you are and the person you're becoming day by day.

You and others

You may not think of it this way, but sometimes you feel that you need to help others and that you're there to inspire them. That's true. But there are other times when actually they inspire you. What may be most important, however, is those close ties with family, who are always there for you every day.

Health and wellbeing

While you, as a Capricorn, enjoy a challenge, including a physical challenge, it's worth noting that gentle movements are as important as those that are vigorous and you may even learn more about your body and yourself if you take a gentler approach.

Goals and challenges

Everybody lists their goals, and most people also note their challenges. The trickiest bit is to embrace those challenges with enthusiasm, knowing that each has come your way to teach you something. And the more enthusiastically you embrace them, the more swiftly you'll learn those lessons.

THIS DAY FOR EVERYONE

By no means are you stubborn, yet you're very attached to certain arrangements, mostly because they've been part of your life for a long time and you rather like the challenges they introduce. Still, these really must come to an end. If you're looking for new challenges, you can expect them soon.

Feelings of passion, whatever their nature, balance my practical side

You

Being an earth sign, when you look at life and your goals from a realistic angle, you think carefully about what you've achieved and, especially, what you haven't. In fact, often you'll have made a list of those objectives, mostly so when each is achieved, you can mark it off and focus on what's next.

If the list isn't actually on paper, there'll certainly be one in your mind. While this is helpful, especially when it comes to deciding what to do first, there's something you'll want to keep in mind. And that's to recognise that life itself is always shifting and, therefore, juggling those goals. So, however, much as you achieve, there's no perfect moment when it's all done – because, of course, life moves on. Your list will change, and so will you.

There is a trick to dealing with this – it's to see those constantly shifting goals as being part of a drama. However, these aren't appearing for your entertainment, but, rather, so you can grow. And once you're viewing them from this angle, and recognising they're a variety of theatre created so you can learn more about life and the world itself, then you won't take it quite so seriously. In fact, you might even enjoy it. And, as you do, you'll recognise that every twist and turn is there for you to learn from – to be entertained by, and to inspire the creative side of your nature.

You and others

It's easy to get lost in the game of life and, especially, to view those around you, from family and friends to colleagues, as part of that story. However, those moments between you and them when you're each experiencing breakthroughs remind you just how deep this process is, and how much each of you is benefitting from it.

Health and wellbeing

As a Capricorn, you'll always be happy with a regime that has to do with how you eat or how you look after yourself. However, there's another activity that will benefit you and it's called relaxation, it's called stopping and simply enjoying life as it is, taking one deep breath after another.

Goals and challenges

Everybody dreads setbacks as an indication that either something has gone wrong or it's a difficult period. Actually it's a bit like if you're hiking up a rather steep hill – setbacks spur growth in you. Note that and you'll not only go for them, you'll grow from them.

26

DECEMBER

THIS DAY FOR EVERYONE

Life has been a bit of a drama lately. While you and others have been struggling, you're still longing for a break. You'll get it, at least in the form of some happy times doing what you love or with those you adore, and within only a few days.

Taking chances is an art – one that isn't about planning, but courage

C / A \ P / R \ I / C \ O / R \ N

27

DECEMBER

You

As a conscientious Capricorn, you're well aware how unwise it is to live life seeking the approval of others. Yet you live in a world where, despite knowing that fact, there are certain individuals you admire for one reason or another. It may be family or friends, somebody who inspires you. Or the setting may be more worldly – somebody who's undertaken a challenge or, as is often the case, an individual in a professional setting whose approval or assistance is vital if you're to achieve more.

All seem important in their own way. Yet there's something else you can do – and that is, give them your approval. You can let them know how much you're learning from them, and how much you appreciate that. Initially, this may seem strange, but once you shift the balance, their approval isn't quite as important and you have, in a way, changed the rules

Instead of a life of challenges to be met, you'll shift from being aware of them to enjoying what's on offer – whatever the setting. While challenges are good, and you grow from them, sometimes the ability to shift the balance is more important. It's a chance not only to grow, but to become more creative. Instead of focusing on knowing most, it's about being wise enough to learn from those challenging situations and those around you.

You and others

Humility is a funny thing. However much certain individuals have accomplished, every once in a while they need the support of others, often about simple matters. Not only will that reveal the necessary facts, it's also a reminder we all have something to learn. And that process of exchanging ideas is more valuable than the facts you already know.

Health and wellbeing

Feeling fit is one thing, feeling energetic when you get up in the morning and being the right weight and shape according to society can be nice, but it depends on what you were born with. What is most important is simply being able to love yourself, to look in the mirror each day and give yourself an embrace.

Goals and challenges

Everybody needs a challenge, especially a Capricorn. As a goat, having a challenge is very much part of your life, but there are many kinds of challenges. Some of them are public, and some of them are private. And on occasion, you don't even know you're dealing with them at the time. It's not until they're history that you realise how much you've achieved.

THIS DAY FOR EVERYONE

For days, if not weeks, you've been avoiding a seriously tricky issue that you quite rightly fear could become explosive. Since this isn't going to vanish in an otherwise quiet period, you're urged to raise and discuss it. Do so now and the odds are good that you'll avoid those dreaded dramas.

Worldly achievements are terrific, but personal happiness is a better companion

You

You, Capricorn, deal with an unusual, in fact rare, combination of drive and desire to achieve in the world you're in. It may not be commercial, it may be your own world.

However, another side of your nature can struggle, if not be amazingly anxious about getting things right. At times, you battle with self-doubt. Some would say that this is the reason you chose to be a Capricorn, to learn from both the challenges and the doubts you're facing. Some question that idea of choosing this.

However, if you choose a way to live, work and look after yourself that suits you, it could well be that you'll have been drawn to life as a Capricorn, with its unique gifts and lessons.

Think of this when fears arise, and you'll not only learn from them, you may well find you're able to share that wisdom with others as well. And, whatever form it takes, this discovery will enable you to both discuss your experiences and recall how much you've benefitted from them.

In each case, recognising that you're not alone in those doubts is one of the secrets of life for you. And when you recognise that, you will be able to deal with your doubts and help others in ways that you can't imagine at the time, and also bring a very special variety of support and help to the world.

You and others

Speaking of doubts, you can sometimes think that others have it easy. But, as you become better acquainted with them, you realise that they're wrestling with exactly the same kind of doubts that you are and, instead of standing back and looking at each other, you can support each other.

Health and wellbeing

Yes, food and exercise are important – and getting those right helps you feel well. But the thing that actually makes you feel terrific when you get up in the morning, and just as terrific when you go to bed at night, is simple happiness – and that comes with accepting who you are today, in the moment. Learn that skill and everything else will fade away.

Goals and challenges

You tend to aim high, which is admirable, but it's vital that you ask the question whether you actually want this goal. Because you tend to aim so high, the goal is often something that touches your heart and your soul. Ask yourself this. The answer may surprise you.

C
/
A
\
P
/
R
\
I
/
C
\
O
/
R
\
N

28

DECEMBER

THIS DAY FOR EVERYONE

With so much in flux, this hardly seems a logical time to reject certain once-appealing options, but the more you learn, the more aware you are that they really wouldn't be a good idea. What's more, the time has come to narrow your options to those that would work in every setting.

Waiting until you know the outcome before taking a chance leads to a very dull life

C
/
A
\
P
/
R
\
I
/
C
\
O
/
R
\
N

29
DECEMBER

You

The question is, are you restless? Do you feel that if you get out and about, see more people and do more things, then you'll overcome those feelings? While that might help, the real problem is that for you, as a Capricorn, you've too much on your mind and a list of things that need to be done, one that's so long you're anxious about getting everything done.

This means you're distracted from everyday life and what you achieve each day, in terms of the tasks you actually deal with. Often, you're virtually unaware of the joys you're experiencing, such as spending time with those who matter most to you or, perhaps, helping certain individuals who need a hand.

This is about life's simple joys. Taking a slow walk rather than hurrying home. Chatting with family or friends. Noting these and savouring them is one of your biggest lessons as a Capricorn.

You've long been convinced achievements of various kinds in a range of settings would bring that joy. While they're wonderful, as is increasingly clear, the ability to pause and experience joy in what you've accomplished recently, what you're doing now and, equally, are planning, is as rewarding.

Add the joy that comes with doing things for others and, whatever the weather, your life will be filled with sunshine.

You and others

Sometimes it's not easy to trust those who seem to want to spoil you. However, certain individuals have an instinct for looking after others and the lucky Capricorn will have at least two or three individuals like that. Let them fulfil their destiny, let them indulge you and, as important, learn to enjoy it.

Health and wellbeing

There are fitness regimes and there are eating regimes, and while a regime can be appealing, the most appealing regime is one that's joyous. If you find something to do or a way to eat that brings you joy, the rest of it will be – if you'll excuse the expression – a piece of cake.

Goals and challenges

Capricorns are famous for their lists: you list what you want to achieve, and you list what you want to do each day, each week, each month and, sometimes, each year. Those lists are fine, but the secret is to rethink and reorganise them regularly. Do that, and not only will you learn a lot, but you will revise your goals as well.

THIS DAY FOR EVERYONE

Watching elements of your life you're fond of, if not very attached to, come undone is no fun. Yet, long ago, you realised that these particular pursuits, activities or even alliances were coming to a natural conclusion. While, understandably, you've battled to keep things going, it's time to say farewell.

GIFTS Solid, Decent, Efficient

CHALLENGES Severe, Grumpy, Melancholic

NUMBER 6

(3+0) + (1+2) = 6

While generosity can be measured, the return it brings is endless.

You

You like to know where you're going and what you'll be doing, so you tend to make a list – possibly on paper, or perhaps in your mind – of your schedule for the day, the week, the month and, to a certain extent, for your life.

This is very efficient, but it also can mean you're so busy getting those things done that you ignore the spontaneity that's essential when it comes to actually feeling great.

True, achieving your goals is important and that boosts your spirits. However, the capacity to act spontaneously allows you to do something that excites you in the moment, to be with somebody who lifts your spirits or who touches you, in a way few do. And if you can manage to balance the two – achievement and moments of joy – then you'll have achieved a rare happiness.

While this is what life is about, there isn't a single right way to organise your life. And that's one of the most powerful insights for any Capricorn. It's understanding that it isn't about achieving that list of goals, but recognising that life itself is a creative exercise. So, however long your list is, and however carefully you plan, you'll probably need to rethink things frequently. And that's the good news, because those last-minute changes in plans will lead you into new exciting and, possibly, unfamiliar, territory.

You and others

Certain individuals come into your life for a special reason. You might say they're good friends or possibly guides; some would call them guardian angels or even gurus. Whoever they are, stay close to them. They are, indeed, there because they're special, and will guide and inspire you.

Health and wellbeing

Feeling good is subjective. Your muscles may be toned and your digestive system may be working or, in fact, you may actually have the flu, but you could still feel fantastic. The trick for your health and wellbeing is to learn to have those fantastic feelings whatever is going on with your body.

Goals and challenges

Of course, as a Capricorn, you like to have everything mapped out and know where you're going. However, sometimes the best challenges are the ones that appear suddenly and the best goals are the ones that get achieved and then vanish. Be willing to revise what you're doing regularly and you'll not only achieve what you want, you'll have a good time doing it.

C
/
A
\
P
/
R
\
I
/
C
\
O
/
R
\
N

30

DECEMBER

THIS DAY FOR EVERYONE

This is one of those strange periods during which minor issues aren't just important, they could reveal misunderstandings that go way back. Invest time in asking a few questions or discussing those issues, and take it slowly. What you learn could prove surprisingly informative.

Surprises can be viewed as a disruption or as a breakthrough in disguise

C
/
A
\
P
/
R
\
I
/
C
\
O
/
R
\
N

31
DECEMBER

You

Of course you like things organised, and for good reason – so you can plunge in, so you know what you're doing, so you can move swiftly. However, as you've noticed, sometimes life has a different idea and those plans get turned upside down, often instantly.

This is where it's important to recognise those changes as giving you an opportunity to take advantage of a gift you've been given – the freedom to act in the moment. True, this may lead to changes; some disruptive, others demanding. You may have to gather facts, organise plans, find people who'll support you.

For you, as a Capricorn, this is challenging simply because you'd rather think ahead, and be organised well in advance. In fact, your independent side likes the idea of not needing anybody else. Yet that can also isolate you.

Instead, situations where you must seek the guidance of someone else are actually a gift opening up the world to you. It's also allowing you to do something that doesn't necessarily come naturally to you, and that is to act spontaneously and with joy and trust.

Begin dealing with whatever arises – whether it's personal, involves your life out in the world or is something new – with an appreciation for those sudden twists and turns, and not only will you handle them wisely, you'll even find yourself enjoying them.

You and others

The capacity to spot people who aren't just friends, but are guides, there to support you and who do it without expecting anything from you, is difficult simply because, as a Capricorn, you live in a world of give and take. Yet once you discover those people, keep them close.

Health and wellbeing

During tricky periods, everyone exchanges recipes for dealing with stress, whether it's a certain kind of exercise, eating a certain way or even meditation, but there's one really simple one – relax. Simply stop, take a few deep breaths and see what happens.

Goals and challenges

Every Capricorn has a list of things to do. What's most important for you, however, is when you make that list, write it in pencil and make sure you have an eraser handy. If you are changing that list regularly, you'll know that you're on the right track.

THIS DAY FOR EVERYONE

There are many ways to say no, but the problem is that certain individuals aren't listening to any of them. What's more, this particular group is working together on a goal that they regard as highly possible, but you have doubts. The only solution is to back out – and to do it now.

Calculating the time tasks will require takes longer than simply tackling them

C
/
A
\
P
/
R
\
I
/
/
C
\
O
/
R
\
N

You

Undoubtedly, celebrating the New Year and a new life is wonderful, and Capricorns born on this date often benefit from that sense of celebration and even the resulting resolutions.

But, most of all, it's important to recognise that this variety of Capricorn to-do list can become restrictive and prevent you from responding to the exciting, if unexpected, events that come your way. However intriguing ideas or offers are, you like to know exactly what you're getting involved in.

Yet when you encounter individuals who are offering things that are beyond anything you know – or opportunities that will take you into new territory in terms of activity, or perhaps mean you'd have to go someplace unfamiliar or learn something new – you'll think about it. Possibly for so long that it's no longer feasible, or, alternatively, you decide that you need to take a course of study in order to do it.

The trick to overcoming this resistance to the new and unfamiliar is to recognise that, actually, these activities constitute a kind of vitamins for you. That is, people who you don't know, who draw you into new territory, or activities that force you to learn new things, are all adding to your life and to your mind and to your future. And these, in turn, spur you on to greater growth and discovery.

You and others

Capricorns needs people around them they can trust. This isn't easy. In some cases, family will do it; you know them and you trust them. But, in other cases, it's those who you draw to you. Learning to do that, learning to build your own family of friends and supporters, can be one of life's greatest skills.

Health and wellbeing

Every once in a while, you say to yourself, "I really must relax." And you mean it, but you don't quite know how to do it, simply because you're probably thinking of a very sophisticated course of meditation or going to a spa. But there is a very simple way to relax, and that is to stop your body and your mind, even if it's only for 10 minutes. The technique? Sit down quietly, then breathe.

Goals and challenges

The most important question to ask yourself regularly is when you last set your goals and whether it's time to review them. If you've been sticking with goals that have been around a long time, it may be time to get a new piece of paper and a new set of goals as well.

01

JANUARY

For ages, you've been trying to find a way around a tricky obstacle and form a rather exciting plan. Yet this may be preventing you from getting more involved. Straightforward as this seems, the actual situation is fraught with issues that could turn into serious problems, possibly overnight.

Showing I care makes me feel vulnerable for minutes, but can pay off for a lifetime

C
/
A
\
P
/
R
\
I
/
C
\
O
/
R
\
N

You

As you move into the New Year, and further into the sign of Capricorn, you'll become aware that you were born under a sign and during a season when life itself changes. If you're in the northern hemisphere, winter will have settled in. And if you're in the southern hemisphere, it will be all about summer.

Whichever the case, it's as if, with that shift in climate, the rules for life have changed. And that, in turn, will call your attention to the importance of reviewing your own "rules for life" regularly, too. As a Capricorn, once you've thought through your objectives and set a plan, you'll stick with it. And you'll regard that persistence as a virtue.

Yet, every once in a while, it's important to notice how what might be called the climate of your life is changing. And, because of that, it's worth reviewing your priorities, the goals you've set, what you're hoping to say farewell to and what you're working hard to achieve.

And, as you proceed, you may well note that some of the things you thought should be on their way out actually fit rather well in your life. And, similarly, certain individuals you thought you wanted to say farewell to also fit very well. But, most of all, you'll realise that certain goals and passions that once meant a lot to you still do, and still deserve your heartfelt attention.

You and others

It's important to recognise that in a range of situations, you are drawn to the opposite type, not because of anything exotic, but simply because they help you understand yourself. As a driven Capricorn, you don't always pause to look within, yet when you spot that inner part of you in another person, you'll learn a lot.

Health and wellbeing

The unexpected could be doing you a big favour, especially if you need to change elements of your life: if you must travel suddenly, or if you've changed your job. It's also time to rethink how you look after yourself. What you learn in the process won't just be about the present, it will bring powerful insights for the future as well.

Goals and challenges

Now and again, it's important to redefine your existing challenges so you can see more opportunities for the future. That may seem strange, because everyone's encouraged to focus on opportunities, but it may be that the way you've defined your challenges has kept you from exploring certain ideas or offers. At least explore them, you'll discover a new excitement.

THIS DAY FOR EVERYONE

There's a fine line between chatting about what you're planning for the future and actually showing interest in what others suggest. It's tricky, at least at the moment, simply because once you begin discussing ideas with certain individuals, they'll expect to be included in future plans.

Hurling myself into a goal I'm passionate about isn't irrational – it's life at its best

♑

You

As a Capricorn, you probably have at least one list – a list of what you need to do today. However, that list may have sub-lists: things from the past that come to mind, goals for the week or of a more long-term nature. You may not have written out that list, if so, it's in your mind, and you repeat it to yourself often.

That's how Capricorns get more done than most other signs. But there's another kind of list – one that's playful, a fantasy list – a list that describes the things you couldn't possibly do. Why not? Because as an earthbound Capricorn, you tend to get so focused on what seems practical and realistic that you don't even consider the possibility of something outlandish. By making two lists, you will release the power of your unconscious, the part of you that is not bounded by the practicalities of being a Capricorn.

And, in doing that, you open the door to different ideas and exploration, of activity, and joy and achievement, that wouldn't otherwise have crossed your mind. True, the next step will be taking action on them.

But, once you've embraced that fantasy part of your nature, the part that enjoys visualising what seems impossible, you'll not only find yourself taking great pleasure in it, you'll discover some of those fantasies are far more possible than you imagined,

You and others

Everybody knows somebody who has a gift that makes life seem magical and who are themselves an inspiration. Knowing them is one thing, but allowing them to influence your vision of what's possible is another matter. Still, let them to help you overcome the sensible side of your nature. You'll be glad you did.

Health and wellbeing

There's an irony about you as a Capricorn. If you feel unwell, you'll tend to be tough on yourself, thinking that that's the best way to overcome either physical ailments or even if you're feeling a bit unsettled. The fact is, a gentle touch is always far better.

Goals and challenges

The question to ask yourself every day, is do you still really want that goal? In some cases, the answer will be an instant and passionate "Yes!". In other cases, the answer may be "I don't know" – and those are the goals it's time to say farewell to.

03

JANUARY

THIS DAY FOR EVERYONE

Making minor changes in your daily routine is one thing, and while it will be disruptive, you don't mind. But major changes are another matter, and you're not happy about these. While that's understandable, these changes affect others as well, and together you can work things out.

Self-discipline isn't about limiting indulgences, it's about selecting the best of them

℞

C
/
A
\
P
/
R
\
I
/
C
\
O
/
R
\
N

04

JANUARY

You

Occasionally, it's useful to look at those who drift from one plan to another, who seem directionless in a way that bothers you, yet who also seem happy. What's more, their lives are functioning smoothly and successfully.

While their approach to life intrigues you, it's also puzzling because it differs from your own more focused way of thinking. As a Capricorn, generally, you'll set a goal, carefully organise a plan to achieve it then stick to it. Yet, there's something to be learnt from others' more casual approach to life and to achieving goals. This is especially important if you've been struggling with certain plans that seem to be going nowhere.

The trick is to view planning as if it were breathing – something you do quite naturally, unthinkingly. If you're breathing heavily, but, for example, not climbing a steep hill, then it's important to ask a few questions. It's the same with plans. If they aren't working out, it's time to pause and consider whether they'd ever work out, or whether you should put your time, energy and, in some cases, heart into exploring others. An initial review is a good start. You may spot a fresh approach, or you may immediately realise that you've better options, possibly right there, awaiting your attention – plans that would be far more rewarding and far more fun to achieve.

You and others

Compromise is a difficult thing for a Capricorn who is settled on a goal or made a plan, whatever it may be. However, once you recognise that there are moments when letting go of what you've organised and considering others is wise. You'll not only do it, but you'll be excited to find out what you discover.

Health and wellbeing

While it's important to look after yourself, everyone agrees it's also important to do what might be termed spoil yourself. Every once in a while, it's essential that you have an indulgent date with people who will be happy to join you in a little joyous excess.

Goals and challenges

Achieving what you have in mind is one kind of challenge. Another more difficult one is actually recognising certain goals just aren't going to work, then letting go of them. Doing that takes courage, but also it frees space in your mind, in your diary and, possibly, in your heart.

THIS DAY FOR EVERYONE

It would be easy to assume that others' lack of irritation with current shake-ups means they don't care about them or the disruption they're causing. Actually, they mean a lot to them. It's just that they're not nearly as expressive as you are about those feelings of frustration, but they definitely do care.

Putting work I love first is easy; doing what I must boosts my self-worth

You

Most Capricorns are rightly proud of being born under your sign, and, even more, of your nature – that is, of both your willingness to work hard but, also, your practical generosity and earthy humour. But there's another side, too. This element of your nature can almost always find something to worry about, or can experience feelings that go up and down or, alternatively, you're always a bit concerned about things going as they should.

This side of your nature is related to the part that can dwell on life's doubts, and recognises stability as a way to avoid those. However, the fact is – and this is something for you to remember, especially as a Capricorn, and an earth sign – is that everything changes. The world around you changes – the seasons, the weather, the trees. While you recognise those changes as something normal and to be embraced, you sometimes forget the seasons in your own life, that is, the ups and downs, are normal. Once you learn to recognise and welcome them, your perspective will improve.

Instead of being anxious when changes arise, you will embrace them with enthusiasm, knowing that something exciting is coming your way and that you're prepared for it. The more optimistic you are, and the more creative you're feeling, the more eager your embrace of the new will be.

You and others

Bouncing ideas off others isn't just wise, it opens up a whole new world to you. Often, you'll retreat to figure out plans, then discuss your final decisions, hoping for their approval. However, with the foundation on which many arrangements are based shifting regularly, the more closely you work with others, the more you'll learn.

Health and wellbeing

When you feel unwell, you'll often head off to the gym or to figure out the best possible diet. However, those unsettled feelings may have to do with the simple fact that your world is changing and so is your life. These ups and downs are nothing more than your body becoming accustomed to a new way of living, thinking and doing things.

Goals and challenges

Organising life is a skill. Organising life when things are changing constantly is more than a skill, it's an art and it's one that is important for you to learn. You probably started out thinking that there would be a single plan. Now that you've learned that that plan is far more exciting than a single plan, being able to embrace change is the skill.

C
/
A
\
P
/
R
\
I
/
C
\
O
/
R
\
N

05

JANUARY

THIS DAY FOR EVERYONE

This is one of those exceptionally tricky periods during which what began as a modest exchange of ideas could burst into a contentious disagreement within moments. The real issue is unspoken tensions. For now, say nothing. This is likely to blow over as swiftly as it surfaced.

Setting aside pressing tasks to support others benefits me as much as them

C
/
A
\
P
/
R
\
I
/
C
\
O
/
R
\
N

06

JANUARY

You

For you, as a Capricorn and somebody ruled by the planet of achievement, Saturn – which is known for the focus it brings but, also, its stern nature – you sometimes struggle with the feeling that, somehow, you should have done more or worked harder. But if you view the actual situations in question logically, you realise you've done all you can, or need to.

Catching this isn't easy, because it's like an automatic recording, one that plays when you've finally dealt with your list of tasks and obligations. The trick is to recognise it's only ideas – or even worrying questions – and not about your own life or the world around you.

The remedy? First of all, pause and look at what you've done. Then, if you still have doubts, ask someone you trust to discuss your concerns with you.

Your ruler, Saturn, is not only the planet of focus and achievement, but also accents doubts of this nature. Recognise that, while Saturn can be a tough planet, it also is about being able to spot and enjoy the cycles of nature. You'll understand that there are times when life is meant to be still, there are times when you're meant to learn things and there are times that are about celebrating what you've achieved.

Embrace this cycle – and everything else will make complete sense.

You and others

Finding balance in life's changes is tough for anybody – it's like walking a tightrope. Yet everybody's life does change. The challenge for you is that you tend to want to control those changes and undertake them according to your own schedule which, as a logical Capricorn, you realise simply isn't going to happen.

Health and wellbeing

Fitness is a very good idea. For you as an earth sign, however, wellbeing is even more important. That is, being able to enjoy yourself, who you are and what you're doing, simply because you are who you are. Make that your priority, and the rest will fall into place.

Goals and challenges

Every once in a while, when you're working on something – and, as a Capricorn, you're usually working on several things – you will be asked how near you are to achieving your goal. The real question is, how can you measure it? Because you change and goals change. The real question is, how much joy are you gaining from the process?

THIS DAY FOR EVERYONE

There's a fine line between sticking stubbornly to long-standing, possibly out-of-date habits or beliefs and giving into the rather pushy attitude of others. While you'd probably be willing to consider changes, you'd rather do it when and how you want. Explain this to others; they may well back off.

However I may view them, no single one of life's joys is better than another

You

Setting goals and standards for yourself is important for every Capricorn. Being ruled by Saturn, the planet of order, it's vital that you know where you stand, in your life, with others, in your role with family or at work, and even more, in terms of your own goals, objectives and ideals. But there's another important question, and that is, whose values will you allow to shape your own? Normally, your parents, your background, your community or your culture will shape those.

But, as life has moved on, you may not have given as much thought to who or what is influencing your thinking, values and priorities in the now. There's plenty to focus on, but are you allowing others' passions to shape yours, personally, professionally or in terms of a cause that's meaningful to you? Each leads to the question: do these activities link with your own personal goals and values?

As a Capricorn, and as somebody who thrives on having a mission – something you can help out with, or a cause you can support – it's vital you review this mission from time to time. The trick is discovering whether what you're doing means as much as it once did, or whether it needs to grow along with you. As for your mission, as you and the world around you change, it may be that commitment will change and grow as well.

You and others

The keyword here is "inspire". That's partly about who's inspiring you. And, also, who you are inspiring with your words and actions. You may not think about this, but as you do you'll realise why certain situations are shifting and begin to discuss new ideas with those around you. And you'll find you're the one who's doing the inspiring.

Health and wellbeing

As a Capricorn, you take a certain pleasure in being disciplined, in fact you can get a bit addicted to them simply because they give order to your life. However, one of the lessons for you is to learn to ease up on them. Make those activities of health and wellbeing emphasise the wellbeing most of all.

Goals and challenges

Many Capricorns have the idea that setting goals and then sticking with them is powerful – it indicates you have a focus. And while sometimes that's true, it's also important to recognise that reviewing and altering those goals isn't weak, it's actually a brilliant idea.

CAPRICORN

07

JANUARY

GIFTS Unflagging, Honourable, Effective

CHALLENGES Over-serious, Sly, Unrelenting

NUMBER 9

(0+8) + (1) = 9

Lasting happiness isn't about what I earn or own, but the result of joy within

You

While the idea of feeling joy is wonderful, as a Capricorn, you tend to think such feelings must be earned through a certain amount of focus or effort or achievement.

There's no arguing that both effort and getting things done merit a reward. Yet it's worth reflecting on your reaction to upbeat feelings of this nature that appear "magically". That is, you can't think of anything you've done to earn them.

Actually, the fact is, joy is there waiting for you at any time. It has nothing to do with what you've achieved or what you've done for others. It exists. And the challenge for you is to overcome the Capricorn doubt that has convinced you that you aren't allowed to feel sheer joy until you achieve certain objectives or overcome certain obstacles or, perhaps, have dealt with the task at hand.

This is a kind of guilt that most Capricorns wrestle with for a while – until they have that amazing breakthrough that is about joy, and about the fact that it's always been there waiting to be discovered. It's just the direction you look in and your sense of the right to have it, and to have it at any time.

Once you know that's true, then nothing and nobody can take it away from you. It will always be there, walking beside you and shedding its light on you.

You and others

Most people have to live in the world with others and the drama that goes on with them can be a compelling one. Both you and others are judges, but also serving each other in some way. It would make a great play, but because it's real life, you're better off approaching it with compassion.

Health and wellbeing

Being fit is great; being able to lift weights, or eating the right thing, or having a trim body is fabulous. All of that is wonderful, especially being able to zip up those jeans. But what about your inner fitness? Because that influences you 24/7, whether or not you've got your jeans on.

Goals and challenges

While most Capricorns will stick with goals, others will keep altering them in the hope of finding something that flows smoothly. The fact is, life isn't designed to flow well. It's designed to be a bit bumpy, and those bumps will be what you've learnt from most and value most in retrospect.

CAPRICORN

08
JANUARY

THIS DAY FOR EVERYONE

When it comes to the issues you're currently facing, timing is everything. While, admittedly, some can't be stopped and, in fact, are best tackled head on, others can and should wait. Assessing this is easier than you think, especially if you trust your instincts. They'll be unexpectedly reliable.

I can challenge myself to face obstacles solo, or I can accept offers of support

You

Most Capricorns are list-makers, and those lists always contain small goals and big goals and often, in fact, your dreams.

While you can achieve those goals one by one, life ensures you have a list against which you can measure your success. Yet the fact is that, however many of those goals you achieve, the thing you're looking for isn't on that piece of paper. And it isn't in your thoughts either.

It could be said to be seated in your heart, and it is actually what might be termed the joy of achievement.

Achievement can have to do with those goals that you have in mind and with the acknowledgment of using your skills.

But, equally, it can have to do with you personally. It can have to do with simply being who you are, or being loved by another, or giving love to another, or simply pausing to observe, and rejoice in, the majesty of nature.

Those components are what's most important. So, when you make that list of those goals, bear that in mind. And, as you live out each day, take a few minutes to experience that joy – the joy in nature, the joy in being yourself and knowing what you personally are offering to the world around you – and to life itself.

You and others

Many Capricorns feel they're responsible for supporting, or being an example to, others – whether to family, to friends or to colleagues. And while often you will inspire people, is that your duty? It's something for you to decide, but you may actually find it is somewhat more of a spiritual calling.

Health and wellbeing

Being fit is fantastic, but if you're joyless, then it doesn't make too much sense. Because fitness includes your inner world, and that's not so much about moving your body or your muscles as putting yourself in a frame of mind that allows you to experience inner peace 24/7.

Goals and challenges

The question is, are all goals worldly? From a Capricorn point of view, as an earth sign, you might think that. Yet every Capricorn who's lived long enough to know that achieving certain goals gives you only so much, is aware there are other varieties of achievement – and they have very little to do with the outer world.

C / A \ P / R \ I / C \ O / R \ N

09

JANUARY

It would be easy to make the mistake of assuming that, when somebody ignored serious issues you raised, they didn't want to discuss them. Actually, the individual in question has been distracted, and may not even have understood what you were saying. Raise it again, and the sooner, the better.

Doubts are best tackled swiftly; putting them off only allows them to grow

C
/
A
\
P
/
R
\
I
/
C
\
O
/
R
\
N

10

JANUARY

You

Often, when you're figuring out what you want to do, you use your background as a foundation for it. Not only is that logical, we all learnt to speak and to think in the language of our background, from the family and the community we come from. Since then, of course, we'll have experienced other people, other settings and, for many, a wider world.

And each of those will have added something to what we consider to be possible, worthwhile and appealing. Yet, every once in a while, it's important to pause and consider whether what you want to do, and what brings you joy, is related to what you've learnt in your background or has an entirely different origin. And, if so, then it may be time for you to begin to explore that.

Of course, as a Capricorn, you'll tend to want to analyse this. However, simply paying attention to what you're drawn to, what excites you and, most of all, what brings you joy, may offer valuable, and possibly unexpected, clues.

After that, you may shift your focus to the here and now, and consider what and whose company inspires you. Then you may think about what you prefer doing anyway and, with very little thought, you'll realise that you're already doing something that enriches your life and which could, quite possibly, become a much more important part of it.

You and others

Eventually, everybody realises that certain individuals in their lives are there because of a relationship, because of an obligation, because they're family. They may not bring much joy, but they're simply there. And then you realise other individuals have something to give to you, a sort of a gift. You know which ones are most important to trust.

Health and wellbeing

There's a lot around these days about fighting ageing. However, there's another approach to it, which is simply retraining the mind not to take the idea of getting old into account at all, but rather to recognise each day as the new birth that it is.

Goals and challenges

As a Capricorn, you love a good challenge every once in a while. It's sort of like a workout, and it may actually be a physical workout or a mental workout. But the important thing is to recognise that, as rewarding as dealing with those challenges is, it's also possible to overdose on them. Enough is enough.

THIS DAY FOR EVERYONE

Annoying as the games others are playing may be – by making, then unmaking plans – they are forcing you to review your thinking about various arrangements. This, in turn, will lead to unexpectedly profitable discussions about what you would like to see happen over the coming weeks and months.

Sticking with the familiar seems wise, but means bypassing unexpected offers

C
/
A
\
P
/
R
\
I
/
C
\
O
/
R
\
N

11

JANUARY

You

Many think of life as being a duty, something that's easier to deal with if you organise your tasks or obligations. Those come first.

Once you've figured them out, you can turn your attention to life's joys – activities that lift your spirits, and the people who bring light to your day.

However, you have a tendency to think that those joys need to be earned, mostly by getting things done. That may seem normal to you, but it's a little like saying breathing must be earned. The fact is, creating a balance between duty and joy in life is important, but it's like that in every element of life.

Many parents encourage their children first to behave, and then to be dutiful. And, often, they make having fun a bonus, a reward for good behaviour. The secret is to begin to rewrite that script, to untangle the notion that joy and fun itself must be earned.

Instead, make those duties fun and, in the process, you can incorporate what you need to do for others. This means rethinking things entirely, but then that is the whole core of it.

It means that you'll spend more time doing what you love with those you love, simply because together you'll be rewriting what might be termed the script for life and its joys, and making those joys the most constructive portion of your life.

You and others

There's a great deal of importance put on being loyal. While that's essential, there's another element. If you can combine being kind, that is helping others or ensuring their needs are looked after, along with being loyal, it's even better. And if you can combine being loyal and being kind with partying, then life is as it should be.

Health and wellbeing

There is something called the deprivation culture, that is, depriving yourself, or having been deprived, is seen as something good, that a tough regime strengthens you. It is a bit of a Capricorn thing, but there's an even stronger kind of regime that you can embrace and it's a regime called loving and being loved.

Goals and challenges

Try setting up temporary goals and seeing what happens. This is totally out of character for you as a Capricorn, but if you want to learn something quickly, it's better to plunge in first, see what happens, and then study your reaction later.

The ability to find joy in the here and now isn't just a gift, it's a passport to freedom

You

The fact is, almost everybody experiences joy of some variety at some time. It's just because it's not discussed much, and because many cultures and settings don't even mention it, they don't notice it.

This may actually be the case in your life. The question is, when was the last time you thought, "What joy I'm feeling!"

However, joy is part of human nature and the more you learn to spot it, the more you'll learn to encourage it in your everyday life – simply by noting it and appreciating it.

And, in fact, that might be described as a good kind of viral growth. The small joys can grow to big ones, and those you can share with others, and the more you experience them and the more you talk about them, the more you can make small alterations in your activities in your own life.

You can organise how you work in a joyous fashion. You can organise time with friends and loved ones in a joyous fashion. And, even more than that, you can create a joyous relationship with the elements of the world that need healing, from the planet to the way people are treated in the world. The more joy you bring to each day, the more joy you will spread. It's that simple. In fact, if you look in the mirror and think of joy, you'll be improving the world that way, too.

You and others

In the contemporary kind of new-age thinking, there's a notion that if you think a thought, then it automatically spreads, which is an interesting concept to consider. So if you look in the mirror and create a moment of happiness and decide to share it, that might work. There's no reason you shouldn't give it a try.

Health and wellbeing

Can you say you feel great in the moment, even if, in fact, you don't? Something is creaking or perhaps you've got a runny nose, but, still, if you think about everything, if you feel great and can think it and even share it with others, then you will be sharing the best possibility of all.

Goals and challenges

As a Capricorn, you probably have a list of goals, but is that list a vision, or is it specific? Probably the most important goals are those that aren't exactly figured out, yet will encapsulate the miracles you're hoping will be coming your way. Take that approach and the odds are good they'll show up soon.

C
/
A
\
P
/
R
\
I
/
C
\
O
/
R
\
N

12
JANUARY

THIS DAY FOR EVERYONE

Usually, when you're enthusiastically discussing ideas with others, the next thing would be to explore turning them into plans. Try to do it, however, and you'll soon realise that the actual situations in question are still too much in flux to think of in lasting terms. For now, enjoy exploring your options.

Listening to others' advice is one thing, knowing whose to follow is quite another

You

As an earth sign, you're very practical and clever, so you tend to make a list of what you intend to do, today, this week, this month and, sometimes, this year. This is powerful and focuses your mind.

However, it can also limit your thinking, because you'll already have defined what you want to do, especially when it comes to long-term plans, goals and objectives. And if you allow your imagination – not the part that's about daydreams, but the part that can envision new ideas and ventures – to take a role in creating that list, then you begin to think in terms beyond what you'd have imagined possible on an everyday basis.

This is a skill that allows you to transform the down-to-earth Capricorn side of your nature into being a kind of visionary, somebody who can see past the restrictions of the present. Somebody who isn't just able to envision miracles, but who can consciously create them. True, everybody has the potential to connect to something beyond themselves, and make that happen.

However, for you, it's about refusing to get hung up in the details and, instead, visualising your goals. Then simply plunge in, even as if those events had already come together. Begin to do that, and you'll be amazed how swiftly they do.

You and others

You're rather good at ensuring you know people who inspire you. But, in this case, you're encouraged to spend time with people who play in a very special way, in that they take you to a land of possibility and encourage you to explore elements of your own mind and possibilities in your life that, otherwise, you'd never have considered.

Health and wellbeing

These days, there are all sorts of things you can do to make yourself feel better, to rejuvenate yourself and to build your energy, but one of the best ones is simply relaxing. Being able to stop and simply be, perhaps to watch a sunset. Try that – it'll be miraculous.

Goals and challenges

As a Capricorn, you were born ambitious. That may have to do with work, but you have a need to achieve what you have in mind. While you may choose those achievements by climbing the highest mountain, why not think of an achievement in your own life, which is much closer and more exciting?

13

JANUARY

The last thing you're in the mood for is dwelling on the past. However, events are calling your attention to long-standing arrangements and you're being prompted to review these. While times have changed, these haven't. Ask questions and you'll soon realise they are holding you back.

Struggling with doubts? Recall when, in the past, you regretted not taking a chance

C
/
A
\
P
/
R
\
I
/
C
\
O
/
R
\
N

14

JANUARY

You

As a Capricorn, and a practical earth sign, you tend to question, if not dismiss, those ideas that suggest that if you simply think of or visualise something, it will happen.

As somebody ruled by the sensible Saturn, this seems a bit too magical for you. Yet you're also drawn to it, and, of course, even more, not only are you aware of those who seem to make things happen exactly that way, you've done it yourself, although unintentionally – that is, you only realised it later, after the fact.

What's more, if they're unfamiliar, you could be anxious about tinkering with such matters. The trick to dealing with all of this is to recognise that you're in a period during which events are forcing you to think in a different way about many areas of your life.

And the more willing you are to do that, the easier it will be to make the best of a cycle that's all about discovery.

These insights will have to do with the practical side of your life, with your everyday discoveries, with the future and, most of all, with what once seemed distant possibilities. The more willing you are to take chances in that way, the better you'll do now and over the coming weeks, months and years. In fact, it might even transform your thinking – and your life.

You and others

Tempting as it is to go along with what others think is a good idea, it's essential that you be true to yourself. But that's tricky, because in some cases it's not until you allow others to tempt you and say no, that you realise what being true to yourself actually consists of.

Health and wellbeing

As an earth sign, you're very sensible. However, that realistic and scientific side of you is also intrigued by certain activities that seem kind of weird, but that also seem to work for other people. The secret? It's simply to be interested in them, learn a bit about them and take it from there.

Goals and challenges

The question is, what brings the greatest rewards? Is it a plan, a plan based on something else that worked? Is it guidance from someone who has achieved? Or is it simply what comes to you when you sit and reflect? Because what plan could be better than the one that you create yourself?

THIS DAY FOR EVERYONE

You're not thrilled that certain arrangements aren't working out as you hoped they would but, judging by the current rather tricky planetary activity, what it reveals will soon lead to things that didn't work out as you hoped. Sudden changes could bring answers for everything, and possibly overnight.

GIFTS Honourable, Industrious, Guarded

CHALLENGES Bitter, Obstinate, Remote

NUMBER 7

(1+5) + (1) = 7

Taking chances is profitable. You will learn from the outcome, whatever it is

C
/
A
\
P
/
R
\
I
/
C
\
O
/
R
\
N

You

True, being able to cross tasks off your list of things to do is both an achievement and satisfying. But, whatever kind of happiness this brings to you, as a Capricorn, it's worth noting there are other equally rewarding activities, and each brings its own variety of satisfaction and achievement, often in ways you wouldn't expect. That's the reason it's vital you think about and recognise, as well.

And, what's more, it offers an opportunity to focus on a side of your Capricorn nature that's very different from the outer world – the tangible world of duty, action and achievement that's so important to you. That portion of your nature is what might be called your inner world; that is, what makes you feel worthwhile, what brings you feelings of accomplishment and what gives you a sense of inner peace.

While this variety of inner peace is unlikely to have been taught in school, achieving a balance between the two – between the outer and inner worlds – isn't just important, it will enhance your view of life. It will inspire you.

Even better, this will touch those around you – family and friends, possibly colleagues and, perhaps even the world around you. Make achieving that balance your primary goal and even better, the rest will fall into place almost magically.

You and others

You're an expert at organising your own life and the world around you. Not everybody cares or, in fact, knows about that powerful but very private inner world. Spotting those who do and making them an important part of your life is one of the most significant steps towards creating that balance, the ongoing balance that will enhance the rest of your life.

Health and wellbeing

Often, people speak of a battle for wellbeing, which may sound like fun and makes it exciting, but is that the way you want to approach your body? You can be kind to it and perhaps love it into wellbeing. That might be a better approach to take.

Goals and challenges

The dream of lifelong achievements versus everyday goals is something to think about, especially for you as a Capricorn, because, often, those goals will dominate your thinking and the choices you make. The fact is, you are only alive in the present, and while achieving those goals some day in the future may be wonderful, your joy in this day is what's most important.

15

JANUARY

THIS DAY FOR EVERYONE

Ordinarily, you'd steer clear of other's battles, mostly because you learnt long ago how easy it is to get caught in the middle of these. However, you may want to keep an eye on what they organise, what they're doing and how it could affect your existing arrangements or plans for the future.

Loving others can be challenging, but it is easy compared to loving yourself

C
/
A
\
P
/
R
\
I
/
C
\
O
/
R
\
N

16

JANUARY

You

Doing what you have in mind and accomplishing it is exciting. However, bizarrely, those achievements can turn into an addiction. This isn't just about your personal sense of achievement, but these become something you can chat about, a conversation you and others enjoy. You can tell them about your goals, they can talk about theirs.

But, at the same time, that achievement can prevent you from exploring other options, things you'd like to do and also activities that take you within. These might be described as more personal goals, such as overcoming doubts or turning tricky issues around. Or this might have to do with your relationship with nature, doing something that benefits the earth, but also satisfies you, possibly in certain ways that are new to you.

What's most important is to realise there's is no right way to do this. It about doing something for the pure joy of it, breaking free from the addiction to achievement that's so important in many people's lives, and especially for you as a Capricorn.

The trick is to seek the joy and the peace that comes from within. Once you're close to that, then you'll realise why it's so important to balance whatever you're doing with that joy. And, in fact, the more joy you have, the more you will enjoy your many achievements.

You and others

Pals from the past can be terrific because, of course, you know each other inside out, but the most important friends you can have when you're in a period of development are those who feed the inner you. Once you learn more about them, and once they understand what you're doing, a relationship can go beyond anything else you could have imagined.

Health and wellbeing

Working out is one thing, but working out as if you were battling your own body won't achieve much. On the other hand, if you overcome that battle and instead make what you're doing an expression of joy and love for your body, it will be an entirely different and hugely rewarding matter.

Goals and challenges

You always set your goals high – it's simply part of your nature. The trick, however, once you know what you'd like to achieve, is to set them a bit lower and make them a bit more manageable and less intimidating. That way you can mark your steps towards achieving those bigger goals with every passing day.

THIS DAY FOR EVERYONE

Somebody seems to think they can win you over to their plans. This is puzzling, because the individual in question doesn't seem to care that much. Your observations are correct – they don't. The fact is, they rather enjoy the game of convincing somebody to go along with their own ideas.

Poetry dwells in the beauties of spring; finding joy in life's darker moments is a real art

C
/
A
\
P
/
R
\
I
/
C
\
O
/
R
\
N

You

As a Capricorn, you're an earth sign, but also, very often, you'll have goals that reach way into what might be termed the heavens.

That is, they're inspired by a part of your character that goes beyond the here and now. If so, then you'll already understand how important it is to balance the two, the part of you that's an earth sign that really enjoys the here and now and has a knack for achieving goals of a practical nature.

But there's also the part that wants to stretch your take on reality, and reach towards feelings some would call joy.

There is that amazing feeling that what you're doing, your ideas or plans, are actually coming together. And, even though not everything has gone as you intended, what's been least expected has been thrilling, and worked out perfectly in the here and now.

And, better yet, you're learning a new skill for you, as a Capricorn. True, it's not the kind of skill you go to university to learn. It may be that nature will teach you, or possibly, you'll encounter somebody who can help you learn about that.

Or simply one day, you'll realise that you've already learnt it, and you'll also realise why being able to recognise joy is such an important contribution to your life, now and in the future.

You and others

Who do you hang out with, and how do they make you feel? While it's wonderful to spend time with people who know you and people who will get you laughing about the past, they won't necessarily lift your spirits or, in fact, add to your self-esteem. Ensure you spend a bit of time with those who don't just inspire you, but who also, indeed, admire you.

Health and wellbeing

The trick to feeling well is to feel really well deep within, and then have those good feelings emerge on the outside. So, eating is good, exercising is great, but finding that place within that gives you what might be termed energy vitamins – that's the place to go.

Goals and challenges

As your horizons broaden, your goals shift quite naturally. This is often the reverse of what many people have been taught, because you're supposed to sit down and list what you want to do, and then figure out what's easiest. However, there's a trick to this, and it's called inspiration. Allow that part of yourself to be inspired and the rest will be easy.

17

JANUARY

THIS DAY FOR EVERYONE

When there was talk of changes to elements of your domestic or working life, you were concerned. This seemed a pointless disruption, but, as you've learnt more, you've also begun to realise these are part of a far-reaching pattern of change, influencing and benefitting others as well as you.

Planning ahead is wise; the ability to embrace the unexpected enthusiastically is a gift

C
/
A
\
P
/
R
\
I
/
C
\
O
/
R
\
N

18

JANUARY

You

As a Capricorn, setting goals is important, but discussing your options beforehand is even more important. You need to organise your mind, and your life, and once you know what you're doing, you can proceed free of concern.

However, as you'll have noticed, sometimes it seems you're not in control – and events almost seem to be telling you what to do. It's as if they're pointing you in a direction that's entirely different from what you had in mind – that may well be the case.

You and the rest of the world are in a period during which you're receiving what might be called coaching from another source, one that is perhaps a little bit larger than your ego and one that wants you to ask for more for yourself. In fact, that's the point.

You're about to become a bigger person – a bigger person in the sense of your heart and your feelings and your mind.

That may sound a bit far out, but as you begin to explore, you'll realise that suddenly, the world seems a much more interesting place and you're more confident. And you're willing to take chances on activities and perhaps even on caring for others in ways that simply wouldn't have been possible, even only recently. This is no bad thing. In fact, you might even find it's the best variety of addiction you could ever have.

You and others

The trick to making the best cycles that are all about growth is to think about who you hang out with. You may or may not know them well, but what you will notice is that when you're around them, you feel more positive, that what seemed unreachable, is suddenly well within your reach and that joy becomes a part of everyday life.

Health and wellbeing

There are stories about how to fight ageing – what you can or cannot do, eat or not eat, or cosmetic treatments. But there's another way to approach it, and that's simply to accept it and, in accepting it, to transcend it, to consider the possibility that if you simply believe it isn't going to happen, it may not.

Goals and challenges

The question is, does achieving your goals, just happen or is it a result of careful planning? As a Capricorn, you'll think it's all about that planning, but, increasingly, you'll realise that both the success you achieve and the happiness you have are the result of a combination of planning and you simply deciding that will be the case.

THIS DAY FOR EVERYONE

There have been many times in your life when you've wished somebody could deal with the tricky matters you're facing. But now it's the reverse, and with certain individuals in charge, you're unsure what to think. Despite your concerns, their intentions are good and you'll be pleasantly surprised.

GIFTS Respectable, Solid, Championing

CHALLENGES Scornful, Grouchy, Sarcastic

NUMBER 2

$(1+9) + (1) = 11 = (1+1) = 2$

Trying to understand others is a challenge. Accepting them for what they are brings joy

You

You're a very special variety of Capricorn because you share the influence of your neighbouring sign, Aquarius. You may not be aware that, for most of history, Capricorn and Aquarius shared Saturn as a ruling planet.

However, in 1781, Uranus was discovered, and it became the ruler of Aquarius. This gives you a rare and powerful link with this remarkable air sign, and accounts for your equally rare capacity to view matters from that practical perspective that comes with being a Capricorn and, also, from the visionary approach of Aquarius.

You also benefit from that link to the planet of innovation, Uranus. If you sometimes find yourself being inspired by ideas so new that you can't imagine where they came from, thank Uranus. Equally, if you're restless or eager to break away from overly sensible pursuits most Capricorns thrive on, you've Uranus to thank.

True, often the practical side of your nature may fret about this adventurous side. Yet, if life's for living, learning from and exploring, then this rare and wonderful balance of planetary energies isn't just of huge benefit to you, it means that every unexpected venture you take up, or surprising encounter you have, will add to that rich experience of blending these two powerful but very different planets, signs and ways of looking at, and living, life.

You and others

It would be no surprise if, gradually, you realise that those around you, from family and friends to, possibly, neighbours or colleagues, all come to you for advice, ideas and suggestions. This isn't just about making wise decisions, but also how to have fun and enjoy the best of life. You've a talent for it, one that's worth sharing.

Health and wellbeing

There are many kinds of health – there's physical health and there's emotional and mental health, but wellbeing itself is all about having an optimistic feeling about what will happen in the next minute, the next hour and the next day, and that's what this chapter of your life is all about.

Goals and challenges

Figuring out what you're going to do next may seem complicated, but, as you're probably discovering, the more you allow something beyond of you to inspire you, whether it's an event or an encounter or simply an idea that comes out of nowhere, the more exciting life becomes. Believe in that very special variety of inspiration because it's the way you'll be living as the future unfolds.

C
/
A
\
P
/
R
\
I
/
C
\
O
/
R
\
N

19

JANUARY

Aquarius

Ruler Uranus
Element Air

Symbol The Water Bearer
Flower Orchid

January 20 – February 18

Aquarius   One of the few human zodiac symbols, Aquarius is the water bearer, the third of the clever air signs. While ruled by Saturn for most of history, when Uranus, the first planet to be discovered in modern times, was spotted in 1781, you acquired a new, edgy ruler. Your flower is an orchid, your spice is chilli and your tree is all those bearing fruit. Not surprisingly, your stone is the aquamarine.

A
\
Q
/
U
\
A
/
R
\
I
\
U
\
S

I'll regard what once seemed a nuisance as an opportunity

You

As a blend of your neighbouring sign, Capricorn, and your own, Aquarius, you have a rare, unusual, yet wonderful mix of energies. Capricorn is an earth sign and very focused on life's practicalities, whereas, of course, Aquarius, as you probably know, is an air sign. That means your thinking and your ideas are far more important to you than being stuck with so-called grounded realities.

However, it's the blend of the two that's so exciting. And this takes you into new and rare territory. It takes you into ways of thinking and doing things that simply don't even occur to others. This is something you won't fully realise until you encounter those who seem so uninterested in the things that touch you, that excite you, that will encourage you to explore.

But, even more than that, because of this unique combination of characteristics, you not only benefit from your own canny ability to observe and understand your own approach to life, you are a natural advisor to others. You're a visionary who sees what's going on far better than those around you.

It's for this reason that people are drawn to you and, often, have questions to ask. While the answers may be as clear to you, they won't always be obvious to others. And this is the reason that, without even realising it, you signed up to be an advisor in this life.

You and others

Your gift for seeing others better than they see themselves makes you good company – simply because even anxious individuals feel comfortable. But you also can be the individual who lights a fire under a person who has something to learn – they will benefit from the confidence you give them.

Health and wellbeing

Unsurprisingly, with your nature, you're drawn to new ways of eating and ways of looking after yourself. Ironically, however, despite the adventurous side of your nature, you can be a creature of habit, falling into eating the same things and doing the same activities every day – something that's worth being aware of.

Goals and challenges

Being a bit of a visionary, you set all sorts of goals for yourself. The irony is that because you get so involved with them, you don't always notice when you've achieved them – it's worth pausing for an occasional review. There's no need to be trying to do what you've already accomplished.

A
\
Q
/
U
\
A
/
R
\
I
/
U
\
S

20

JANUARY

THIS DAY FOR EVERYONE

Luck is in the air. It's true. However, there are unexpected twists and turns in the air, and it's unlikely you'll benefit from these once you've dealt with them and any unsettling issues. Knowing that, tackle them now, possibly focusing on one a day. These will prove far easier than you imagined.

GIFTS Unconventional, Rousing, Tolerant

CHALLENGES Contrary, Obstructive, Determined

NUMBER 4

(2+1) + (1) = 4

Each day I discover something new and exciting

You

As January 21ˢᵗ Aquarius, you're always interested in what's going on around you and what people are doing. They don't just fascinate you, they inspire you to ask questions because you want to hear about their ideas, plans and what's motivating them. This process of learning about others, and their direction and intentions, isn't just intriguing – you'll sometimes make important observations. You may notice they're restless or, alternatively, that others seem to get stuck doing the same thing, again and again.

Yet the fact is that you, too, can be a creature of habit. This is because you're one of the four fixed signs of the zodiac, born in the middle of each season – something you share with Taurus, Leo and Scorpio. While this gives you stability, you can become such a creature of habit that you don't even realise you could live differently, work differently or even look after yourself differently. You'll get into eating the same thing and going to the same places.

But once you spot that habit, while you'll benefit from the "stick-to-it-ness" that comes with being a fixed sign, and you'll also have the luxury of exploring what you could do, going to places, meeting intriguing people and generally making a point of ensuring that every week and, if possible, every day, you discover something new in life.

You and others

As an Aquarius, you're a natural affiliate. That means you're not just a friend to people, you'll stick by them during periods of change or challenge. And you will both grow. The important thing to recognise is that they also will be of benefit to you.

Health and wellbeing

You're intrigued by so much that's going on around you, in terms of what to eat and what to do and how to look after yourself. Yet another part of you says routine makes life easier. While that's true, try to achieve a balance between the two. In fact, making discovery part of your routine is the ideal.

Goals and challenges

It may well be that in your youth, you learnt it's unwise to measure yourself against others. The reason for this is that, as an Aquarius, you're more inquisitive than most, and more willing to venture into new territory. If you recognise that, then you'll realise you can only measure yourself against the unique you.

A
\
Q
/
U
\
A
/
R
\
I
/
U
\
S

THIS DAY FOR EVERYONE

Only days ago, you thought certain plans were settled, and in detail. Since then, however, events have made it clear you must reassess them. As much of a nuisance as this seems, once you begin, you'll realise how much circumstances have changed and, because of that, your own plans need a rethink.

21

JANUARY

GIFTS Trend-setting, Resolute, Unique

CHALLENGES Unresponsive, Impersonal, Withdrawn

NUMBER 5

(2+2) + (1) = 5

I'll rethink my everyday routine and make life an adventure

You

By nature, you are a seeker. You'll get involved in a way of living, working or even loving that becomes core to your life. Yet because the particular process of discovery you're drawn to – that of being a seeker – is so natural, it seems each day you find something else you need to learn about, someone intriguing to meet, or simply a tiny change in your life that will become a great discovery.

And that is indeed core to the nature of being an Aquarius. It is, on one hand, about finding a routine that allows the fixed-sign part of your nature to experience the stability that's so important for you.

But having achieved that – and having learnt to maintain it – you'll finally feel you're able to venture out into new territory, and in a number of ways.

This involves exploration in a range of forms. It's all about what you do, and what you learn as a result. It's about the people you meet, and various elements of your activities. Many Aquarians benefit from living what might be described as a number of lives packed into one. They may have multiple careers, they may go through different stages in their personal life, or they may even experiment with their identity. Whatever the case, this is a joyous voyage of discovery that was almost designed for you as an Aquarius.

You and others

Most Aquarians always seem to have lots of people around them. That's because you're interested in others, you attract them. It's unique to you, as you'll notice, when few of those around you share your own genuine interest in the world and in discovering the people who are in it.

Health and wellbeing

One of the most wonderful characteristics of your nature is your inquisitiveness and your joy at discovering life. However, as you may have noticed, it can mean that sometimes you get so involved in that process of exploration, you forget to eat and look after yourself. Of course, the challenge is finding a balance between the two.

Goals and challenges

When in childhood, everybody's asked what they want to be when they grow up, even if they don't have any particular interest in a special activity. That's a big question. For you, it's the other way around. You'll find one thing you want to do, and as a fixed sign, you could get stuck in it – as if you have no option. But for you, the question is as an adult: what do you want to be when you grow up?

THIS DAY FOR EVERYONE

Recently, when you were discussing plans, you sidestepped certain details. You weren't being careless or, as some suggest, secretive. It's just that you knew things would change, including precisely these details. If others are concerned, explain slowly and, in fact, in detail.

A
\
Q
/
U
\
A
/
R
\
I
/
U
\
S

22
JANUARY

As much as I value old friends, if they're dull they get only so much time

You

Some of those born under the sign of Aquarius seem fairly conventional and lead what appears, on the surface, to be an ordinary life, while others born under your sign are genuine, if sometimes discreet, rebels. However, deep within the core of your nature is that unconventional, if not rebellious, character.

You're probably not aware that you were born under the rulership of the planet Uranus, the first to be discovered in modern times, in 1781. So, of course, you'll see things from your own, unique angle, and differently from the rest of the world – from the other signs – but even from other Aquarians. That's because, in a way, you're creating an entirely new identity for yourself and for your sign.

This isn't just about what you do and how you think of yourself, but how you live your life, from your activities out in the world and your relationships in general, to your or career, your view of finances and your goals and objectives. For this reason, when you make decisions about the present and the future, it's worth regarding them as tentative, if not an experiment.

However, as one of the fixed signs of the zodiac – those stable signs in the middle of each season – you sometimes overcommit to plans. The trick is to recognise that, by nature, you were born to be an explorer.

You and others

Many come to you for guidance and ideas. You don't realise this until you compare notes with those around you. And this is useful for them, not just because you have a rare capacity to spot the potential in others, but also because you learn so much from every conversation you have with them.

Health and wellbeing

As an air sign, you enjoy feeling well and free. However, the routine of looking after your body isn't something that comes naturally, so you need an activity that combines mind and body. That may sound strange, but if you find something you can do that will stimulate both, you'll enjoy it for a lifetime.

Goals and challenges

Many people figure out a system to live by, values to have, things to go for. But as an Aquarius, because you're inquisitive, that changes, and the system itself needs to be all about discovery. Once you understand that, then instead of trying to find the perfect thing to do, you'll realise that those discoveries are what you're meant to be doing.

A
\
Q
/
U
\
A
/
R
\
I
/
U
\
S

23

JANUARY

THIS DAY FOR EVERYONE

Saying no to something or, indeed, somebody, when things won't work has never been a problem. You'll usually explain your thinking and the reason why, and then move on to other topics. But now somebody is determined to change your thinking. Listen once, thank them, then, as before, move on.

Finally, I'll swap my current routine for a new, adventurous one

A
\
Q
/
U
\
A
/
R
\
I
/
U
\
S

24

JANUARY

You

As an air sign, you are by nature witty. All the air signs – Gemini, Libra and Aquarius, – enjoy exploring ideas, those that are familiar as well as new concepts. And humour isn't just important, it can be an antidote for the practical side of all those ideas, and often adds a welcome sense of the absurd.

Sometimes it may be just a quiet laugh, but there are other times when actually getting silly and feeling hysterical about something – belly laughter, as it's often called – isn't just fun. It makes you feel terrific. This capacity to see humour in life is vital.

However, you're always fascinated to discover that not everyone understands – or even appreciates – humour. In fact, some people would rather analyse dull matters in detail than benefit from the variety of laughter that, often, gives life itself a timely perspective.

Once you're aware of this, you'll also spot those who might be termed "laughing pals", that is, people you can hang out with when you're in that mood. But, also, you'll be increasingly aware of certain individuals who, whatever you say, take life very seriously.

The fact is, they probably aren't an air sign, like you, so they almost speak a different language than you do. Still, give it a try. The irony is that, for them, the conversation could prove life-changing.

You and others

You have a rare capacity to celebrate life's oddities and the quirks that you experience. But, also, you've probably learnt that not everybody can, and the capacity to spot irony in even very difficult situations doesn't exist in everyone's personality. In those cases, you may have to learn to be sympathetic.

Health and wellbeing

The idea of eating well is useful, and many Aquarians do, but the idea of getting up and moving vigorously is a little less interesting for most air signs. A type of movement that sparks your intuition or excites you may have to do with dancing, dancing of any kind. How about the tango? Have you ever given it a try?

Goals and challenges

You have a low boredom threshold. Once you know how to do something, you often see no reason to stick with it, which means that you need to alter your goals. This is not something you share with others, which means also you need to find those with whom you can discuss exploring new goals, and do it regularly.

THIS DAY FOR EVERYONE

There are many ways to agree to plans, and at the moment you're being rushed into arrangements you still question. The fact is, you are tinkering with things that are still in transition, and whatever is arranged over the weeks, if not the months to come, they are bound to evolve.

GIFTS Contemporary, Clever, Easy-going

NUMBER 8

CHALLENGES Hermit-like, Erratic, Unapproachable

(2+5) + (1) = 8

Suddenly, I realise that somebody who seemed dull is actually amazing

You

The irony of being an air sign is that you're inquisitive about everything. You love observing the world around you, especially what others are doing, their characteristics, what they go for, and, equally, what they avoid and all their quirks and oddities.

However, you often don't stop to observe your own characteristics in the same way. You like what and whom you like, and you dislike what doesn't suit you, and that's that. Why would you want to challenge or change that? You've observed other restless individuals as they set out to broaden their horizons in ways they find exciting. But, often, you've regarded it as just plain odd.

This is indicated by the fact that Aquarius is one of the four fixed signs, those born in the middle of the season. While this gives you amazing stability, you can settle into a pattern and become so familiar with it that you'll avoid making changes when actually they'd lead to something new and, often, beneficial.

And this is exactly what you'll be able to spot in somebody else, yet is one of your own lessons. It's about a new variety of inquisitiveness. Once you learn it, a whole new world of options will open up before you.

Discover that fixed side of your nature, begin to shake it up a bit, and the world will become a far more interesting place.

You and others

Your circle of friends or, probably, your family and even colleagues isn't just important – the time you spend with them is nourishing to you. They support you, but, also, it's their voices you trust when you have questions and, equally, it's their capacity to reassure you that's crucial.

Health and wellbeing

These days, there's a lot of talk about mind, body and spirit, and finding the balance for you. This isn't just a good idea. It's actually vital, because you wander off in your thoughts and forget about your body and looking after it. But also you can forget about the part of yourself that knows inner peace.

Goals and challenges

Even setting goals is odd for someone like you, who is restless and inquisitive by nature. Yet because the world shifts, and often those goals shift, that's you too. And the trick is to find those goals that do naturally shift, because it prevents you from getting stuck.

A
\
Q
/
U
\
A
/
R
\
I
/
U
\
S

THIS DAY FOR EVERYONE

For ages, you've been trying to win over one particularly stubborn individual regarding plans you know they'd enjoy. The problem is that they won't even listen to what you have to say. Back off. Force them to ask you about your ideas. It will require patience, but it will also work.

25

JANUARY

GIFTS Quick-thinking, Empathetic, Sociable

NUMBER 9

CHALLENGES Forceful, Unnerving, Formal

_(2+6) + (1) = 9_

Those who are fun to chat with now get priority

You

As you've probably noticed, you don't just have an active and inquisitive mind. There are times when you're not merely in an inquisitive mood, but your mind seems to escape, and it's all over the place – you're thinking about so much, you can't concentrate on any one thing. However, it's important for your mind to work that way, simply because being ruled by Uranus, the first of the newly discovered planets, means you – as an individual – are always discovering things yourself.

And often, these sudden insights are the result of almost overwhelming moments of enthusiasm and exploration. Some of what arises will be important to you, but some may be important to those around you – your circle, if not the world. And this is the trick to discover – that while you're always intrigued in the now and what you're doing, very often what you discover, what you enjoy, will be important to you and important to the wider world as well.

Most of all, you are here to learn to live life anew every day. While habits may streamline what you do, if you decide to do a single thing differently every day, to alter a minor habit or even a major one, then you'll avoid falling into the rituals that prevent you from the kind of discovery that you, as an Aquarius, were born to experience on a regular basis.

You and others

You're fiercely loyal to those closest to you; family, but also friends. This is an important and valuable characteristic, but something that's essential you review from time to time. Check it out. Not everyone is reliable, and you may discover that certain individuals aren't as loyal to you as you are to them.

Health and wellbeing

Most Aquarians understand the importance of being physically fit. They like being able to get up and move around quickly. But boredom is a problem, simply because many regimes are exactly that – boring. The trick is to include mind, body and spirit in your activities. That takes a lot of fitting in, but it's worth the effort.

Goals and challenges

In order to have goals, you need to set them. However, many Aquarians stumble over what they're doing in life, whether it's at home or with family or a career, and only later discover that what they're doing has discovered them, which may actually be the best approach.

AQUARIUS

26

JANUARY

THIS DAY FOR EVERYONE

If you've already talked about what you'd like to do and hope to achieve and are running out of enthusiasm, it's probably time to change the subject. In fact, judging by the rather tricky planetary activity you're facing, you're better off sidelining those plans and savouring each day for the pleasures it offers.

GIFTS Objective, Ingenious, Stylish

NUMBER 1

CHALLENGES Dictatorial, Immovable, Distant

(2+7) + (1) = 10 = (1+0) = 1

I've run out of excuses for not making long-overdue changes

You

You have a love-hate relationship with habits. They allow you to organise life in such a way that you don't have to think about every single thing you're doing. At the same time, as an inquisitive air sign, you need to explore. Ideas are like a kind of vitamins for you. The trick, therefore, is to ensure that those habits involve things that keep life going smoothly.

Ironically, you might have to develop a habit of breaking habits. That is, from time to time, you think about whether there's anything you do regularly – so regularly that it would prevent you from getting to know somebody interesting or exploring something new. The habit-breaking method is simple. It's about ensuring that you always do something new and unaccustomed, at least every couple of days.

This also will allow you to stumble across new ideas, intriguing people and, possibly even activities that otherwise wouldn't have crossed your mind. As an inquisitive Aquarius, you're also one of the fixed signs, so can easily get caught in the kind of habits that are restrictive. Those are the ones you want to watch out for.

Once you find that balance between the habits that stabilise you and the habit of exploration, you'll have organised a life that allows you to be efficient, yet also to discover something new regularly, if not every day.

You and others

Who is the ideal friend for an Aquarius? Those who say to you, "Come along with me. Let's explore this. Let's try this. Here's a new idea." While you are inquisitive about everything, someone coming to you with something you haven't stumbled across isn't just a good idea. Those individuals are a gift.

Health and wellbeing

By now, you have probably come to realise that just because healthy is printed on the label of something, that doesn't mean it's good for you. However, how do you discover what is healthy? Actually it doesn't have so much to do with what you eat or drink as how you look after yourself.

Goals and challenges

Every once in a while, it's important to review your goals, simply because what once seemed important isn't any more. When you discover that, you can chuck out those goals, slim down your list of objectives and pursue what you care about most with passion.

A
\
Q
/
U
\
A
/
R
\
I
/
U
\
S

27

JANUARY

THIS DAY FOR EVERYONE

Long ago, you learnt to live with and, in some cases, to disagree with certain individuals. But if you are going to take various complex plans to the next stage, you have no choice but to find a way to deal with the issues and conflicts that arise – and in detail. This won't be easy, but it is a vital skill.

GIFTS Even-handed, Inventive, Quirky   NUMBER 2

CHALLENGES Single-minded, Wacky, Rebellious   *(2+8) + (1) = 11 = (1+1) = 2*

If I'm the most interesting person in a conversation, I need new friends

A
\
Q
/
U
\
A
/
R
\
I
/
U
\
S

You

You delight in the world around you – people, and what they do – fascinates you. But also it fascinates you how some people seem to complain with every breath. It's almost as if that's their perspective on life. They get up each morning and push the start button on their complaint mode. When others, and indeed, you, are joyous, they're complaining, if not miserable.

As an Aquarius, what might be referred to as your "joy temperature" goes up and down depending on your mood. That's normal. However, those around you who aren't very joyous are a big lesson in how to organise your life, and also how to shape your thinking, because often that joy has to do with how you approach life itself. As an air sign, it is easy to fall into analysing what you do, as opposed to paying attention to the ups and downs that actually give you a sense of purpose and enthusiasm about life, particularly during those moments when challenges, when life's uphill climbs are a bit overwhelming.

Once you've mastered that skill then, when you encounter those challenging moments, or longer periods, you'll recognise that while they may seem overwhelming at the moment, dealing with this is a skill – and that skill is making the best of each day, with its uphill climbs and twists and turns.

You and others

It's said that you discover your true friends during periods of challenge. And while that is true, you also discover your true friends when they are challenged, because if they settle into doing nothing but complaining, there isn't much you can do for them, as a friend. Choosing those closest is about both your characters.

Health and wellbeing

As an inquisitive Aquarius, you are always experimenting, not only with what you do, but with how to feel well, how you eat, with fitness, with diet. But what's most important is actually your viewpoint about your wellbeing. If you put that first, everything else will fall into place.

Goals and challenges

You need new challenges regularly to keep that active Aquarian mind of yours going. However, you also need enough stability that you are able to enjoy being yourself each and every day. Out of all the 12 signs, you are probably best at doing exactly that.

THIS DAY FOR EVERYONE

Sooner or later, you will need to take a tough line with somebody who is difficult on the best of days. While it is understandable that you are putting off tackling the issues in question, these won't vanish. You may, in fact, be better off taking things in stages. Slowly but surely you will get there.

GIFTS Neutral, Championing, Unwavering

NUMBER 3

CHALLENGES Impersonal, Impatient, Iron-willed

(2+9) + (1) = 12 = (1+2) = 3

Same plans again this weekend?
It's time for a complete change

You

You may not notice this – at least, you may not notice it right away – but of course, you have always been you. The fact is, you are more inquisitive than others – and more observant. You discover more simply by observing the world around you, by looking at nature. But, even more, you learn about people by watching them, those you may see on the street and those you see regularly – family, friends, neighbours or colleagues.

In fact, often you might know more about them than they do themselves. However, turning that mirror on your own life and on what and who you put first is what is most important – but not quite as easy.

Initially, you may not find yourself particularly interesting, but if you fall into the rather typical Aquarian habit of doing the same thing, a routine, then it is essential that you use your wisdom to examine your own life and to break the behaviours that could settle into what often are termed "the habits of a lifetime". Instead, make a point of breaking a habit a week, if not a habit a day.

Once you begin doing that, then you will give yourself the freedom that you, as an air sign, not only want, but the freedom that will make life itself all the more exciting – exciting enough that you will wake up each day with a sense of eager anticipation.

You and others

Many Aquarians don't notice a difference between those around them, because it is not your nature to compare or judge people. Yet, occasionally in conversations, you notice that others do that. Don't judge or compare, but make a note of how wonderfully able you are to enjoy those around you, whatever their quirks.

Health and wellbeing

The feeling of being at one with yourself – so settled in who you are that you don't feel the need to change anything – is rare and wonderful. And it is something that, for you as an Aquarius, is within your grasp. The challenge, however, is to ignore those people that say, "If you change X or do Y in your life, you will feel much better." For you, it is simply not necessary.

Goals and challenges

The fact is, you need a new challenge from time to time. This is by no means negative – it is almost as if you were taking vitamins. Having a small challenge – not something overwhelming, or negative – will give you an opportunity to exercise your muscles of being inquisitive and being clever in a way that is very useful indeed.

A
\
Q
/
U
\
A
/
R
\
I
/
U
\
S

29

THIS DAY FOR EVERYONE

Tempting as it is to sidestep dull facts and even more tedious rules and regulations, they really can't be ignored. It may seem you have got away with it, but things are likely to catch up with you. So invest time in dealing with these now, before they become any more complicated.

JANUARY

I won't wait for others to believe in my ideas; I'll plunge in on my own.

You

The phrase "the joy of discovery" is a wonderful one. And to say that is something you have, something you were born with, is even better. This means that you're interested in others in a way that they sometimes aren't themselves. And you are interested in the world around you in a manner that not everybody is. Occasionally, you are shocked – and surprised – to discover how little interest those around you have in the world, from the people in it to the events taking place.

You may try to get them excited about things – and a few may, indeed, respond, but not always for long. The fact is, you were born to be the person you are. And that means inquisitive – interested in others and curious about their lives and activities. This innate interest is not only your greatest asset. It is something that allows you a variety of joy that is rare and wonderful to experience. And it comes with being an Aquarius, perhaps the most inquisitive sign of the zodiac and also the sign that is ruled by the planet, Uranus – the first planet to be discovered in modern times.

This, itself, is a symbol of your nature. Enjoy yourself simply for who you are. And while it isn't your habit to compare yourself to others, if you begin to do so, realise that actually, it is not only unwise, it is unnecessary.

You and others

It may take you a while to realise, but you will soon discover that there are two groups of people. There are those who are inquisitive, like you, and then there are those who don't particularly care about anybody else. It is not difficult for you to figure out who you should be hanging out with.

Health and wellbeing

When it comes to looking after yourself, variety is important. Many people get into a routine, both with what they eat and with exercise. But, while the routine itself is not a bad idea, you need something to challenge that vital mind of yours. And if that means changing those routines, all the better.

Goals and challenges

When you are chatting with others about what you have in mind to do, you may have noticed that their idea of a goal is very different from yours. Compare notes if you want, but recognise that you, as an Aquarius, are seeking something very different from most of the world – and what you are seeking has to do with having a broader and brighter horizon.

A
\
Q
/
U
\
A
/
R
\
I
/
U
\
S

30

JANUARY

THIS DAY FOR EVERYONE

It is said that you should never go to bed without settling differences. And, as is the case now, you want to at least express hope you will reach an accord with others. Even saying that might be challenging, but when you wake up in the morning, you will be glad you did.

GIFTS Free-thinking, Idiosyncratic, Offbeat

CHALLENGES Controversial, Autocratic, Withdrawn

NUMBER 5

$(3+1) + (1) = 5$

It's time I freed the adventurer within me to explore

You

As an air sign, you have a restless mind and, sometimes, a restless body as well. You've a powerful need to get out and about, possibly merely in your neighbourhood, or maybe to explore the wider world. And when you do, you're often surprised, if not shocked, by what others seem happy to settle for.

This makes you aware of how little interest many people have in broadening their horizons, even slightly. But it also makes you realise that, oddly, in certain areas of your own life, you can be very predictable.

This is, of course, because you are born under one of the four fixed signs of the zodiac – Leo, Taurus, Scorpio and Aquarius. And, in fact, once you develop certain habits, while it seems they streamline your life, they also feel very comforting – except you, personally, can begin to feel stifled or suffocated by them.

The trick is to develop certain habits that benefit you but, at the same time, to develop the habit of always exploring something new, every week if not every day. Balance those two, and that fixed side of your nature will lend you a stability that is very useful for you as an inquisitive air sign. However, it will also mean that you are always making sure that you are not allowing yourself to get stuck in any restrictive habits or ways of thinking.

You and others

As an Aquarius, you need people in your life. But what you mostly need are individuals who have restless minds, who ask you why you are doing what you are doing, who encourage you to explore and who will inquire with you about what is new. They are not only good friends, they are assets.

Health and wellbeing

There is nothing better than getting up in the morning knowing what you are going to eat and what kind of physical activity you will undertake during the day. However, for you as an Aquarius, variety is an important kind of vitamins, along with what you do and what you eat. Ensure that you have lots of options.

Goals and challenges

Most children are asked what they want to be when they grow up, as if somehow, as a child, you would know. But for you, in particular, as an Aquarius, life is itself a voyage of discovery. Make that voyage your priority. And instead of trying to settle on one destination, you will enjoy each and every place you go.

A
\
Q
/
U
\
A
/
R
\
I
/
U
\
S

31

THIS DAY FOR EVERYONE

It's true, you're often reluctant to make changes, especially if you can't understand why you should bother or what you'll get from them. The fact is, you've no choice. The situation in question involves others as much as you and, ironically, they're eager to take things to the next stage.

JANUARY

GIFTS Unshakeable, Uncommon, Detached

NUMBER 3

CHALLENGES Uncompromising, Austere, Aloof

(0+1) + (2) = 3

I will do something new at least once a week, but try for every day

A
\
Q
/
U
\
A
/
R
\
I
/
U
\
S

01
FEBRUARY

You

You're naturally inquisitive. You don't think of it, until you're chatting with others, and realise how little they observed about a particular place, about somebody you both met or an event of some kind. However, your interest in the world, and life itself, is part of being an Aquarius. Of course, not everybody born under your sign takes advantage of this special variety of curiosity. What's more, even a single change in plan can be an invitation to look at life differently. True, initially, you may be irritated, as the fixed sign side of your nature struggles with change. Yet, as an Aquarius and an air sign, you thrive on new ideas, meeting new people and, in fact, having to solve new problems. And this is what comes with organising a life that itself brings you twists and turns. If those aren't part of your daily routine at home or in your working life, then you can invite those twists and turns into your experience of exploring something new. It doesn't have to be a single way or a single regime and ideally, in fact, you will experience different reasons for different twists and turns over the years of your life. What is most important is that, as they occur, instead of worrying and saying, "Oh no, not another change," you will embrace them with the enthusiasm that comes with knowing that this is yet another adventure in your life.

You and others

One of the great turning points in your life is understanding that those around you truly don't see things like you do and, in fact, have no interest in viewing things from your perspective. As an Aquarius, you are always fascinated to know how other people think, but it is a characteristic that the rest of the world doesn't necessarily share with you.

Health and wellbeing

It is easy for you as an Aquarius to be seduced by exotic physical routines and diets. In fact, the more complicated they are, the better. And you can become obsessed with them, but the fact is that is a kind of seduction that distracts you from the most important thing, which is how well you are feeling.

Goals and challenges

On occasion, when others are talking about what they are doing in their lives, you aren't just intrigued, you are envious. You want to be drawn into their lives and their goals. But there is an important thing to remember – as thrilling as these activities are for others, the individuals in question aren't you.

THIS DAY FOR EVERYONE

Sometimes discussions are about an exchange of ideas. At the moment, however, it would seem that your main role in several such situations is as a listener. Tempting as it is to offer advice, it is really not wanted or, in fact, helpful. The individual in question needs to talk and talk and talk.

GIFTS Unbiased, Freewheeling, Exciting

CHALLENGES Unnerving, Unapproachable, Awkward

NUMBER 4

(0+2) + (2) = 4

I'll listen to what others expect me to do, then deliberately do something else

You

For an Aquarius, the phrase "joy of discovery" will no doubt appeal – but it's important to remember that what others enjoy discovering won't be the same as your own variety of joy. However, you may share a restless appreciation of the new, and those individuals may be perfect companions with whom to explore and to pursue new ideas. And when you connect with somebody like that, it's great.

Still, at the same time, part of your life is about discovering that each individual is truly taking a unique journey, one that's designed for their own character, and what they're meant to learn.

While all Aquarians are inquisitive, each of you benefits from a unique path and, as a result, may end up somewhere very different, doing something very different.

There are those who say they have done it all, explored it all, and now they know where they are going to be and it is unnecessary for them to ask any more questions. And for certain individuals, that is true.

However, for you as an Aquarius, there is always something more to discover. It may be out in the world around you. It may be about humanity, or it may be about yourself. Whatever it is, for you, life is an exquisite journey of discovery, one that has gems waiting for you along the way.

You and others

It is a very rare Aquarius who is meant to go through life on their own. Some will be surrounded by family, some by friends, some by colleagues, even occasionally by those you encounter here and there. In every case, these individuals aren't just companions. They are there for you to bounce ideas off and to learn from.

Health and wellbeing

As an air sign, you love nothing more than a quick fix for your wellbeing, whether it is an eating regime or activities – and the more complicated it is, the better. But the big discovery is actually paying attention to what makes you feel well. There is no better regime than that.

Goals and challenges

For you, as an Aquarius and somebody who might be termed an original, it's vital that you be true to yourself. Simply defining the term goal for yourself may be one of life's greatest challenges. It will take time, but what you learn will remain with you all of your life, and bring rewards each and every day.

A
\
Q
/
U
\
A
/
R
\
I
/
U
\
S

02

THIS DAY FOR EVERYONE

The last thing you want is to disappoint people and leave situations undone. But certain individuals have ignored your advice and are now blaming you for their problems. Explain once, and firmly, where you stand, then withdraw from discussions. There really is nothing more to say.

Joy isn't in knowing what's coming; it's about making life an adventure

You

One of the gifts of being an Aquarius is your genuine interest in others. On occasion, you realise that most people pay little attention to those around them, even family and loved ones. Your inquisitiveness comes naturally. And not only do you listen to what they have to say, think about it and ask questions, you actually pay attention and are fascinated with elements of the lives of others.

While you tend not to compare yourself to others, you learn about yourself from the differences between your approach to life and theirs. This, in turn, allows you to think about doing things in a new way and exploring new activities. Yet certain individuals may also provoke you into asking questions about yourself – and this is where it is worth pausing to consider whether that is necessary.

Many Aquarians have managed to find an inner balance, one that is rare and allows you to be who you are without hours of pointless poking at your own psyche or your ego, which so many do. This is because having been born under perhaps the most inquisitive sign of the zodiac and the sign that is all about exploration, you do that naturally.

Appreciate this element of your character and, when others are struggling, you will realise why you are not – then you can appreciate yourself all the more.

You and others

Most Aquarians love having people around them. It may be family, if you have an extended one, or they are nearby. It may be neighbours. It may be colleagues, or even pals. But being able to brush up against others isn't just fun – it reminds you of the beautiful diversity that life offers in the form of the people around you.

Health and wellbeing

There are all sorts of ways to look after yourself, but one of the best ones has to do with actually hanging out with friends and seeing what they are doing. They will take you into new territory, not just in terms of fitness, but in terms of how you eat and what you think. And often, a few days spent with pals will constitute a proper workout.

Goals and challenges

It is important that, as one of the fixed signs of the zodiac, you are aware that you can easily repeat the same challenge in a different form. Be alert to that, because if you are thinking about doing something differently, you might as well learn something new too.

AQUARIUS

03

FEBRUARY

THIS DAY FOR EVERYONE

There is no tidy way to make sudden and, in some cases, dramatic changes in long-standing arrangements. Others may complain, but they, too, are being influenced by the changes triggered by this period. Unsettling as these changes are, there is no arguing the fact that things must move on.

Instead of complaining that life is predictable, I'm going to spice it up

You

Those around you may be complaining about challenges in their own lives. This is a term used these days to mean that things are difficult, and actually these people are not merely seeking your advice, but also your help in some form. However, it is important for you to consider whether, indeed, this is merely a matter to be discussed and if you can, or should, do anything to help them.

In some cases, these individuals need to deal with their own challenges – that's the whole point of them. In other situations, it's about you pointing them in a particular direction, then leaving them to get on with it. But, also, it is essential that you recognise that being distracted by others in this way may be preventing you from looking at your own life, your own restlessness and your need to find something new to do as a way of beginning the next chapter of your life.

As one of the four fixed signs of the zodiac, born in the middle of each season, along with Taurus, Leo and Scorpio, you can get stuck in your own habits. And if you find yourself drawn into other's crises, it may well be that actually this is an invitation for you to begin to explore and to shake things up in your own thinking and your own life. Do so, and you'll discover a new world of activities, ideas, and people just waiting for you.

You and others

Aquarians tend to have a gift for making friends, whether it's neighbours, family or even colleagues. It's important, however, that you make a point of linking up with those who are always interested in the world around you and always out there discovering something new and intriguing. While, that's your instinct, they'll encourage that in you.

Health and wellbeing

There are many ways of assessing your health and, of course you can look after how you eat and how you exercise. But also, there's the influence of an unsettled mind and how much it can disrupt things. If that's the case, you don't need to do a major meditation course. What might be termed mini-meditations, that is brief ones, can do the trick.

Goals and challenges

Being somebody who's inquisitive by nature, it's easy for you to line up a set of goals. This gives you not only a sense of purpose, but enthusiasm and variety. However, it's worth ensuring that those goals are realistic otherwise you also risk being overwhelmed.

A
\
Q
/
U
\
A
/
R
\
I
/
U
\
S

04

THIS DAY FOR EVERYONE

FEBRUARY

There's a difference between a possible solution for a problem, and you've lots of those. Then there's the kind that you can be sure will last. At the moment, nothing quite fits. While others are impatient, your instincts are correctly telling you that it's vital you wait until more worthwhile ideas surface.

GIFTS *Unique, Stylish, Electrifying*

NUMBER 7

CHALLENGES *Bloody-minded, Volatile, Shocking*

$(0+5) + (2) = 7$

Agreeing with others may win friends, but clashing with them gets me thinking

You

It may have been recently, it may have been ages ago – or, possibly, at New Year – when you set goals or resolutions. Whatever form these take, for you, as an air sign and somebody who has an instinctive sense of the future unfolding – perhaps greater than any other sign – whatever form this process takes, it's an important one.

While this vision is about what you could be doing over the coming months or even years, it's also vital to discuss your existing ideas and objectives. Some may go back ages, yet you haven't reviewed them. These may no longer be relevant to who you are now, or today's world. The trick is to have a clear out. You may be clinging to once-cherished but unrealistic objectives. As you declutter, consider whether your current goals need an update, too. This may lead to a rethink of what setting goals looks like. You may regard them more as an experiment, taking you into unknown but exciting territory.

Most of all, it's about being flexible. The more you explore, the more you'll discover. Make discovery your theme, and instead of worrying about setting the right goal or achieving it, you'll enjoy every twist and turn of the journey, simply because of what you've experienced, who you've met and what you've learnt.

You and others

There are certain people you click with and life is easy, but it's also important to recognise that certain individuals have a capacity to prevent you from settling into habits in the way that you like to, instead encouraging you to come with them on a voyage of discovery.

Health and wellbeing

Knowing what you're going to do the next day and the next week may be reassuring, but it doesn't necessarily mean it's good for your mind or your body. In fact, sometimes surprises are the best possible gift, whatever form they take.

Goals and challenges

It's good to have the perfect setup, but in some ways it actually hampers you – simply because if you're sticking with that perfection, you're prevented from exploring. And for you, as an inquisitive Aquarius, exploration of that nature is like taking a deep breath.

A
\
Q
/
U
\
A
/
R
\
I
/
U
\
S

05

FEBRUARY

THIS DAY FOR EVERYONE

Welcome as current ideas or offers coming your way may be, inevitably they'll be disruptive. While in some cases it's about having to rethink the timing of plans, in others, changes are seriously unsettling. Although, obviously, you've no complaints, you can't help wishing things weren't so rushed.

GIFTS Objective, Unswerving, Lenient

NUMBER 8

CHALLENGES Impersonal, Unyielding, Unresponsive

(0+6) + (2) = 8

It may be tiny or a big deal, but each day I'll do something very different

You

As one of the three air signs – Gemini, Libra and Aquarius – you're fascinated by what's going on in the world around you and in your own life, and learn from what you observe.

But when it comes to actually making changes, it's not so easy. This is partly because you want to ensure that you have freedom in your own life, which, in turn, means that if you commit to one avenue of activity, you'd be missing out on others.

Yet, every once in a while, it's important to not only make a change, but to break away from a path so familiar that you know exactly what awaits you around every corner. This is one of the tricky issues for you as one of the fixed signs of the zodiac – born in the middle of each season. You fear that in taking that first step in a new direction, while you're breaking old and, perhaps, restrictive, patterns, you're plunging into the unknown.

In a way, you are. That's the point. For you, the world of discovery is a vital one. In fact, as an air sign and an Aquarius, discovery, experimentation and growth are as natural to you as breathing. Sticking with what you know seems safe, but it's like remaining in an increasingly stuffy room when you could throw open the door and walk outside into the fresh air. The more skilled you become at discovery in life, the more you will enjoy life itself.

You and others

Most Aquarians have a large circle of friends and enjoy the company of others. The tricky bit is how much time you spend listening to what they're doing and their dramas versus the time you spend exploring together. Think carefully about that, then think carefully about who you put first when making plans.

Health and wellbeing

Discussing dilemmas is easy and, in fact, many people enjoy the process. Allowing them to take over your thinking and to turn into ongoing anxiety is, however, something that's important to watch out for. Choose what you discuss, who you discuss it with and, most of all, choose what you put your mind to.

Goals and challenges

It's easy to set things up that will impress everybody else. Not that you do for that reason, but simply because their enthusiasm brings enthusiasm out in you. The trick is discovering what really excites you. As an Aquarius, you're a unique individual, and that process of discovery may take a while, but it's worth the patience and the effort.

A
\
Q
/
U
\
A
/
R
\
I
/
U
\
S

06

FEBRUARY

THIS DAY FOR EVERYONE

The planetary activity ahead won't just be exciting. Much of what's coming your way could turn into something worthwhile and of a long-term nature. However, that won't be clear at the time, which means you owe it to yourself to explore everything, including what seems unappealing.

Instead of complaining that life's predictable, I'll turn it into an adventure

You

As an Aquarius, you benefit from an inquisitive mind, a powerful imagination and a rare sense of vision. Even more than that, you have a restless and very real interest in the world around you and in others. You'll chat with others, learn about them and what they're doing.

Yet, ironically, that doesn't necessarily trigger an interest in making changes in your own life. On the contrary, you compare what you're doing to the activities of others, then are pleased with certain elements of your life – and this can lead to you becoming a creature of habit.

Spend time with those individuals. And if you also make a point of ensuring that what you're doing isn't merely interesting, but is also rewarding for you personally, you'll realise that certain individuals may chat a lot and talk about interesting ideas, but these don't in any way involve you.

As a fixed sign, born in the middle of each season of the year, you'll happily settle into routines, often inspired by others' interests. As a result, it doesn't occur to you to explore, even in matters that mean a lot to you. It may be you're unaware what you're missing until, suddenly, you're longing for them. This is one of the most important journeys for you – to acknowledge and embrace your own passions.

You and others

Being able to discern between individuals who are interesting and warm and those who are focused on their own missions and have no interest in yours, is one of the greatest skills you can develop. When you've learnt to find and spend time with those who are passionate about you, then life will take on a new joy.

Health and wellbeing

There are many who say that your wellbeing is all in your head, that it has to do with how you think about yourself. And in some cases, that's really true. If you allow yourself to get involved in worries or to dwell on anxieties, then it's unlikely you'll feel great. The trick is to begin with loving who you are and what you're doing.

Goals and challenges

Everybody needs a new challenge. If you don't have one, it will simply appear. If, on the other hand, you set a challenge for yourself – or possibly even make a list of what you'd like to do or to achieve – then you can tick them off one by one, knowing each has been your own selection.

A
\
Q
/
U
\
A
/
R
\
I
/
U
\
S

07

FEBRUARY

THIS DAY FOR EVERYONE

Admitting you're wrong is no problem. However, certain individuals insist their facts are right and you need to apologise. The problem is they're looking for a battle and have chosen the topic, which involves you. Say nothing. Those individuals will soon turn their attention elsewhere.

GIFTS Empathetic, Neutral, Fair

CHALLENGES Uninterested, Distant, Bigoted

NUMBER 1

$(0+8) + (2) = 10 = (1+0) = 1$

Today I'll rearrange my day, just for the fun of it

You

As an air sign, you love thinking about ideas and discussing what's going on in the world around you with others. You'll touch on all sorts of possibilities, some familiar, others so new you're still learning about them.

For you, as an Aquarius, being up to date is exciting and makes you think about what you could do next. However, once you begin thinking about the practical side of embracing those possibilities, your enthusiasm dies down, mostly because getting involved would mean making changes you regard as overwhelming, if not just plain impossible.

So those discussions remain exactly that – an exchange of ideas. The trick? It's to recognise that it's impossible to discuss a future that's as unfamiliar as it is exciting. This is where, in the past, you've backed out of promising plans, personal or otherwise.

However, certain individuals have a knack for being guides. You may not be able to do it alone. Trust them. At least chat with them. They'll help you imagine how those changes could work. In the past, you've often said, "Yes, but…", then done nothing. It's the same with relationships. Here, too, you tend to look for what you know. But, as an Aquarius, your life's about experiencing a broader world and once you decide to do it, not only will you learn, you'll enjoy every step of the journey.

You and others

You enjoy meeting people who are interesting and settling into habits that might be termed the rituals of meeting. But that alone can be restrictive. The trick is to have at least one person who kicks you out of those habits and forces you into doing something new, and regularly.

Health and wellbeing

There is a concept circulating about healthy addictions. Those kind of addictions are the ones that encourage you to undertake activities, ways of thinking or even ways of eating that will benefit you and which you don't even have to think about every day. Focus on those and you'll notice the difference.

Goals and challenges

You tend to repeat different versions of the same activities, whether they're professional activities or the way you organise your life. The trick is to become interested in truly new ones. Find a friend who will join you in that pursuit. You'll never regret it.

A
\
Q
/
U
\
A
/
R
\
I
/
U
\
S

08

FEBRUARY

THIS DAY FOR EVERYONE

There's a difference between making tentative plans and lasting commitments. The problem is, one particular individual views every arrangement as final. Gently but firmly help them understand that, at the moment anyway, plans are flexible and that will be better for everybody concerned.

GIFTS Unbiased, Collaborative, Clever

NUMBER 2

CHALLENGES Formal, Unpredictable, Confrontational

$(0+9) + (2) = 11 = (1+1) = 2$

Every day, I'll think of something I'd "never" do – then do it

09

FEBRUARY

A
\
Q
/
U
\
A
/
R
\
I
/
U
\
S

You

You have the rare situation of being one of the signs that acquired a new ruling planet – the first in modern history. That planet was Uranus, which was discovered in 1781. This means that, along with its new planetary influence, your own sign has developed new characteristics, and is continuing to do so.

While once you were ruled by the cautious Saturn, now life is about discovery – and in many ways. And, even more, it's about doing what some would describe as reinventing yourself. In the past, if you found an approach to doing things that worked, and that streamlined your life, you'd stick with it.

However, you feel restless – and you should. Being an Aquarius is about discovery, both as you explore the world around you, and, just as much, rethink elements of your own life. And if things become too predictable, you may just make a few changes for the fun of it.

For you, as an inquisitive air sign, you need at least one or two activities that shake you out of those habits and that challenge you to solve problems, to do things in a new way and encourage you to meet people, possibly the kind of people you wouldn't otherwise have encountered. Make that your single objective in life, and the rest of what follows will not only make life more interesting, it will make it more rewarding as well.

You and others

You have a natural ability to connect with those who will bring a sense of warmth to you – your family and friends and, if you work, colleagues. However, it's important to ensure that this circle broadens, and broadens gradually. The new individuals in your life will enrich your life as you add them to your circle.

Health and wellbeing

Many people get into a fitness regime when they're young and stick with it through the rest of their life. Yet you as an individual have changed – and how you look after yourself, how you eat and what you do should change as well. The ideal is to adopt a new fitness regime and, possibly, even a new sport every couple of years.

Goals and challenges

As an inquisitive Aquarius, you have many options in life, options to do new things and reinvent yourself. The question is, will you? There may be a part of you that prefers to stick with what you know, the new being so disruptive. But the part that's in your best interests will embrace the new and unfamiliar.

THIS DAY FOR EVERYONE

Few things are more precious than time with loved ones and family. Now, suddenly, somebody you care about is putting others first. Before you get hurt or angry, ask what's going on. They have an obligation they haven't mentioned. Once they explain, you'll understand exactly what they're dealing with.

GIFTS Innovative, Contemporary, Edgy

CHALLENGES Eccentric, Provocative, Cheeky

NUMBER 3

(1+0) + (2) = 3

If I can't change my entire wardrobe, I'll begin with one new colour

You

No sign is more interested in others, in the world around you, in life and what people are doing in the community that those born under the sign Aquarius. Yet, at the same time, all those interests can become a distraction, one that prevents you from doing something even more important. And that's focusing on your relationship with yourself. That may sound like psychobabble, but it's the best way to describe the importance of pausing regularly to reflect on how you feel – in the moment, whatever the setting, and whoever you're with.

You probably don't think of it this way, which is the reason it's important to pause and consider who you're spending time with, and the places you're going, and whether they add to your life. This may seem selfish, but the fact is those activities, those thoughts and even those companions constitute a variety of vitamins for your mind and spirit.

They may also introduce you to new activities or pursuits that you wouldn't otherwise encounter and, in that way, add to your life. As an intellectually restless Aquarius, allowing those individuals to bring new ideas to you isn't just efficient. It means that you're broadening your horizons and will be able to do so in return with others, creating a circle of growth and development – one that, in certain cases, will last a lifetime.

You and others

There are all sorts of reasons to have companions. Some are fun. Some are relaxing. But ensure you always have one individual in your life who encourages you to break habits. You don't notice that, indeed, you are a creature of habit, until that individual asks you why you're doing the same thing yet again.

Health and wellbeing

It's worth taking a few moments to consider how fit you are. You may eat well. You may walk a lot. But there are other kinds of fitness that have to do with your resilience and your zest for life. Ensure that you include in your activities those that add that particular variety of vitamin to your life as well.

Goals and challenges

Any new goal is a challenge, and any new challenge is worthwhile. The point isn't whether it will be successful or not – although if you would like it to be, that's good. The simple act of breaking patterns when you embrace a new challenge will add to your life.

A
\
Q
/
U
\
A
/
R
\
I
/
U
\
S

10

FEBRUARY

Usually there's no wrong way to express concern about a matter somebody is struggling with. However, one particular individual is presenting an upbeat façade to the world and would be upset if they thought you saw through it. What they will need is somebody to talk to. That person could be you.

I'll surprise my friends, and myself, when they ask if I want "the usual" and I say no

You

Obviously, experiencing joy as an everyday part of your life is an appealing idea. But as an air sign, you'll easily get lost in analysing the past and its influence, and you'll consider what worked and what didn't.

Yet, as you'll be aware, it's vital that you broaden your horizons in terms of what you do and the people you're meeting in the here and now. The fact is, every element of your life – from the individuals you spend time with, to the activities you pursue and, especially, your goals – is like a form of vitamins. They nourish you, in a unique way, and for that reason, you need a dose of them regularly, if not every day. And, every once in a while, you need a different formula.

If things aren't working, then it isn't about just simply exchanging one activity for another. It's about facing what hasn't worked and recognising some tough facts before you begin to consider your options.

Otherwise, you will simply do the same thing again. It's a little bit like getting fit and using new muscles. It aches initially, and you may even have to be taught to do it. But in this case, the muscle you're using is being inquisitive about life, people and places in a new way. Once you understand that, if what you're doing aches a little, you'll also know you're doing exactly the right thing.

You and others

During times of change, certain individuals may seem to be unsympathetic, if not just plain bullying. Ordinarily, that's not welcome, but in certain situations, it's true friends who are preventing you from settling into old patterns, forcing you to do things in a new way and introducing you to those new activities.

Health and wellbeing

Many people are encouraged to get in the habit of looking after themselves in a particular way – eating in a particular manner and working out in a particular way. But life changes. Your body changes. And so must the way you look after yourself.

Goals and challenges

Even if you're happy with what you're doing, every once in a while a shake-up is important. Not because there's anything wrong, but because it helps you to spot what's working and what isn't, and, even more, it helps you to spot what you want to reach for next.

A
\
Q
/
U
\
A
/
R
\
I
/
U
\
S

11
FEBRUARY

THIS DAY FOR EVERYONE

For ages, you've managed to keep a particularly tricky issue under wraps. It hasn't been easy, but you've felt strongly that this was nobody else's business. But now, it is the business of others. And you need to ensure certain individuals are aware of the full facts, including why you've said nothing until now.

Changing the first thing I do in the morning seems pointless – until I actually try it

You

As a chatty and friendly Aquarius, it's amazingly easy for you to get caught up in talking about "doing". That may sound strange, but talking about what you could be doing, or might be doing soon, isn't the same as actually undertaking those new activities.

It isn't about changing habits. It's about the idea of doing it. And for you as an air sign – and, especially, as an Aquarius – ideas can be incredibly stimulating.

However, if your objective is to alter elements of your life, you also have to be prepared to actually make those changes – whatever their nature, whether it's in habits, how you live, your routine, the clothes you wear or the places you go. And, of course, it may have to do with your activities out in the world or your job, if you go to one.

The trick is understanding that this isn't about a major change. Sometimes a minor alteration to your habits will begin the process of shaking things up, which in turn gets you considering options that, only recently, you never would have thought of.

This isn't about a single occasion. It's about developing the habit of exploring regularly. Once you begin doing that, life will suddenly become a much more exciting place, one full of opportunities and adventures that previously you hadn't spotted.

You and others

Hanging out with old friends and family can be wonderful, but new individuals add spice. Those that are the most important, however, are the ones who challenge you to go somewhere new, do something new, and break those reassuring yet restrictive habits.

Health and wellbeing

The emphasis is often on what you eat and how you work out. The single idea of learning a new skill regularly is brilliant. It not only gets you interested in things, it's a form of mental push-ups. It exercises your mind in ways you might not otherwise be doing.

Goals and challenges

Many people have long-standing goals in their lives. Some have to do with an aspect of their career. Others are personal,. Particularly for you, as an Aquarius, that goal may be shining in front of you. It may also be that it's something you actually no longer care about. If so, it's time to say farewell to that and think about something entirely different.

AQUARIUS

12 FEBRUARY

THIS DAY FOR EVERYONE

Obviously, you're not thrilled about admitting you made an unwise decision. This is especially the case, because this involves a matter where you'd battled to have things your way. However, the actual circumstances have changed. Acknowledge you got it wrong, apologise, and move on.

GIFTS Inventive, Tolerant, Progressive

CHALLENGES Withdrawn, Strange, Unstable

NUMBER 6

(1+3) + (2) = 6

Instead of expecting others to be passionate about what I love, I'll explore their passions

You

As an Aquarius, you enjoy getting to know about people, and for that reason, you are confident, you're good company. Most Aquarians have a natural understanding of others. And your genuine interest in them makes you charming. What's more, you enjoy exploring ideas and talking to people.

Yet there's one small issue, and that is, as broad-minded and inquisitive as you are about others, you can get stuck in certain situations that aren't just repetitive, they are so predictable that even you are getting bored. The problem is, you're unsure what to do about it. This comes from being one of the four fixed signs of the zodiac, those born in the middle of each season – Taurus, Leo, Scorpio and Aquarius.

While you benefit from amazing stability, once you get into a habit you can either be comfortable with it and never even try to change it, or, if you do try to break it, you struggle – and to a puzzling extent.

This is both your challenge and your opportunity. The trick isn't to figure it out, but to merely make one change. A single alteration in the hour you get up, in the way you eat, perhaps even in the order in which you do things in the morning, will begin to alter how you use your mind. That's the first step, not towards changing your routine, but towards beginning a new chapter of your life.

You and others

Note that there are certain individuals in your life who encourage you to take chances. Spend time with those individuals on occasion, simply because they're not only there for good fun. They're there to help usher you into the next chapter of your life.

Health and wellbeing

Familiar activities are comforting, but they can also lead to a trap. They can lead to powerless feelings versus the excitement of taking chances, altering the way you live, the way you eat, the way you think – and even the way you love.

Goals and challenges

The big question is, how long ago did you set the goals you're living by? If it was a while ago, maybe the time has come for a revision. In fact, maybe the time has come for a proper top-to-bottom revolution.

A
\
Q
/
U
\
A
/
R
\
I
/
U
\
S

13

FEBRUARY

THIS DAY FOR EVERYONE

There's a distinction between facts – that is, things that are true – and what is often termed the full facts, which means every element of a situation. Acknowledge this, and you'll realise why some discussions seem to turn into battles. It's not about who's right or wrong, but about your perspective.

GIFTS Campaigning, Detached, Idiosyncratic

CHALLENGES Insistent, Remote, Peculiar

NUMBER 7

$(1+4) + (2) = 7$

I'll create a "discover something new" club, then act on my commitment

You

Your birthday falls, as you may be aware, on Valentine's Day, which, in many parts of the world, is about the ideal of the perfect romance. However, as everybody knows, while there may be a few of those around, living life with other human beings can have its ups and downs. And even the most perfect romance may be the result of dealing with and finding a way around those difficult points that arise when interacting with any other human being over a long period of time.

However, the notion of romance complicates this, because the simple phrase "falling in love" suggests that it's pure destiny, and the individuals in question have no responsibility to make things work in practical terms. In fact, it's not that easy to deal with those in your life, from family and friends to colleagues, and even those you meet. With each, it's about discovering what they're like.

This interest in individuals is natural. It comes with being an Aquarius. And for you, one of the most disillusioning days is the moment you realise that many people have little interest in those around them – including you. When you come across someone who shares an interest in humanity, and in you, not only is that an individual to value, it's someone to cherish. Whatever the relationship, keep them close to you and cherish them.

You and others

There are those individuals who are easy to deal with. And then there are those who always challenge you, who ask why you're doing what you're doing, who encourage you to make changes and who even, in some cases, badger you to do something new. They are your true friends and allies.

Health and wellbeing

It's easy to get lost in the regime of looking after yourself, of eating well, and particularly the kind of exercises that go on at the gym, where there are all sorts of machines. However, it's easy to get lost in those machines and let your Aquarian mind wander. If so, you might as well not be exercising, but living in a dream.

Goals and challenges

Some say that sticking with the same goals your entire life is wise. However, it's worth noting that, with the world around you changing, what you're seeking must change too. There are many kinds of growth. And the growth that has to do with allowing your goals to grow is one of the most important.

A
\
Q
/
U
\
A
/
R
\
I
/
U
\
S

14

FEBRUARY

THIS DAY FOR EVERYONE

Recently, life has been so demanding and so complicated that each day has felt like a battle. And, equally, it's meant you've had little time to think of yourself, or your own plans and arrangements. Review these now. Ironically, all that you've already dealt with will mean this is surprisingly easy.

GIFTS Even-handed, Inspirational, Rousing

NUMBER 8

CHALLENGES Indifferent, Obstructive, Volatile

(1+5) + (2) = 8

I'll admit familiar habits are holding me back – then I'll change them

A
\
Q
/
U
\
A
/
R
\
I
/
U
\
S

You

Most Aquarians are sociable by nature. People fascinate you, and often simply observing them when out and about will keep you interested for hours. However, being on your own is quite another matter, and, as much as you enjoy your own company, facing life without family nearby, a companion or even roommates can be a challenge for you.

Yet it also gives you a chance to think. As an air sign and somebody who thrives on bouncing ideas off others, often you'll learn most from those around you, or so it will seem. But it's not until you're able to sit and reflect on those insights that you'll gain clarity about where they're taking you. This is an important thing to be aware of, because as somebody who's one of the four fixed signs of the zodiac – Taurus, Leo, Scorpio, and Aquarius, the signs in the middle of each season – you can settle into a routine. One that may be reassuring, but also prevents you from sticking your head above the parapet and looking around to see what's out there.

Ideally there will be certain individuals in your life who don't just encourage you to explore, but who challenge you to do new things, to break patterns, to break habits that seem reassuring, but actually have become a bit of a trap. For you, as an Aquarius, those individuals are more precious than diamonds.

You and others

It's easy to stick with the familiar. Sticking with those who encourage you to break habits won't be quite as easy, but they are the ones who will turn your life into a journey of growth, joy and discovery.

Health and wellbeing

Your theme is discovery. And, as you know, as an Aquarius and an air sign, you can either forget to eat or stick with pretty much the same menu, even for weeks on end. Yet at the same time, you love to discover you thrive on new experiences. It's essential some of those discoveries have to do with your daily routine.

Goals and challenges

Thinking about the things you intend to do is one thing, but it's essential you write them down. Not so much so you can achieve them in a metaphysical way, but so you can read what you wrote down a week later and revise those goals. Then continue to revise them as you broaden your goals and your horizons.

THIS DAY FOR EVERYONE

It's not that you mind others making decisions in situations that involve you. Actually, it's often a relief. However, you prefer to take part in discussions, mostly because others lack your knack for telling those around you what's up. While this is tricky, you'll soon find a way to deal with those problems.

GIFTS Unconventional, Modern, Exciting

NUMBER 9

CHALLENGES Weird, Unapproachable, Outrageous

(1+6) + (2) = 9

Once, joy was meeting the same person at the same place. Now it's about exploration

You

For you, those around you – family, friends, and occasionally colleagues – aren't just people you know, they're what could be termed provocateurs. They are vital, simply because, from time to time, one will ask a question or another will point out that you've been doing something the same way for a very long time. And, in each case, they are gently but firmly challenging you to change habits that are familiar. So familiar that, in a way, they numb your mind.

Even if it doesn't seem to be the case at the time, these habits prevent you from exploring in ways that are important for you, as an Aquarius and an air sign. And, while others' words may be irritating, deep down you know they're doing you a favour. If they didn't provoke you, if they didn't point out what you said you wanted to do, but haven't taken action on, they wouldn't be true friends.

Remember this when you're annoyed with them, and instead of flaring up, as you have in the past, you might even thank them.

But even more than that, if possible, get them to join you in those adventures. For you, an Aquarius and an air sign, life is about discovery, and every time you do something in a new way, every time you break a familiar habit, you're taking another step towards delightful discovery.

You and others

Some place deep in your mind, you have a feeling that those who are true friends should be people you can hang out with and simply enjoy without any kind of conflict. But, of course, the point is, those who are true friends or family members who love you will actually challenge you. They're concerned about your being stuck. This may not be welcome, but it's the biggest favour they could do you.

Health and wellbeing

There are all kinds of ways to ensure that you feel better. There are various kinds of exercise, from walking to yoga to jogging to things you haven't even heard of. And there are different ways of eating. But there's another way that you, as an Aquarius and an air sign, can often fall into, and it's called daydreaming. If you do that it may feel good, but it probably won't do your body much good.

Goals and challenges

Tempting as it is to revive goals from your past that once meant a great deal to you, deep down you know they are indeed from the past. The trick is to pay attention to those that are in the present and in the future and glimmer in front of your eyes. Those are the ones to go for.

A
\
Q
/
U
\
A
/
R
\
I
/
U
\
S

16

FEBRUARY

THIS DAY FOR EVERYONE

In their enthusiasm to tell you about certain new ideas or offers, one particular individual could be overly zealous. They may even seem to be bullying you. Despite that, what they have in mind would actually be in your best interests, but you won't know that until you do a little exploration.

Do I say no before I even realised it?
That's an invitation for a breakthrough

You

Often, as an Aquarius, you have several plans or projects on your mind, some of which are actually happening, and others that you're thinking about. Yet for somebody ruled by Uranus, the planet of innovation, life is about breakthroughs. And it's vital to consider whether what you're doing and planning has to do with the past, and past successes, and is similar to what others around you are doing, or is it actually about taking an entirely different approach to some element of life.

Those new pursuits may involve a range of activities, but they all share something in common – what might be described as a form of vision. That is, they're not about things that you've already done or have already experienced, but are new.

And that's the most important thing about them for you – they inspire you. Some may have to do with work, some may be practical, some may be social.

But in every case, they remind you that there's a world out there that you can change – in small ways and in big ways. And for you, being an Aquarius and somebody who not only has vision, but who can be a visionary, this is important.

Undertake that – ideally with those you care about – and life won't just be exciting, it will be extraordinarily satisfying.

You and others

Nothing is better than hanging out with people who spur your thinking and get you going. They may be family, work colleagues or people you're involved with. Whatever the case, this process of exchanging ideas isn't just stimulating, it's about taking a step into the future.

Health and wellbeing

It's worth bearing in mind that, as much as you enjoy getting focused on ideas and ideals, it's easy to forget about looking after your body. Yet you'll need that body in order to take things to the next stage. So looking after it is as important as looking after those exciting changes.

Goals and challenges

Be wary of those around you who describe what you're doing as idealistic. As an Aquarius, you were born to be exactly that. Even if you have a fairly boring day job, some element of your life needs to have an idealistic thread running through it. For you, that's like health-giving vitamins.

17

FEBRUARY

THIS DAY FOR EVERYONE

In some situations, fast action is vital, but in at least one, you're urged to wait until you have clarity, in terms of both hard facts and your own feelings, and that comes with having dealt with things and thought them through. Until then, explore your options, but avoid lasting decisions.

GIFTS Offbeat, Trend-spotting, Team player

NUMBER 2

CHALLENGES Aloof, Unpredictable, Outlandish

$(1+8) + (2) = 11 = (1+1) = 2$

Certain places and people bring me joy, so I stick with them. But others might, too

You

You're always ready to explore and try new things. In fact, there's a part of you that rather enjoys doing something that isn't just a bit of an experiment but that will, in some way, change the world. It may be modest; in fact, it may be your very private experiment. You may have fantasies about it leading to exciting things.

Yet there's another part of you that enjoys having a routine. It's familiar, and as an air sign and somebody who is easily distracted, knowing what's next grounds you. During times of transition, it's essential that you give yourself what might be termed elbow room. A chance to alter that routine, or perhaps even create a new one.

In doing so, that will reprogramme the way you use your mind and your brain, and allow you to think about those goals and activities in a new way as well. This probably is the reverse of your thinking. You feel that if you can stick to the same routine at home, say in the morning, or when you go to bed, then you can venture out further. But actually it's the reverse. This is one of the greatest skills for you, as an Aquarius, to learn. To not only play games with your mind, but to train your mind as if you were taking it to a gym. To exercise it and to work with new ideas. Do that regularly, and you'll be amazed how much fun you have.

You and others

Don't be surprised if those around you are suddenly asking you a lot of questions, or perhaps even referring to you as someone who is guiding them. This isn't necessarily what you set yourself up to be. But the fact is, you are often more observant and closer to the trends than others, and your guidance will indeed be helpful for them.

Health and wellbeing

There's a phrase that it's important for you to edit from your thinking and your habits. And that phrase is "I always need to…". Whether it's what you eat or what you do, this is what might be termed an addiction. And even if it's a healthy addiction, exercising in a certain way or eating certain foods, at this point in your life, flexibility is more important than habits.

Goals and challenges

There are many kinds of goals, but for you, the most important one is discovery. And that means not setting the goal itself, but simply deciding you're on a journey during which, every week, every day or as often as possible, you'll encounter something new, something inspiring and something that reassures you that you're on the right path.

A
\
Q
/
U
\
A
/
R
\
I
/
U
\
S

18

FEBRUARY

THIS DAY FOR EVERYONE

Unsettling as sudden changes may be, what's coming your way now and over the coming weeks isn't just exciting. Those events could be the answer to persistent problems. However, they won't seem that promising when they arise. Make a point of exploring everything. You'll be surprised what works out.

Pisces

Ruler Neptune
Element Water

Symbol The Fish
Flower Waterlily

February 19 – March 19

Pisces   Symbolised by a pair of fishes, you, as a Pisces, born under this often charismatic and highly intuitive water sign, can view almost any situation from two angles. While Pisces was originally ruled by Jupiter, Neptune's discovery in 1846 changed that. Your flower is waterlily, your food and flavours are mosses and lime and your tree is the fig. Your stone is misty blue-green jade.

P
\
I
/
S
\
C
/
E
\
S

GIFTS Intuitive, Liberal, Spontaneous

NUMBER 3

CHALLENGES Unworldly, Fantasizer, Indirect

$(1+9) + (2) = 12 = (1+2) = 3$

Dawn is a reminder of nature's capacity to forgive humanity

You

You were born on a very special day – the first day of the sign of Pisces, a sign that has reinvented itself. You're probably aware of your symbol, which is two fishes swimming in different directions. And those fishes actually saved the goddess Aphrodite when she was born in the sea and brought her up into the air.

But also your sign has reinvented itself because in 1846 it acquired a new ruling planet, Neptune, which, of course, is appropriate for your sign. It could also be said to inspire you to be the Pisces you are today, whereas before, it seems Pisces seemed to live a life that depended on circumstances. With Neptune, you've stepped out as someone who's very interested in having a positive impact on those around you, from close family to the world itself. And that impact has to do with helping people be the best selves they can be.

This is a wonderful mission, but at times can lead to confusion in relationships and friendships. And that's the balance you're seeking – to be able to inspire others, yet encourage them to be independent. It's as if you're watching an infant learn to walk – firstly, you help them take their first few steps, holding your hand, then you back off and leave it to them. This is one of the best gifts you can give others – your support. And there's nothing like support from a Pisces.

You and others

A lingering friendship between an individual and a Pisces is a great treasure. You're an inspiration, and your presence in the life of another can help them turn a good idea into something wonderful – something that inspires others and, on occasion, could even benefit the world as well.

Health and wellbeing

As you're aware, as a Pisces you can get so involved in what you're doing that you simply forget to eat or even sleep. Finding that balance – between being an inspiration to others and for them, in turn, to inspire people themselves – can be challenging. However, when you manage to do it, you'll increase what you're able to give to the world.

Goals and challenges

Having the ability to care for others is a gift, but being able to care for yourself and deal with what you need to do at the same time can be a challenge. However, it's a challenge that, in some way, you designed for yourself as a Pisces. While it won't always be an easy one, it's one you're equal to and will profit from.

P
\
I
/
S
\
C
/
E
\
S

19

FEBRUARY

THIS DAY FOR EVERYONE

It's not that you've been trying to escape certain burdens and responsibilities, but rather you didn't know which to tackle first, so did nothing. However, now events have kick-started a cycle of action, each day will bring something new, exciting and wonderful to focus on and to deal with.

GIFTS Redemptive, Extrasensory, Flowing

CHALLENGES Unreachable, Naive, Vague

NUMBER 4

(2+0) + (2) = 4

At the right moment, even a seemingly minor gesture touches a Piscean heart

You

While you're sympathetic by nature, when the moment calls for it, you can be very firm, if not actually tough – with others and with yourself. What's more, you also benefit from a powerful practical streak. In fact, when it comes to big matters, it's amazing how clear you can be.

However, the sympathetic streak that is also a part of your nature surfaces from time to time and can distract you. That means, when you're doing something, however modest, the real challenge isn't figuring out what to do. You can rely on your instincts for that. It's balancing that vision with the portion of your nature that gets so obsessed with tiny details or which can, at times, be so hurt by someone else's unthinking behaviour, that you're distracted from your objective.

As a water sign, while you're idealistic, you can take things personally – from others' unwitting comments to the peculiar attitude of certain individuals. Most Pisceans learn to spot this and, before you take things to heart, either speak up or, if that's not possible, make a decision to ignore them.

This is a skill – but then all of life is a skill. And the better you get at dealing with such distractions, whatever their nature, the better you'll be able to use your extraordinary ability to touch others – and to transform the world around you that comes with being a Pisces.

You and others

Dramas around you can be distracting, but once you learn to spot them you'll learn to ask the question, "When is enough?" It's as if you were enjoying the warmth of the sun, but then realise if you stay out too long, you're likely to get burnt. Dealing with those who could undermine your confidence is the same. The trick? It's to ignore them.

Health and wellbeing

As a water sign, while you look after yourself, you sometimes forget about the toll being around those who have a tendency to undermine you can take. This not only causes concern, it can also lead to worry about other things. The trick is to discuss the matter clearly and firmly and in a way that you, as a Pisces, wouldn't usually do.

Goals and challenges

Every once in a while, you pause and organise yourself, your thinking and your life, so know what's working and what isn't. And that will last for a while. However, one individual will then draw your attention and pull your balance away. The trick is to go back, as swiftly as you can, to that balance – because that balance is one of the most precious elements of your life.

P
\
I
/
S
\
C
/
E
\
S

Understandably, you're in no mood to argue with somebody who, on the best of days, is difficult to deal with. But if you don't tackle the issue in question now, it will be assumed that you're happy with things as they are, when that is by no means the case. Speak up now. You won't regret it.

20

FEBRUARY

A spring leaf, an infant, a new love – all remind us of life's promise

You

Pisceans take great joy in being able to make the world better, whether it's one person at a time, one situation at a time or even bigger projects. But for you, as a Pisces, it isn't easy to maintain this as your main activity.

With the world around you changing – and with those who are involved shifting – there are bound to be many twists and turns, and of many varieties. Even those whose main profession is doing exactly this variety of humanitarian work know they need to balance that with other activities in their own life and, equally, with family or hobbies.

So it's important for you to be aware of the need for that balance. These individuals and activities are an essential part of your life. They are, in fact, a variety of emotional vitamins and you need them just like you might need actual vitamins. In this case, those activities and those individuals help you keep your perspective and, when necessarily, realign your thinking and remind you what's actually in your best interests. They help you rediscover your core, your centre.

Not only do these individuals benefit you, but they give you the strength you need to go on to the next day, the next week and the next month, and to make the world better in the way that you like to, but to do so without having to pay a price yourself.

You and others

You're probably aware you're sentimental, but you don't notice how much the attitude of others matters to you. If they're uncaring, it can be hurtful. Be aware of this and steer clear of those who are thoughtless. Instead, ensure those closest support you in the way they, and you, know is vital.

Health and wellbeing

While some Pisceans are naturals at working out, most aren't. If you're one of the latter, then finding ways to move that aren't really exercise is vital. And it can be fun. Seek out something that's magical and, ideally, musical. Do that, and you'll appreciate the next time you can get out there and shake with those vibes, exercising your body at the same time.

Goals and challenges

Setting goals is one thing. Pursuing them is another matter. However, list those goals, ideally on paper, and you know what you expect to do. But, actually, combining these with your own personal desires can be an even bigger challenge. The solution? Ask someone to stand beside you when you need that support. It's worthwhile.

THIS DAY FOR EVERYONE

While you'd have every right to be annoyed with certain thoughtless individuals, the fact is they are unaware of the impact of their words or actions. Raise this gently but frankly, and invest time in the process. The resulting discussions will be astonishingly informative for everybody concerned.

P
\
I
/
S
\
C
/
E
\
S

21

FEBRUARY

Discern between those in need and complainers, who are louder and more persistent

You

You are, of course, living by your own set of ideals. This is something that you, as a Pisces, will have figured out probably from your earliest days. And as you've lived over the years, these ideals have become clearer.

You've also tended to assume that others have ideals, too. But gradually, you've come to realise that not only do others not have ideals, many don't even care. This is disillusioning, but this also explains quite a lot about certain people in your life and why, when you're talking about something you hope to do because it is an ideal, they look at you blankly.

Once you understand that, then you will understand why certain individuals are easier to live with, work with and do things with. Whereas others may require more time and effort, until you reach the point of simply telling them what you expect them to do and not explaining why it's good for them, or the world.

This variety of insight – this variety of being able to deal with others – is one of the greatest skills for you as a Pisces. It means you'll stop trying to get those who have no capacity for empathy towards others to be that way. And, equally, you will recognise who has earned your attention, your friendship and, in some cases, your love.

You and others

It's becoming clear that certain individuals hear what you say in different ways. Some understand your vision, and that what you're describing is steps towards that. But others just see life as a long list of things to do. Once you realise that, then simply tell them, and don't expect them to share your vision, because it's unlikely they will.

Health and wellbeing

The idea of stopping to look after yourself is difficult for Pisceans, partly because, as a water sign, you don't really notice if you're hungry or tired until you're almost falling over. But also, looking after yourself in terms of activities may seem strange. Yet if you begin to question how you feel about it, then it may be quite different. Fall in love with some kind of activity and eating well. The rest will be easy.

Goals and challenges

As a Pisces, you're a visionary. And for that reason, you may have had a sense of exactly what you wanted to be when you grew up. But even if you didn't, you will still have been drawn towards certain activities. Stick with them. Even if you have to redefine them every couple of years, they will still be core to your sense of achievement and of who you are.

P
\
I
/
S
\
C
/
E
\
S

THIS DAY FOR EVERYONE

Usually, rethinking plans at the last minute is no problem. In fact, you rather enjoy the challenge. But reorganising arrangements when they're advanced – as is the case now – is complicated, disruptive and time-consuming. Once you've begun, you'll realise how necessary these changes are.

22

FEBRUARY

GIFTS Fluid, Self-sacrificing, Charitable

CHALLENGES Cryptic, Martyred, Profligate

NUMBER 7

(2+3) + (2) = 7

Nobody is better at spotting those who need help and knowing exactly what to do

P
\
I
/
S
\
C
/
E
\
S

You

If you're into astrology, then you'll know that, as a Pisces, you're one of the three water signs, along with Cancer and Scorpio. And as a water sign, you have the power to understand the feelings of others often better than they do, and to recognise that your own feelings and emotions can be very powerful.

Not only that, you're idealistic. And you feel – and hope – that if you can work out a way to make your own life and the lives of others better, you can also have a greater impact on those around you, or maybe even the world.

While this is irrational and emotional, it's also visionary. And, very often, vision can override obstacles simply because you leap over the practicalities that so many others live with, and begin to work at turning that vision into a reality.

If there are those who question your capacity to achieve that, thank them for telling you. But go on doing what you believe in, because, as a Pisces, some would say you were born under that sign to benefit from that vision in whatever form it takes.

And it's true. That form may shift over time, but that doesn't matter. As you grow, it will change as well. But, most of all, the important thing is to never, ever give up believing that miracles are possible. If anyone can make them happen, it's a Pisces.

You and others

All Pisceans have an intuitive side, and a belief in others. The funny thing is, often you'll have more belief in those around you than they have in themselves. Avoid arguing with them about what you see, but simply be there as they begin to recognise the characteristics that you spotted long ago. This is something you will do regularly throughout your life. And many will thank you for it.

Health and wellbeing

One of your greatest gifts is your capacity to commit to a person, a cause or a plan. And you do it so much that you forget about your own energy and body. The trick is to catch yourself before you go too far. Hurl yourself into something with passion – but at the same time, know when to stop.

Goals and challenges

Most Pisceans have a list of goals they want to achieve. If there's a problem, it's a tendency to line up new ones too soon. While on one hand, that makes sense – because you want to be preparing for the next – it can also mean that goals seem relentless. The secret? It's to celebrate each one as they're achieved.

23

FEBRUARY

THIS DAY FOR EVERYONE

There have been all sorts of excuses for the increasing distance between you and somebody who was once an important part of your life. While it's true you've been busy and so have they, the fact is you simply haven't made time for them. Do it now. Once you're together again, you'll be glad.

Often, simple gestures say more about feelings than grand gifts

You

In most areas of life, you have an ideal – a vision for yourself, for others or possibly for an organisation. It may be simple or it may be ambitious. But, in every case, there will be a phrase that's involved with this, which is, "One day, when…"

This may have to do with work, or relationships, or something that you care deeply about. However, if you're waiting until that one day when things are a certain way, then you aren't able to enjoy it in the here and now. And the odds are good that when you get there, whatever there is with that plan or project, you'll already be thinking about something else new.

For many Pisceans, this is tricky. And for many Pisceans, being in the here and now – and enjoying what you're doing with the people that you're with – is a real challenge.

Yet if you can manage to do this, that is, manage to enjoy the incomplete plans and the not-quite-done goals, but the fact that you're working on them, and if you can manage to enjoy the presence of the people you're with, again the relationship may not be perfect, but you're still enjoying them. That's a victory. And that too will add to what might be called your joy vitamins. Goals move along, but if you ensure you take your joy vitamins every day, then you'll be fine.

You and others

Pisceans tend to gather others for support when necessary. While, mostly, that's good, it's about who's reliable or trustworthy. The challenge? It's to recognise that, while certain individuals are supportive, they don't do much. Others may not be good company, but are reliable. Once that's dealt with, you'll have exactly the kind of support you need.

Health and wellbeing

It's easy to meet someone and grab a cup of coffee. But that's not really spending time with them. Yet, with life ever more complicated, when is there time? The secret? Make a grown-up playdate, to set aside what's often called quality time with others. This isn't just pleasant, it will give you a very special variety of emotional vitamins.

Goals and challenges

Pisceans are the dreamers of the entire zodiac, but that doesn't mean you should completely ignore reality. The trick is to recognise that, one day, reality will hit – and you need to welcome it, because the insights it gives you will enable you to ensure that your dreams do become reality.

P
\
I
/
S
\
C
/
E
\
S

It would be easy to assume that the silence of others means they disagree with you, dislike your plans or, perhaps, are angry and unwilling to communicate. Equally, it could be a simple misunderstanding. But you won't know if you don't ask. Do exactly that – ask. And the sooner, the better.

24

FEBRUARY

Pisces understanding is infinite, unless faced with cruelty. That's a game-changer

You

You don't think of yourself as an idealist until you talk to others and realise they don't care nearly as much as you do about the world, or about people's wellbeing or individuals being happy. While you've assumed others also cared about such matters, the fact is, they live in very different worlds, and their feelings aren't the same as yours.

Once you get over being disillusioned, the trick is to learn to speak their language. If you want their support in some way, you need to be very clear, because they won't be swept up in the way you are by your passion for the cause. Yet if you tell them exactly what you need, they'll probably be not only be happy to help, but may even give you worthwhile advice.

Ironically, this will also help you to broaden your own contacts and interests, because when people don't respond to your Piscean enthusiasm for what matters to you, you assume they're not interested. Yet, when you take another approach, you'll learn a lot about that. This isn't just about those activities you're passionate about. It's about almost any kind of relationship with others.

Those in the world around you speak a very different language from the language of Piscean idealism. And once you realise that, then you'll understand them far better – and they will understand you far better as well.

You and others

Most of us are born surrounded by family and friends who remain part of life but who don't necessarily understand us. It's about longevity, being part of our lives. That clarifies why they may not share your views. Ironically, they may be most informative when they disagree with you. Discuss why and you'll learn a great deal about the viewpoint of others.

Health and wellbeing

Everybody has ideas about eating well and the right way to achieve physical perfection. But there's something exciting you can do. It will suit you whatever the season, and wherever you are. And that is simply walk. Take a short walk, take a long walk; walk on your own or walk with a friend. Doing that will remind you of just how magnificent the world itself can be.

Goals and challenges

Achieving the goals you want at the level you want isn't going to be easy, and others have no idea what you're thinking of. Their view of something done well is only about 75% of what you have in mind. Once you understand that, instead of being shocked, you'll realise they are just being themselves.

P
\
I
/
S
\
C
/
E
\
S

25

FEBRUARY

THIS DAY FOR EVERYONE

You haven't exactly been patient, but you have been forced to recognise that no matter how unfair circumstances have been, there's no single solution. While sudden events will eliminate obstacles, these matters still can't be rushed. Continuing to be patient won't be easy, but it will pay off – and big time.

Sometimes the kindest thing you can do for another is accept their generosity

You

Life as a Pisces can be complex. The irony is that if things are going too well, you begin to feel guilty. And if you're having too much fun, you may even begin to unconsciously undermine certain things you're doing so you have to work harder. In fact, that means you have to rethink your timing and do more for duty and relax less.

Of course, this side of your nature keeps changing, so it's hard to spot it. Yet, if you recognise those moments when whatever was going smoothly gets undermined, then think about whether there was something that you committed to suddenly, or someone you've got close to who takes a lot of time, then you'll recognise the part of you that can undermine progress.

You'll also learn how to organise things in a very different way, and possibly even sideline that side of your nature and those individuals.

As a Pisces, you have a unique vision, one that is often beneficial to the world in many ways. Apply that vision to your own everyday life, excluding those individuals, those activities or those obsessions that could undermine things and prevent them happening.

Not only will you be able to contribute to the world in the wonderful ways that you do as a Pisces, but you'll be able to do so without dramas and with ease.

You and others

Defining joy may be challenging. But it's simply knowing you're happy with what you did yesterday, you're pleased with today and you're pretty excited about tomorrow, too. The trick? Not to allow anything to disrupt that joy. It isn't easy, but it's up to you alone to determine this. It may sound complicated, but actually it's very simple.

Health and wellbeing

Currently, there's an obsession about getting things done. But for you, as an intuitive Pisces, it's clear what you need to do. Despite that, you sometimes get so involved in what you're doing, you forget about eating or sleeping. It's easy to get back on track. Just sit quietly, reflect and remember who you are and what's in your best interests.

Goals and challenges

Every Pisces has the notion, deep in their mind, that they can achieve amazing goals – what others might call fantasies. However, some say you must sacrifice something. That's an old story. But, actually, as a Pisces, you were born to have that vision. All you need to do to achieve it is ignore those who either try to undermine it or laugh at it.

P
\
I
/
S
\
C
/
E
\
S

There's a fine line between discussing the best option and having an exchange of ideas that descends into a battle about who's right and who's wrong. Neither you nor anybody else is likely to give in. The solution? Allow the evaluation process to unfold as it must – then wait and watch.

26

FEBRUARY

Usually, trust must be built slowly. Except when it bursts on the scene like fireworks

You

Every sign of the zodiac is said to have a ruler, a heavenly body that's linked with it, mythically and astrologically. This practice goes back thousands of years. Yet over the past couple of hundred years, three signs have acquired new ruling planets, including yours.

Until 1846, Pisces was considered to be ruled by Jupiter. But that year the appropriately named Neptune was discovered, and it became your ruler. This is especially appropriately because your symbol is two fishes, swimming in opposite directions. And that's one of your big lessons as a Pisces. Neptune is not only about vision but also intuition; it's helping you align those two fishes, one of which is going in a practical direction, and one of which is going in an intuitive direction.

Learn to balance the two; that is, the practical side that needs to align with your intuition, the side that's more about feelings. As a Pisces, you have rare access to both. You can create a beautiful life in the physical world, but also reach to the heavens, and sometimes deep into humanity's core.

Certain individuals have a role to play in others' lives, whatever the setting. It may be among family, or in the wider world. And it may change at times. Whatever it is you're doing, you'll bring a special touch, which is your Piscean capacity for caring.

You and others

Urgent as remedying others' problems seems, the fact is, they probably aren't yours to deal with at all. Some people are born knowing what they want to do, while others develop that vision over life. Many have family and friends guiding them, and sometimes telling them what to do. Be cautious of others becoming too dependent on you.

Health and wellbeing

As a Piscean, you're easily touched by others, and if there is tension – if they have tension in their own lives, or if there's tension between you that you can feel deeply – the trick is not to try to solve it. Instead, you need to realise that if there isn't anything you can do at the moment, back off and let things be as they are.

Goals and challenges

Setting goals can be difficult. Yet being true to yourself is essential. And as you understand yourself better, those goals are likely to change. Don't feel you've got to stick with the same ones when you've shifted; those goals should shift then as well.

P
\
I
/
S
\
C
/
E
\
S

27

FEBRUARY

THIS DAY FOR EVERYONE

Few things annoy you more than trying to organise plans with somebody who refuses to focus on the big picture and instead thinks only about details. Actually, this is ideal. You dread fine-tuning matters of this nature, but are superb at dealing with the overview – so now you can split your duties.

GIFTS Calming, Insightful, Compassionate

CHALLENGES Escapist, Assumptive, Unreadable

NUMBER 3

(2+8) + (2) = 12 = (1+2) = 3

Quiet joys go deepest and are longest lasting

You

As a water sign, you're influenced by your feelings, of course. However, you're also influenced by the world around you, by the people you're talking to and by circumstances.

And all of those can mean that you rethink what once were very clear plans, a vision for what you want to do and achieve. But, even more than that, if you chat with others too much about your own goals, it's easy to allow them to influence you, simply because they want to understand your vision. But then, of course, they aren't you. Even if they are Pisceans, your own vision is very much an extension of yourself. It may seem antisocial when others talk about things to say, "Well, I totally disagree with you."

However, it's worth noting that many Pisceans are actual artists – they're actors or performers – and they use their intuitive side to create roles.

In your case, if you find others are always trying to tell you what to do, it may be that it's important for you to dig deeper into your own nature and discover what your role is in life.

Equally, it's important to recognise that the right role at one particular moment may change or evolve. Because, of course, we all grow over time. When you recognise that, then instead of worrying about getting it right, you'll enjoy the process as it unfolds.

You and others

Discussions can sometimes be difficult, because others don't seem to understand that your views are completely different from theirs. However, if you run into one of those rare individuals who not only celebrates the uniqueness of your views, but encourages you to nurture them, then keep that person close to you. They're the one you want nearby as you're exploring your options.

Health and wellbeing

There are those who feel that if you have your health well in hand, then life will run smoothly. But for a Pisces and a water sign, ups and downs are natural. There will be times when you eat enthusiastically and sleep well, and others when you're restless or not hungry. That's all about being a Pisces, experiencing the ebb and flow of being a water sign.

Goals and challenges

Basically, there are two ways to achieve what you want. One is to set a goal and go after it. But there's another that's far more Piscean, and that is to wake up and sense what you should do next. Gradually, you'll learn how powerful intuition can be, and how following it can shorten the path to achieving those goals.

P
\
I
/
S
\
C
/
E
\
S

Life would be a lot easier if you could sidestep certain obligations that are as tricky as they are tedious. However, tempting as it is to put these off, they won't just vanish. In fact, they could become more complicated. The sooner you tackle them the better – and the easier it will be.

28
FEBRUARY

This rare and special date accents unique gifts and charms

You

This is a very special birthday. Not only because it only occurs every four years, but also because in numerology, your number February 29th, two and nine add up to 11, which is considered to be one of the master numbers. This indicates that you were born for a special reason.

And, as you live your life, all sorts of intriguing opportunities will arise. It may also be that you have your own particular vision – many Pisceans do, but you may be drawn to a certain activity. You may have a certain talent, a gift or a characteristic that adds not only to your life but to the lives of those around you – and possibly even to the lives of everyone else on the planet.

In many cases, you may sense this when you're young. In others, it will come about and in some cases it will morph, it will reshape itself as you live out the days of your life. But what's most important for you to realise is that, while each of us comes into this life with a gift, as someone who is a February 29th Pisces, you have a very special gift. One that it's important to share with the world, but also one that it's even more important to embrace and enjoy as the individual that you are.

Simply being you will add to the environment you're in – every day and in more ways than you can imagine possible.

You and others

Feeling you have something special to offer may seem bizarre or even arrogant, but the fact is, you do. You don't need to define it or say it, but chatting with certain individuals will leave them changed – and you as well. Every time you do it, you'll be contributing to the wellbeing of others and of the planet – and you'll bring greater joy to your own life as well.

Health and wellbeing

Finding ways to look after yourself can be difficult, because often you're sensitive or perhaps have unusual energies different from everybody else. All you need to do is check in with yourself on any particular day and sense what you need. It may be you need to rest. It may be you need food. It may even be that you need a large ice cream cone. Whatever the case, give yourself that gift and listen in the same way every day.

Goals and challenges

Many in the world want to make things better. The practical earth signs have one set of ideas and the air signs have another. But you, as a special Pisces, have what might be described as a golden touch. And when you make a suggestion, it might work out to be nothing short of miraculous.

P
\
I
/
S
\
C
/
E
\
S

29

FEBRUARY

THIS DAY FOR EVERYONE

You're in no mood to take care of tasks or obligations as boring as they are rewarding. However, these aren't just your responsibility. Once you're involved, you'll realise how much you have to learn from them. That alone will justify the time and effort required, but also you'll soon begin to enjoy them.

Most arguments are mere differences, but a few are a way of showing love

You

Part of your nature, as a Pisces, is that of the searcher. You're searching for all sorts of things. You're searching for that vision that is yours, but you'll also be searching in other ways, in practical ways and personal ways, that have to do with friendships – that special gift for somebody, something that will make their life easier, or even an introduction that you can make, the right person meeting the other right person at the right time.

And that element of perfection is also core to your life. There's a tendency to feel that if you can just line up the energies, then things will fall into place. And that would be true if you were in a world where everyone had the same intention. But, as you have seen, some people almost have an instinct for turning relatively smooth arrangements upside down, and they do it all on their own.

If you take responsibility for that, then you'll be distracted from who you are, which is someone who's there to align events and the thoughts of others and to make things happen.

The trick is to continue to search, but forget about perfection. Then, you'll draw to you those individuals who somehow always manage to turn things upside down, and instead you will make the best of every day and every hour and every moment, simply because that's your intention.

You and others

Every once in a while, you'll come across somebody who's quite special. In fact, those individuals might become what you could call co-searchers. That is they, too, have a sense that there's something to be discovered – not through struggle, but through a quiet intention to encounter something wonderful. You might spend a day with them, or a lifetime. But you will change each other's lives.

Health and wellbeing

There's one characteristic of the true searcher, and that is someone who has a vision. Your energy extends into the world, looking for what you can do and how you can share those experiences with others. There's no formula for it, but there is a formula for enjoying it. And it's to realise that each morning when you wake up, you'll be experiencing something new.

Goals and challenges

Many people have no understanding about you. It's as if you speak a different language. The fact is, you do. They don't understand about vision or about search. They only understand about today and tomorrow – and life's practicalities. Acknowledge that simple fact, and the rest will be easy.

P
\
I
/
S
\
C
/
E
\
S

Obviously, you'd rather not stand your ground with somebody who's difficult in the best of circumstances, but not only is it wise, the individual in question knows they're in the wrong, yet is too proud to admit it. Gently but firmly challenge them, and they'll not only respond positively, they'll thank you.

01

MARCH

If somebody is being demanding, do nothing until you observe how they treat others

You

The word idealism is so often used when talking about Pisceans. Of course, certain individuals insist they're idealists, but they're probably a little bit different from your brand, simply because their idea of things going well has more to do with politics and economics than it does with yours. It is the sense that there is a vision, a way of living life, where, instead of things being a struggle, they can work out and, in some cases, fall into place.

And that is entirely possible, except it's mostly only Pisceans, or those for whom the sign is very strong in their astrological chart, who can deal with that. It's also important for you to recognise the difference between those who share your vision and those whose version of idealism might be more, shall we say, practical or even academic.

When you understand that, then you'll also understand there are actually two languages you need to use. The one you use with the fellow true idealists, and the one with those who are trying to live up to their version of that. And when you understand that there are two brands of idealism, then, also, you'll be more relaxed about it. The fact is, with those who are following their "not-quite-Piscean" brand of idealism, their hearts are good, as are their intentions. Embrace that – and the rest will be easy.

You and others

Finding a way to talk things over with those whose view is very different can be tricky, until you realise it's as if you're speaking different languages. When that's clear, you'll realise that their values, ethics and objectives are very different. Then you'll be able to talk about things the way they understand them, and may even be able to add a few intriguing thoughts to their approach to life.

Health and wellbeing

As a Pisces, the possibility of catching something from someone isn't just about a cold; you can catch someone's bad mood. However, it's easy to shake off, because if you remember the best of your vision for the world, you will quickly reshape your mood.

Goals and challenges

Explaining to somebody else what you'd like to achieve can be difficult. As a Pisces, you have your own unique values and viewpoints. Understand that and then, when you're talking with others, you'll realise that occasionally you need to say things in a different way for them to understand the vision that you have in mind.

P
\
I
/
S
\
C
/
E
\
S

THIS DAY FOR EVERYONE

You're facing a range of decisions. Some are minor and easy to deal with. Others are so complex that you've no idea where to begin. Urgent as things seem, there's no rush to deal with these. Invest time in asking questions. What you learn will clarify matters more swiftly than you'd imagined possible.

Nobody understands the power of love better than a Pisces

You

What does it take for you to say life is good? You'd think you know the answer. Many want a home, love, a job, friends – and those are important. But for you, as a Pisces, while of course those things matter a great deal, there's also part of you that wants those around you, or possibly the entire world, to be free from pain and struggle. That's your Piscean idealism at work.

And if you can't remedy them, you might have a tendency to say you can't be happy until the world is free of whatever it is that's worrying you.

It's worth thinking about that, because that means that you won't be able to add your personal happiness to the world until certain world issues are dealt with.

If you had infinite powers, then that's understandable. But the odds are that you don't. And, therefore, the trick is to recognise there are things going on in the world that you're not happy about, but that their existence doesn't need to, and shouldn't, undermine your own contentment.

It's a tricky thing to recognise that, when you say you won't be happy until X problem or Y situation is solved, but it will also bring powerful insights about the way certain parts of your mind can undermine your own joy.

You and others

We all have a gift to give to the world. In some cases it has to do with family, loved ones or friends. It may be raising children. It may be being a valuable friend to others. But in every case, it's essential to think about what you can do and give each day. It may seem so ordinary to you that you don't actually realise how truly extraordinary it is.

Health and wellbeing

There are lots of ways we're advised to maintain our health – vitamins, the right food and exercise. But there's another way that's important for you as a Pisces. And that is to have a good time. Because when you're having fun, when you're relaxed, when you're happy, you're calling on the best, most healing elements of your nature. They will put you right and scare away any shadowy thoughts fast. Try it, and you'll see how well it works.

Goals and challenges

Certain individuals dismiss you as not being very practical – because they're realists. However, some would say that each of us has created our own world with our own vision, at least in terms of how we see things. That's an entirely different view, but it's one that is well worth reflecting on for you as a Pisces.

P
\
I
/
S
\
C
/
E
\
S

Last-minute changes are one thing, but having to abandon plans you've explored in depth and discussed with others isn't just annoying – it's been a waste of your time. Your irritation is understandable. Still, when new options arise, those facts and insights will prove to be hugely valuable.

03

MARCH

Love, at its purest, is life-changing. The trick? Recognising that purity

P
\
I
/
S
\
C
/
E
\
S

You

Many Pisceans believe in miracles, or what might be termed amazing possibilities, if you're not into religion or words like that. Whatever the case, you'll have had experiences, small and large, where what seemed to be impossible situations were dealt with magically. That's another word you can use.

It's the capacity for there to be a leap of events, something completely unexpected that shows up and seems to follow you around. Actually it's possible for everybody. But as a Pisces, and someone who's intuitive you have a gift for drawing this kind of, shall we say, magical event into your life. And it seems to occur often.

As you're aware, there are those around you who think it's wonderful and are delighted to hear you talk about it. Yet there are others whose reaction could only be defined as a "harrumph" and who simply won't discuss it, if you insist on being illogical.

The fact is, you are who you are. And you have that vision. You also have a knack for picking up a situation with that Piscean energy, and transforming it in some magical or miraculous way. If there are those who don't believe in it, that is up to them. For you, the capacity is something that you not only have every right to enjoy, you also have every right to exercise it as frequently as you like.

You and others

You like to talk about what goes on in your life, and there are those around you who sometimes hear about what some would call abnormal occurances. That is, those very special miraculous events. Talk about them all you want, because the more you talk about them, the more normal they become. And, quite possibly, the more frequently they will occur. That's what being a Pisces is all about.

Health and wellbeing

There are many ways to feel great. There's fitness and there's eating well, which are both important. However, as a Pisces, you'll know the way to feel your best is to be in a sunny mood. Even if the day isn't sunny, if your mood is, you'll have a bounce in your step.

Goals and challenges

There are those who regard themselves as real intellectuals, who live a life based on facts. It's hard to tell when they fall in love, because that's difficult to prove with facts. But when you talk about your own view of the world, which can range from scientific facts to the more intuitive side of your nature, their vocabulary is stretched. You need to consider just how long you want to chat with these doubters.

THIS DAY FOR EVERYONE

Few things are more disappointing than being let down by someone you trust. In the past, you've accepted an apology without discussion. It's now time for this to change. Ask what's behind these sudden developments. What you learn and ultimately talk over will be amazingly informative.

04

MARCH

GIFTS Mysterious, Graceful, Saintly

CHALLENGES Aloof, Reclusive, Impractical

NUMBER 8

(0+5) + (3) = 8

Ignore those who question your vision; trust your instincts over others' doubts

You

The word promise means different things to different people and signs. For instance, to a Gemini or Sagittarius, "I promise" means "Maybe" or, "I hope so". But when you as a Pisces promise to do something, you mean it absolutely and you'll do everything you can to make it happen. It comes from the heart as much as from the mind.

However, this perspective, more of a belief than an idea, reflects your way of looking at life that is unique to you. While many regard facts as unchangeable, as a Pisces, you believe deeply that your intention – your vision of what's possible – accompanied by hard work or effort, is what makes life happen.

While this isn't just different from most signs, it's unique to your nature as a Pisces. What's more, your perspective often clashes with the reality others live with, which leads to ongoing confusion between you, as a Pisces, and the rest of the world – it's as if you're speaking two different languages.

And, in fact, it's true. Of course, every once in a while, you'll come across those born under other signs but whose personal chart is strongly influenced by Pisces, and this is how they think, too. Recognising this special vision of life and of what's possible is important, because it isn't just your way of looking at life – it embraces the magic of being a Pisces.

You and others

While your idealism is core to your way of thinking and living, it's vital that you recognise the rest of the world doesn't think this way. So if things aren't falling into place, realise that you'll need to take an approach that allows you to make plans without the dramas.

Health and wellbeing

Being disappointed by others is inconvenient. Equally, when you're unable to live up to commitments, you suffer from knowing others have to reschedule. But everybody has a different attitude towards such commitments, and you care more than most. Of course, you can't change the world right away, but you can learn to understand others better.

Goals and challenges

Whatever you're doing, you always aim high. You don't even think about it, it comes so naturally. But you aren't always prepared for twists and turns and surprises, the unexpected events or, even, those who say they will absolutely be there for you but then aren't. The problem? It's simply their idea of loyalty is very different from yours.

P
\
I
/
S
\
C
/
E
\
S

THIS DAY FOR EVERYONE

Certain individuals don't really care about facts, even when getting things wrong would inconvenience others. While ordinarily this doesn't matter, current arrangements involve the two of you and perhaps others as well. Explain that it will be easier if you deal with the details, then do exactly that.

05

MARCH

While giving love is easier than accepting it, receiving it changes everybody's life

You

It's a question you ask yourself again and again – who comes first? Many signs simply act in their own best interests and don't even think about it. But, as a Pisces, it's another matter – one connected to your symbol of two fishes swimming in different directions.

You're always conscious of the circumstances of others and how you can help them or support them but, also, what do you need to do for yourself? And that leads to confusion. Often, there's your loyalty to others. Whether it's family, offspring or close friends, it's fierce. What's more, you're proud of those values. It could be said that, as you swim through the waters of life, your focus is intense. You're looking after your own interests and, just as much, focusing on those of others.

However, every once in a while, you need to pause and question who and what you're putting first and, especially, whether those activities and those goals are as important or meaningful as they once were. As a Pisces, you can commit deeply to goals; yet life changes, times change and so do you. And sometimes your focus on certain goals needs to change, if not come to an end. If there's anything that's become an obstruction or isn't falling into place for you, it's worth examining the situation. Try it. What comes to light could begin an exciting new cycle.

You and others

Very often you're the one rescuing others when they're facing difficulties, and when they need support, you're there. But there are times when you need others to rescue you. Not in the sense of the same kind of drama, but in the sense of helping. This is something that you face from time to time. And when you do, it's important to recognise that their support isn't just valuable, it is essential.

Health and wellbeing

As a Pisces, you'll be aware that life can involve emotional ups and downs that can be draining, which means if you've been through a period like that, you may not be as clear as you could be. This is when the support of others is so important – not necessarily to resolve the problems, but simply to help you find that centre, the core of your being again.

Goals and challenges

Putting yourself first sounds simple, and many signs are good at it. However, for you as a Pisces, it can be difficult, because you can feel guilty when you tell others they'll have to wait because you have something you need to think about in your own life first. Still, do it.

P
\
I
/
S
\
C
/
E
\
S

THIS DAY FOR EVERYONE

Few things are more boring than dealing with practicalities but, as you know, ultimately you'd regret leaving these in the hands of somebody else. Once you're involved, you'll realise how exciting this is and how creative you can be, both with existing arrangements and plans for the future.

GIFTS Extrasensory, Empathic, Dazzling

CHALLENGES Diverting, Lost, Irresponsible

NUMBER 1

(0+7) + (3) = 10 = (1+0) = 1

Little is better than making a life-changing suggestion and everything working out

You

As a Pisces, you're a natural organiser. Many people don't recognise this, because you're very discreet in your approach. While certain signs are heavy-handed, you have a way of making others feel important and, in fact, you'll get them to shoulder responsibilities in a way that will boost their confidence.

What's more, you're also superb at fitting in, so, even if there's chaos, you'll inspire others. Suddenly they'll realise they can help get things organised or even contribute to imposing order on chaos.

And that is your gift as a Pisces. It's not just your capacity to connect with and inspire others to stand up for themselves. Better yet, you encourage them to discover and offer the best of who they are.

This has to do with life, with what's being organised, but also it has to do with all sorts of relationships – with family, with loved ones, with friends and with the wider world.

And this gift you have is something that is meant to be used. Even though you may not think of it as that much of a gift, it enables you to encourage or guide others to be the best they can be.

But, even more than that, encouraging them to grow allows you to grow too, in satisfying ways. In modern-day talk, it could be said to be a win-win for everybody.

You and others

There are certain individuals who will decide that you are responsible for what they do. They'll play a game with you – they'll ask your advice, then they'll ask even more advice, and before you know it, you'll be in charge. Watch out for that. Of course, you'll know what to do, which is, quite simply, back off.

Health and wellbeing

As you know, from time to time, you can get so involved in doing something, partly because it's fun, that you don't realise you're overdoing things and you're ignoring your energy levels, and your effort. This is particularly important when you're doing something where you recognise that others are benefitting. It seems obvious, but it doesn't always occur to you.

Goals and challenges

The ability to exit from an arrangement is a rare skill. There are certain individuals who will pick a fight to make it happen, while others just fade away. Because you have the gift of being able to turn rather unworkable situations into something remarkable, it's also vital that you acquire the skill of saying a gracious but firm farewell at the right moment.

P
\
I
/
S
\
C
/
E
\
S

07

While you don't particularly enjoy changes in long-standing arrangements, you've accepted that they are sometimes unavoidable. Changes in close alliances with family and loved ones are another matter, but here, too, things are moving on. Embrace even unwelcome changes – they are vital.

MARCH

Hoping for magical events is one thing, but a surprise appearance is something else

P
\
I
/
S
\
C
/
E
\
S

You

As you're aware, your symbol – the fishes swimming in two directions – can indicate confusion. It's true that, at times, as a Pisces, you can be indecisive. Yet, at the same time, you have an amazing ability to deal with a range of situations – some practical, others sentimental and dramatic. This capacity to juggle tricky circumstance is one of your Piscean skills.

It's just that, at times, others can become dependent on you for dealing with such matters. This is where it's tricky, because while this skill is very rare, you can impart this ability to others and, gradually, hand the responsibility over to them.

True, they may not be quite as good at it as you are, but that doesn't matter. They'll be adept enough that they can deal with tricky situations wisely and creatively. This capacity to create happy situations and opportunities for growth isn't just important. You'll be giving yourself a way out of arrangements where others have been dependent on you.

While they'll have been rewarding, each must change as the circumstances move on. If the sense of intimacy you've developed makes everyone feel like they want to hang out for longer, that can be easily done. The skill? Learn when and how to walk away with a fond farewell, and you'll have learnt a skill that will benefit you for a very long time.

You and others

The fact is, you have a magic touch, and when you remember to use it, it's very powerful. The trick is to use it with intention, then stop. Otherwise, certain individuals will assume that you'll continue to organise their life in a way that's just as magical as what you've done recently. Make it very clear that this isn't a service that can be rented, whatever the cost.

Health and wellbeing

As a water sign, you're somebody who concentrates more on their feelings than their body. It's vital you look after yourself, even though it doesn't come naturally. Enough sleep, the right kind of food and getting away from people who drain you all seem simple, but when you're in the midst of something that is exciting, you tend to forget it. The trick is to say goodbye at the right moment.

Goals and challenges

There's a difference between knowing what you want to do and setting goals. As a Pisces, sometimes you're able to do what might be termed "magic up" the situation you need. However, if you put a little thought into defining what you'd like to do – that goal, and how you'd like it to happen – then that magic can occur all the more swiftly.

08

MARCH

THIS DAY FOR EVERYONE

You're by no means a control freak, yet you dislike allowing others to make decisions that really should be yours to decide. For now, leave things to them. What they opt for may be very different from what you'd have chosen. But you can reorganise everything later.

GIFTS Kind, Meditative, Rescuer

CHALLENGES Neglectful, Indirect, Interfering

NUMBER 3

$(0+9) + (3) = 12 = (1+2) = 3$

Anonymous generosity is typically Piscean, but it causes both confusion and joy

You

From time to time, you're faced with a range of dilemmas, each of which is chaotic in some way. While, intuitively, you sense you can put them in order, it's bound to be complicated.

Yet with your trademark intuition and with the two Piscean fishes being able to view the situation from two directions, you'll soon spot where there are "Yeses" and "Nos" to be dealt with. And, equally, recognise where issues are the fault of certain individuals, while others will simply be the result of circumstances.

And, in every case, it seems that where others are unable to examine the facts or make a grounded analysis, you'll be able to. This is one of your greatest gifts as a Pisces.

However, your challenge is to get involved, talk about the facts, examine matters in detail but, at the same time, make it clear you're involved only to a certain extent. And, equally, you'll ensure others are aware you're not going to look after the circumstances forever, nor will you babysit any tricky individuals involved.

This may disappoint those who see you as being the great rescuer, but the fact is you're there to help the individuals in question deal with, and learn from, these and any other tricky matters, and that's that.

And, just as much, you'll be there to help them be clear in their own minds about what they must, and need to, do.

You and others

There is a part of your nature, and a part of the nature of others, which doesn't just thrive on a variety of chaos, it enjoys it. There is an intellectual challenge and there is an emotional challenge. It requires a kind of vision you rarely get to employ in life. Use it wisely, and encourage others to use theirs, so when you've got everything sorted out, you can walk away with a clear mind.

Health and wellbeing

It may seem strange to say you need sleep, but when you are involved in something, you almost forget. But the fact is you're still living in a human body and you will still allow those worries to make your mind work overtime. So even if you're in bed, your mind will keep on dancing around. Being able to stop is always important, and when you're in the midst of something overwhelming, it's essential.

Goals and challenges

As an idealist, you're only really interested in something if it offers inspiration to the people involved. Yet sometimes the challenge is so appealing that you can't resist getting involved. While you may be able to do wonders, it could mean it's more about ego than the kind of vision that is your Piscean trademark.

P
\
I
/
S
\
C
/
E
\
S

Every once in a while, you need to stand up to somebody. While you did this before, it was about a particular matter. Now the issue has to do with the arrogant and often dismissive manner of certain individuals. The point is to register a complaint and that's all. Within days, you'll see why.

09

MARCH

GIFTS Free, Natural, Friendly

NUMBER 4

CHALLENGES Vague, Chameleon-like, Cool

(1+0) + (3) = 4

Even the most eloquent Pisces will struggle to explain generosity to somebody unkind

P
\
I
/
S
\
C
/
E
\
S

You

You say you're longing for an ordered life, to have things going the way you expect, to have balance. Yet, at the same time, there's a part of you, that part which is the two fishes swimming in different directions, that gets a bit bored if what you're doing or those you're dealing with are too predictable. For you, as a Pisces, the disruption, the feelings that come with it and the process of finding the solutions for the resulting disarray are part of the drama of life. Fixing things, finding the potential for perfection in disarray – whether it's in your work, day-to-day life or close relationships – is all hugely rewarding to you.

However, the trick is to have something else that's a little bit dramatic, whether it's rescuing a situation or perhaps supporting somebody who needs to learn and to deal with everyday life. Why? Because this prevents you from being drawn into the unconscious dramas that are familiar to those who know you; the sudden dramas that are the Pisces signature.

They occur frequently , especially when you're bored. Take that approach, and you'll keep the two Piscean fishes well occupied, because they'll both have to paddle madly to keep up. Meanwhile, you can deal with the dramas that are necessary to keep your watery, rather emotional, rather dramatic Piscean nature happy.

You and others

If you're trying to figure out what makes you tick, that is about the elements of your character that are very much part of what's going on, the fact is you won't necessarily be ready to analyse things. Yet, at the same time, it's all about looking at who you're drawn to, the kind of person who's giving you the kind of fun you love, which, if it's serious drama, means you're rather enjoying it.

Health and wellbeing

The art of looking after yourself in the midst of upheaval is a skill, and it's one that, as a Pisces, you sometimes ignore, because for you living out the ups and downs is exciting, especially in a world that seems to try so hard to walk on a level playing field. As a Pisces, you're not just a visionary, you have a strong dramatic streak. Think carefully about how you use it. There are many kinds of art to life.

Goals and challenges

Deciding what to say to certain individuals who you know are going to be difficult is seriously challenging. Ordinarily as a Pisces, you'd already be calculating ways to work around them. There's another approach – and that is to say an uncompromising no.

10

MARCH

THIS DAY FOR EVERYONE

Usually there's no point in debating issues you have strong views about, as do others. Yet, judging by the planetary activity ahead, which accents discussion and, even more, expansive thinking, you could achieve a shared perspective on even serious differences.

In so many settings, simply saying yes is life-changing. A refusal shatters joy in seconds

You

As a Pisces, you're designed for multitasking. As one of the mutable water signs – the signs born at the end of each season, who have a talent for juggling a range of interests and tasks, but also as a water sign and somebody who is able to tune into others in a rare way – you're able to use your skills in a range of settings. What's more, you're adaptable, so can deal with even rather difficult people, although you may not want to do it full-time.

However, you're easily bored, and for this reason you often move from one task or setting to another. Even if you're in business, you'll begin doing one thing, then another, and often the next after that. All of this is fine, except certain situations and individuals place great value on sticking with things.

As a clever and tactful Pisces, you're usually able to find a way around such dilemmas. This is, in fact, one of your greatest gifts – in every area of your life.

You've a knack for rethinking elements of your life, yet making others feel important. That way, you're always doing something new, but it makes life itself much more fun.

The trick to all of this, therefore, is to ignore those who give solid business advice and tell you to stick to one thing. Instead, use your imaginative Piscean vision. It's one of the best allies you'll ever have.

You and others

There are many kinds of friendships and love, and, as a Pisces, you know many people who have experienced a range of feelings about you. Some of them will declare their feelings, others will simply hang around a lot, but this kind of devotion, appealing as it is, may not be in your best interests especially because you can get drawn into dramas. Finding somebody who cares about you, and finding friends and family members, who have that quality isn't just wise, it's essential.

Health and wellbeing

If there's a single phrase that's part of your approach to life, it's "overdoing it".When you have a passion about an individual or a project, you'll hurl yourself into it. That is your nature as a Pisces. However, the trick is to also be aware when enough is enough.

Goals and challenges

While you may stick with the same way of living, even the same job, for a long time, it's important that your goals shift, because you thrive on finding new ways to do things, and the trick is to be flexible. That means you're able to tackle new activities, meet new people and go to new places, all of which feed that inquisitive side of your nature.

P
\
I
/
S
\
C
/
E
\
S

Thinking back, it was only a while ago that you felt you had no choice but to stand your ground against ideas, events or changes that would create nothing but disruption. These happened anyway, and you've realised how thrilling they are now, and will be in the future.

11

MARCH

While Piscean kindness is infinite, receiving is another, far less comfortable, matter

You

As a Pisces, your enthusiasm is a trademark. It emerges from your inquisitive nature and it's in your approach to everything, from the circumstances you're dealing with to the individuals you meet or the ideas that excite you. You respond to these naturally and deeply.

Sometimes those feelings are emotional but, also, they'll be creative or even intellectual. They constitute a variety of vitamins, in that they make you feel better and stronger, and that life is more exciting, more worth living. And the trick to dealing with this, whatever the setting, is to bring it your idealism.

As a Pisces and a water sign, you go with the flow. Imposing order on a situation or others doesn't come naturally. Yet, in certain matters, you've no choice, especially when practical obligations, money or commitments are involved. These aren't fun, but ignoring them only leads to complications. So if you dealt with that practical side of things early on, and organised things in a way that seems very dull indeed, you'll be glad you did.

You will, in fact, discover you're free to be all the more creative and to encourage others to be as well. This is one of the great paradoxes of being a Pisces. While some of your greatest gifts have to do with being highly intuitive, if not a little crazy, one of the greatest safeguards for you is strong organisation.

You and others

Pure Piscean energy is about inspiration. Where you take that and how you use it is up to you, and that has to do with figuring things out in practical terms. If you don't, you'll continue to bounce ideas off others, which has its own particular kind of high, but often doesn't compensate you in terms of time or money.

Health and wellbeing

Pisces tend to overdo things, and this can occur in lots of ways. You get too enthusiastic, don't sleep enough, give too many ideas, spend too much time with somebody. Only later do you realise you're exhausted and, quite possibly, haven't been compensated for your efforts. Figure out the practicalities first – that is a message from the heavens.

Goals and challenges

Aiming impossibly high is very much part of your Piscean nature. But so that you can enjoy the ride – and as you do, are able to look down on what you're doing from the point of view of being on a high – you'll realise that certain things need to change and improve. And that's the best approach – turning something that's already exciting into something absolutely amazing.

P
\
I
/
S
\
C
/
E
\
S

12

THIS DAY FOR EVERYONE

Not only is planning ahead wise, organising your schedule lets you relax and focus on what you're doing in the here and now. Still, however carefully you've planned, the current twists and turns make you rethink things, often at the last minute. Ironically, what's least expected could be very exciting.

MARCH

Discreet gestures backed by deep love can bring life-transforming change

You

As a restless Pisces, as someone who is intuitive by nature, and as someone who enjoys drama, it's possible for you to get involved in situations where everything is happening at the same time. You may even lend a hand to others who are struggling. It's not just about people; you even nurse struggling plants back to health. In each case, that drama is appealing.

But, still, it's essential that you balance it with situations that allow you to use your remarkable creative energy, your kindness and your generosity without the price that comes with those dramas. Initially this may seem rather dull, until you begin to recognise that without the dramas it's far easier to concentrate on what you want to get done.

While, often, people think of this in terms of the arts, many Pisceans are fantastic at business as well and will excel – as long as they're not distracted by those dramas. The trick? It's being able to spot those difficulties before you get involved. And that has to do not only with the circumstances involved, but the people as well. Certain individuals seem perfectly rational until you get drawn in, then their dramas become yours to deal with, and sometimes you have to look after them, too. The trick? It's to use that Piscean intuition as best you can. You'll not only benefit from it. You'll avoid yet more unnecessary drama.

You and others

Spotting those who can give to you – friends who can support you and help you block out those who are realistic or demanding – is difficult. But it's a skill that's worth developing, because, as you become ever more creative and ever more the marvellous Pisces you are, those who depend on you will be drawn to you. And saying no can be rather difficult.

Health and wellbeing

It's easy to say you'll rest later. It's something you've done as life becomes more fulfilling, more demanding and more exciting. But it requires time and organisation. You can't save up sleep like you can money in a bank account. The trick is to learn how to balance things. Even if it's having somebody close to you who tells you when it's time to go to bed.

Goals and challenges

When there's a lot going on, even if it's rather simple – it doesn't need to be a big business, it could be local theatre – but when there are those who are very creative around, they can take over and use your creative abilities. This is where it's tricky, because it means setting your own goals. This may not make you popular in the short term, but it's essential in the long run.

P
\
I
/
S
\
C
/
E
\
S

Unsettling as sudden changes may be, they're often clearing the way for something better. This applies to links with those individuals who've been part of your life for ages, but who recently have been more of a burden than a joy. Saying farewell won't be easy, but it may be for the best.

13

MARCH

Being generous once is noble; frequent generosity with the same person is worrying

You

Some people are argumentative and enjoy battling because it's fun. It's like breathing for them. But for you, as a Pisces, when you fight for something or somebody it's because you believe in it, so you take it more personally than others. In fact, you're intuitive and it's quite difficult for you to have the kind of argument that many do when they're sitting around, don't have much to talk about and perhaps have a drink in their hand.

In your case, you'll battle for something or somebody you're passionate about. And, if you get caught up in those situations, you can end up in a battle, simply because the other individual doesn't care about the matter in question, they're just enjoying the noise and the conflict. Backing out of such situations is, however, surprisingly difficult for you.

And that's one of your major lessons. It's to differentiate between what you really care about and other less important matters. Yet what you learn will also lead you to other activities and people who light up your day, your life and even your soul, in the sense that once you are involved with them, you'll realise their passion doesn't come from enjoying an argument. If they differ from you, it's only because they care just as much as you do about whatever it is you're working on. And that alone will light up your life.

You and others

Dealing with dramas is your choice. But, even more than that, your choice enables you to learn more about joy. In some cases, those dramas aren't joyous at all, but you realise that behind that, there is the promise of something deeper and more rewarding. And that's what will make the difference.

Health and wellbeing

When you're in the middle of exciting things, exciting discussions, exciting dramas, or doing something you care passionately about, stopping seems a waste of time. But in your case, as a Pisces and somebody who's more vulnerable than you like to admit, stopping won't just be important. It will allow you to make the best of what you're dealing with over the weeks, months and even years ahead.

Goals and challenges

Other people rate achievements in terms of how much they'll impress others. But the only real achievement that's important is something that matters to you, as a Pisces and an idealist. It may not have to do with anything artistic or imaginative. It may have to do with business. But if it's something that lights up your life and touches your soul, then that's exactly what you should be doing.

P
\
I
/
S
\
C
/
E
\
S

THIS DAY FOR EVERYONE

Theoretically, facts are reliable. However, certain things you believe to be true for ages are being challenged by recent discoveries, or certain individuals are embracing new ideas. Tempting as it is to dismiss these, ask what they're about. What you learn will be interesting, if not life changing.

14

MARCH

Those who question your faith in others should look in the mirror

You

As a Pisces, the question you need to answer is, why do you struggle to please others, those who want you to make a single plan, when, in fact, your symbol is two fishes swimming in different directions.

There's another sign that's similar: Gemini, which is the twins. Both signs share the same rare capacity to look at any situation from at least two different angles.

While that's a gift, it isn't necessarily recognised by the other individuals who are in your world. They simply want you to make a plan and then stick with it. While that may be easy for the Capricorns and Virgos of this world, your nature is always to see both sides of something.

And that is a great gift. If others are unhappy with it, very politely tell them that you will inform them when and how you can commit, but you can't transform yourself.

And this is very much part of the realisation of your own gift, as well. Then you realise that those who don't appreciate your vision are actually at a loss – and it's too bad for them.

While you can't, and shouldn't, explain what they can't see, you can, and will, help them as best you can. And then, having done that, you can quietly back off, spend time with those who appreciate you and enjoy being yourself. That is the greatest gift of all.

You and others

The simple fact of recognising that others can't see as much as you can – and, even more than that, don't care that they can't see – is difficult. Yet, at the same time, there are few things that will free you as much as a simple realisation that your vision of the world is far broader and more inspiring than many of those who think they know more than you do.

Health and wellbeing

Dealing with periods when you're overwhelmed is tricky. The exhaustion is one thing, but there are also the demands of others who refuse to acknowledge you need to take a break. Do what you can, but no more. Then put yourself in a setting where you are free from demands of that nature. This is all about rest and recovery.

Goals and challenges

Choosing your own goal, deciding what you want to do, seems easy. But if you happen to be in a world of those whose view of life is based on a struggle and a perspective that is alien to yours, then it'll be tricky. What's most important, however, is that in choosing a goal, you pick one that is yours and yours alone.

P
\
I
/
S
\
C
/
E
\
S

THIS DAY FOR EVERYONE

You're in the uncomfortable position of having to confront somebody about their facts being wrong. In this case, the individual in question tends to speak without thinking. And the matter in question involves you. Address this firmly and, out of character as it may be, don't apologise.

15

MARCH

Pisceans often help out those who are struggling, but prior investigation is worthwhile

You

To say that happiness is fluid may sound very strange, but as a water sign, you understand that very well. You understand that, on one hand, circumstances shift – some things work out, some don't – but your own mood has its ups and downs as well. So what seemed great one day doesn't seem so great the next, and is the last thing you want on the day after that.

However, those around you don't understand, because these less-imaginative individuals have the same definition of happiness day in, day out and year in, year out. And from your point of view, that's absolutely fine.

Yet, at the same time, you're dealing with others, and your relationships also have their own ups and downs. Not so much negativity, but with a world in flux and with the peaks and valleys of modern life, it's natural that there are moments when things flow, and others when they don't.

And this is something that's obvious to you as a Pisces, who has as your symbol the two fishes swimming in opposite directions. Yet, every once in a while, you have to explain it. Using the fish as an example might not work, but you'll have enough examples in the world to make it very clear to others that the kind of stability they are demanding is simply unlikely to happen in today's world.

You and others

What you understand, but others don't, is that in a world of change, when life is redefining itself, relationships themselves will shift. This doesn't mean you care any more or less. It just means the way you communicate with others, the way you see them and the time you spend with them, changes. In many cases, the world's shifting only deepens those relationships.

Health and wellbeing

As a Pisces, a water sign, and somebody who has a fascination for drama, a regular regime can be dull, but that doesn't have to be the case. It's simply that with so much happening around you, it's vital that you rest enough, eat well, and do things that let your body thrive.

Goals and challenges

Life used to be a lot simpler. Goals could be clearly defined and it was easy to figure out a way around challenges. But, with every passing year, that version of what is a challenge and what's an opportunity is itself changing. The fact is, challenges to others may actually be gifts to you. Recognise that when others talk about difficult circumstances, they may well be the ones you're thriving on.

P
\
I
/
S
\
C
/
E
\
S

16

MARCH

THIS DAY FOR EVERYONE

It's not that you've been secretive, despite what certain individuals suggest. But between changes in circumstance and your own equally changeable feelings, you simply didn't know what to say. Fortunately, now that things have reached a turning point, you have a clear sense of those feelings.

The concept of quiet joy is Pisces at its purest and most inspiring

You

It's easy to get drawn into discussions of the visions and goals of others, as well as your own. It's something you quite enjoy, as a Pisces and someone who's a bit of a visionary. You also enjoy comparing notes.

However, when it comes to getting things organised, it's completely different. In fact, it's two different processes – because once others simply made a plan and stuck to it, but the shifting foundation on which plans themselves are based is ideal for you.

As a Pisces, with your two fishes swimming in different directions, you have a broader view of what's possible than others. And those who insist on making a complete and detailed plan for whatever's going to be done can often be distracting. But, of course, the trick is to avoid those conversations and, instead, recognise that each step will need to be taken as you take it, and then the next one after that. And with each step, you will learn a lot.

If others learn something too, that's great. But if they are determined to travel with you, it's essential you make it clear to them that it will be on your terms. That may sound pushy, but many individuals who are accustomed to achieving may insist on doing things their way. That could be the old way. And it may be a way that will hold you back. As a Pisces, be loyal to one thing – and that is to your vision.

You and others

Are you facing a cynic? Somebody who laughs at others, especially those who care deeply and have vision. You don't have to deal with them, but if you do, you don't have to like them. You need to set goals that are as clear as theirs. And be as tough, Ironically, that encounter may transform your perspective.

Health and wellbeing

There is a single four-letter word for you: Stop. That's difficult, because when you've lots to do, it's always just one more thing – an experience, discussion or task. And that's not stopping. It means taking more on when you simply need to say enough If there's a motto you'll want to live by as you go through life's twists and turns, it's "Keep it simple."

Goals and challenges

Every once in a while, it's important to question for whom you're achieving your goals. It may be that you're involved with an organisation or a business, or even a family, and you've set goals that are in accordance with theirs. If so, pause and think a little more about those goals. Are they truly yours – in your heart and your soul? If so, continue. If not, it's time to rethink them.

P
\
I
/
S
\
C
/
E
\
S

THIS DAY FOR EVERYONE

When sudden changes arose, they seemed unsettling, but also relatively uncomplicated. Since then, you realise they involved far more than you anticipated, and they're taking you into new and exciting territory. Yet you almost rejected them. Make a mental note of this, so you can recall it in the future.

17

MARCH

Every Pisces knows they've healing power, and they'll use it without saying a word

You

Pisces often live a life of extremes, not so much that others would see, but more gentle extremes of joy and disappointment, of recognising what you could do – and what others could do. And while at times there's excitement, there are also dramatic changes. The trick here is to know when to make those changes and what demands to make.

There will be those around you who will think they can remedy your difficulties by making them more like theirs. But unless they're a Pisces, they probably won't understand why you've chosen to organise elements of your life in the way you have. You needn't explain it to them. All you need to do is sidestep those individuals who are quite sure they know how to be you far better than you do. This is a particularly important challenge for you as a Pisces, simply because those around you do have good intentions, but they don't realise that everybody is an individual. And that in being true to yourself, you're able to be the best you can be.

As a Pisces, you're instinctively aware of that. You'll have had to argue that point a lot, yet you'll also have learnt more about the importance of that personal truth. Make that your goal – far beyond achieving the kind of goals that others go for – and you'll always make the right decision.

You and others

Those who have in mind some other project are thinking in terms of their own goals, not yours. Don't argue, just do something that you as a Pisces are so good at, and that is withdraw quietly to another setting. Perhaps you won't pick up the phone for a while – whatever it takes to be true to yourself – but if ever there was a time to do it, it's when others are trying to tell you how to live your life.

Health and wellbeing

There are many ways of being fit and perhaps the most important one, during periods when you are experiencing growth and change, is to do what feels best to you. There are those who will offer various regimes – walking, dieting, certain foods or supplements – but none will give you the strength in the core of your soul that doing what you feel is best will achieve.

Goals and challenges

If anyone can achieve astronomically high goals, you can. But if you don't feel like doing what those around you are encouraging you to do, then avoid the subject. The fact is, your vision is extraordinary. And what seems not particularly exciting will one day turn into something remarkable, because as a Pisces, you have an instinct for that sort of thing.

P
\
I
/
S
\
C
/
E
\
S

18

MARCH

THIS DAY FOR EVERYONE

Joy comes in many forms. It can be organised and scheduled. However, what's coming your way is likely to be as surprising as it will be delightful. Because they're unexpected, you might not recognise events for what they are when they first appear. The secret to spotting them is whatever lifts your spirits.

GIFTS Visionary, Telepathic, Charitable

CHALLENGES Inattentive, Noncommittal, Wasteful

NUMBER 4

(1+9) + (3) = 13 = (1+3) = 4

The biggest challenge? Believing in yourself.
The biggest reward? Also believing in yourself

You

Your birthday is a celebration of balance, going from the subtle nature of the water sign Pisces to the fiery Aries. In the northern hemisphere, it's about waking from winter's chill and darkness and going into spring, while the southern hemisphere also calls attention to the power of nature's cycles.

The move by the Sun from Pisces to Aries is about a shift in your viewpoint, as well. As a Pisces, you're a visionary. But throw in a little of the fire of Aries and you change the game entirely. You have a rare gift of being able to turn the subtlety of the Piscean vision into something that moves swiftly and brings powerful insights.

The trick is to believe entirely in yourself. If those around you want to reassure you, that's fine. However, you'll be increasingly aware that you know better than anybody else what you should be doing with your time, your energy, your passions, your love and your creativity. There are many who are born around your time of year who have done remarkable things.

And, whether what you achieve is visible to the world or not, you will be one of them. Believe in yourself in this extraordinary way, because to be born on this date gives you a rare gift, a gift that you will use in many ways, and in many settings throughout your life.

You and others

While it's important to discuss your ideas, be careful not to share too much with others. While they may make suggestions, those may not be helpful. If anything, you can use them for contrast and gain greater confidence about your own ideas.

Health and wellbeing

If you're going to be in good health, there's a single word that will make all the difference. And that word is joy. It's the joy that comes from doing what you want, recognising you're being the person you're meant to be and not allowing anything or anyone to draw you from that truth. It may sound pretty dramatic. But for you as an individual, being able to live out that truth isn't just vital, it will be thrilling.

Goals and challenges

Goals are important because they allow you to define what you want to do. Yet, in fact, you may not even define them to yourself until you look back later and realise certain decisions you made weren't just important, they were life-changing. What's significant, however, is that, as you live out each minute of your life, you're true to yourself.

P
\
I
/
S
\
C
/
E
\
S

THIS DAY FOR EVERYONE

19

Having had to defend yourself from blame for others' poor decisions, you're increasingly cautious. You've also been comparing notes with those involved. This isn't so much for their advice as to ensure that everybody is aware of your objectives and long-term plans and is happy with them.

MARCH

About Shelley

I was born and grew up in Hollywood and, while my parents weren't in showbusiness, it was around me from my earliest days. Although I recognised the glamour of it, I was fascinated by philosophy, and read about and studied it long before I reached my teens.

My recollection of my introduction to the heavens, in terms of both astrology and astronomy, is vivid. I was about eight years of age, at the Griffith Park Observatory in the hills above Los Angeles, waiting to go into a planetarium show on the heavens. In the foyer, there was a pendulum, and above it were frescoes – paintings of the images of the gods, signifying each of the planets.

At that moment, I knew they'd be part of my life. It was clear. The ancient myths, the subtleties of astrology and even the science of astronomy – about which I'm knowledgeable enough to hold my own in an exchange of ideas with experts – have become a joy and a passion. They are central to my life, as a career, and – as anybody who looks at my social media accounts will know – my passion for the heavenly bodies is as enthusiastic as it is extensive.

Today's distractions, on all sorts of screens, mean that even astrological enthusiasts don't actually look up at the heavens; they may note the power of the Full Moon, but they won't have a chat with the heavenly body – that luminous magnet that, in ancient times, was herself regarded as a goddess. Even today, we honour the Moon with a range of names – Selene, Diana, Artemis and Phoebe – and it's the same with most of the planets.

Similarly, we cite the planets every time we speak of somebody being unpredictable or mercurial (Mercury), or jolly, generous and jovial (Jupiter). They're woven into our culture and way of thinking, even for those who don't "believe" in astrology.

These days, it's become as much a tool for self-reflection and gaining an awareness of others as it is about prediction, although many columns, including mine, feature that.

But we're living in a time that balances the knowledge of science with several forms of ancient wisdom, including astrology. It is, after all, the study of cycles, of the rhythms of nature around us and our lives, collectively and individually.

And, I hope, when reading this book and its entries, you'll not only recognise an accurate and insightful portrait of yourself and others, but also a testimony to this ancient art that honours the year's cycle, day by day.

Today, books like this are only part of the conversation. In addition to writing for publications, I speak to groups and talk on matters from personal awareness to business; recently this has focused on untangling – and making sense of – the dramatic changes reshaping our world.

Some would say, and I agree, this is the beginning of a new cycle, the Age of Aquarius we've heard so much about. While it may, indeed, lead to a more peaceful era, on the way to creating it, humanity will have to grapple with a few of its most disruptive characteristics.

Also, some astrologers, including me, suggest that the clearer your own self-awareness is, the greater your power will be to usher in a new, more harmonious and productive way of thinking, being, living – and running a planet.

If you're interested to know more about yourself or about astrology, I've listed some publications and organisations that would be a good place to start.

Questions about the dates of the signs? Find out more at shelleyvonstrunckel.com.

References

If you want to know more about yourself, visit my website, shelleyvonstrunckel.com, where you can read your own daily, weekly and monthly stars.

You can also order your own personal chart: a map of the heavens for the exact date, year and time (if known) you were born, and the exact place. The resulting astronomically accurate maps of the heavens is your personal birth chart and is regarded as a "mirror" of your nature. It comes with an interpretation of your character written by a trained professional for your chart – or that of a family member, child, or even your boss.

These are wonderfully easy to read and understand; I've had amazing feedback. Order them from my website.

Astrological charts about children are also available. Parents have told me how helpful they are, and they're also a great gift. You can also order charts and a yearly analysis of your own chart. All are done to order, just for you.

If want to know more about astrology itself, there are some great magazines you can read, books to delve into and organisations that are worth getting to know.

Do you want to learn more?

An excellent website for books is wessexastrologer.com. Those seeking guidance about what to read or where to study and learn more can email info@wessexastrologer.com

The Mountain Astrologer is a terrific journal, published in the USA but of international interest. For subscriptions/enquiries in the UK and Europe:
wessexastrologer.com/product-category/the-mountain-astrologer/

And for enquiries in the USA and ROW, as well as digital subscriptions:
mountainastrologer.com/tma/

There is also a Wessex Astrologer YouTube channel, which is being added to all the time:
youtube.com/channel/UCLYJ58jI-5MwkNNa47ClhMw

Schools

London School of Astrology
General: londonschoolofastrology.co.uk
Online courses: londonschoolofastrology.com

The Faculty of Astrological Studies
astrology.org.uk/

The Mayo School, led by Wendy Stacey
mayoastrology.com/

American Federation of Astrologers
astrologers.com/

Kepler College
keplercollege.org

International Society for Astrological Research
isarastrology.org/en-gb/

National Council for Geocosmic Research
geocosmic.org/

The Astrology University
astrologyuniversity.com/

DK LONDON

Publishing Director Katie Cowan
Senior Acquisitions Editor Stephanie Milner
Editor Alison Thomson
Art Director Maxine Pedliham
Managing Art Editor Christine Keilty
Designer and Illustrator Abi Read
Senior Production Editor Tony Phipps
Production Controller Rebecca Parton

DK DELHI

Pre-production Manager Sunil Sharma
CTS Designer Umesh Singh Rawat

First published in Great Britain in 2020 by
Dorling Kindersley Limited
DK, One Embassy Gardens,
8 Viaduct Gardens,
London, SW11 7BW

A CIP catalogue record for this book
is available from the British Library.
ISBN: 9780241455852

Printed and bound in Latvia

For the curious
www.dk.com